Rainbow Days

1

Story and Art by
Minami Mizuno

CONTENTS

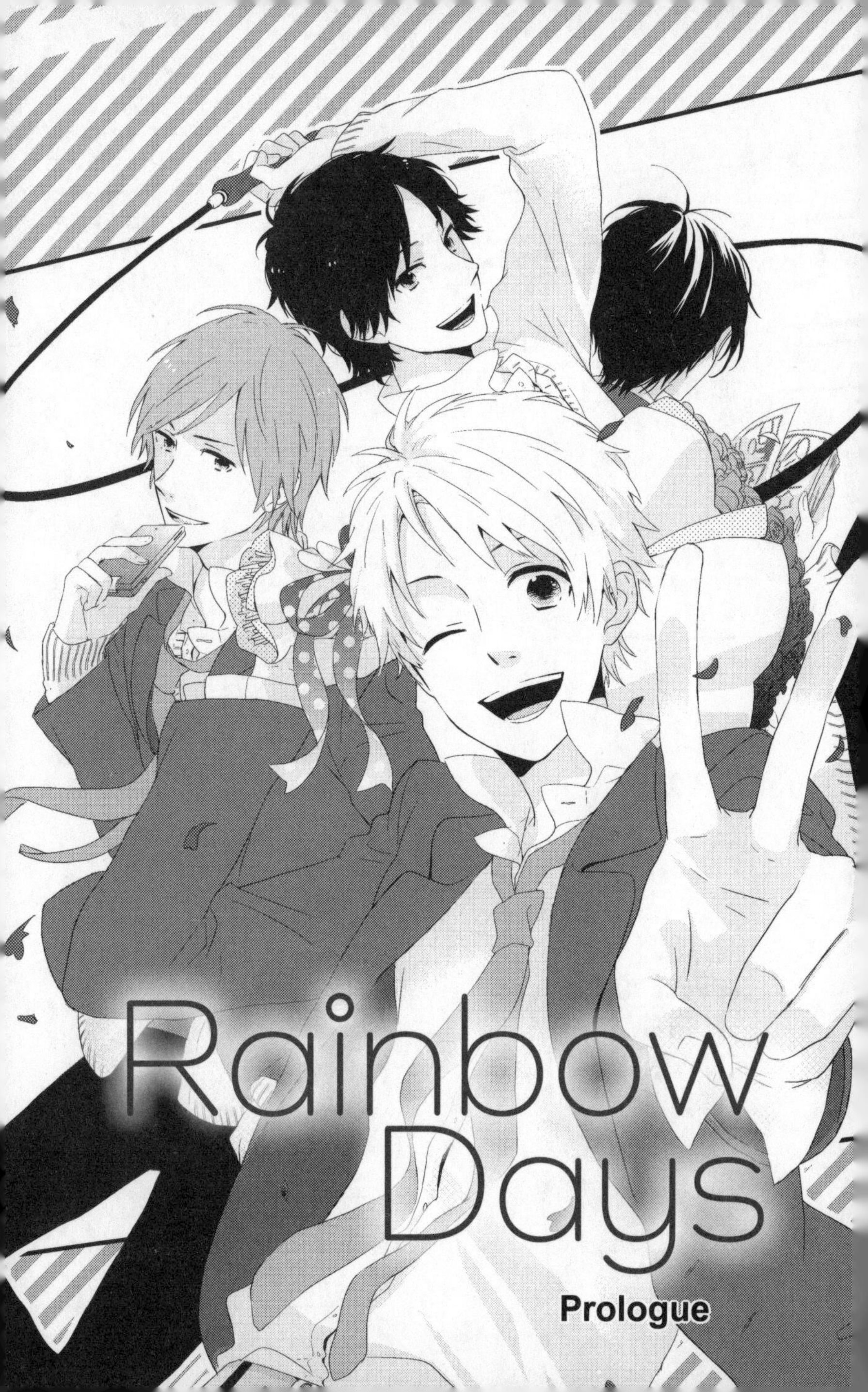
Rainbow
Days
Prologue

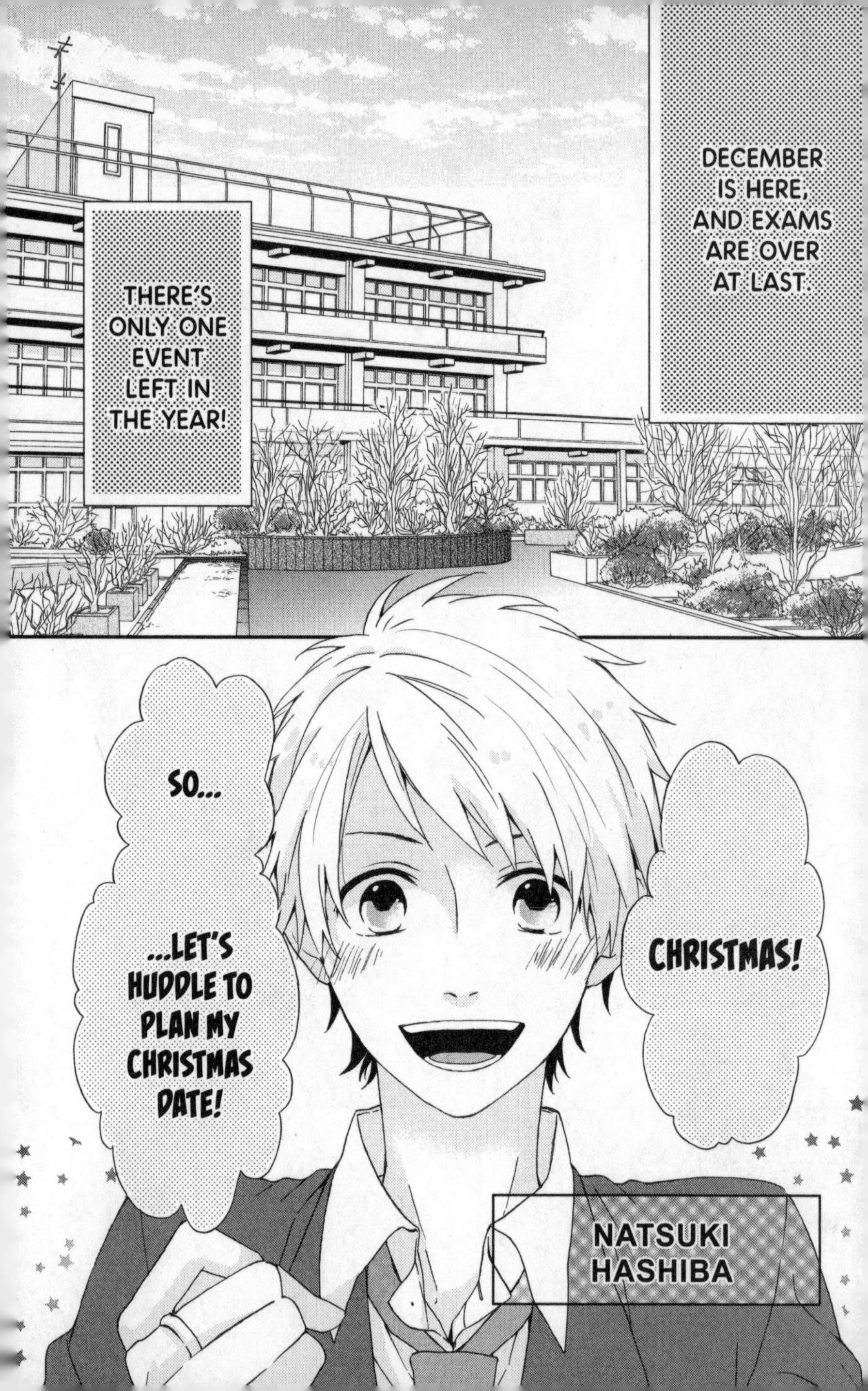
DECEMBER IS HERE, AND EXAMS ARE OVER AT LAST.
THERE'S ONLY ONE EVENT LEFT IN THE YEAR!
CHRISTMAS!
SO...
...LET'S HUDDLE TO PLAN MY CHRISTMAS DATE!
NATSUKI HASHIBA

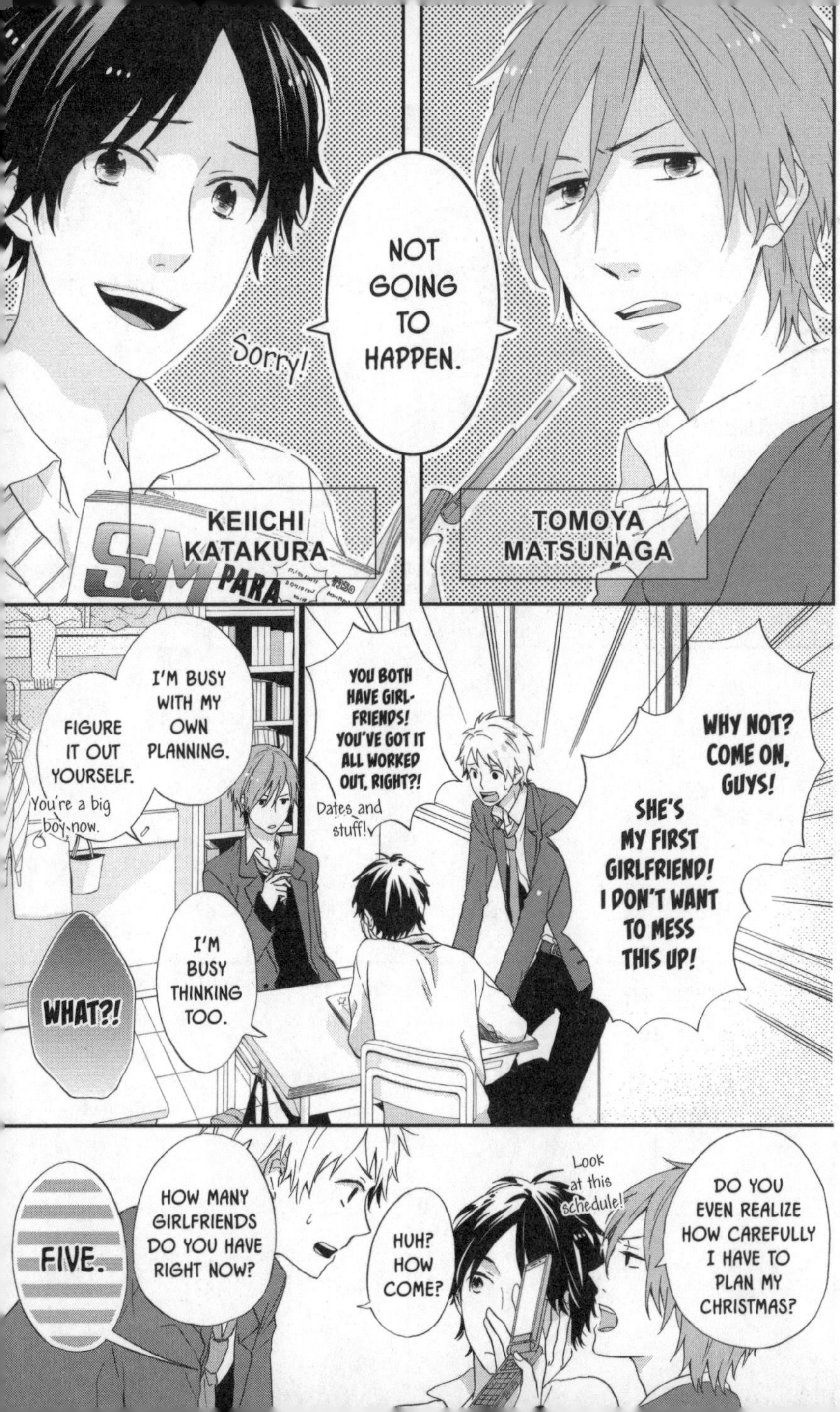
NOT GOING TO HAPPEN.
TOMOYA MATSUNAGA
Sorry!
KEIICHI KATAKURA
S&M PARA
WHY NOT? COME ON, GUYS!
SHE'S MY FIRST GIRLFRIEND! I DON'T WANT TO MESS THIS UP!
YOU BOTH HAVE GIRL-FRIENDS! YOU'VE GOT IT ALL WORKED OUT, RIGHT?!
Dates and stuff!
I'M BUSY WITH MY OWN PLANNING.
FIGURE IT OUT YOURSELF.
You're a big boy now.
I'M BUSY THINKING TOO.
WHAT?!
DO YOU EVEN REALIZE HOW CAREFULLY I HAVE TO PLAN MY CHRISTMAS?
Look at this schedule!
HUH? HOW COME?
HOW MANY GIRLFRIENDS DO YOU HAVE RIGHT NOW?
FIVE.

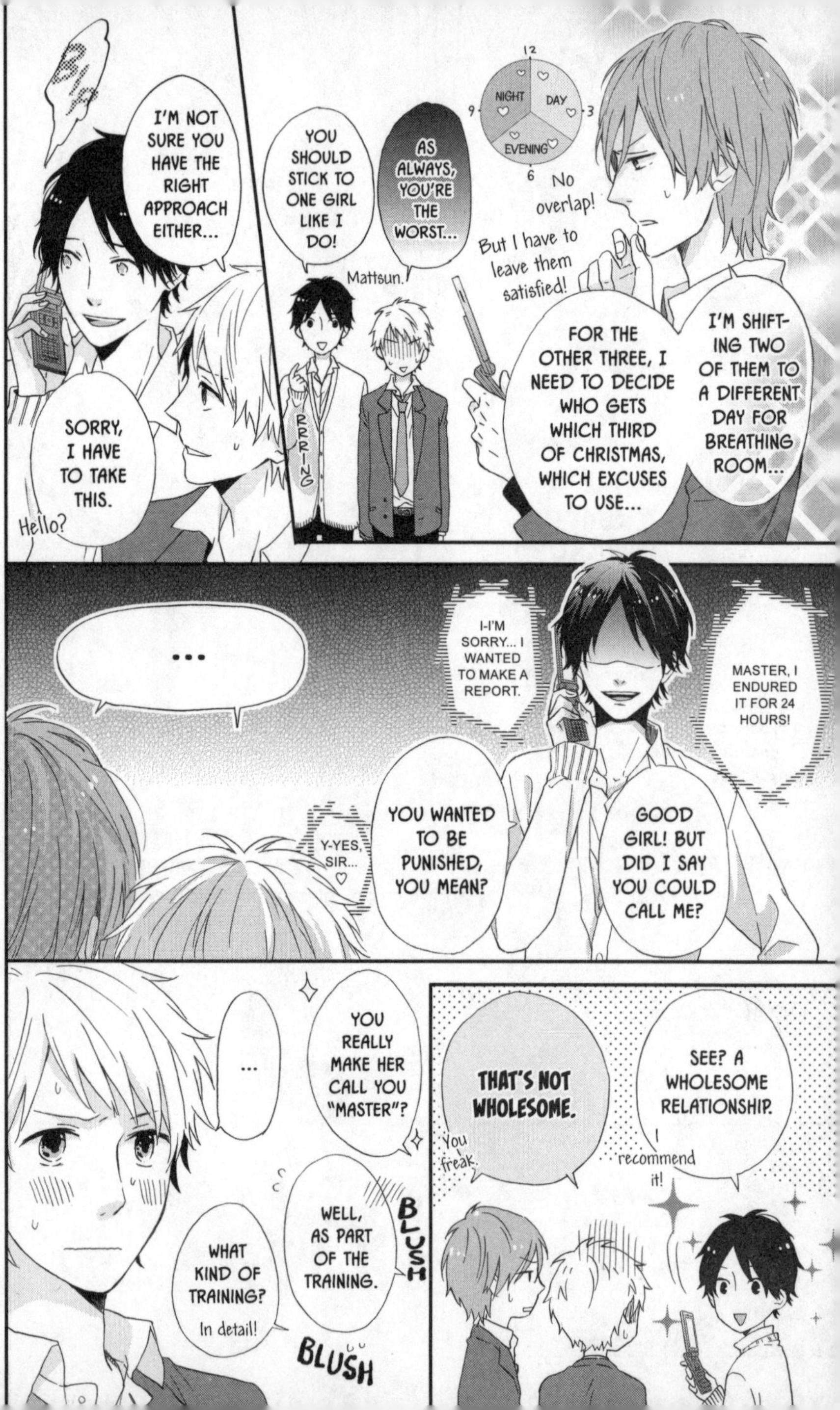
I'M SHIFTING TWO OF THEM TO A DIFFERENT DAY FOR BREATHING ROOM...
FOR THE OTHER THREE, I NEED TO DECIDE WHO GETS WHICH THIRD OF CHRISTMAS, WHICH EXCUSES TO USE...
But I have to leave them satisfied!
12
NIGHT
DAY
9
3
EVENING
6
No overlap!
AS ALWAYS, YOU'RE THE WORST...
Mattsun.
YOU SHOULD STICK TO ONE GIRL LIKE I DO!
RRRING
I'M NOT SURE YOU HAVE THE RIGHT APPROACH EITHER...
SORRY, I HAVE TO TAKE THIS.
Hello?
MASTER, I ENDURED IT FOR 24 HOURS!
GOOD GIRL! BUT DID I SAY YOU COULD CALL ME?
I-I'M SORRY... I WANTED TO MAKE A REPORT.
YOU WANTED TO BE PUNISHED, YOU MEAN?
Y-YES, SIR... ♡
...
SEE? A WHOLESOME RELATIONSHIP.
I recommend it!
THAT'S NOT WHOLESOME.
You freak.
YOU REALLY MAKE HER CALL YOU "MASTER"?
...
WELL, AS PART OF THE TRAINING.
BLUSH
WHAT KIND OF TRAINING?
In detail!
BLUSH

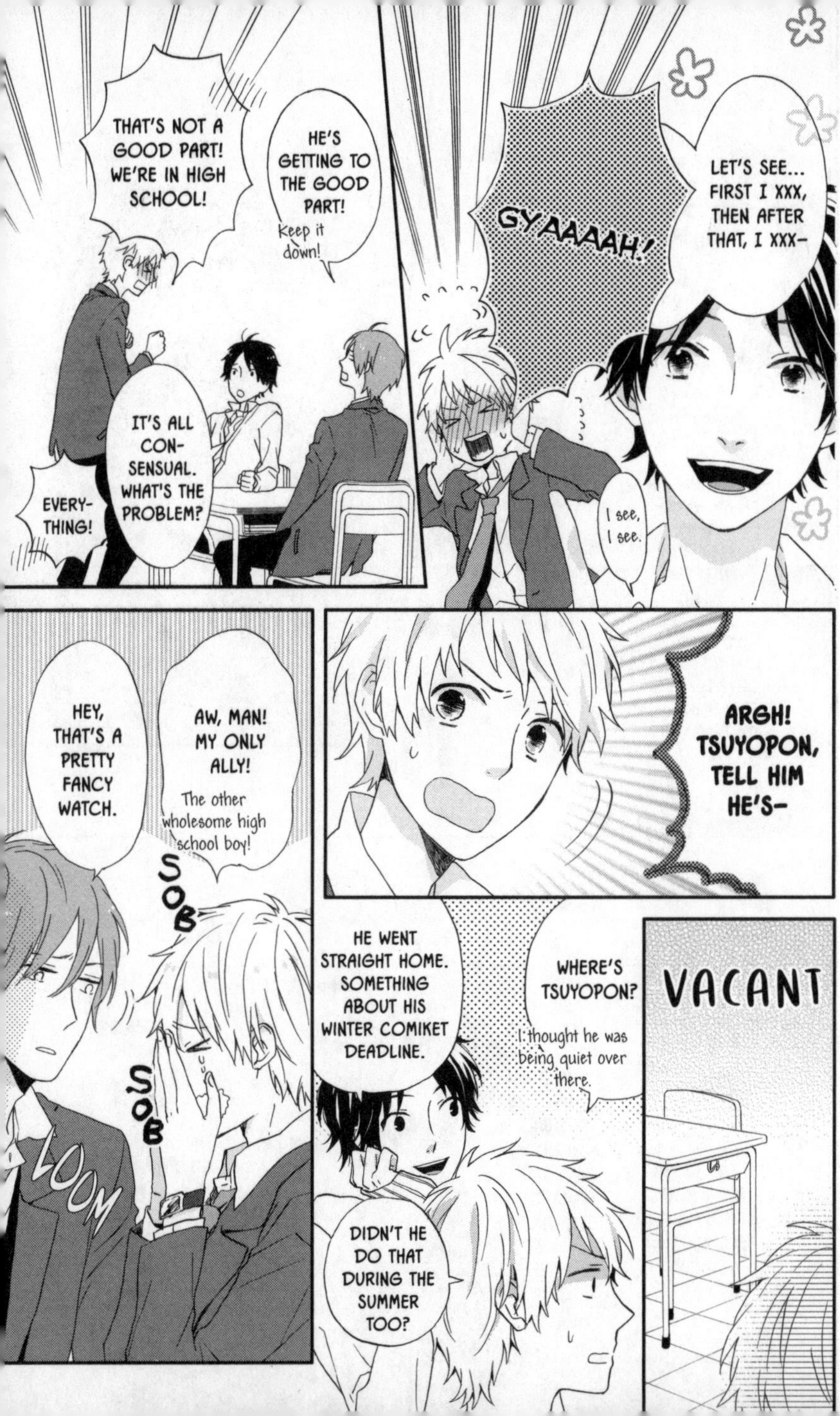
LET'S SEE... FIRST I XXX, THEN AFTER THAT, I XXX–
GYAAAAH!
I see, I see.
HE'S GETTING TO THE GOOD PART!
Keep it down!
THAT'S NOT A GOOD PART! WE'RE IN HIGH SCHOOL!
IT'S ALL CON-SENSUAL. WHAT'S THE PROBLEM?
EVERY-THING!
ARGH! TSUYOPON, TELL HIM HE'S–
VACANT
WHERE'S TSUYOPON?
I thought he was being quiet over there.
HE WENT STRAIGHT HOME. SOMETHING ABOUT HIS WINTER COMIKET DEADLINE.
DIDN'T HE DO THAT DURING THE SUMMER TOO?
AW, MAN! MY ONLY ALLY!
The other wholesome high school boy!
HEY, THAT'S A PRETTY FANCY WATCH.
SOB
SOB
LOOM

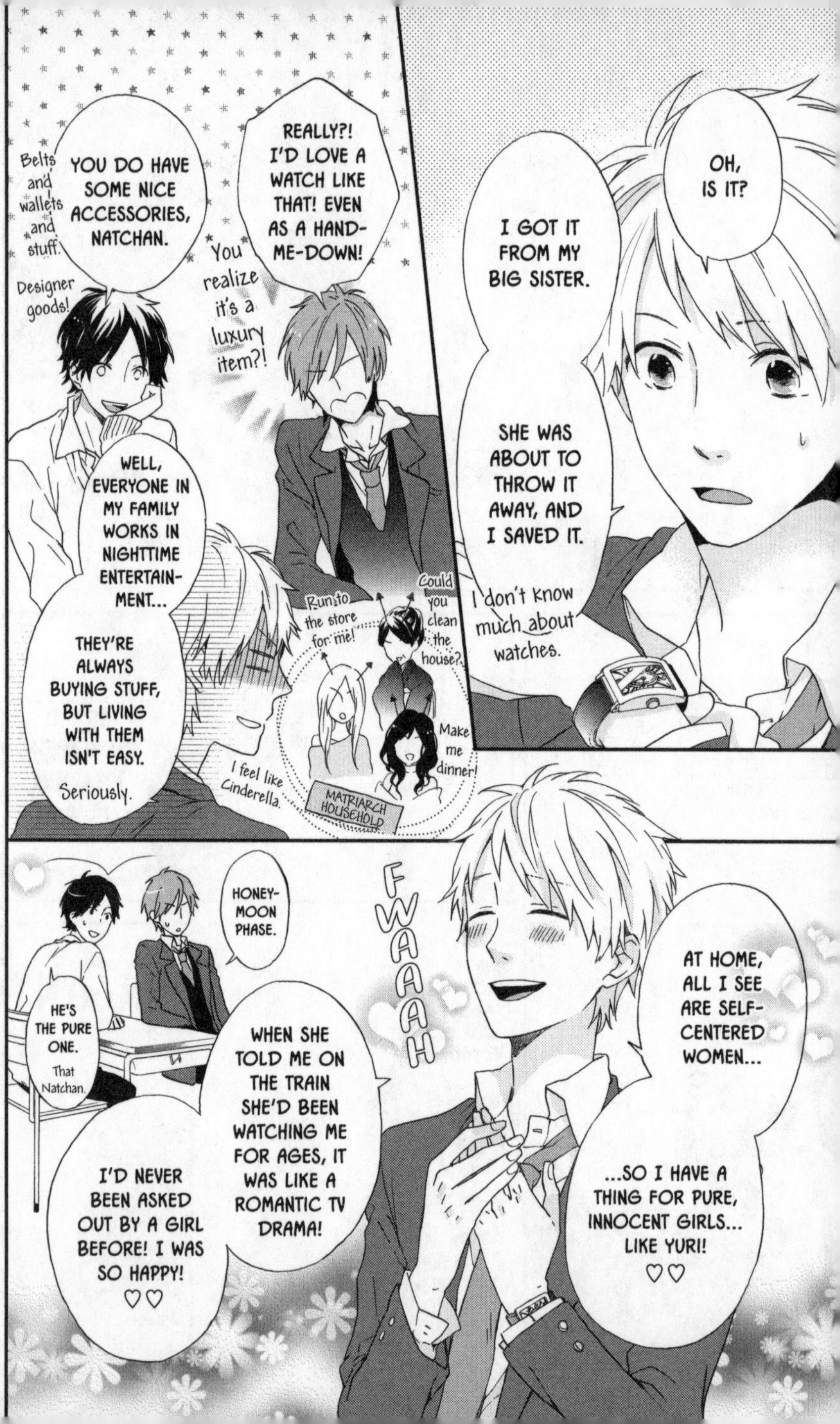
OH, IS IT?
I GOT IT FROM MY BIG SISTER.
SHE WAS ABOUT TO THROW IT AWAY, AND I SAVED IT.
I don't know much about watches.
REALLY?! I'D LOVE A WATCH LIKE THAT! EVEN AS A HAND-ME-DOWN!
You realize it's a luxury item?!
YOU DO HAVE SOME NICE ACCESSORIES, NATCHAN.
Belts and wallets and stuff.
Designer goods!
WELL, EVERYONE IN MY FAMILY WORKS IN NIGHTTIME ENTERTAINMENT...
THEY'RE ALWAYS BUYING STUFF, BUT LIVING WITH THEM ISN'T EASY.
Seriously.
Could you clean the house?
Run to the store for me!
Make me dinner!
I feel like Cinderella.
MATRIARCH HOUSEHOLD
FWAAAAH
AT HOME, ALL I SEE ARE SELF-CENTERED WOMEN...
...SO I HAVE A THING FOR PURE, INNOCENT GIRLS... LIKE YURI! ♡♡
WHEN SHE TOLD ME ON THE TRAIN SHE'D BEEN WATCHING ME FOR AGES, IT WAS LIKE A ROMANTIC TV DRAMA!
I'D NEVER BEEN ASKED OUT BY A GIRL BEFORE! I WAS SO HAPPY! ♡♡
HONEY-MOON PHASE.
HE'S THE PURE ONE.
That Natchan.

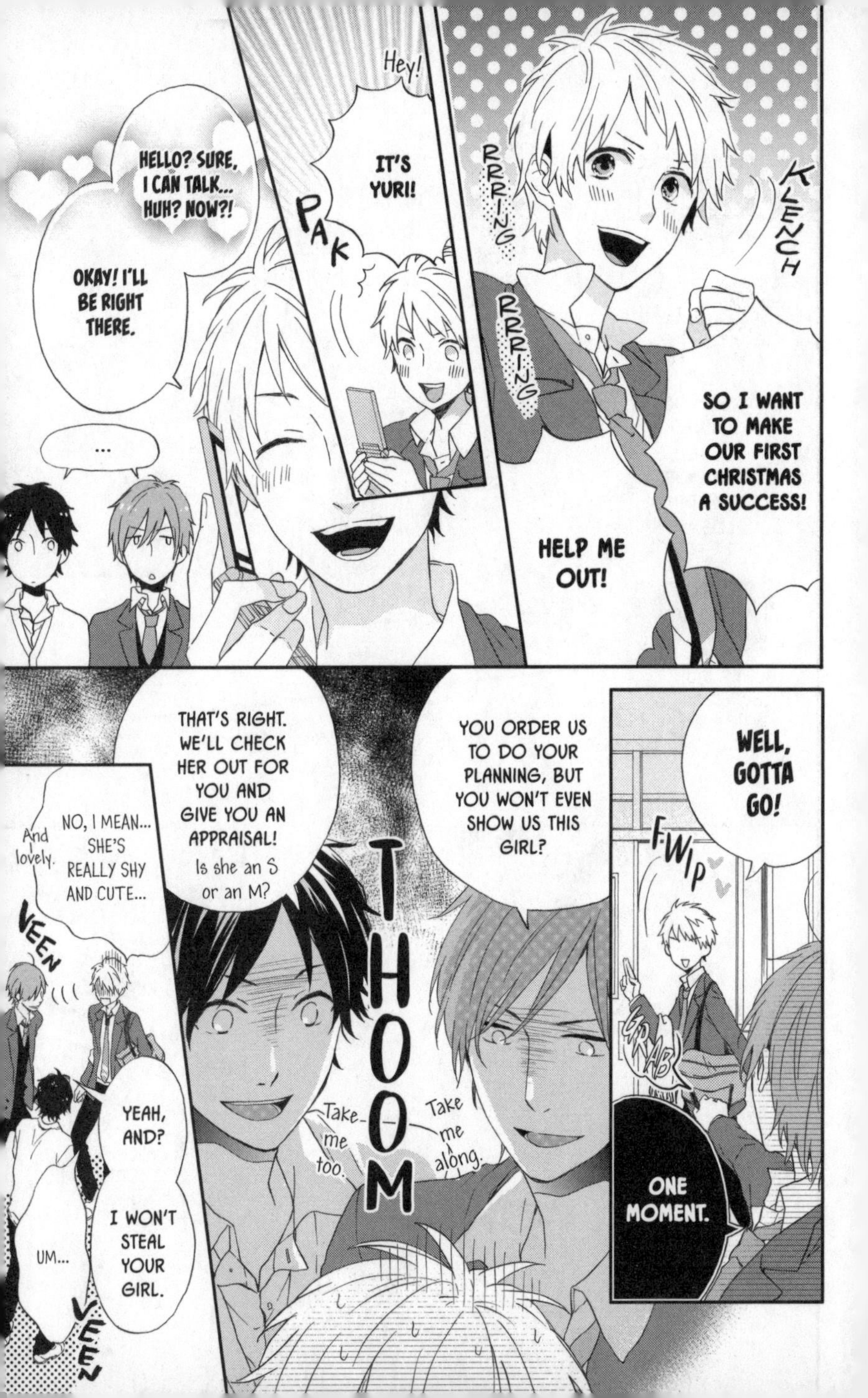
RRRING
RRRING
KLENCH
SO I WANT TO MAKE OUR FIRST CHRISTMAS A SUCCESS!
HELP ME OUT!
Hey!
IT'S YURI!
PAK
HELLO? SURE, I CAN TALK... HUH? NOW?!
OKAY! I'LL BE RIGHT THERE.
...
WELL, GOTTA GO!
FWIP
GRAB
ONE MOMENT.
YOU ORDER US TO DO YOUR PLANNING, BUT YOU WON'T EVEN SHOW US THIS GIRL?
THAT'S RIGHT. WE'LL CHECK HER OUT FOR YOU AND GIVE YOU AN APPRAISAL!
Is she an S or an M?
THOOM
Take me along.
Take-me too.
NO, I MEAN... SHE'S REALLY SHY AND CUTE...
And lovely.
VEEN
YEAH, AND?
I WON'T STEAL YOUR GIRL.
UM...
VEEN

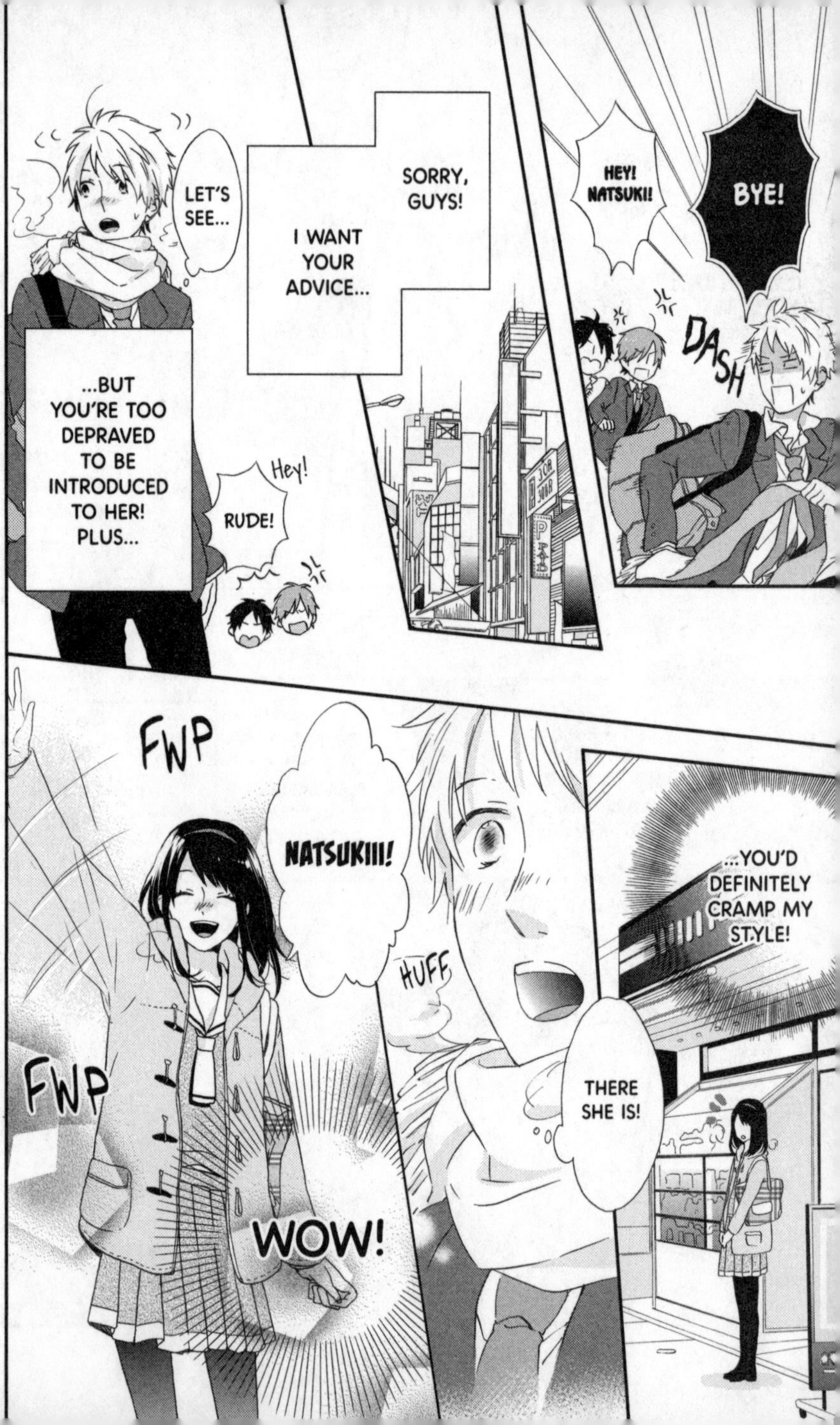

BYE!
HEY! NATSUKI!
DASH
SORRY, GUYS!
I WANT YOUR ADVICE...
LET'S SEE...
...BUT YOU'RE TOO DEPRAVED TO BE INTRODUCED TO HER! PLUS...
Hey!
RUDE!
...YOU'D DEFINITELY CRAMP MY STYLE!
THERE SHE IS!
NATSUKIII!
HUFF
FWP
WOW!
FWP

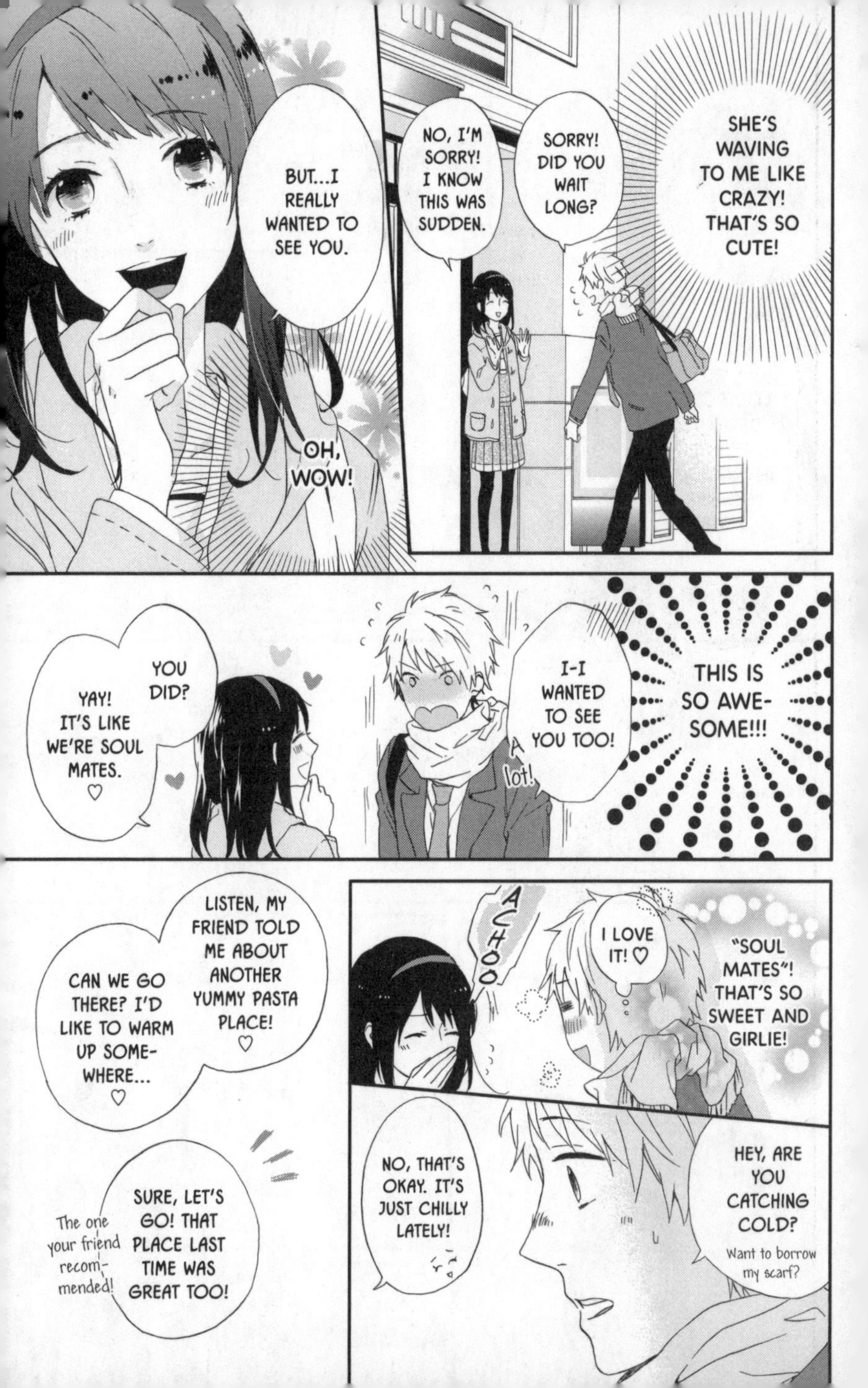
SHE'S WAVING TO ME LIKE CRAZY! THAT'S SO CUTE!
SORRY! DID YOU WAIT LONG?
NO, I'M SORRY! I KNOW THIS WAS SUDDEN.
BUT...I REALLY WANTED TO SEE YOU.
OH, WOW!
THIS IS SO AWE-SOME!!!
I-I WANTED TO SEE YOU TOO!
A lot!
YOU DID?
YAY! IT'S LIKE WE'RE SOUL MATES. ♡
"SOUL MATES"! THAT'S SO SWEET AND GIRLIE!
I LOVE IT! ♡
ACHOO
HEY, ARE YOU CATCHING COLD?
Want to borrow my scarf?
NO, THAT'S OKAY. IT'S JUST CHILLY LATELY!
LISTEN, MY FRIEND TOLD ME ABOUT ANOTHER YUMMY PASTA PLACE! ♡
CAN WE GO THERE? I'D LIKE TO WARM UP SOME-WHERE... ♡
SURE, LET'S GO! THAT PLACE LAST TIME WAS GREAT TOO!
The one your friend recom-mended!

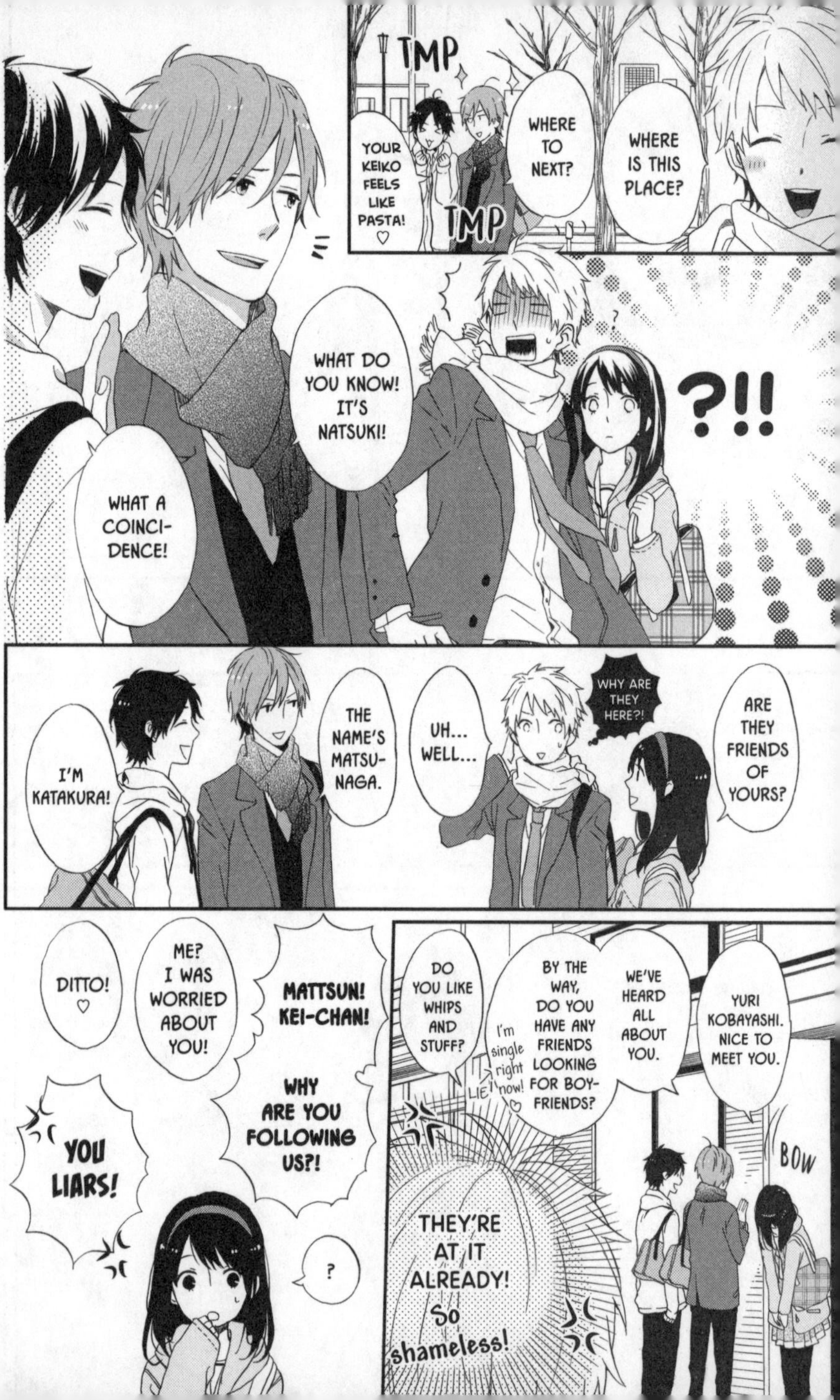
WHERE IS THIS PLACE?
WHERE TO NEXT?
TMP
TMP
YOUR KEIKO FEELS LIKE PASTA! ♡
?!!
?
WHAT DO YOU KNOW! IT'S NATSUKI!
WHAT A COINCIDENCE!
ARE THEY FRIENDS OF YOURS?
WHY ARE THEY HERE?!
UH... WELL...
THE NAME'S MATSUNAGA.
I'M KATAKURA!
BOW
YURI KOBAYASHI. NICE TO MEET YOU.
WE'VE HEARD ALL ABOUT YOU.
BY THE WAY, DO YOU HAVE ANY FRIENDS LOOKING FOR BOYFRIENDS?
I'm single right now! ♡
LIE
DO YOU LIKE WHIPS AND STUFF?
THEY'RE AT IT ALREADY! So shameless!
MATTSUN! KEI-CHAN!
WHY ARE YOU FOLLOWING US?!
ME? I WAS WORRIED ABOUT YOU!
DITTO! ♡
YOU LIARS!
?

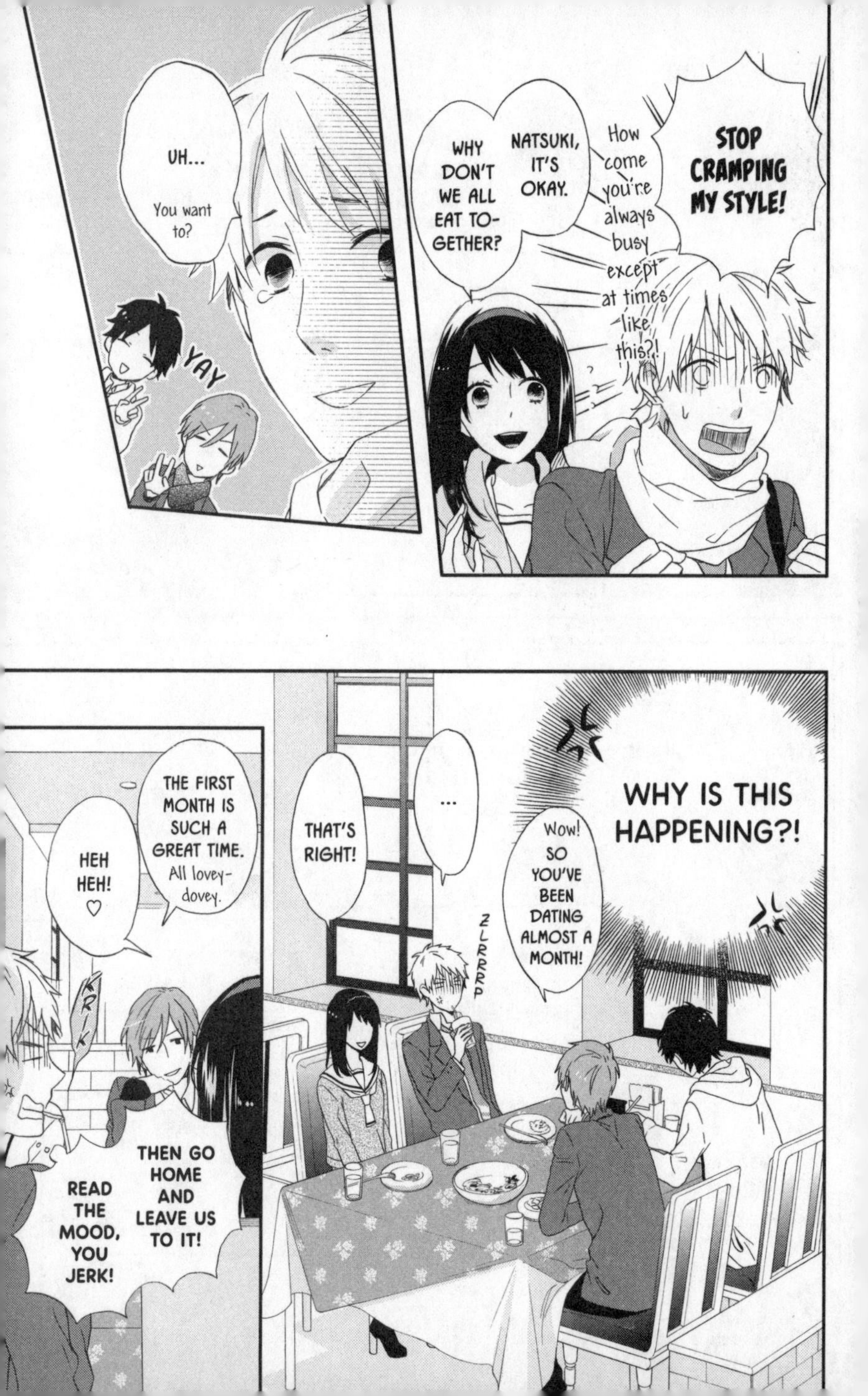
STOP CRAMPING MY STYLE!
How come you're always busy except at times like this?!
NATSUKI, IT'S OKAY.
WHY DON'T WE ALL EAT TO-GETHER?
UH...
You want to?
YAY
WHY IS THIS HAPPENING?!
Wow! SO YOU'VE BEEN DATING ALMOST A MONTH!
ZLRRRP
...
THAT'S RIGHT!
THE FIRST MONTH IS SUCH A GREAT TIME. All lovey-dovey.
HEH HEH! ♡
KRIK
THEN GO HOME AND LEAVE US TO IT!
READ THE MOOD, YOU JERK!

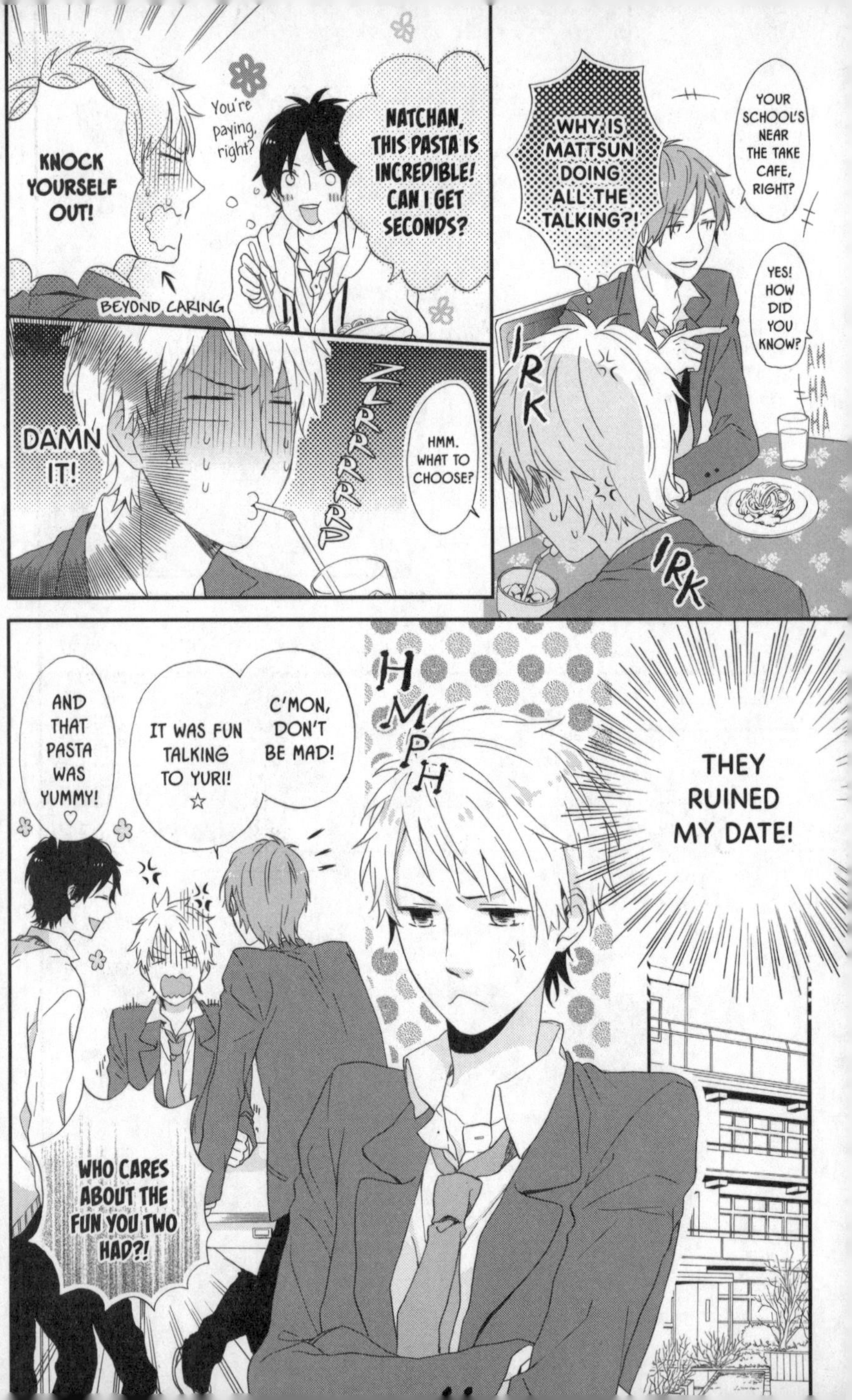
WHY IS MATTSUN DOING ALL THE TALKING?!
YOUR SCHOOL'S NEAR THE TAKE CAFE, RIGHT?
YES! HOW DID YOU KNOW?
AH HA HA
IRK
IRK
NATCHAN, THIS PASTA IS INCREDIBLE! CAN I GET SECONDS?
You're paying, right?
KNOCK YOURSELF OUT!
BEYOND CARING
HMM. WHAT TO CHOOSE?
ZLRRRRRRP
DAMN IT!
THEY RUINED MY DATE!
HMPH
C'MON, DON'T BE MAD!
IT WAS FUN TALKING TO YURI! ☆
AND THAT PASTA WAS YUMMY! ♡
WHO CARES ABOUT THE FUN YOU TWO HAD?!

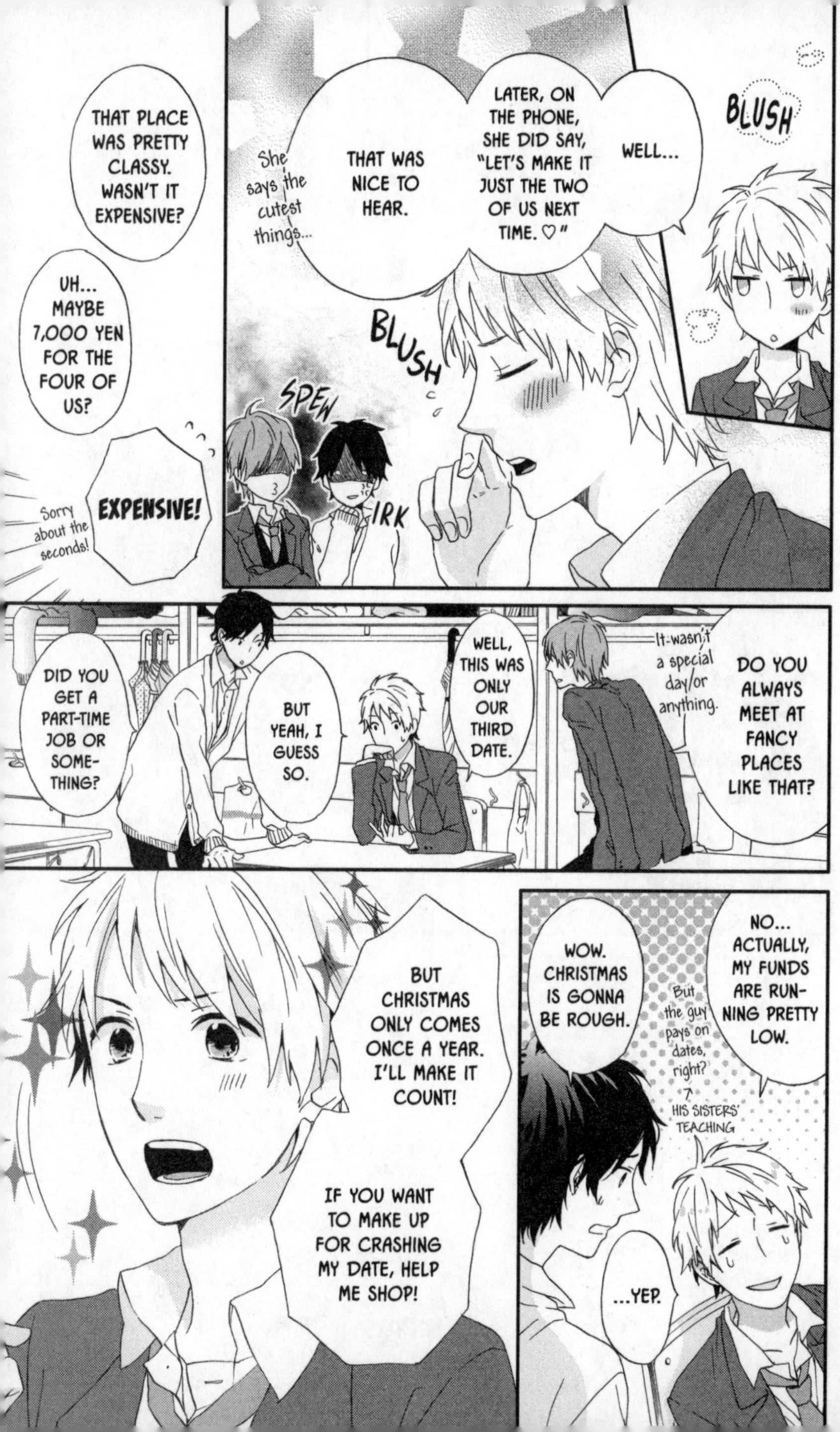
BLUSH
WELL...
LATER, ON THE PHONE, SHE DID SAY, "LET'S MAKE IT JUST THE TWO OF US NEXT TIME. ♡"
THAT WAS NICE TO HEAR.
She says the cutest things...
BLUSH
SPEW
IRK
THAT PLACE WAS PRETTY CLASSY. WASN'T IT EXPENSIVE?
UH... MAYBE 7,000 YEN FOR THE FOUR OF US?
EXPENSIVE!
Sorry about the seconds!
DO YOU ALWAYS MEET AT FANCY PLACES LIKE THAT?
It wasn't a special day/or anything.
WELL, THIS WAS ONLY OUR THIRD DATE.
BUT YEAH, I GUESS SO.
DID YOU GET A PART-TIME JOB OR SOME-THING?
NO... ACTUALLY, MY FUNDS ARE RUN-NING PRETTY LOW.
WOW. CHRISTMAS IS GONNA BE ROUGH.
But the guy pays on dates, right?
HIS SISTERS' TEACHING
...YEP.
BUT CHRISTMAS ONLY COMES ONCE A YEAR. I'LL MAKE IT COUNT!
IF YOU WANT TO MAKE UP FOR CRASHING MY DATE, HELP ME SHOP!

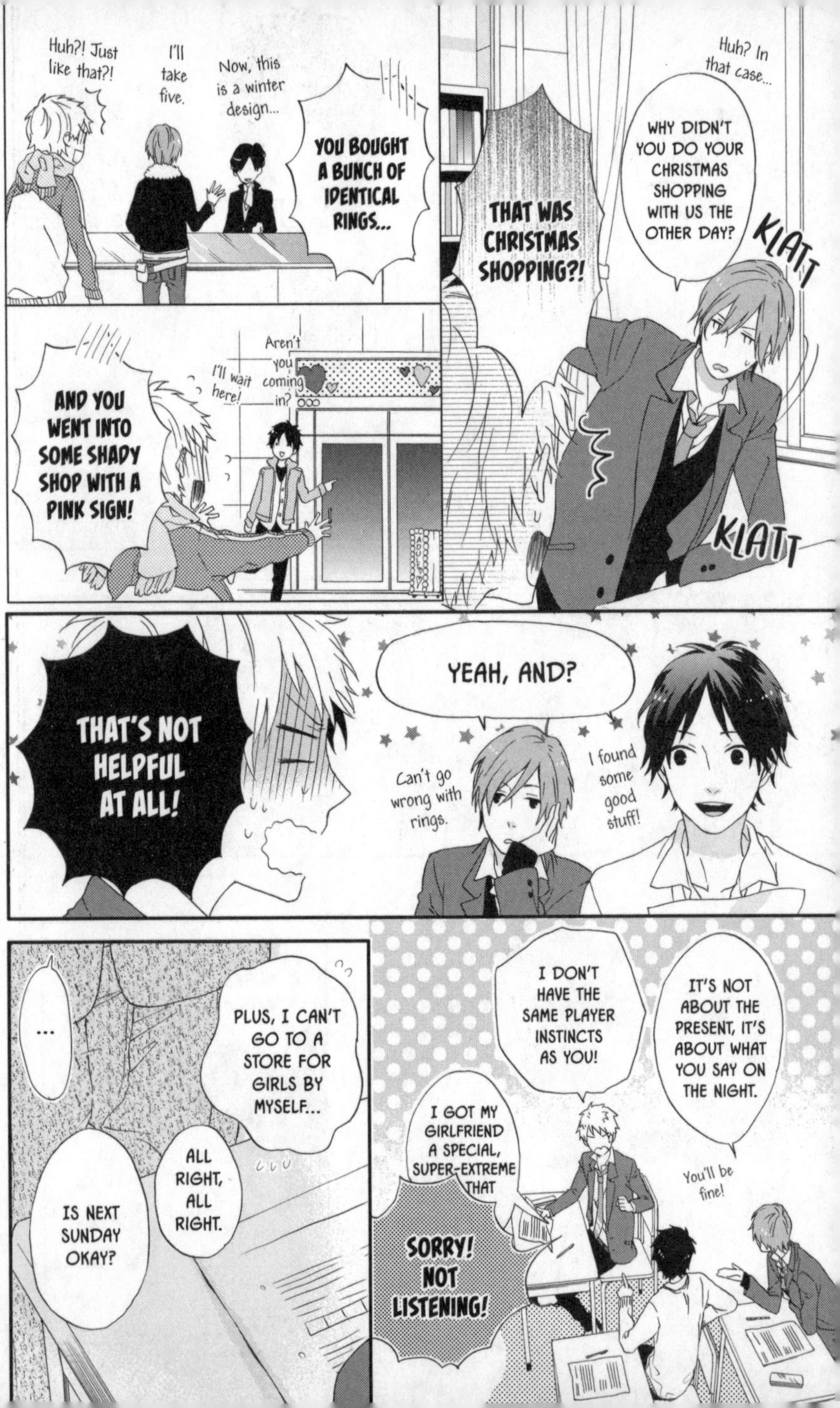
Huh? In that case...
WHY DIDN'T YOU DO YOUR CHRISTMAS SHOPPING WITH US THE OTHER DAY?
KLATT
THAT WAS CHRISTMAS SHOPPING?!
KLATT
YOU BOUGHT A BUNCH OF IDENTICAL RINGS...
Now, this is a winter design...
I'll take five.
Huh?! Just like that?!
Aren't you coming in?
I'll wait here!
AND YOU WENT INTO SOME SHADY SHOP WITH A PINK SIGN!
I found some good stuff!
YEAH, AND?
Can't go wrong with rings.
THAT'S NOT HELPFUL AT ALL!
IT'S NOT ABOUT THE PRESENT, IT'S ABOUT WHAT YOU SAY ON THE NIGHT.
I DON'T HAVE THE SAME PLAYER INSTINCTS AS YOU!
You'll be fine!
I GOT MY GIRLFRIEND A SPECIAL, SUPER-EXTREME THAT
SORRY! NOT LISTENING!
PLUS, I CAN'T GO TO A STORE FOR GIRLS BY MYSELF...
...
ALL RIGHT, ALL RIGHT.
IS NEXT SUNDAY OKAY?

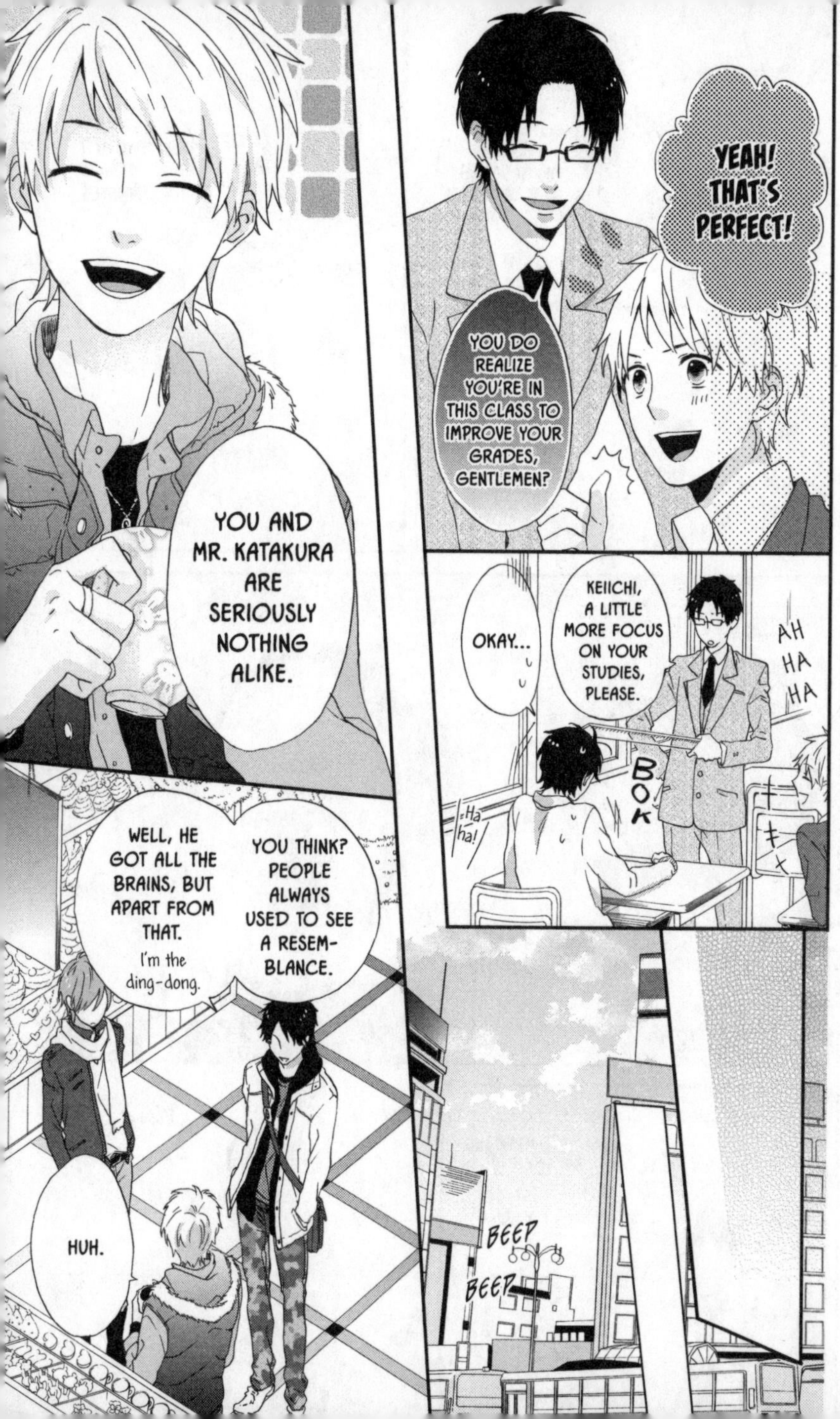
YEAH! THAT'S PERFECT!
YOU DO REALIZE YOU'RE IN THIS CLASS TO IMPROVE YOUR GRADES, GENTLEMEN?
AH HA HA
KEIICHI, A LITTLE MORE FOCUS ON YOUR STUDIES, PLEASE.
OKAY...
BOK
Ha ha!
YOU AND MR. KATAKURA ARE SERIOUSLY NOTHING ALIKE.
BEEP
BEEP
YOU THINK? PEOPLE ALWAYS USED TO SEE A RESEM-BLANCE.
WELL, HE GOT ALL THE BRAINS, BUT APART FROM THAT.
I'm the ding-dong.
HUH.

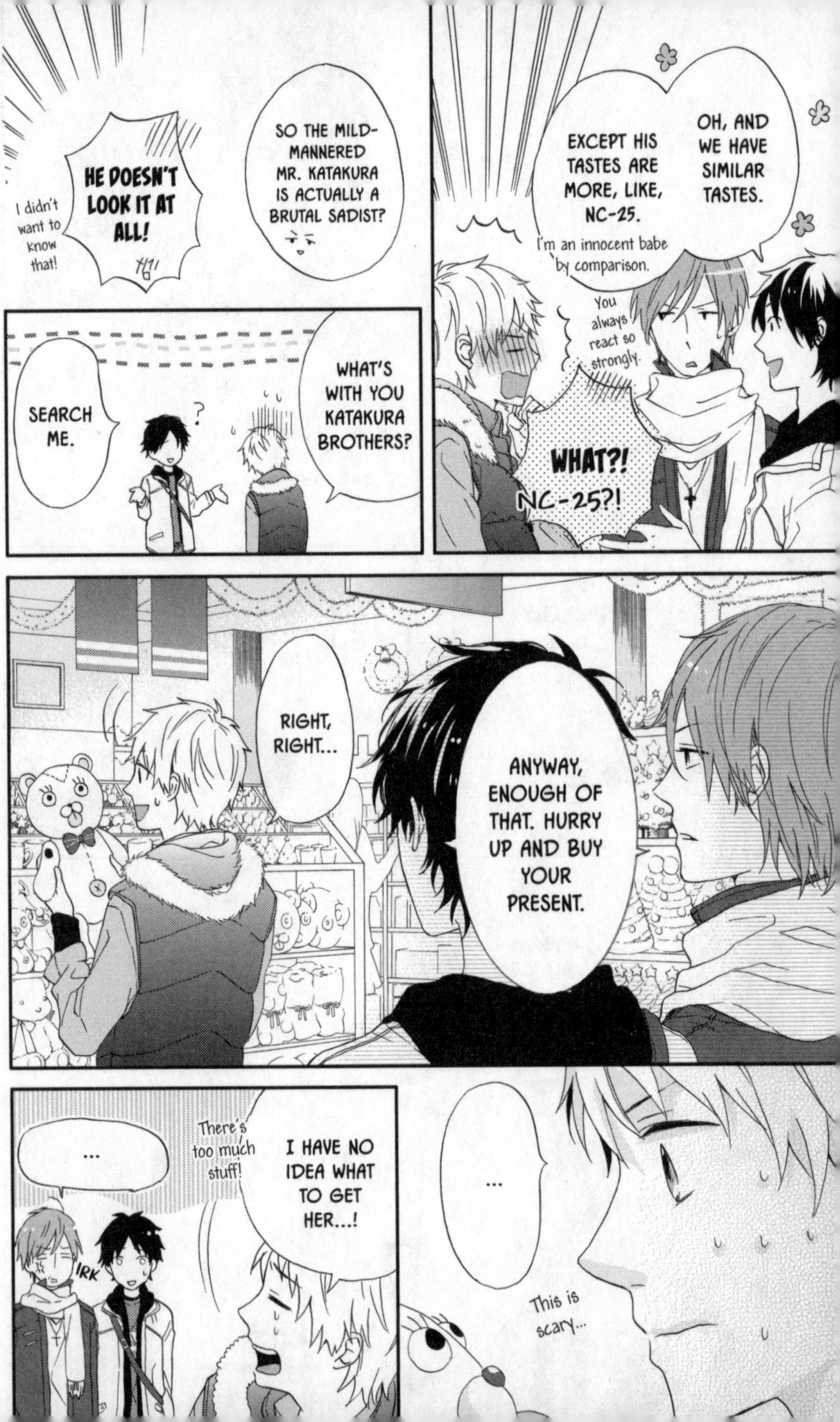
OH, AND WE HAVE SIMILAR TASTES.
EXCEPT HIS TASTES ARE MORE, LIKE, NC-25.
I'm an innocent babe by comparison.
You always react so strongly.
WHAT?! NC-25?!
SO THE MILD-MANNERED MR. KATAKURA IS ACTUALLY A BRUTAL SADIST?
HE DOESN'T LOOK IT AT ALL!
I didn't want to know that!
WHAT'S WITH YOU KATAKURA BROTHERS?
SEARCH ME.
ANYWAY, ENOUGH OF THAT. HURRY UP AND BUY YOUR PRESENT.
RIGHT, RIGHT...
...
This is scary...
I HAVE NO IDEA WHAT TO GET HER...!
There's too much stuff!
...
IRK

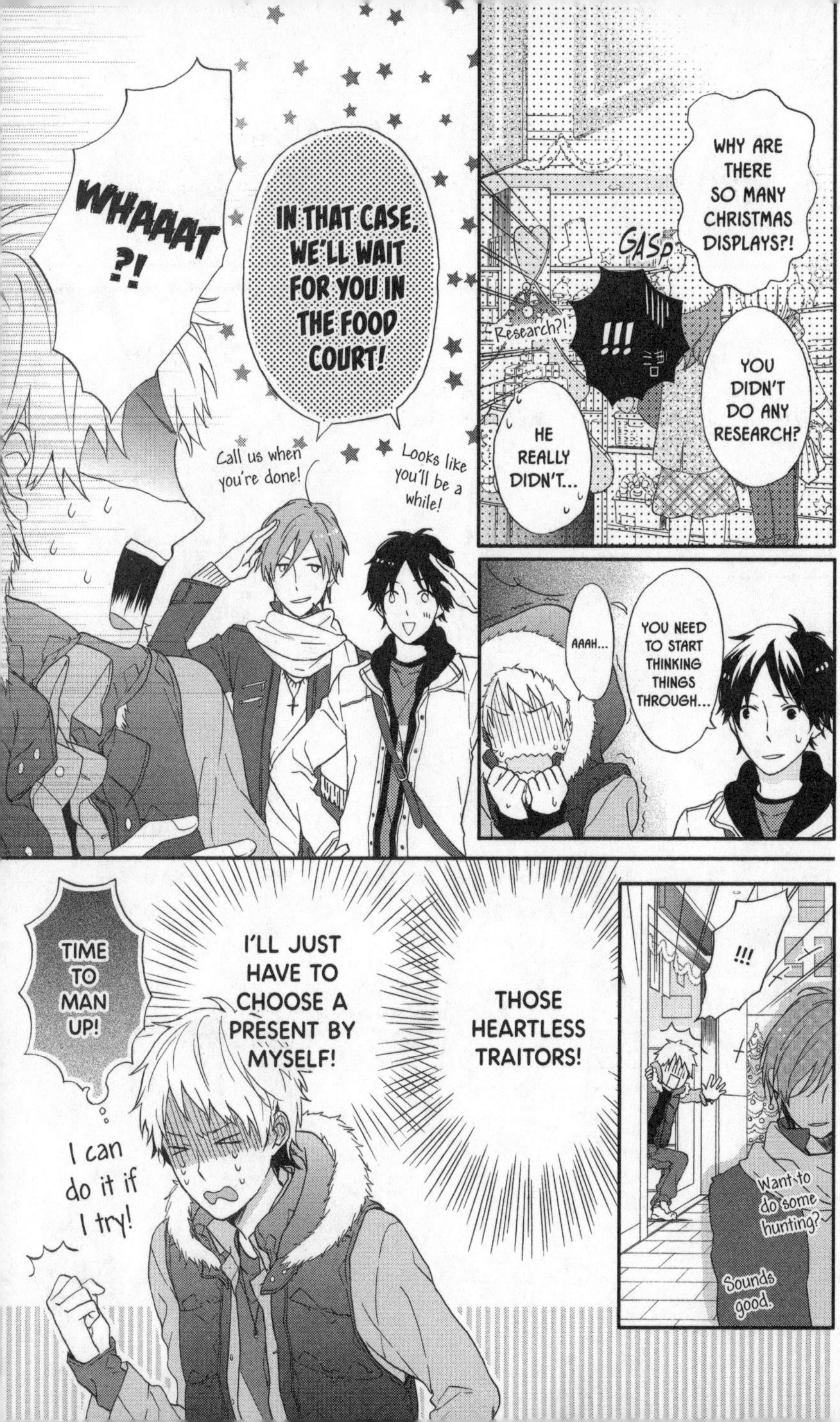
WHY ARE THERE SO MANY CHRISTMAS DISPLAYS?!
GASP
!!!
Research?!
YOU DIDN'T DO ANY RESEARCH?
HE REALLY DIDN'T...
AAAH...
YOU NEED TO START THINKING THINGS THROUGH...
IN THAT CASE, WE'LL WAIT FOR YOU IN THE FOOD COURT!
WHAAAT ?!
Looks like you'll be a while!
Call us when you're done!
!!!
Want to do some hunting?
Sounds good.
THOSE HEARTLESS TRAITORS!
I'LL JUST HAVE TO CHOOSE A PRESENT BY MYSELF!
TIME TO MAN UP!
I can do it if I try!

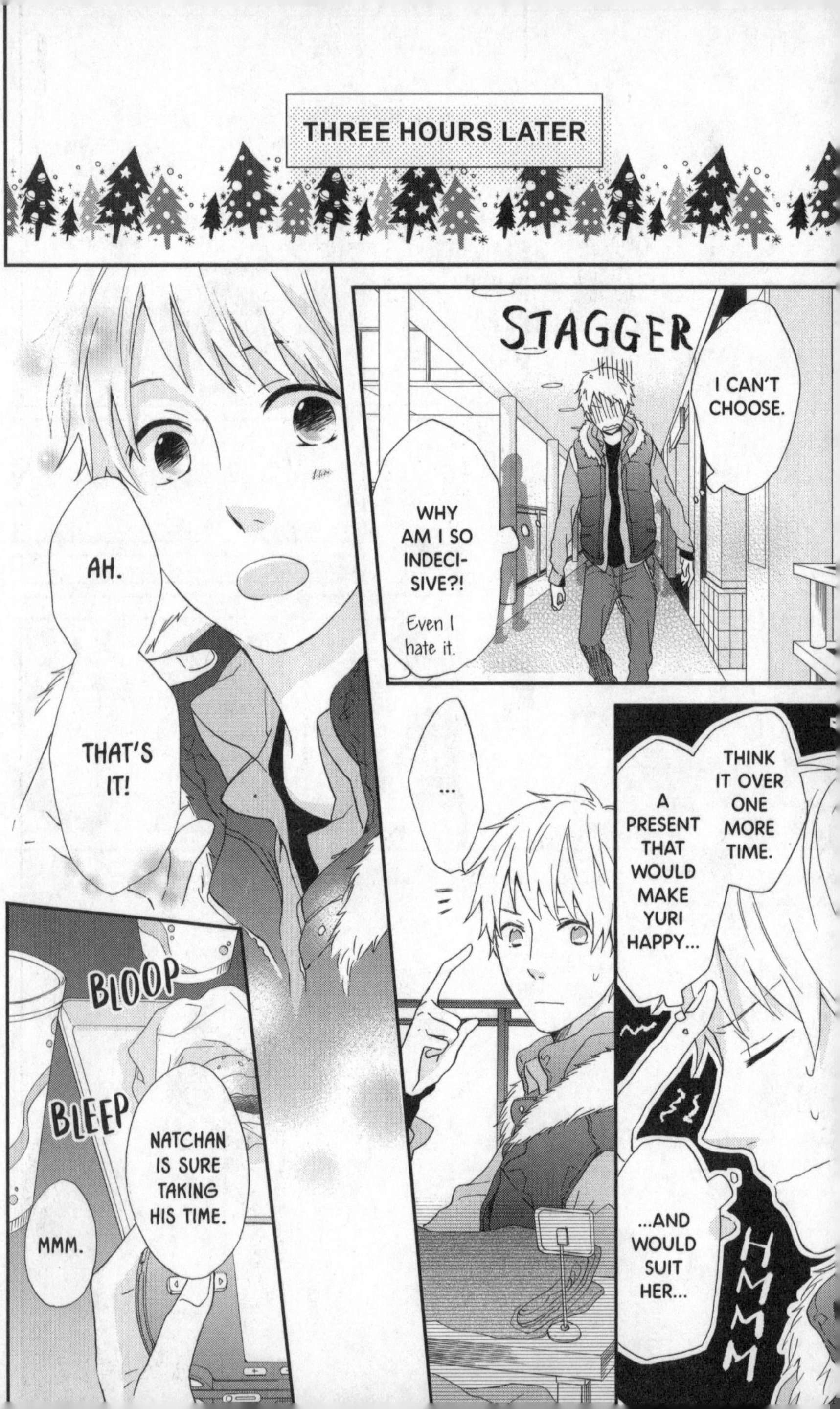
THREE HOURS LATER
STAGGER
I CAN'T CHOOSE.
WHY AM I SO INDECISIVE?!
Even I hate it.
THINK IT OVER ONE MORE TIME.
A PRESENT THAT WOULD MAKE YURI HAPPY...
...AND WOULD SUIT HER...
HMMM
...
AH.
THAT'S IT!
BLOOP
BLEEP
NATCHAN IS SURE TAKING HIS TIME.
MMM.

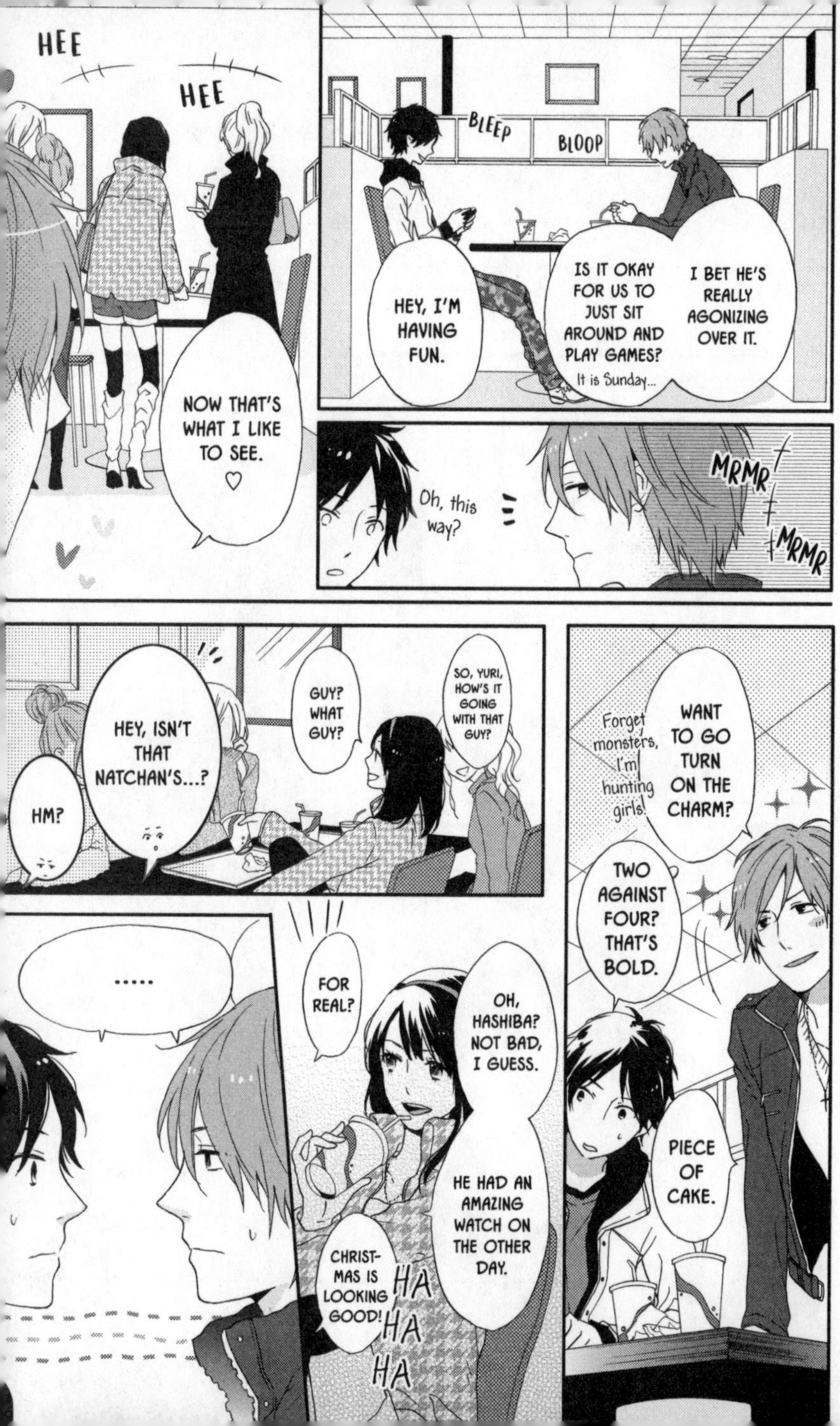
BLEEP
BLOOP
I BET HE'S REALLY AGONIZING OVER IT.
IS IT OKAY FOR US TO JUST SIT AROUND AND PLAY GAMES?
It is Sunday...
HEY, I'M HAVING FUN.
MRMR
MRMR
Oh, this way?
HEE
HEE
NOW THAT'S WHAT I LIKE TO SEE. ♡
WANT TO GO TURN ON THE CHARM?
Forget monsters, I'm hunting girls!
TWO AGAINST FOUR? THAT'S BOLD.
PIECE OF CAKE.
SO, YURI, HOW'S IT GOING WITH THAT GUY?
GUY? WHAT GUY?
HEY, ISN'T THAT NATCHAN'S...?
HM?
OH, HASHIBA? NOT BAD, I GUESS.
FOR REAL?
HE HAD AN AMAZING WATCH ON THE OTHER DAY.
CHRIST-MAS IS LOOKING GOOD!
HA
HA
HA
......

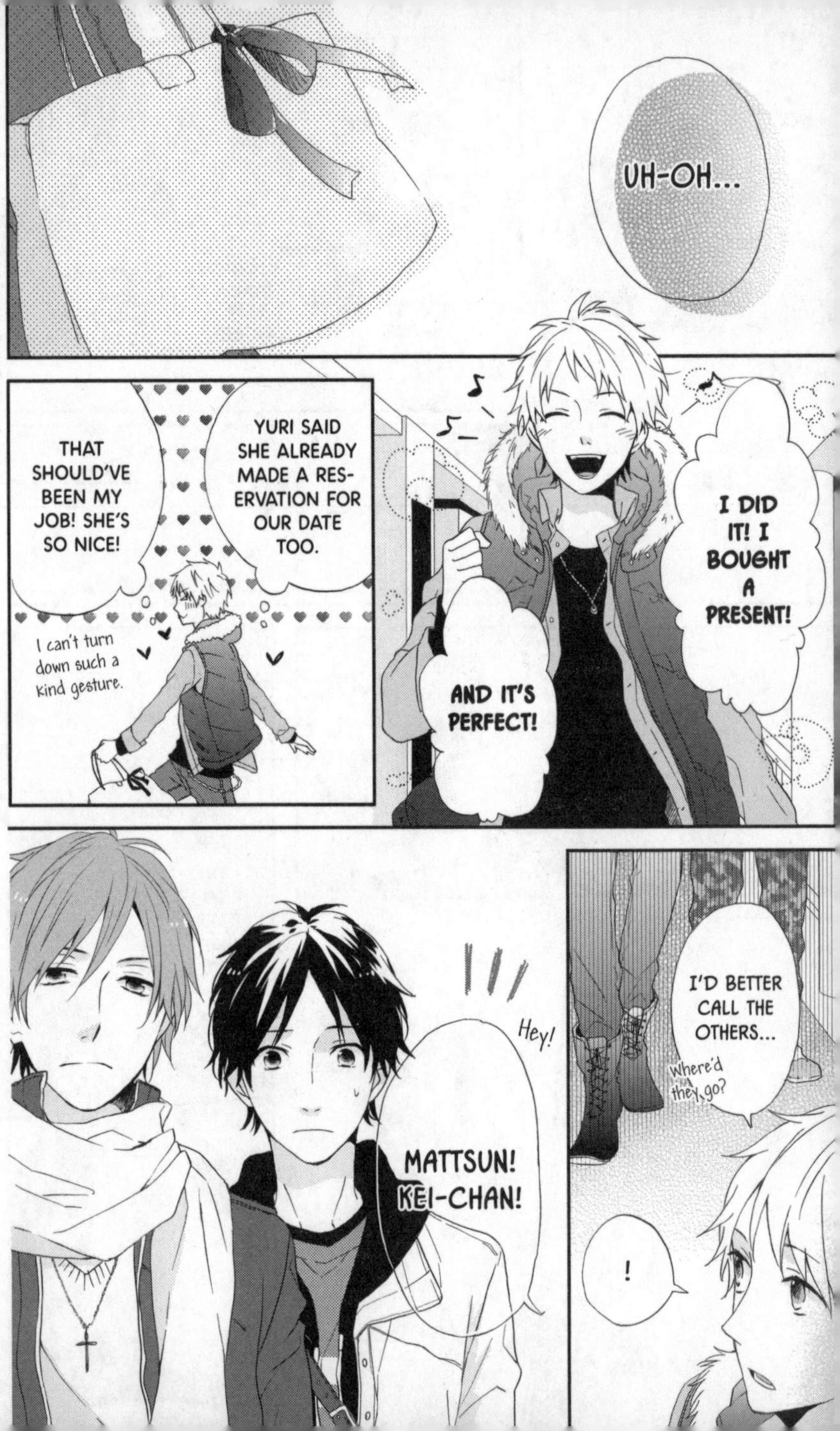
UH-OH...
I DID IT! I BOUGHT A PRESENT!
AND IT'S PERFECT!
YURI SAID SHE ALREADY MADE A RES-ERVATION FOR OUR DATE TOO.
THAT SHOULD'VE BEEN MY JOB! SHE'S SO NICE!
I can't turn down such a kind gesture.
I'D BETTER CALL THE OTHERS...
Where'd they go?
!
Hey!
MATTSUN! KEI-CHAN!

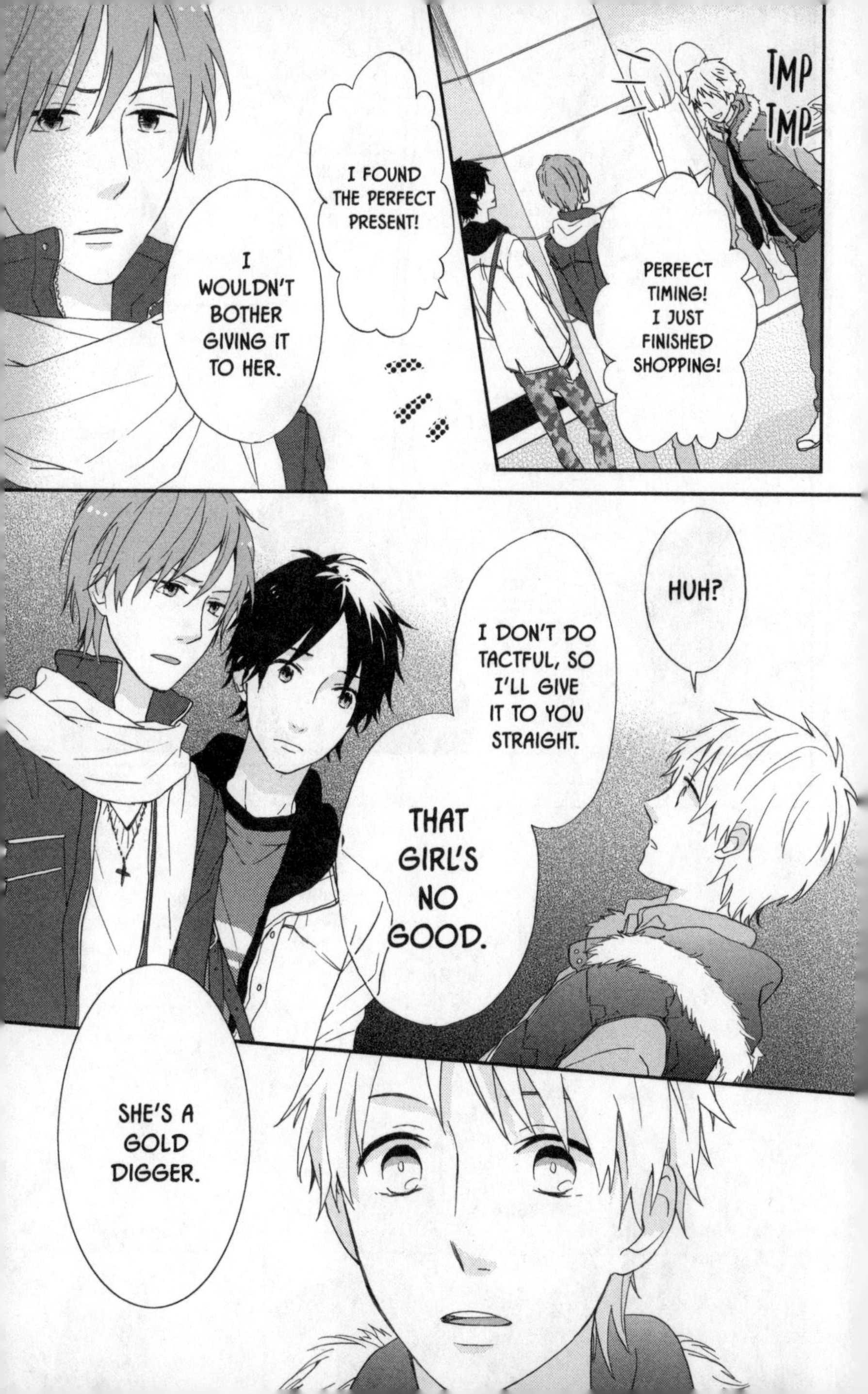
TMP
TMP
PERFECT TIMING! I JUST FINISHED SHOPPING!
I FOUND THE PERFECT PRESENT!
I WOULDN'T BOTHER GIVING IT TO HER.
HUH?
I DON'T DO TACTFUL, SO I'LL GIVE IT TO YOU STRAIGHT.
THAT GIRL'S NO GOOD.
SHE'S A GOLD DIGGER.

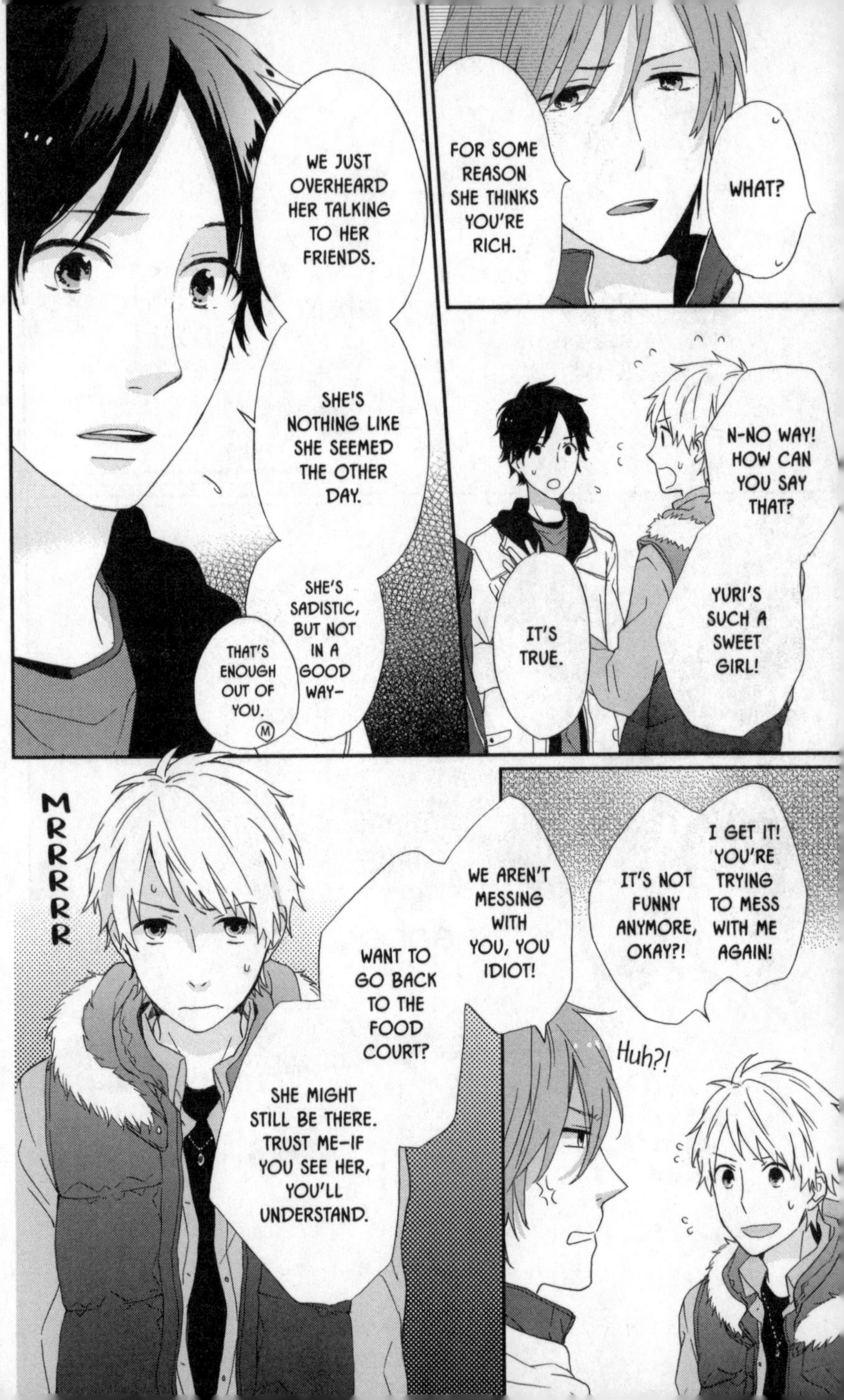
FOR SOME REASON SHE THINKS YOU'RE RICH.
WHAT?
N-NO WAY! HOW CAN YOU SAY THAT?
YURI'S SUCH A SWEET GIRL!
IT'S TRUE.
...
WE JUST OVERHEARD HER TALKING TO HER FRIENDS.
SHE'S NOTHING LIKE SHE SEEMED THE OTHER DAY.
SHE'S SADISTIC, BUT NOT IN A GOOD WAY–
THAT'S ENOUGH OUT OF YOU.
I GET IT! YOU'RE TRYING TO MESS WITH ME AGAIN!
IT'S NOT FUNNY ANYMORE, OKAY?!
WE AREN'T MESSING WITH YOU, YOU IDIOT!
Huh?!
MRRRRR
WANT TO GO BACK TO THE FOOD COURT?
SHE MIGHT STILL BE THERE. TRUST ME–IF YOU SEE HER, YOU'LL UNDERSTAND.

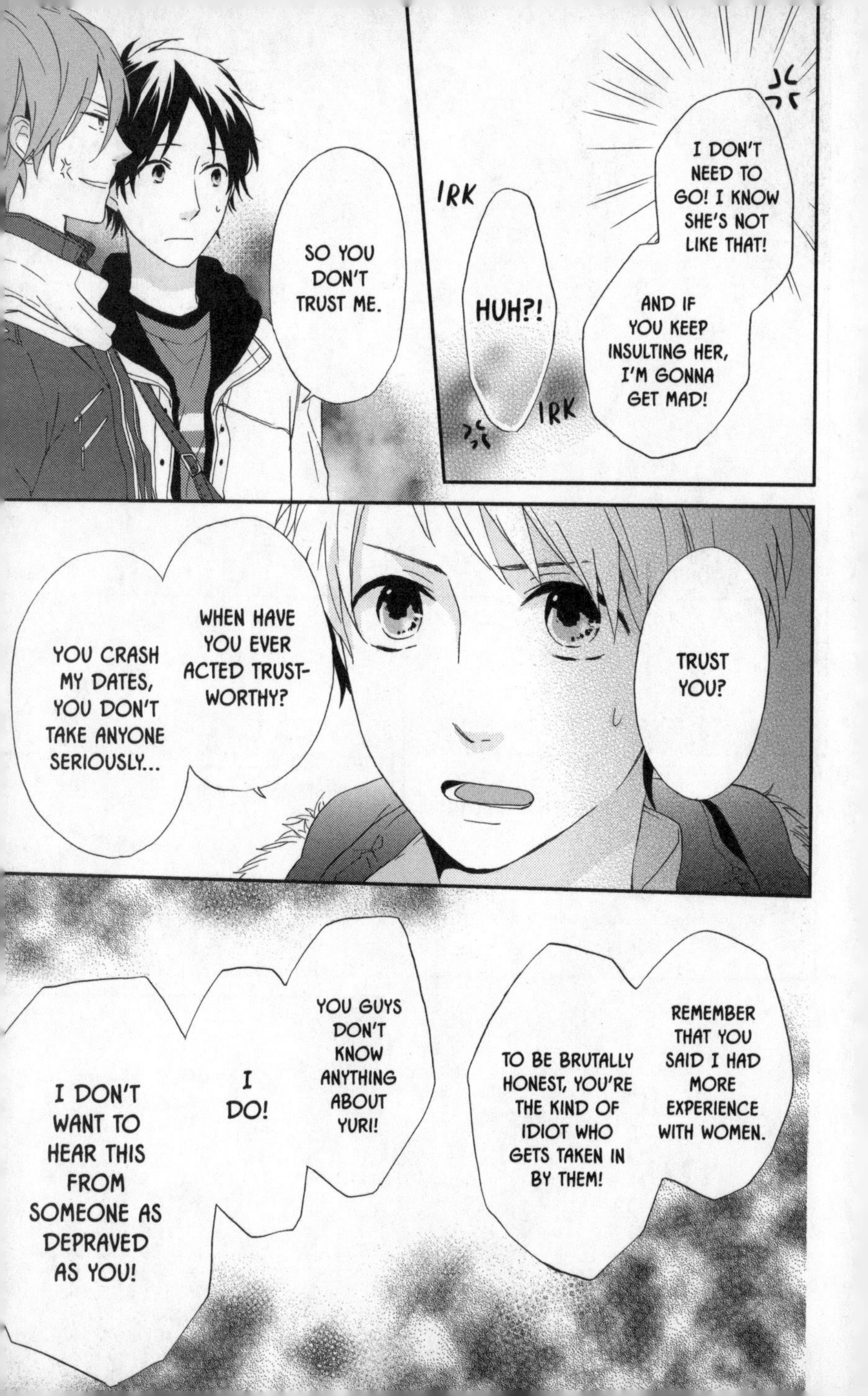
I DON'T NEED TO GO! I KNOW SHE'S NOT LIKE THAT!
AND IF YOU KEEP INSULTING HER, I'M GONNA GET MAD!
IRK
HUH?!
IRK
SO YOU DON'T TRUST ME.
TRUST YOU?
WHEN HAVE YOU EVER ACTED TRUST-WORTHY?
YOU CRASH MY DATES, YOU DON'T TAKE ANYONE SERIOUSLY...
REMEMBER THAT YOU SAID I HAD MORE EXPERIENCE WITH WOMEN.
TO BE BRUTALLY HONEST, YOU'RE THE KIND OF IDIOT WHO GETS TAKEN IN BY THEM!
YOU GUYS DON'T KNOW ANYTHING ABOUT YURI!
I DO!
I DON'T WANT TO HEAR THIS FROM SOMEONE AS DEPRAVED AS YOU!

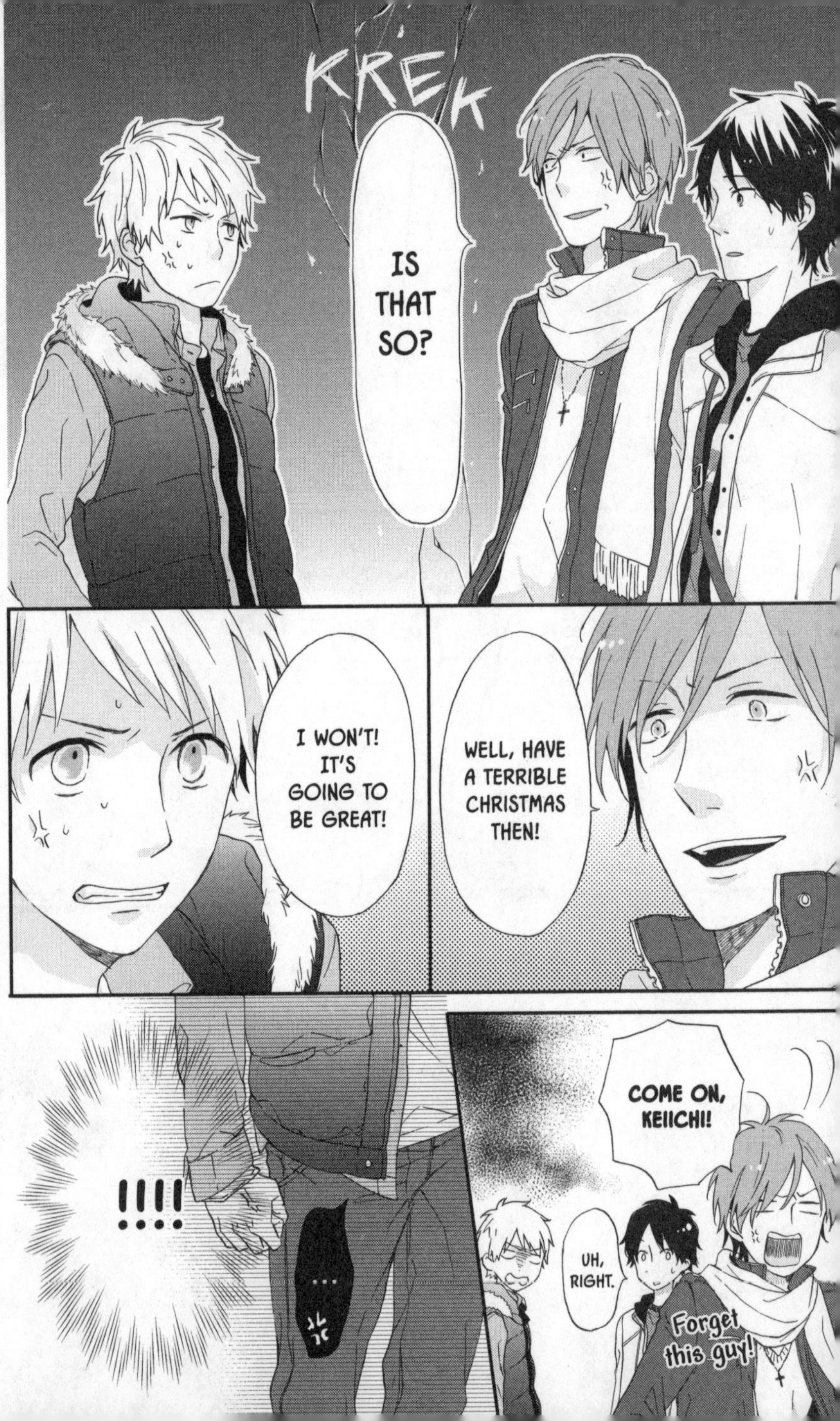
KREK
IS THAT SO?
WELL, HAVE A TERRIBLE CHRISTMAS THEN!
I WON'T! IT'S GOING TO BE GREAT!
COME ON, KEIICHI!
Forget this guy!
UH, RIGHT.
!!!!
...

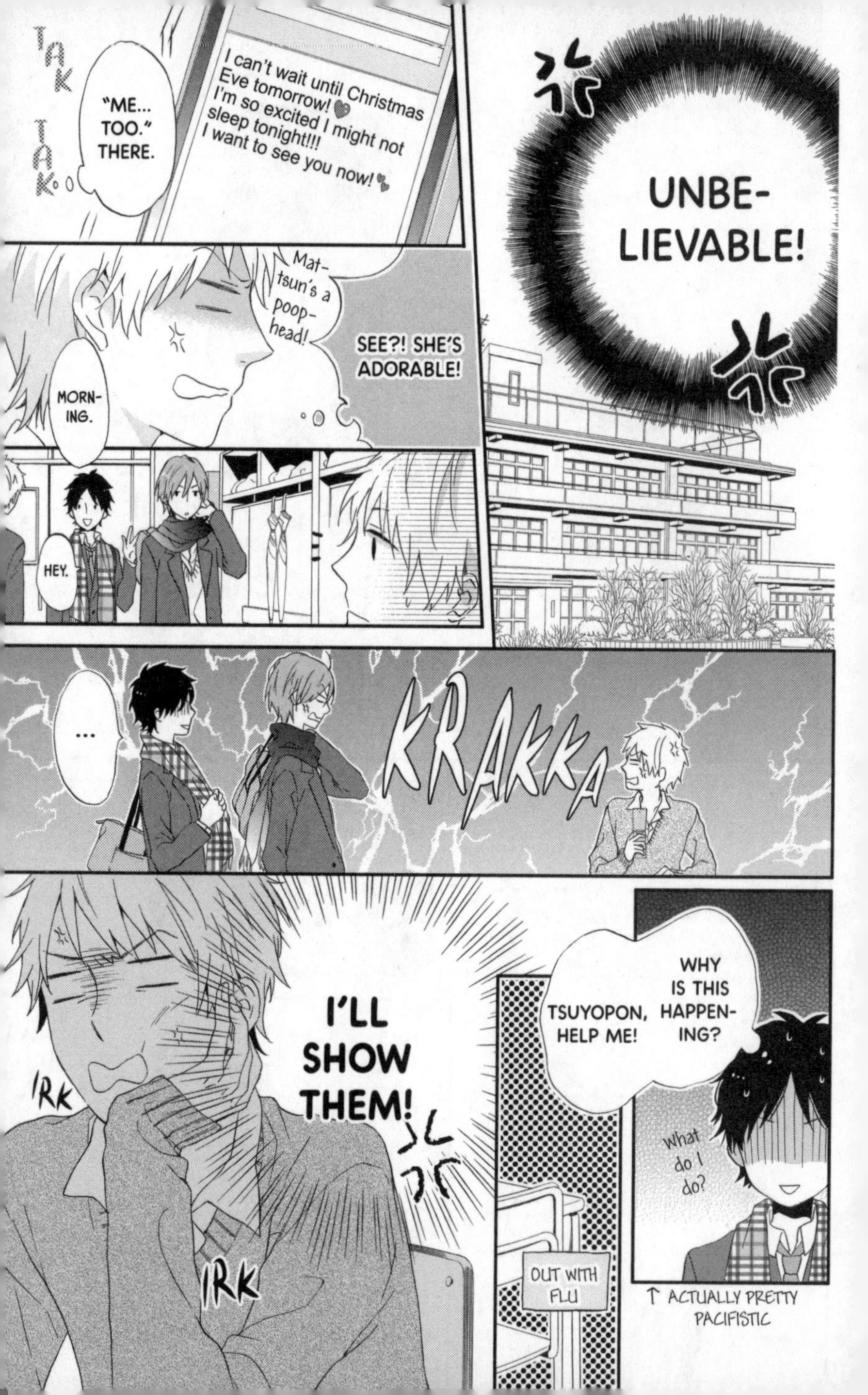
UNBE-LIEVABLE!
I can't wait until Christmas Eve tomorrow! ♥ I'm so excited I might not sleep tonight!!! I want to see you now! ♥
"ME... TOO." THERE.
TAK TAK
SEE?! SHE'S ADORABLE!
Mat-tsun's a poop-head!
MORN-ING.
HEY.
KRAKKA
...
WHY IS THIS HAPPEN-ING?
TSUYOPON, HELP ME!
what do I do?
↑ ACTUALLY PRETTY PACIFISTIC
OUT WITH FLU
I'LL SHOW THEM!
IRK
IRK

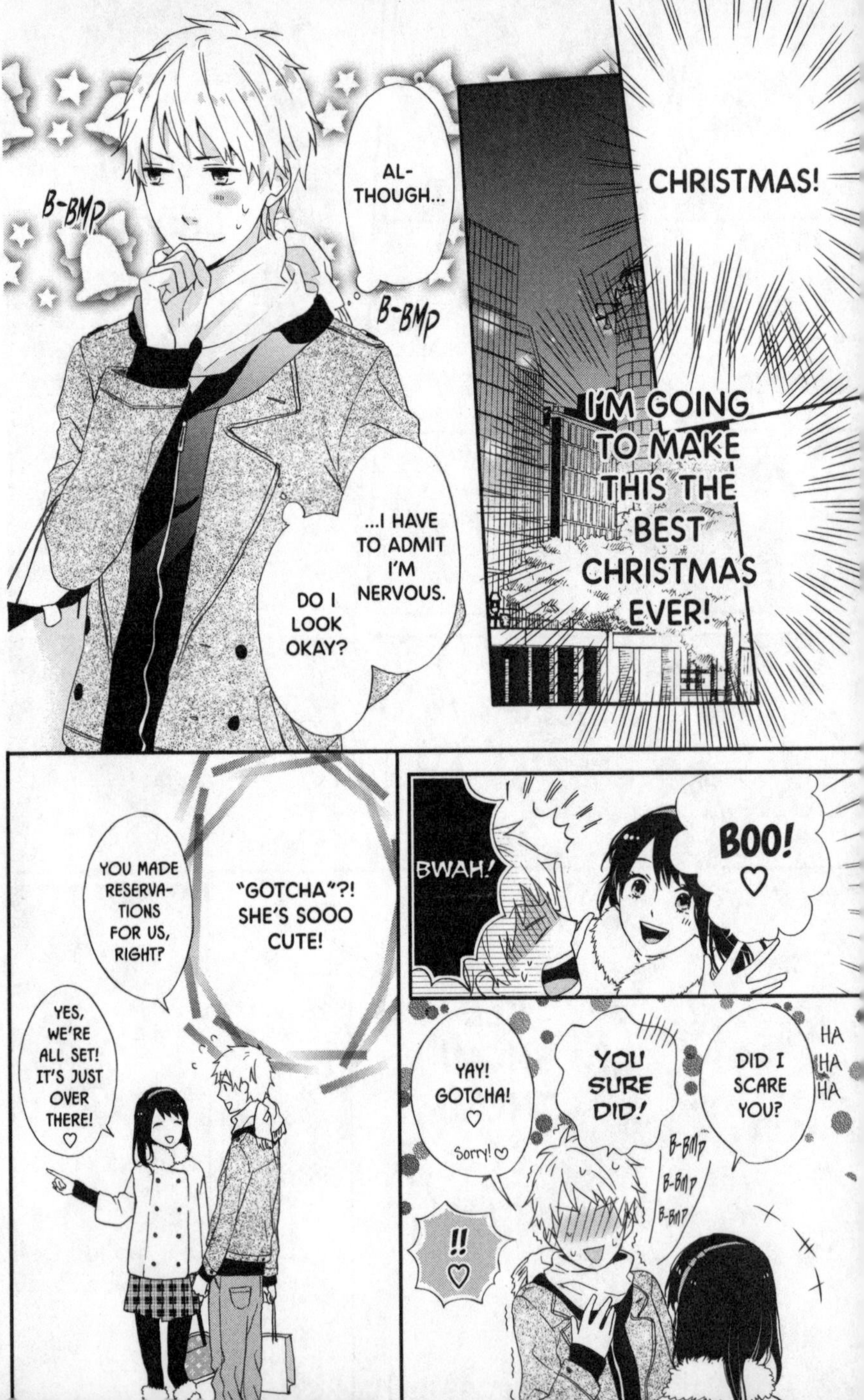
CHRISTMAS!
I'M GOING TO MAKE THIS THE BEST CHRISTMAS EVER!
AL-THOUGH...
B-BMP
B-BMP
...I HAVE TO ADMIT I'M NERVOUS.
DO I LOOK OKAY?
BOO! ♡
BWAH!
HA HA HA
DID I SCARE YOU?
YOU SURE DID!
YAY! GOTCHA! ♡
Sorry! ♡
B-BMP
B-BMP
B-BMP
!! ♡
"GOTCHA"?! SHE'S SOOO CUTE!
YOU MADE RESERVA-TIONS FOR US, RIGHT?
YES, WE'RE ALL SET! IT'S JUST OVER THERE! ♡

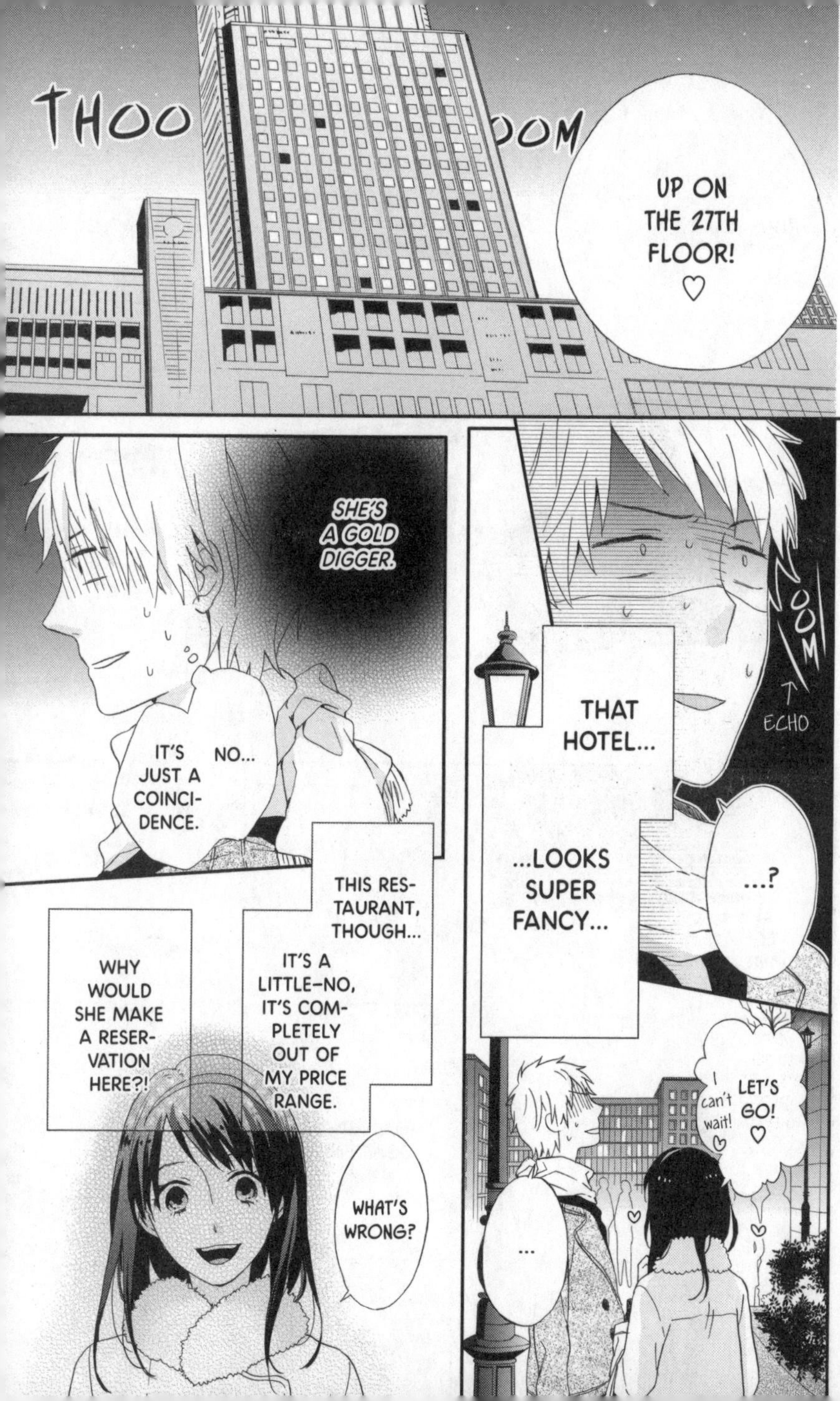
THOO
OOM
UP ON THE 27TH FLOOR! ♡
THAT HOTEL...
...LOOKS SUPER FANCY...
...?
OOM
ECHO
NO...
IT'S JUST A COINCIDENCE.
SHE'S A GOLD DIGGER.
THIS RESTAURANT, THOUGH...
IT'S A LITTLE—NO, IT'S COMPLETELY OUT OF MY PRICE RANGE.
WHY WOULD SHE MAKE A RESERVATION HERE?!
WHAT'S WRONG?
LET'S GO! ♡
I can't wait! ♡
...

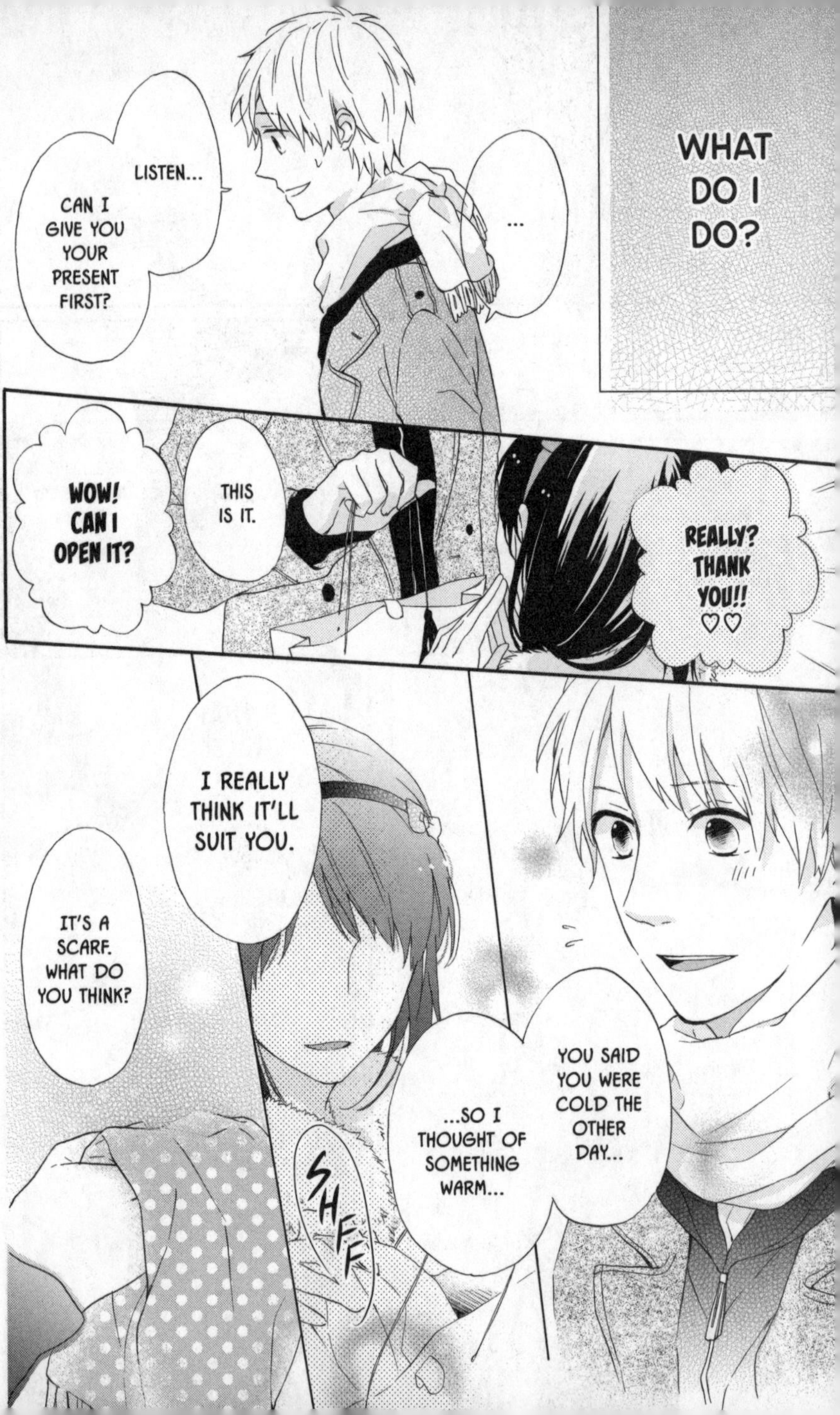
WHAT DO I DO?
...
LISTEN... CAN I GIVE YOU YOUR PRESENT FIRST?
REALLY? THANK YOU!! ♡♡
THIS IS IT.
WOW! CAN I OPEN IT?
YOU SAID YOU WERE COLD THE OTHER DAY...
...SO I THOUGHT OF SOMETHING WARM...
I REALLY THINK IT'LL SUIT YOU.
IT'S A SCARF. WHAT DO YOU THINK?
SHFF

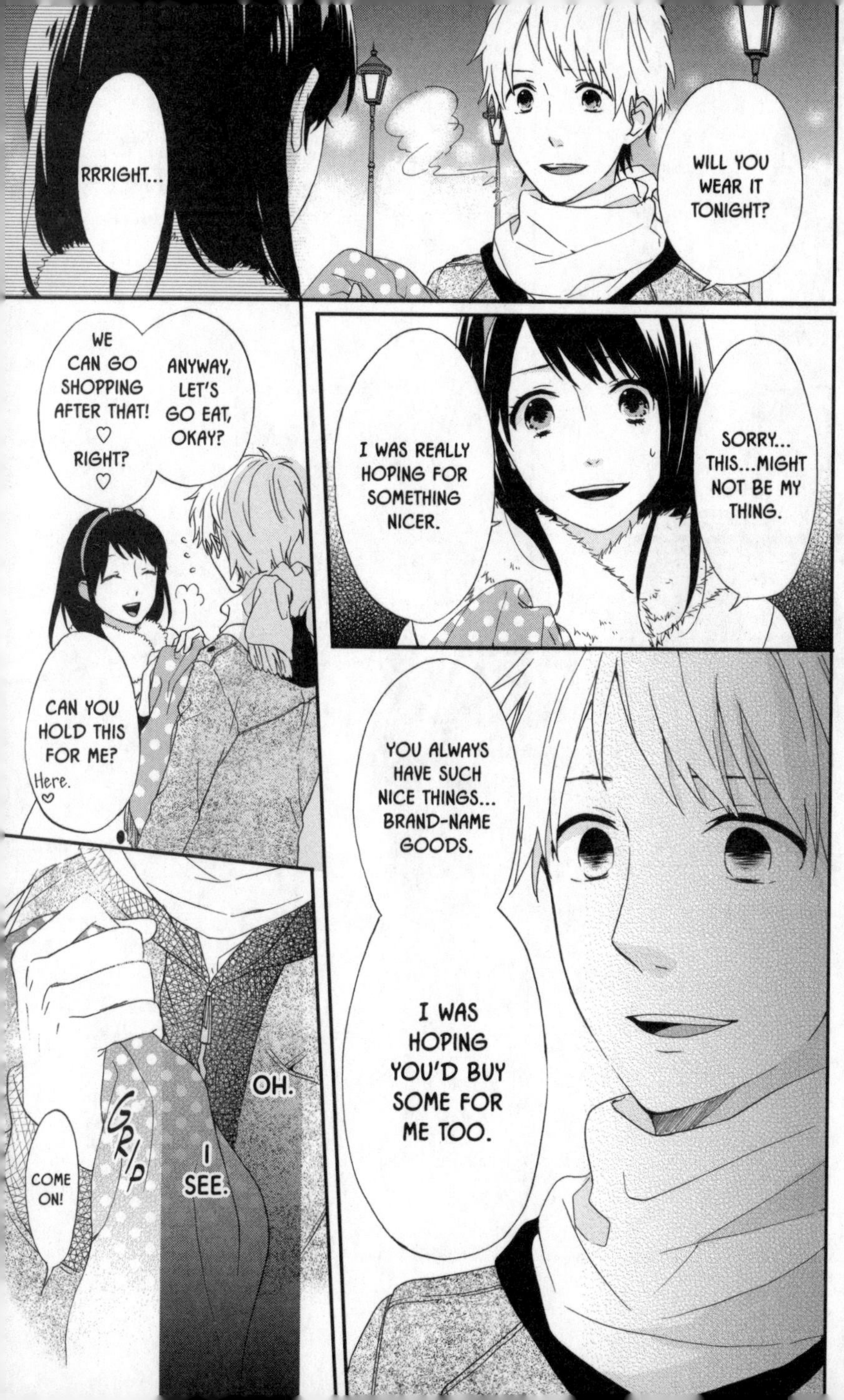
WILL YOU WEAR IT TONIGHT?
RRRIGHT...
SORRY... THIS...MIGHT NOT BE MY THING.
I WAS REALLY HOPING FOR SOMETHING NICER.
ANYWAY, LET'S GO EAT, OKAY?
WE CAN GO SHOPPING AFTER THAT! ♡ RIGHT? ♡
CAN YOU HOLD THIS FOR ME?
Here. ♡
YOU ALWAYS HAVE SUCH NICE THINGS... BRAND-NAME GOODS.
I WAS HOPING YOU'D BUY SOME FOR ME TOO.
OH.
I SEE.
GRIP
COME ON!

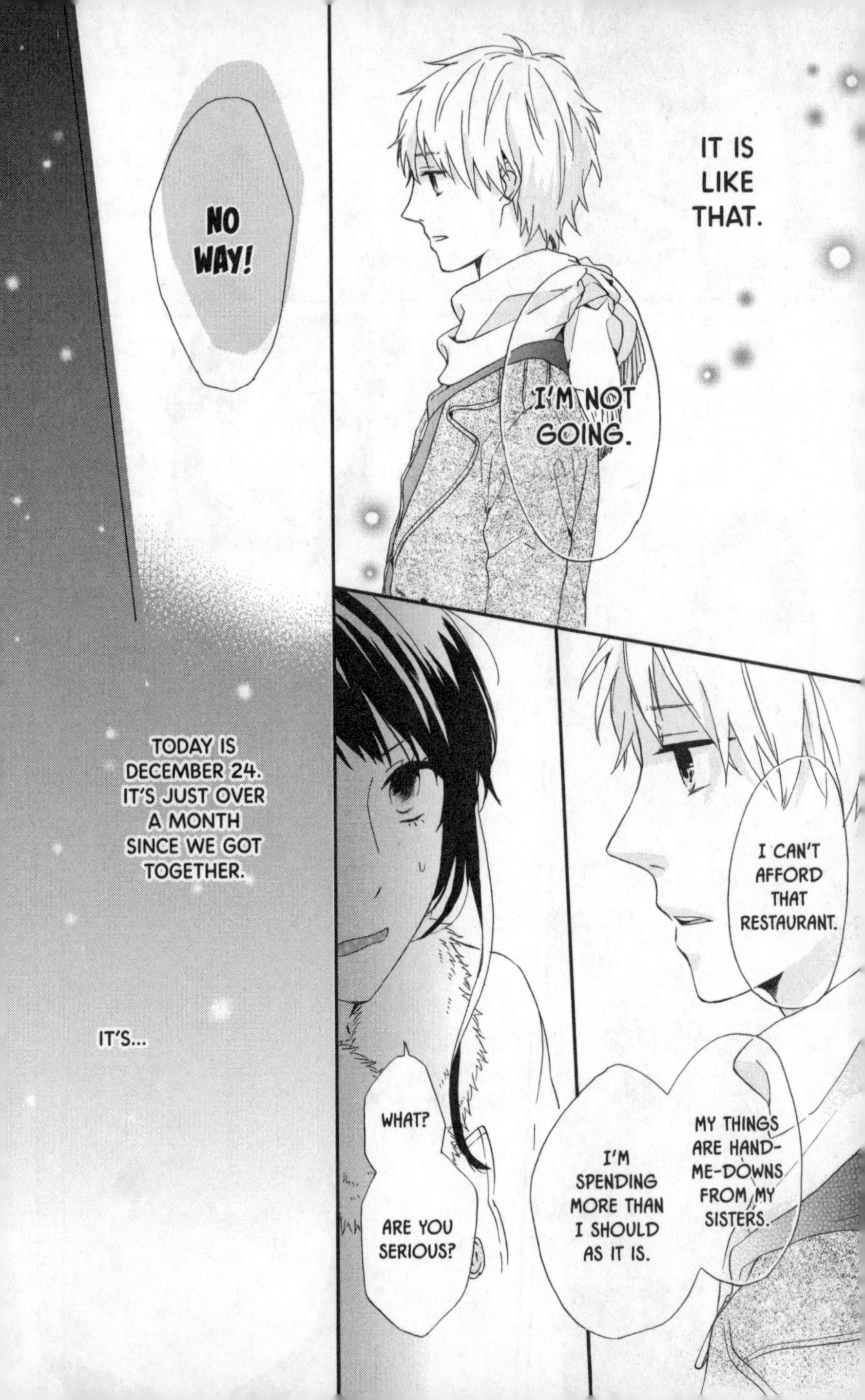
IT IS LIKE THAT.
I'M NOT GOING.
I CAN'T AFFORD THAT RESTAURANT.
MY THINGS ARE HAND-ME-DOWNS FROM MY SISTERS.
I'M SPENDING MORE THAN I SHOULD AS IT IS.
WHAT?
ARE YOU SERIOUS?
NO WAY!
TODAY IS DECEMBER 24. IT'S JUST OVER A MONTH SINCE WE GOT TOGETHER.
IT'S...

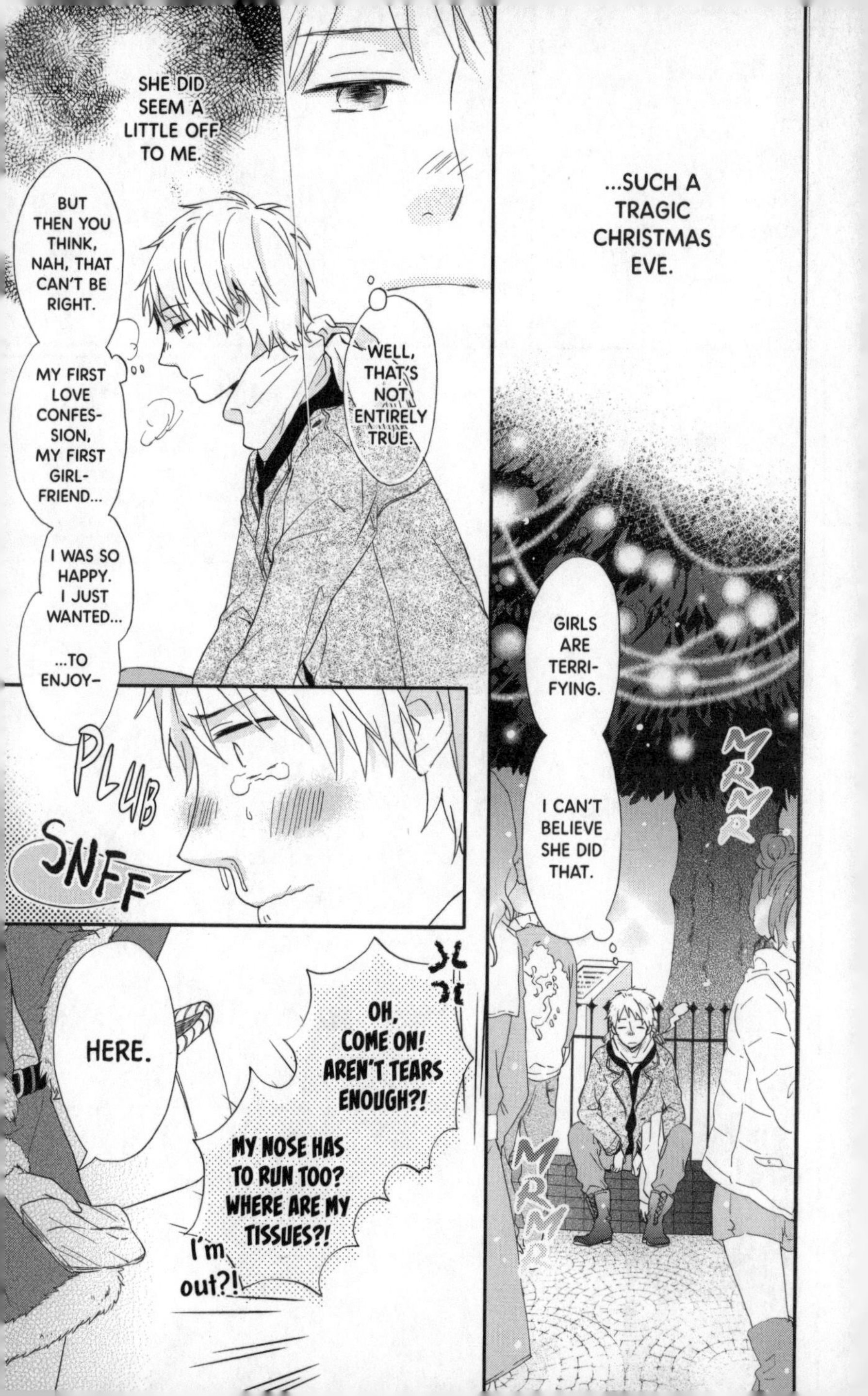

...SUCH A TRAGIC CHRISTMAS EVE.
GIRLS ARE TERRI-FYING.
I CAN'T BELIEVE SHE DID THAT.
MRMR
MRMR
WELL, THAT'S NOT ENTIRELY TRUE.
SHE DID SEEM A LITTLE OFF TO ME.
BUT THEN YOU THINK, NAH, THAT CAN'T BE RIGHT.
MY FIRST LOVE CONFES-SION, MY FIRST GIRL-FRIEND...
I WAS SO HAPPY. I JUST WANTED...
...TO ENJOY—
PLUB
SNFF
OH, COME ON! AREN'T TEARS ENOUGH?!
MY NOSE HAS TO RUN TOO? WHERE ARE MY TISSUES?!
HERE.
I'm out?!

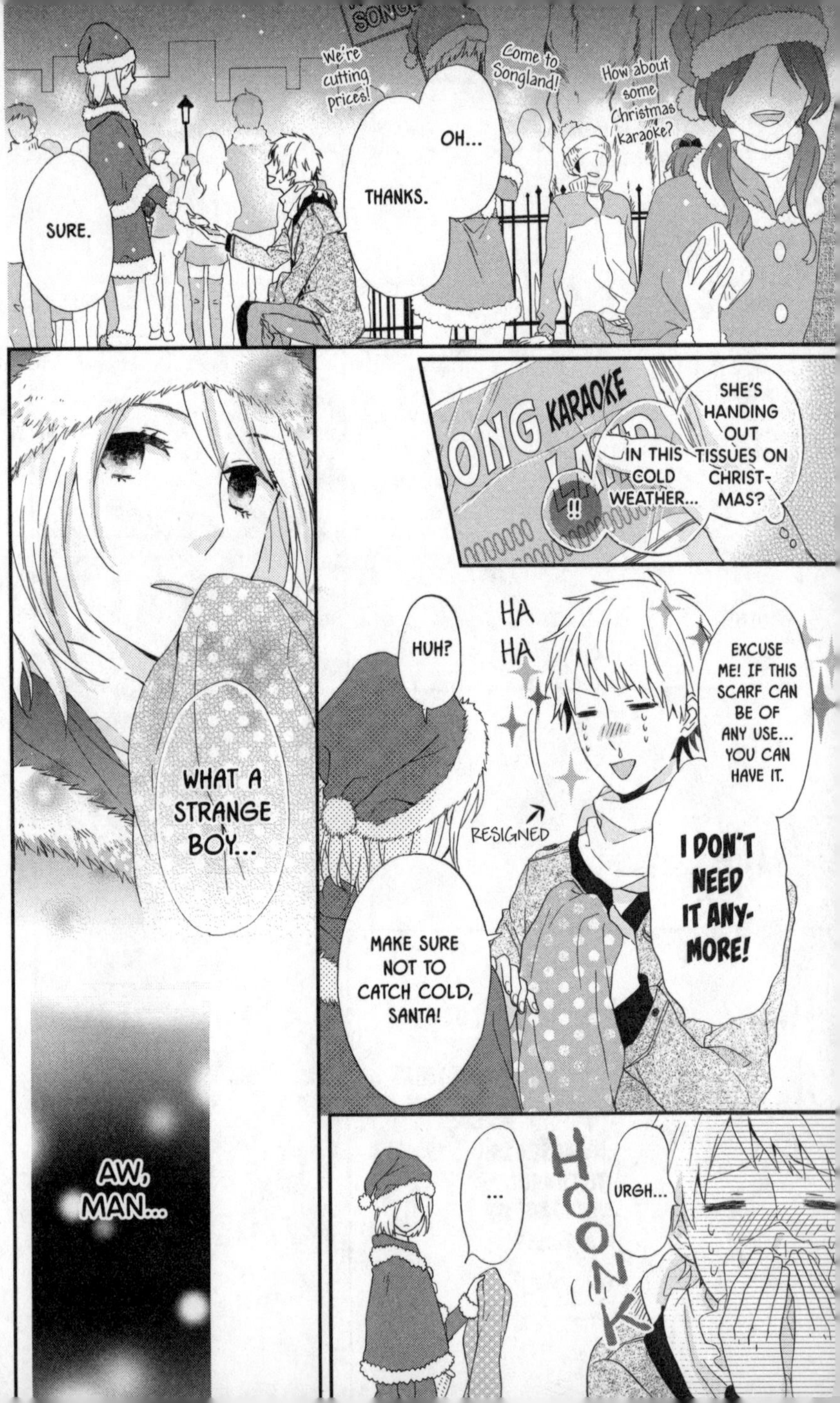
How about some Christmas karaoke?
Come to Songland!
We're cutting prices!
OH... THANKS.
SURE.
SONG KARAOKE
SHE'S HANDING OUT TISSUES ON CHRIST-MAS?
IN THIS COLD WEATHER...
!!
EXCUSE ME! IF THIS SCARF CAN BE OF ANY USE... YOU CAN HAVE IT.
I DON'T NEED IT ANY-MORE!
HA HA
RESIGNED
HUH?
MAKE SURE NOT TO CATCH COLD, SANTA!
URGH...
HOONK
...
WHAT A STRANGE BOY...
AW, MAN...

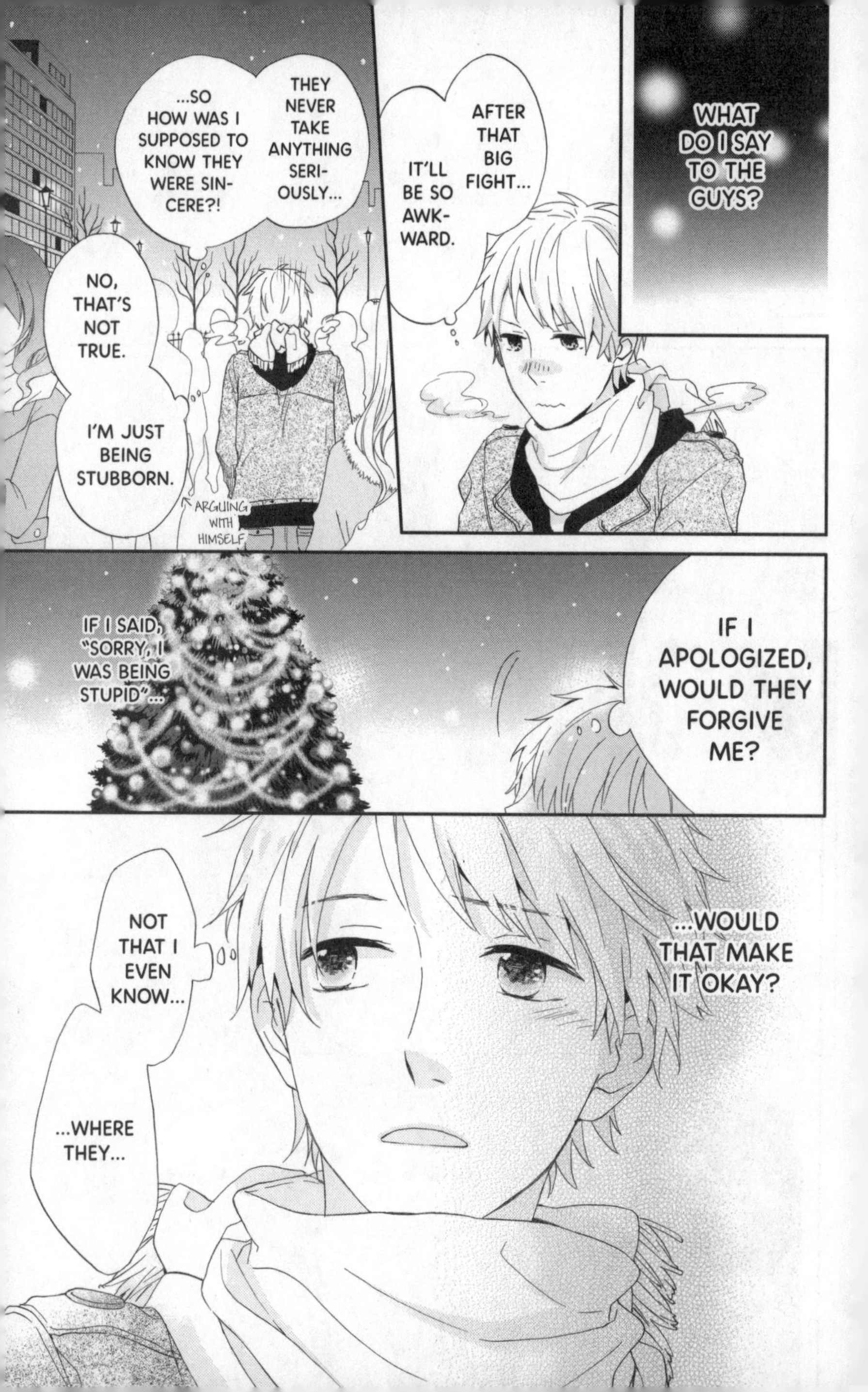
WHAT DO I SAY TO THE GUYS?
AFTER THAT BIG FIGHT...
IT'LL BE SO AWK-WARD.
THEY NEVER TAKE ANYTHING SERI-OUSLY...
...SO HOW WAS I SUPPOSED TO KNOW THEY WERE SIN-CERE?!
NO, THAT'S NOT TRUE.
I'M JUST BEING STUBBORN.
ARGUING WITH HIMSELF
IF I APOLOGIZED, WOULD THEY FORGIVE ME?
IF I SAID, "SORRY, I WAS BEING STUPID"...
...WOULD THAT MAKE IT OKAY?
NOT THAT I EVEN KNOW...
...WHERE THEY...

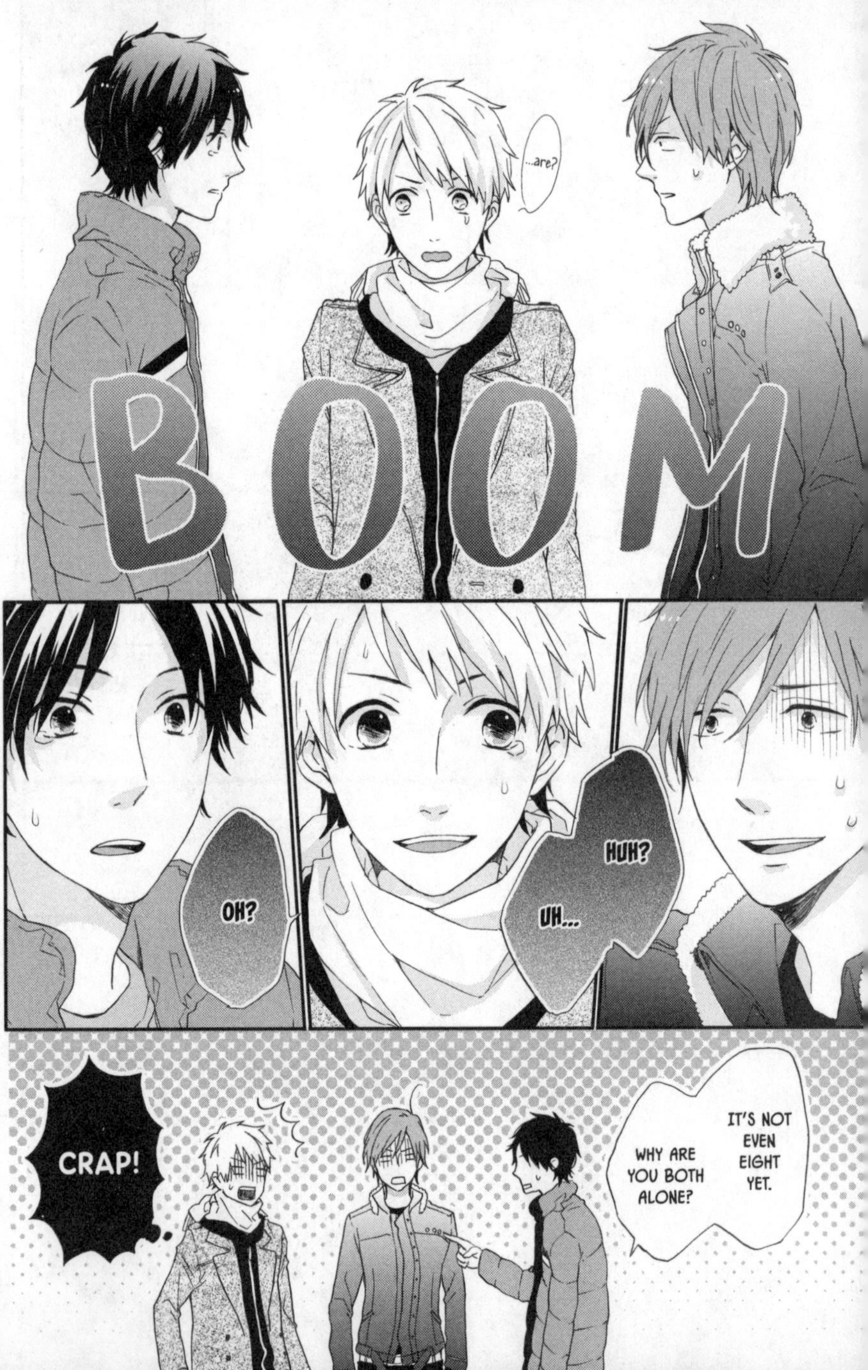
...are?
BOOM
HUH?
UH...
OH?
IT'S NOT EVEN EIGHT YET.
WHY ARE YOU BOTH ALONE?
CRAP!

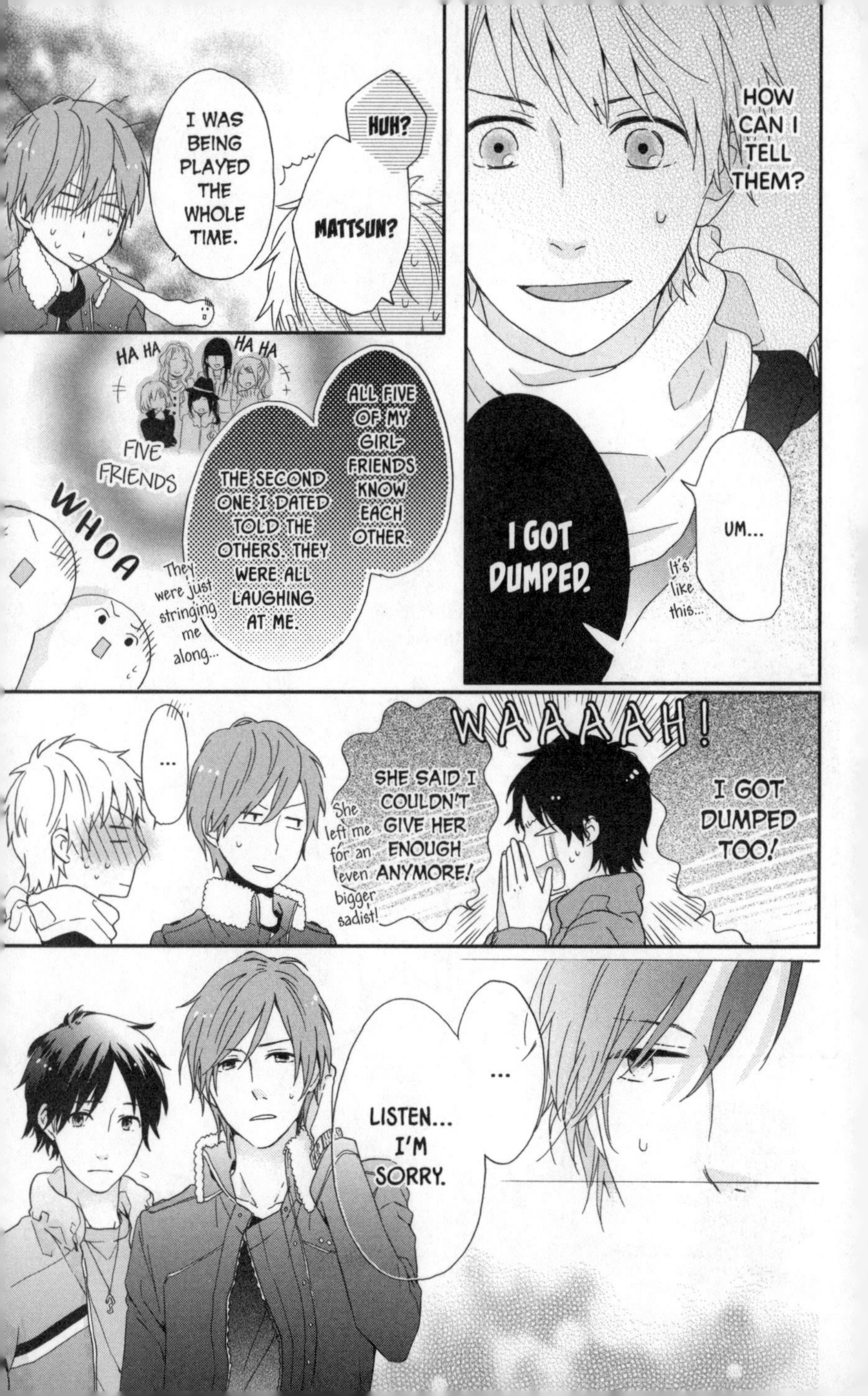
HOW CAN I TELL THEM?
UM...
It's like this...
I GOT DUMPED.
HUH?
MATTSUN?
I WAS BEING PLAYED THE WHOLE TIME.
ALL FIVE OF MY GIRL-FRIENDS KNOW EACH OTHER.
THE SECOND ONE I DATED TOLD THE OTHERS. THEY WERE ALL LAUGHING AT ME.
They were just stringing me along...
HA HA
HA HA
FIVE FRIENDS
WHOA
WAAAAH!
I GOT DUMPED TOO!
SHE SAID I COULDN'T GIVE HER ENOUGH ANYMORE!
She left me for an even bigger sadist!
...
...
LISTEN... I'M SORRY.

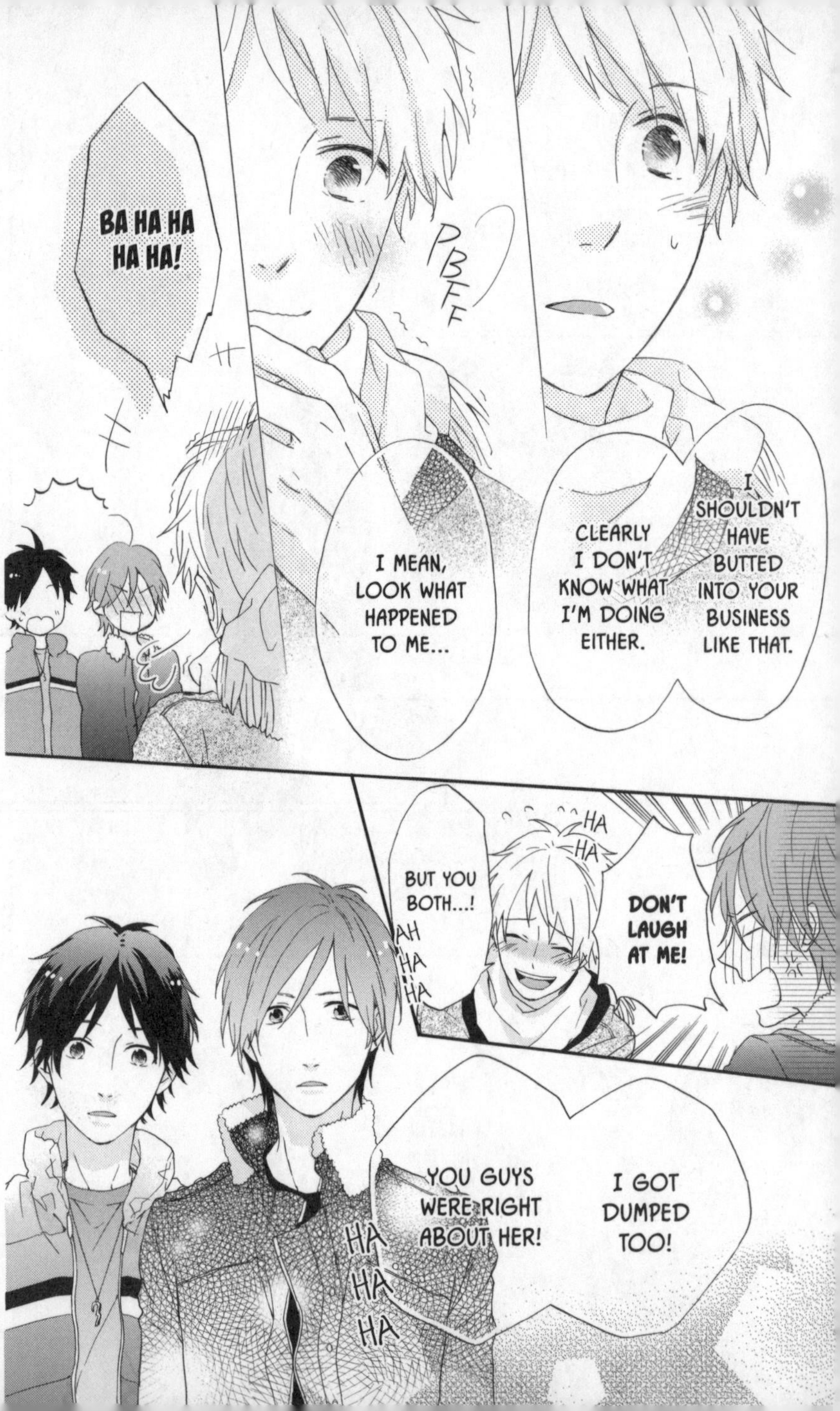
I SHOULDN'T HAVE BUTTED INTO YOUR BUSINESS LIKE THAT.
CLEARLY I DON'T KNOW WHAT I'M DOING EITHER.
PBFF
I MEAN, LOOK WHAT HAPPENED TO ME...
BA HA HA HA HA!
DON'T LAUGH AT ME!
HA HA
BUT YOU BOTH...!
AH HA HA
I GOT DUMPED TOO!
YOU GUYS WERE RIGHT ABOUT HER!
HA HA HA

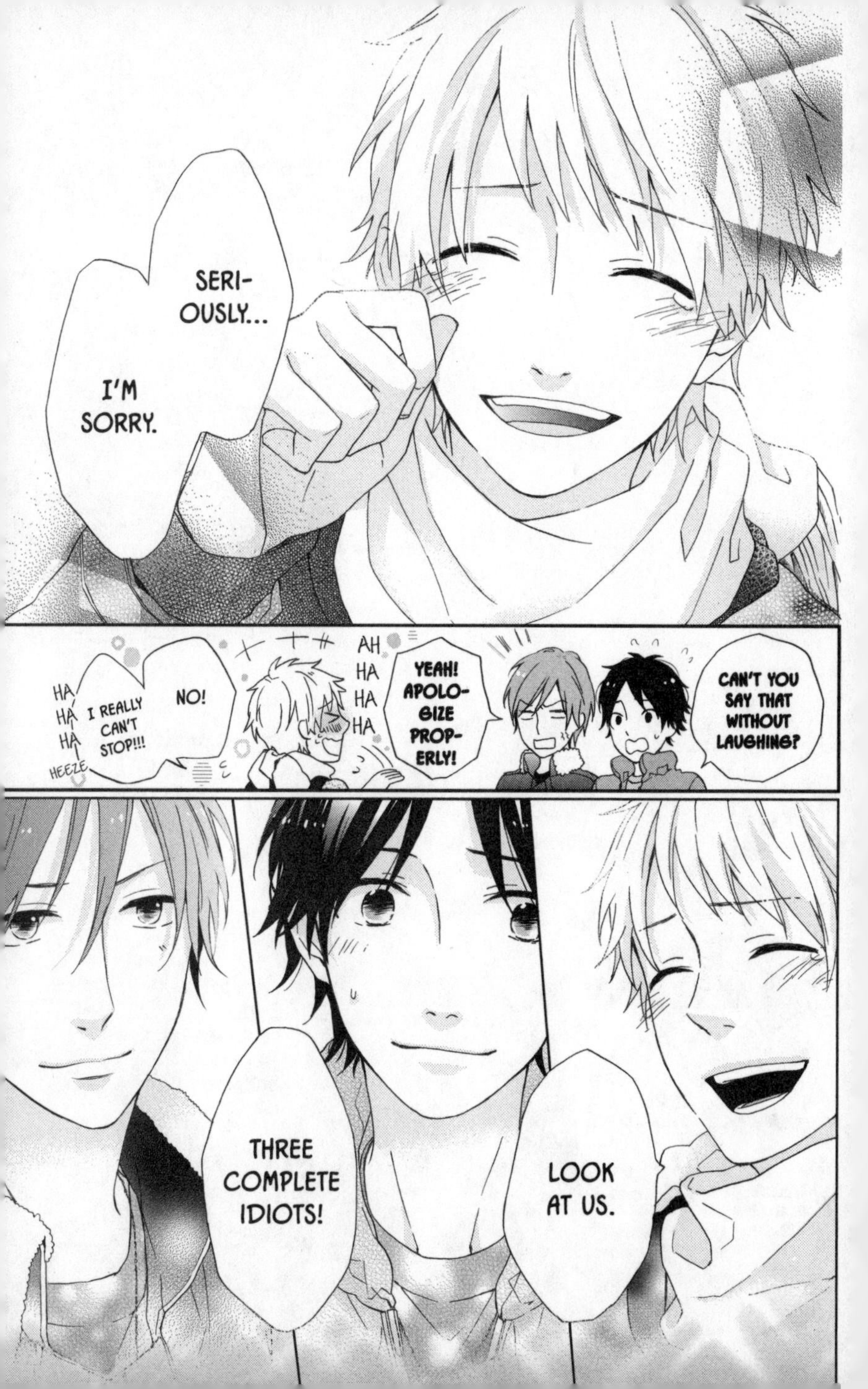
SERI-OUSLY... I'M SORRY.
CAN'T YOU SAY THAT WITHOUT LAUGHING?
YEAH! APOLO-GIZE PROP-ERLY!
AH HA HA HA
NO!
I REALLY CAN'T STOP!!!
HA HA HA HEEZE
LOOK AT US.
THREE COMPLETE IDIOTS!

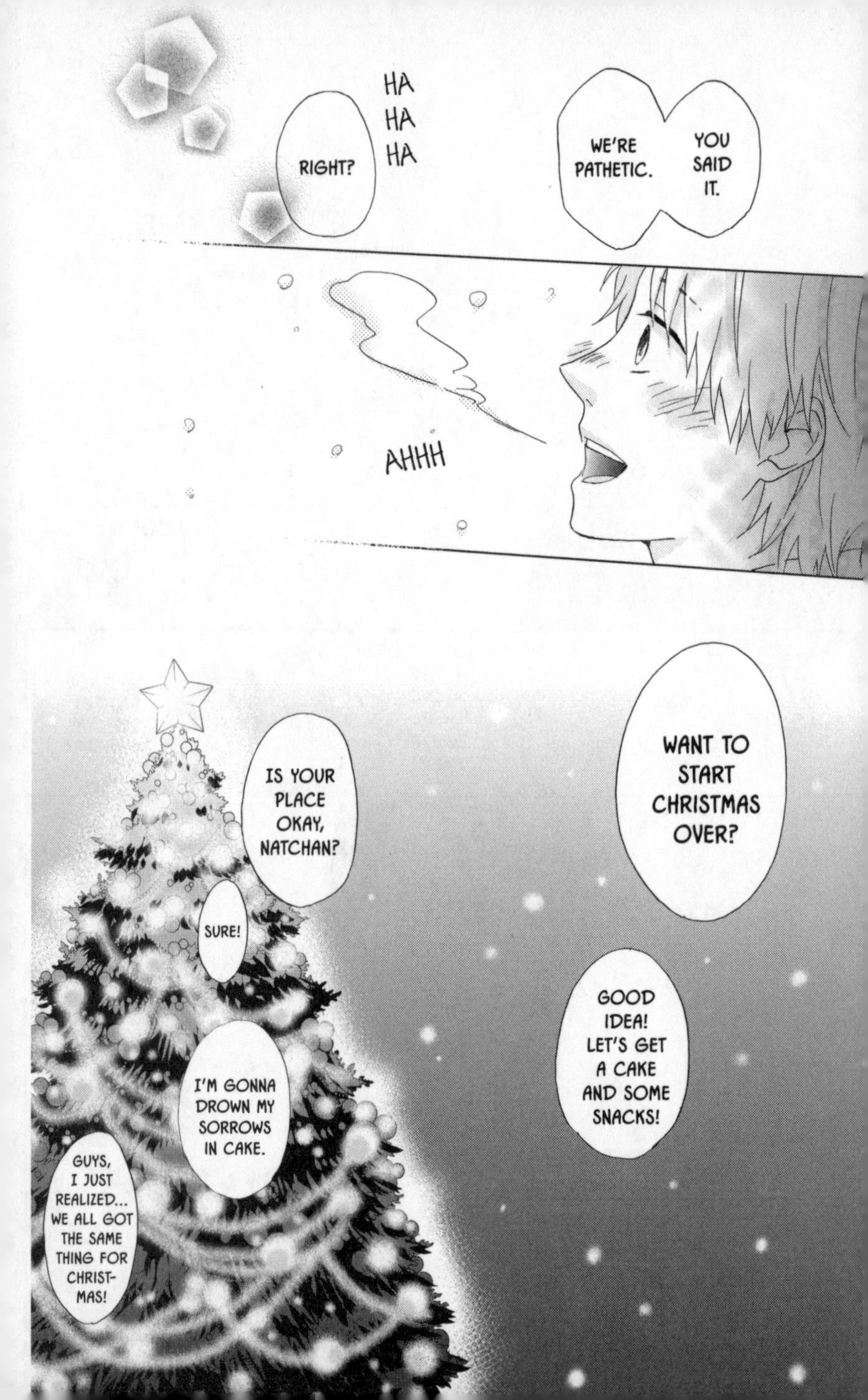
YOU SAID IT.
WE'RE PATHETIC.
HA HA HA
RIGHT?
AHHH
WANT TO START CHRISTMAS OVER?
GOOD IDEA! LET'S GET A CAKE AND SOME SNACKS!
IS YOUR PLACE OKAY, NATCHAN?
SURE!
I'M GONNA DROWN MY SORROWS IN CAKE.
GUYS, I JUST REALIZED... WE ALL GOT THE SAME THING FOR CHRIST-MAS!

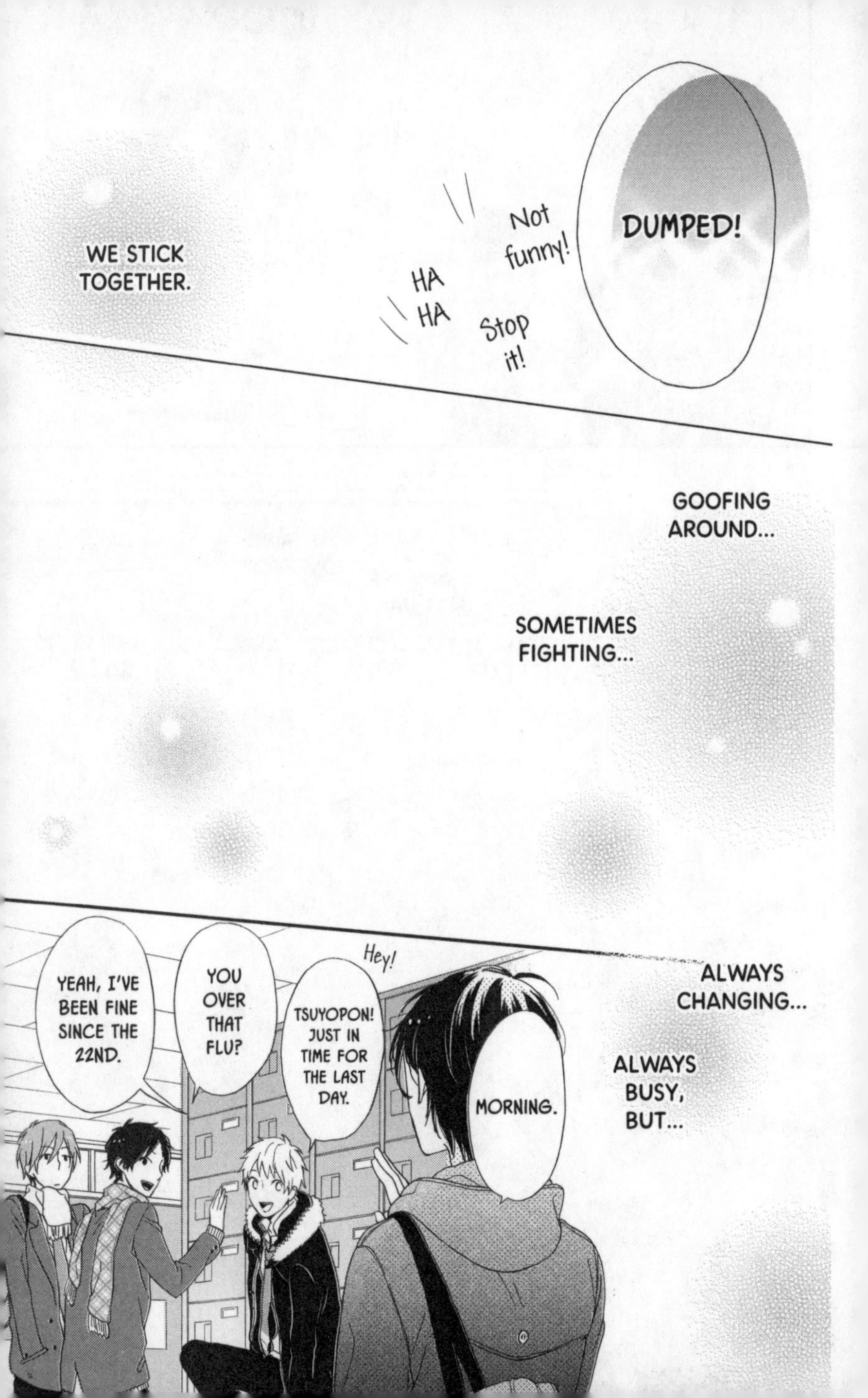
DUMPED!
Not funny!
Stop it!
HA HA
WE STICK TOGETHER.
GOOFING AROUND...
SOMETIMES FIGHTING...
ALWAYS CHANGING...
ALWAYS BUSY, BUT...
MORNING.
Hey!
TSUYOPON! JUST IN TIME FOR THE LAST DAY.
YOU OVER THAT FLU?
YEAH, I'VE BEEN FINE SINCE THE 22ND.

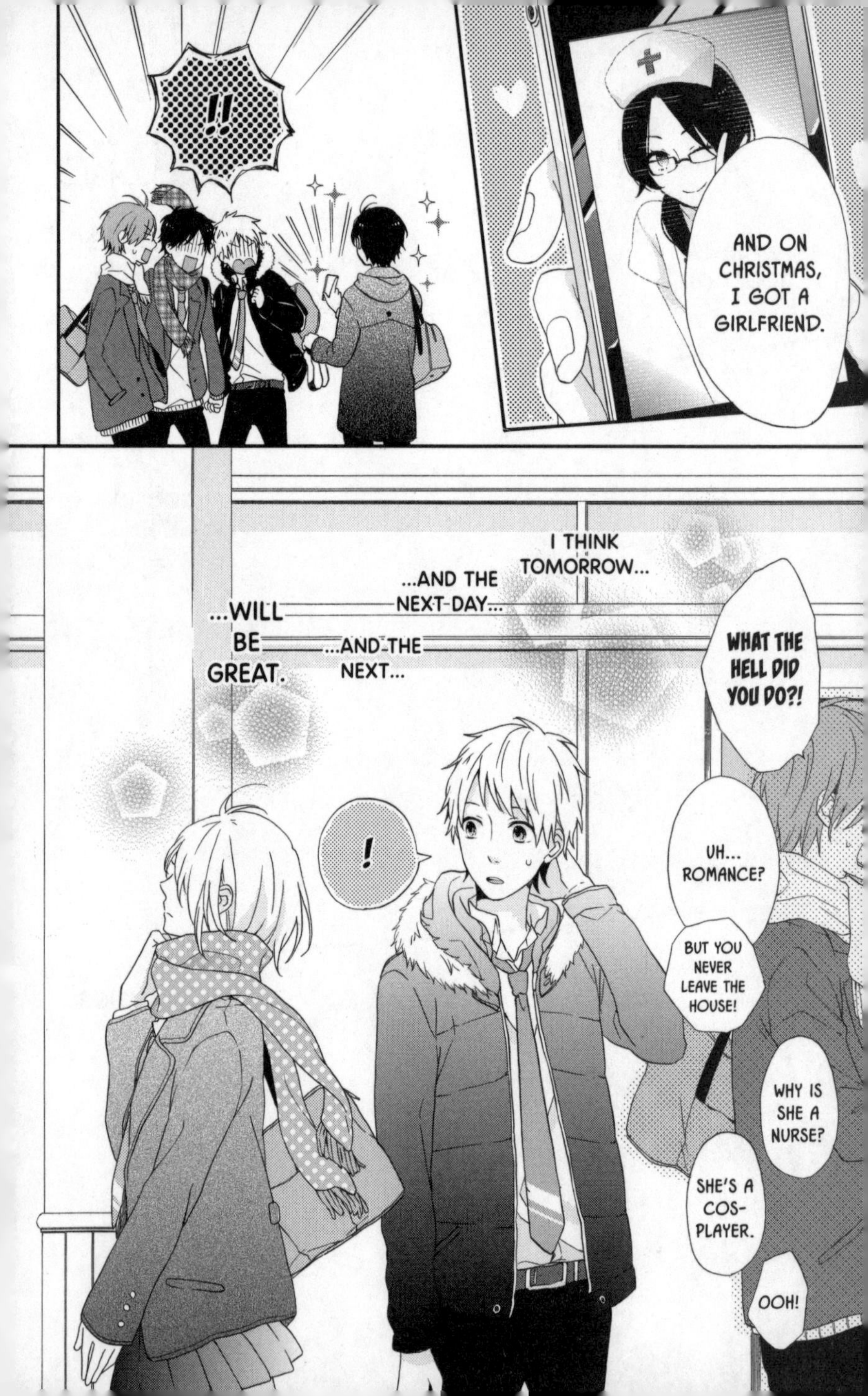
AND ON CHRISTMAS, I GOT A GIRLFRIEND.
!!
WHAT THE HELL DID YOU DO?!
UH... ROMANCE?
BUT YOU NEVER LEAVE THE HOUSE!
WHY IS SHE A NURSE?
SHE'S A COS-PLAYER.
OOH!
I THINK TOMORROW...
...AND THE NEXT DAY...
...AND THE NEXT...
...WILL BE GREAT.
!

Rainbow Days

Chapter 1

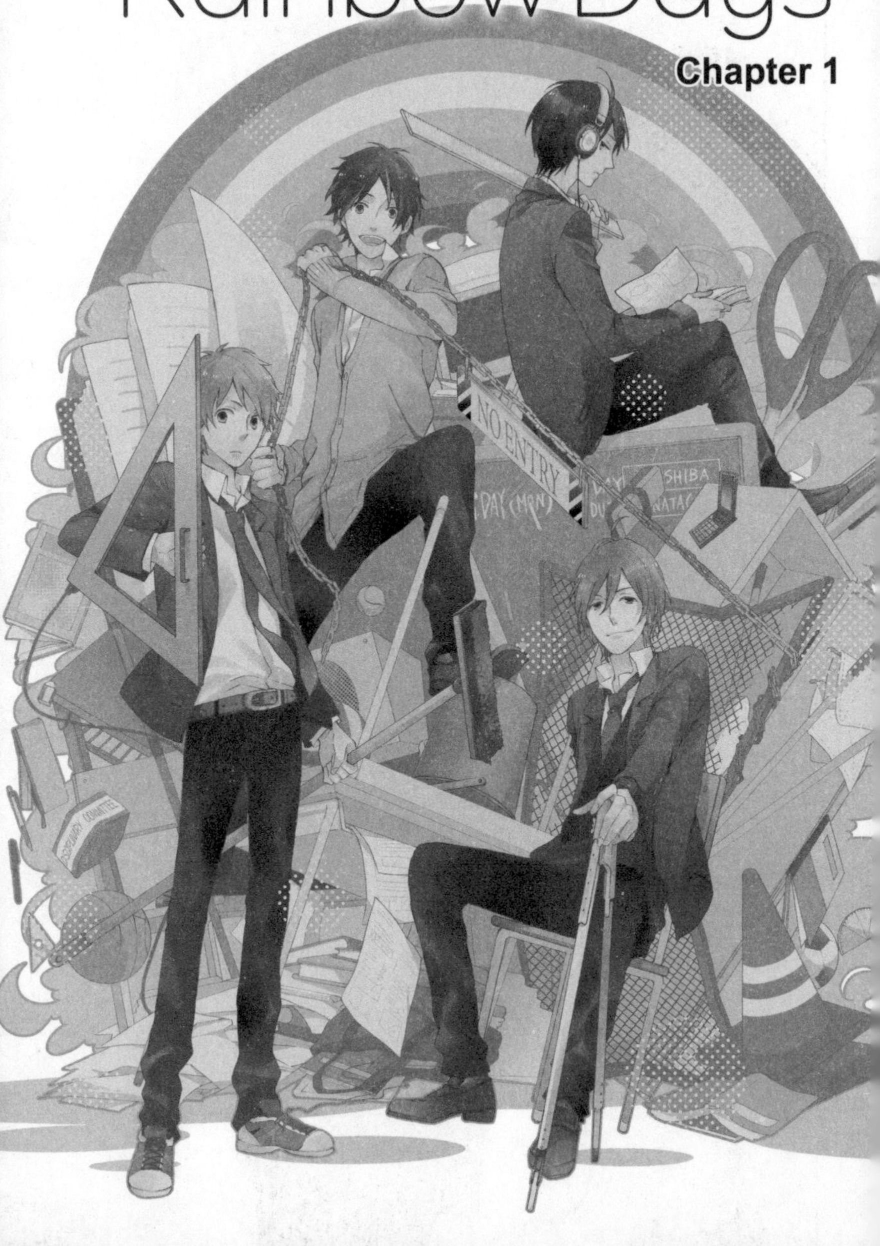

NO ENTRY
SHIBA

Rainbow
Days

■ ■ ■ ■ ■ ■ ■

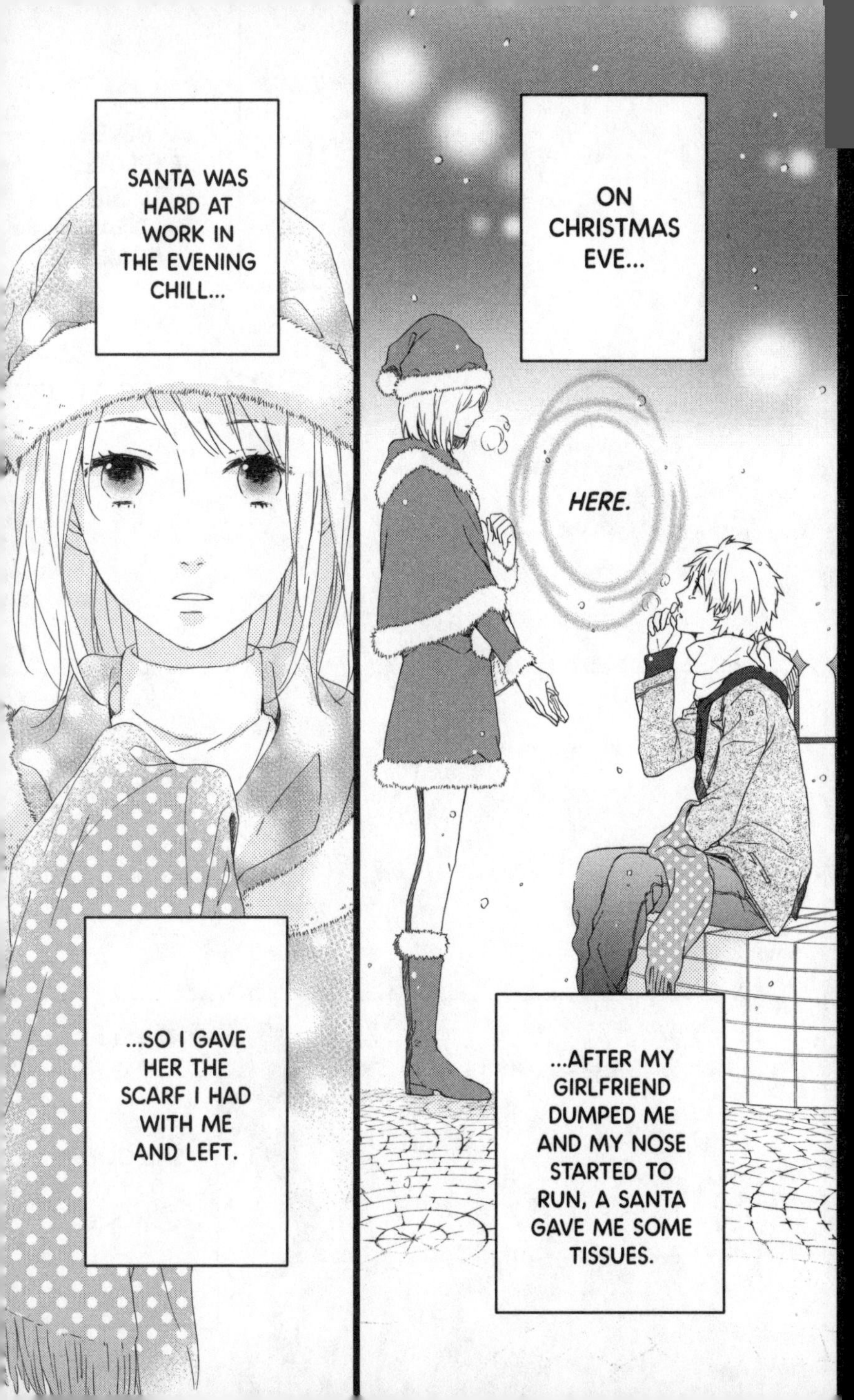
ON CHRISTMAS EVE...
HERE.
...AFTER MY GIRLFRIEND DUMPED ME AND MY NOSE STARTED TO RUN, A SANTA GAVE ME SOME TISSUES.
SANTA WAS HARD AT WORK IN THE EVENING CHILL...
...SO I GAVE HER THE SCARF I HAD WITH ME AND LEFT.

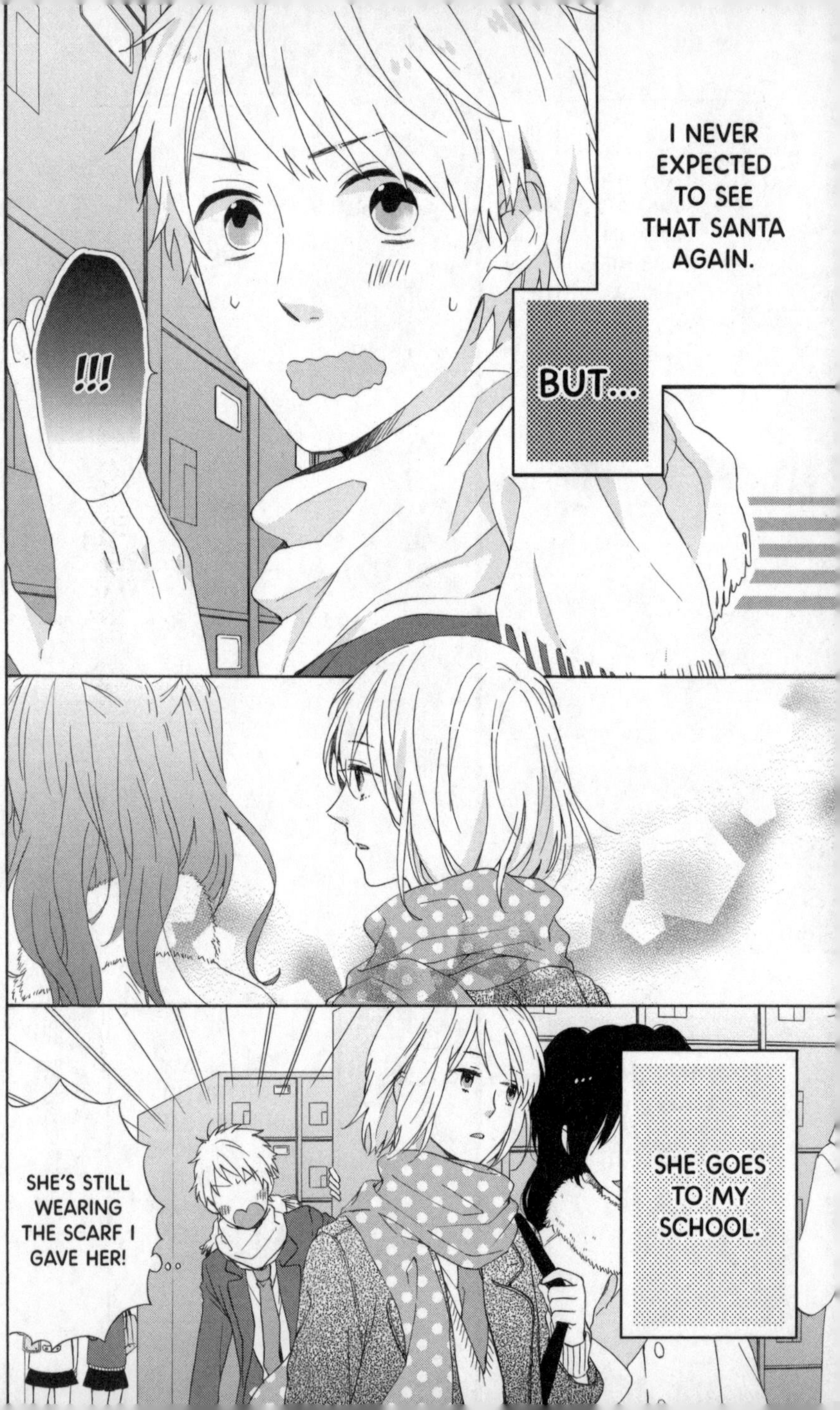
I NEVER EXPECTED TO SEE THAT SANTA AGAIN.
BUT...
!!!
SHE GOES TO MY SCHOOL.
SHE'S STILL WEARING THE SCARF I GAVE HER!

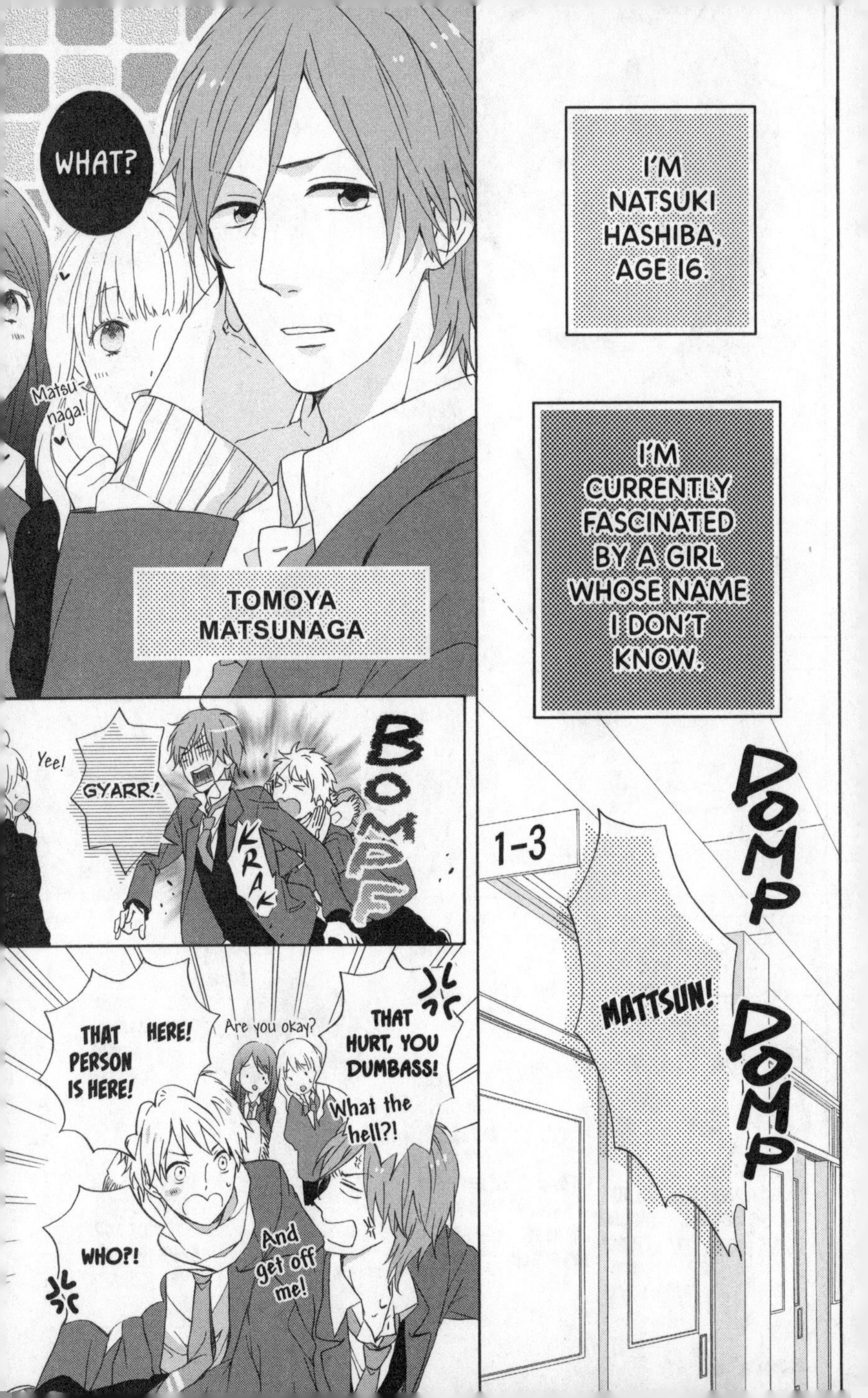
I'M NATSUKI HASHIBA, AGE 16.
I'M CURRENTLY FASCINATED BY A GIRL WHOSE NAME I DON'T KNOW.
1-3
DOMP
MATTSUN!
DOMP
WHAT?
Matsu-naga!
TOMOYA MATSUNAGA
BOMPF
KRAK
GYARR!
Yee!
THAT HURT, YOU DUMBASS!
What the hell?!
Are you okay?
HERE!
THAT PERSON IS HERE!
And get off me!
WHO?!

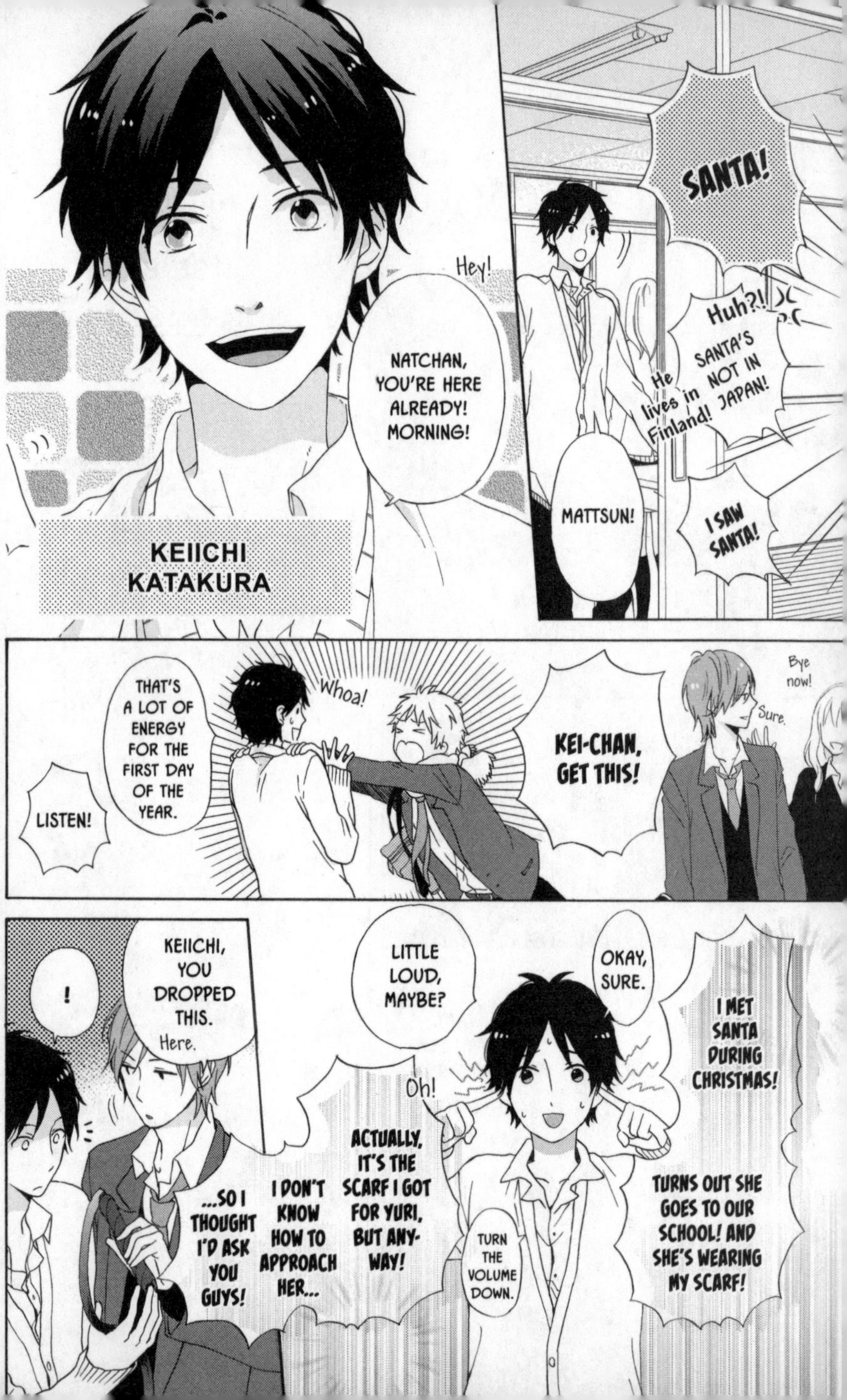
SANTA!
Huh?!
SANTA'S NOT IN JAPAN!
He lives in Finland!
I SAW SANTA!
MATTSUN!
Hey!
NATCHAN, YOU'RE HERE ALREADY! MORNING!
KEIICHI KATAKURA
Bye now!
Sure.
KEI-CHAN, GET THIS!
Whoa!
THAT'S A LOT OF ENERGY FOR THE FIRST DAY OF THE YEAR.
LISTEN!
I MET SANTA DURING CHRISTMAS!
OKAY, SURE.
TURNS OUT SHE GOES TO OUR SCHOOL! AND SHE'S WEARING MY SCARF!
LITTLE LOUD, MAYBE?
TURN THE VOLUME DOWN.
ACTUALLY, IT'S THE SCARF I GOT FOR YURI, BUT ANYWAY!
I DON'T KNOW HOW TO APPROACH HER...
...SO I THOUGHT I'D ASK YOU GUYS!
Oh!
KEIICHI, YOU DROPPED THIS.
Here.
!

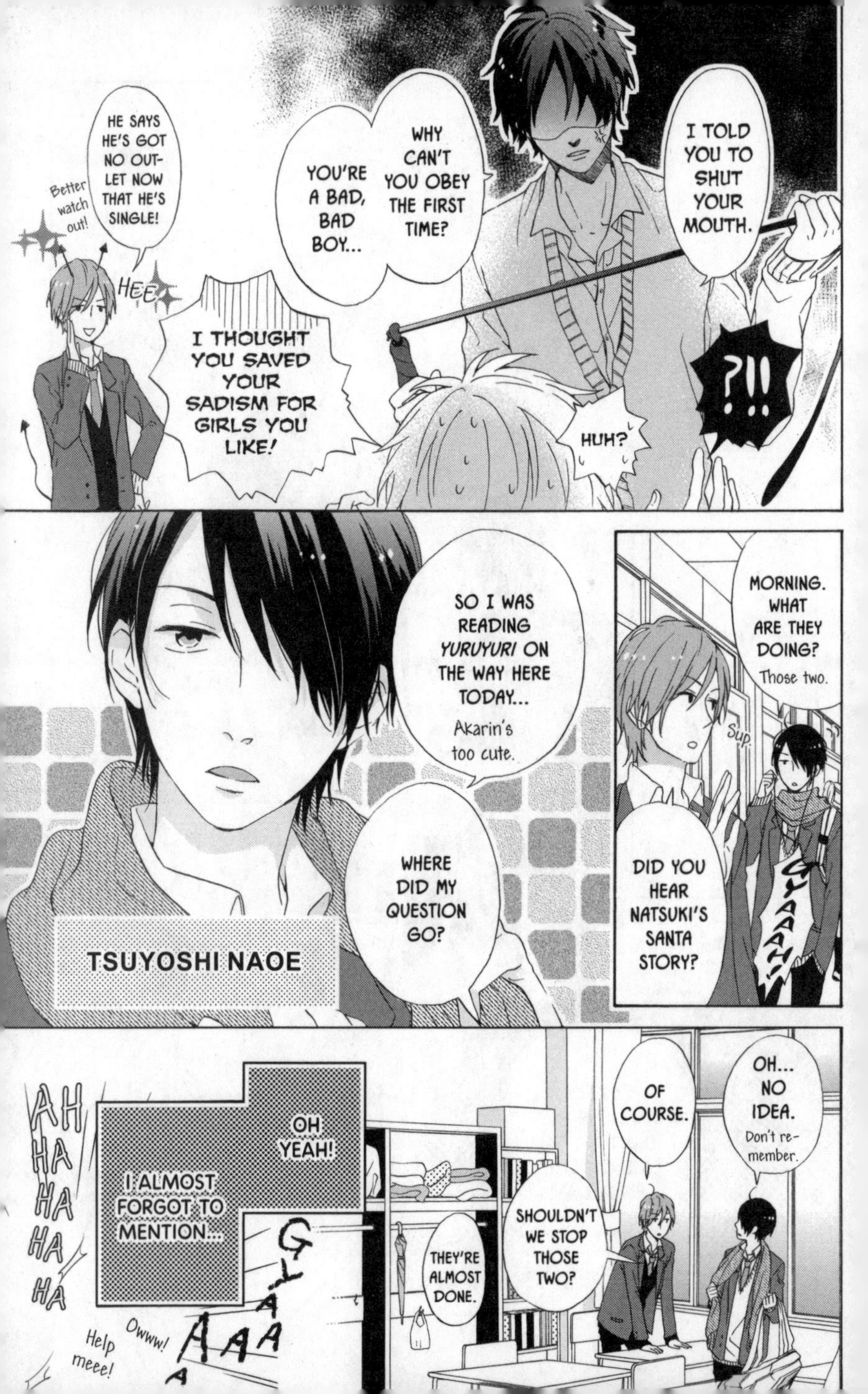
I TOLD YOU TO SHUT YOUR MOUTH.
?!!
WHY CAN'T YOU OBEY THE FIRST TIME?
YOU'RE A BAD, BAD BOY...
HUH?
I THOUGHT YOU SAVED YOUR SADISM FOR GIRLS YOU LIKE!
HE SAYS HE'S GOT NO OUT-LET NOW THAT HE'S SINGLE!
HEE
Better watch out!
MORNING. WHAT ARE THEY DOING?
Those two.
Sup.
DID YOU HEAR NATSUKI'S SANTA STORY?
GYAAAAH!
SO I WAS READING YURUYURI ON THE WAY HERE TODAY...
Akarin's too cute.
WHERE DID MY QUESTION GO?
TSUYOSHI NAOE
OH... NO IDEA.
Don't re-member.
OF COURSE.
SHOULDN'T WE STOP THOSE TWO?
THEY'RE ALMOST DONE.
GYAAAAA
OH YEAH!
I ALMOST FORGOT TO MENTION...
Owww!
Help meee!
AHAHAHAHAHA

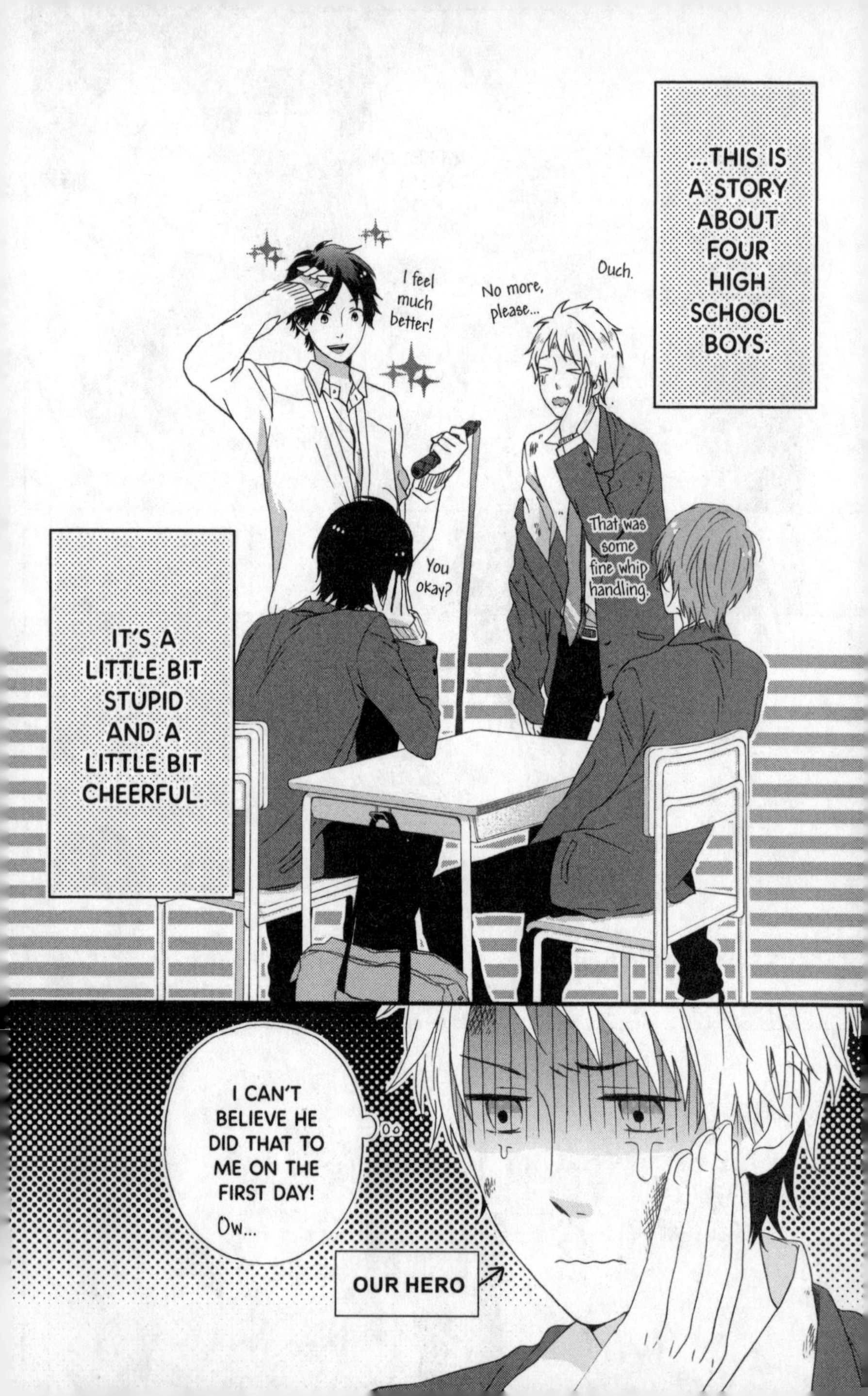
...THIS IS A STORY ABOUT FOUR HIGH SCHOOL BOYS.
Ouch.
No more, please...
I feel much better!
That was some fine whip handling.
You okay?
IT'S A LITTLE BIT STUPID AND A LITTLE BIT CHEERFUL.
I CAN'T BELIEVE HE DID THAT TO ME ON THE FIRST DAY!
Ow...
OUR HERO

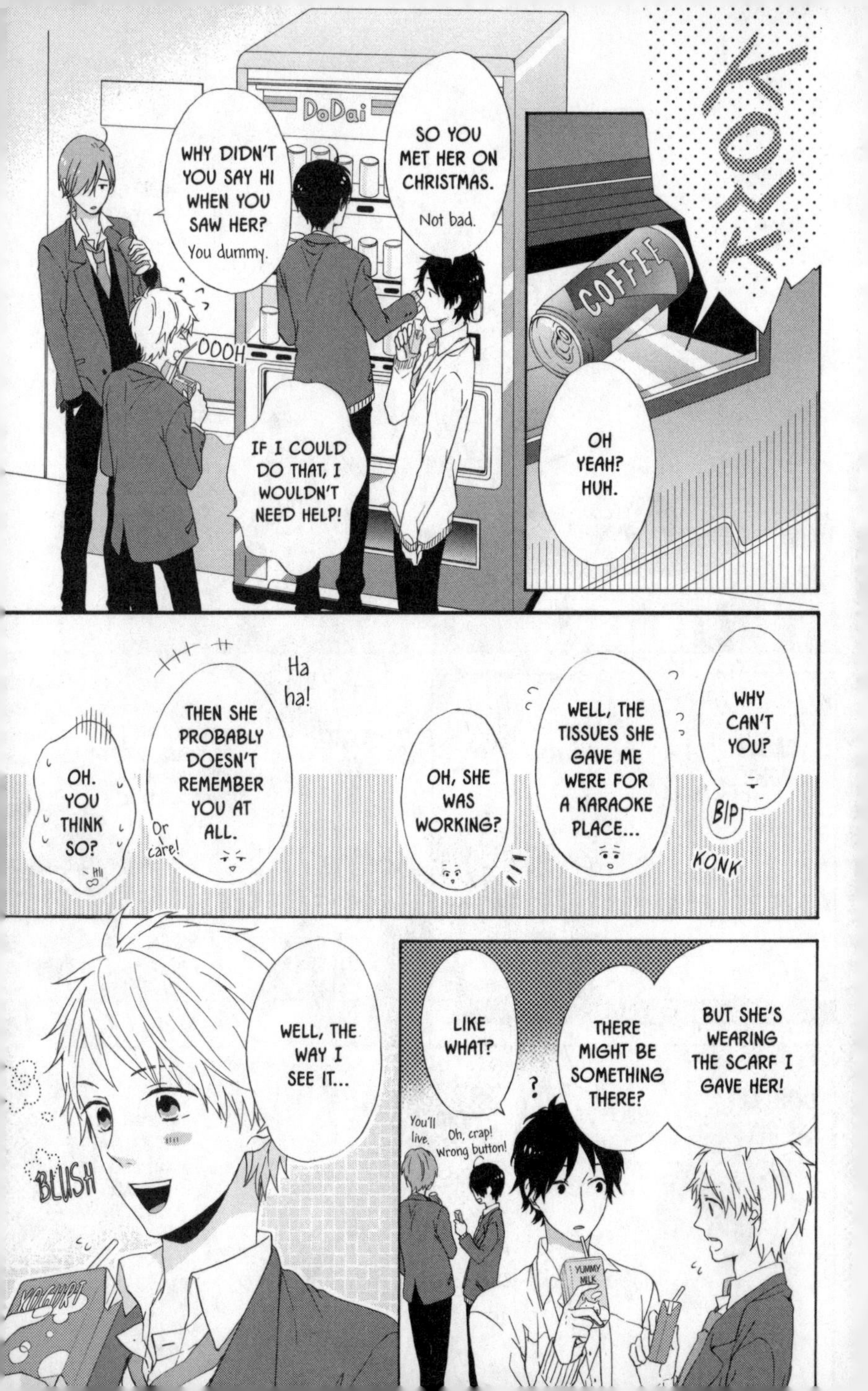
KONK
COFFEE
OH YEAH? HUH.
DoDai
SO YOU MET HER ON CHRISTMAS. Not bad.
WHY DIDN'T YOU SAY HI WHEN YOU SAW HER? You dummy.
OOOH
IF I COULD DO THAT, I WOULDN'T NEED HELP!
WHY CAN'T YOU?
BIP
KONK
WELL, THE TISSUES SHE GAVE ME WERE FOR A KARAOKE PLACE...
OH, SHE WAS WORKING?
Ha ha!
THEN SHE PROBABLY DOESN'T REMEMBER YOU AT ALL.
Or care!
OH. YOU THINK SO?
BUT SHE'S WEARING THE SCARF I GAVE HER!
THERE MIGHT BE SOMETHING THERE?
LIKE WHAT?
Oh, crap! Wrong button!
You'll live.
YUMMY MILK
WELL, THE WAY I SEE IT...
BLUSH
YOGURT

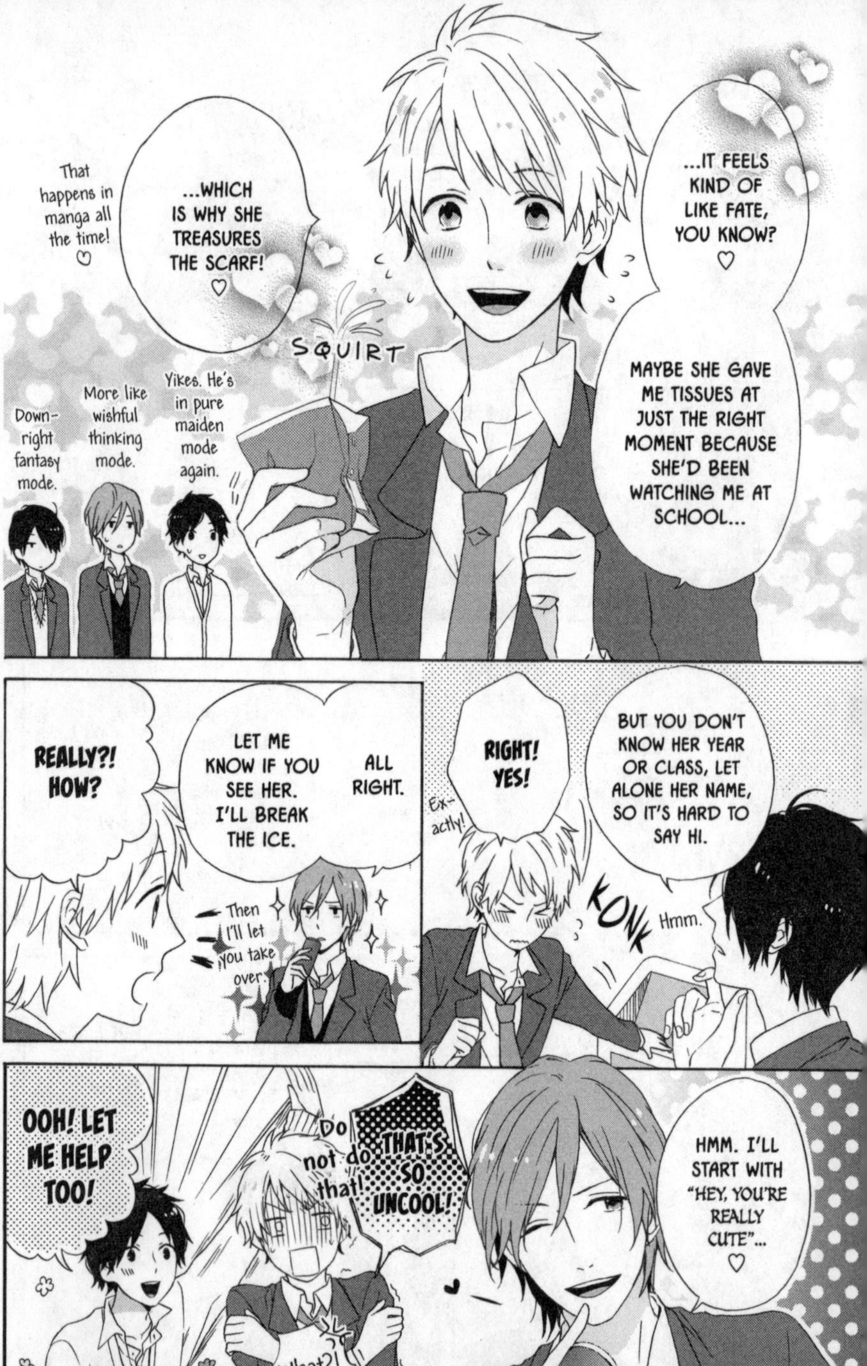
...IT FEELS KIND OF LIKE FATE, YOU KNOW? ♡
MAYBE SHE GAVE ME TISSUES AT JUST THE RIGHT MOMENT BECAUSE SHE'D BEEN WATCHING ME AT SCHOOL...
SQUIRT
...WHICH IS WHY SHE TREASURES THE SCARF! ♡
That happens in manga all the time! ♡
Yikes. He's in pure maiden mode again.
More like wishful thinking mode.
Downright fantasy mode.
BUT YOU DON'T KNOW HER YEAR OR CLASS, LET ALONE HER NAME, SO IT'S HARD TO SAY HI.
Hmm.
KONK
RIGHT! YES!
Exactly!
ALL RIGHT.
LET ME KNOW IF YOU SEE HER. I'LL BREAK THE ICE.
REALLY?! HOW?
Then I'll let you take over.
HMM. I'LL START WITH "HEY, YOU'RE REALLY CUTE"... ♡
THAT'S SO UNCOOL!
Do not do that!
What?!
OOH! LET ME HELP TOO!

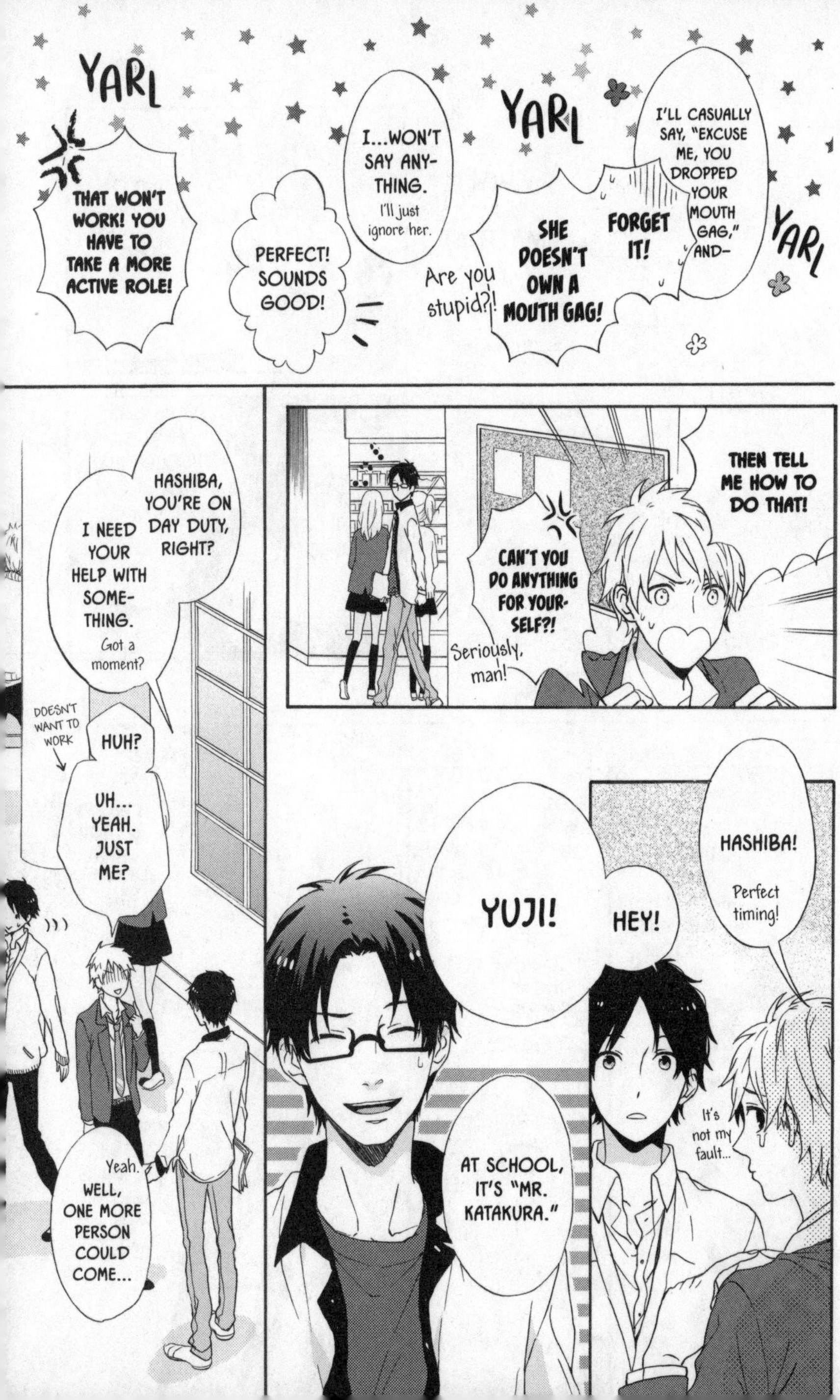
YARL
I'LL CASUALLY SAY, "EXCUSE ME, YOU DROPPED YOUR MOUTH GAG," AND—
FORGET IT!
SHE DOESN'T OWN A MOUTH GAG!
Are you stupid?!
YARL
I...WON'T SAY ANY-THING. I'll just ignore her.
PERFECT! SOUNDS GOOD!
YARL
THAT WON'T WORK! YOU HAVE TO TAKE A MORE ACTIVE ROLE!
THEN TELL ME HOW TO DO THAT!
CAN'T YOU DO ANYTHING FOR YOUR-SELF?!
Seriously, man!
HASHIBA! Perfect timing!
HEY!
YUJI!
It's not my fault...
AT SCHOOL, IT'S "MR. KATAKURA."
HASHIBA, YOU'RE ON DAY DUTY, RIGHT?
I NEED YOUR HELP WITH SOME-THING. Got a moment?
HUH?
DOESN'T WANT TO WORK
UH... YEAH. JUST ME?
Yeah.
WELL, ONE MORE PERSON COULD COME...

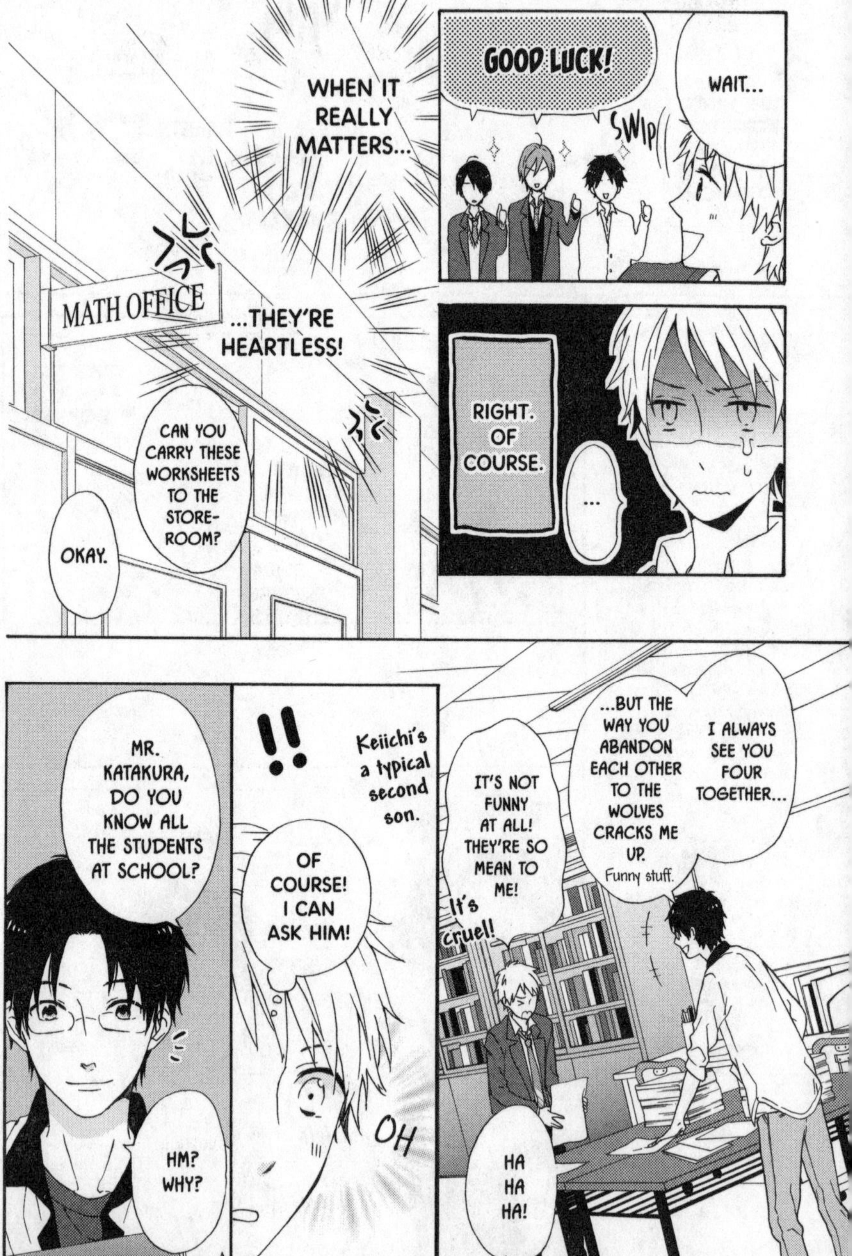
WAIT...
SWIP
GOOD LUCK!
RIGHT. OF COURSE.
...
WHEN IT REALLY MATTERS...
...THEY'RE HEARTLESS!
MATH OFFICE
CAN YOU CARRY THESE WORKSHEETS TO THE STOREROOM?
OKAY.
I ALWAYS SEE YOU FOUR TOGETHER...
...BUT THE WAY YOU ABANDON EACH OTHER TO THE WOLVES CRACKS ME UP.
Funny stuff.
IT'S NOT FUNNY AT ALL! THEY'RE SO MEAN TO ME!
It's cruel!
HA HA HA!
Keiichi's a typical second son.
!!
OF COURSE! I CAN ASK HIM!
OH
MR. KATAKURA, DO YOU KNOW ALL THE STUDENTS AT SCHOOL?
HM? WHY?

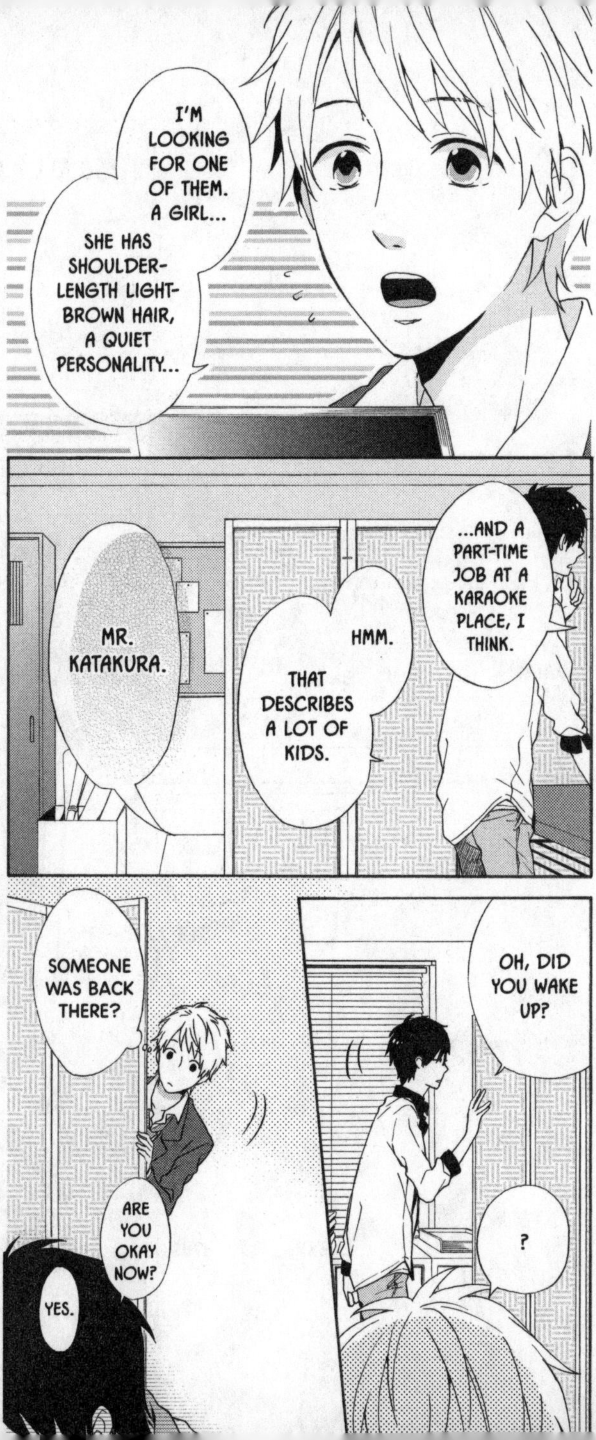
I'M LOOKING FOR ONE OF THEM. A GIRL...
SHE HAS SHOULDER-LENGTH LIGHT-BROWN HAIR, A QUIET PERSONALITY...
...AND A PART-TIME JOB AT A KARAOKE PLACE, I THINK.
HMM.
THAT DESCRIBES A LOT OF KIDS.
MR. KATAKURA.
OH, DID YOU WAKE UP?
?
SOMEONE WAS BACK THERE?
ARE YOU OKAY NOW?
YES.

1

Hello! Mizuno here. My official comments are at the end of the book...but welcome to this sidebar. It's been ages since I wrote one of these! My hand-writing is still awful! Sorry!

Lately(?) I've been finishing my drawings digitally. The last all-analog work I did was *Rasen no Vamp*.

Sometimes people think I work 100 percent digitally, but up through the inking stage I'm still analog. I like how it feels to draw with an analog pen. ♡
I love my G-pen. ♡

With digital, scanning and cleanup is a pain, but it's superconvenient when you live outside Tokyo.
You can send the data from your house!! You don't have to go to the airport with your finished pages!! You don't have to get on a train with no makeup or get your mother to take half a day of PTO to drive you to the airport!! And you can use the time you would have spent getting ready and commuting on work instead!! (This is pretty important.)

Those are the reasons I started doing things digitally. (*laugh*)

Even so, I still haven't mastered Comic Studio at all. I need to study up...

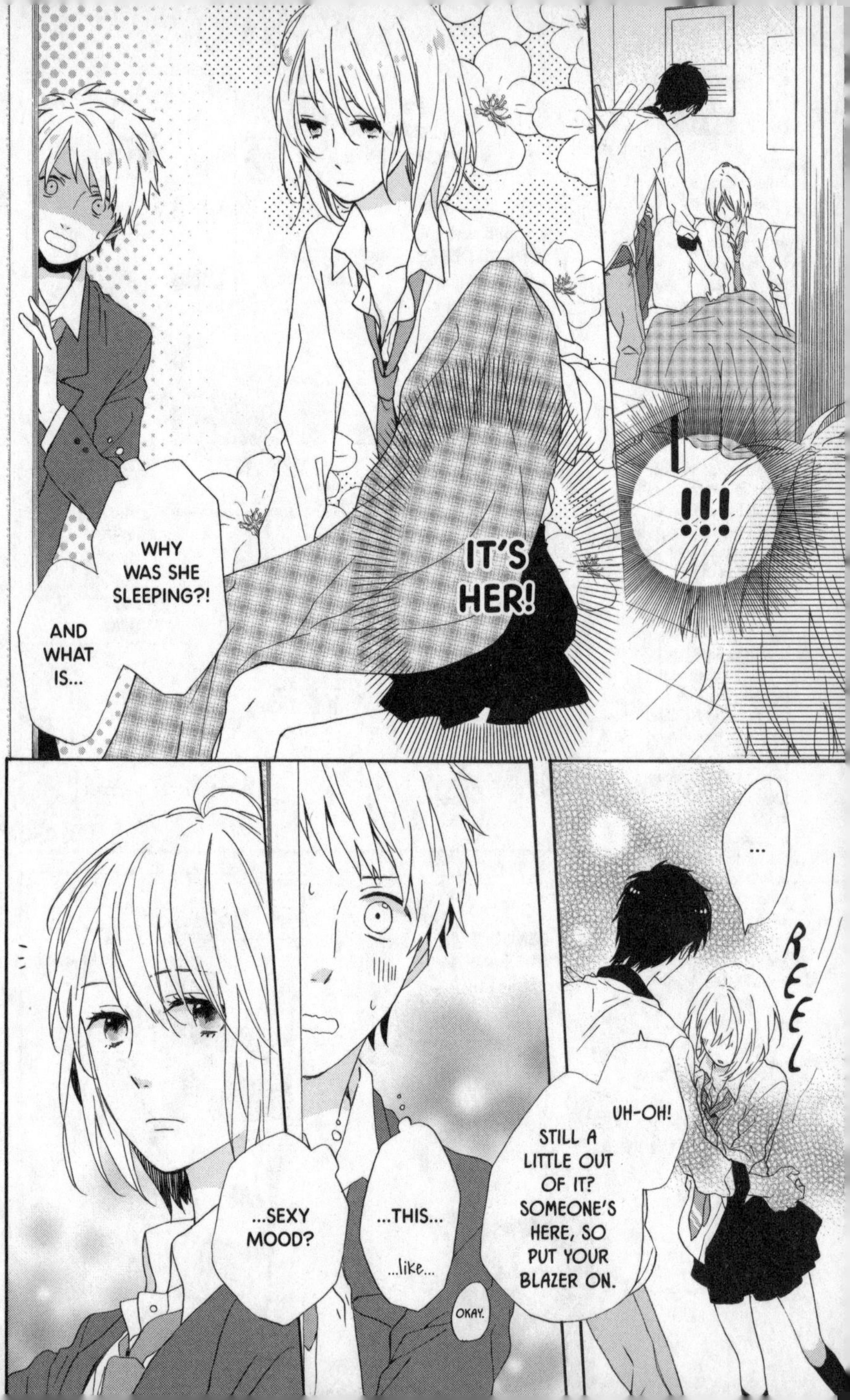
!!!
IT'S HER!
WHY WAS SHE SLEEPING?!
AND WHAT IS...
...
REEL
UH-OH!
STILL A LITTLE OUT OF IT? SOMEONE'S HERE, SO PUT YOUR BLAZER ON.
OKAY.
...THIS...
...like...
...SEXY MOOD?

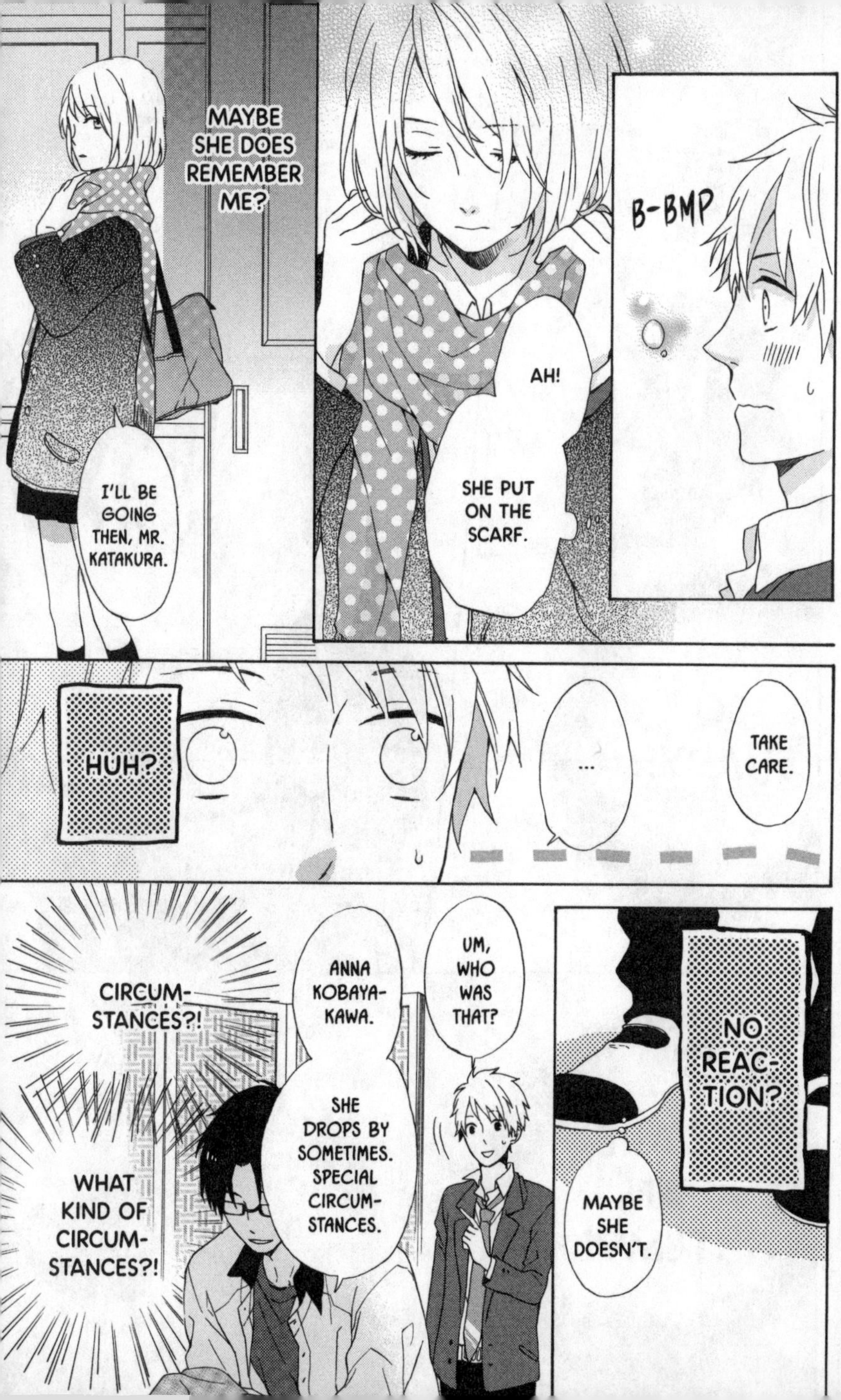
B-BMP
AH!
SHE PUT ON THE SCARF.
MAYBE SHE DOES REMEMBER ME?
I'LL BE GOING THEN, MR. KATAKURA.
TAKE CARE.
...
HUH?
NO REACTION?
MAYBE SHE DOESN'T.
UM, WHO WAS THAT?
ANNA KOBAYAKAWA.
SHE DROPS BY SOMETIMES. SPECIAL CIRCUMSTANCES.
CIRCUMSTANCES?!
WHAT KIND OF CIRCUMSTANCES?!

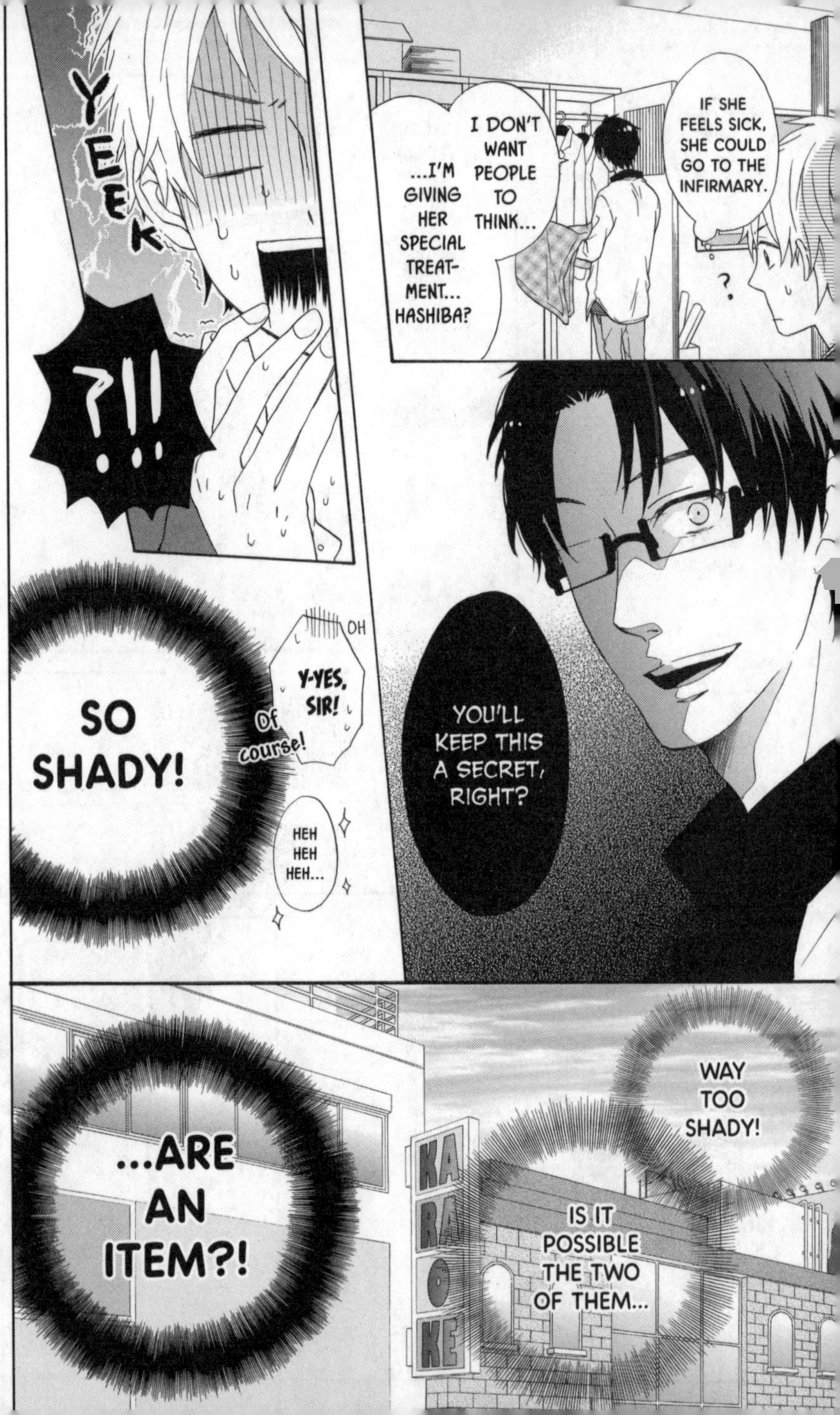
IF SHE FEELS SICK, SHE COULD GO TO THE INFIRMARY.
?
I DON'T WANT PEOPLE TO THINK...
...I'M GIVING HER SPECIAL TREATMENT... HASHIBA?
YEEEK
?!!
YOU'LL KEEP THIS A SECRET, RIGHT?
OH
Y-YES, SIR!
Of course!
HEH HEH HEH...
SO SHADY!
WAY TOO SHADY!
KARAOKE
IS IT POSSIBLE THE TWO OF THEM...
...ARE AN ITEM?!

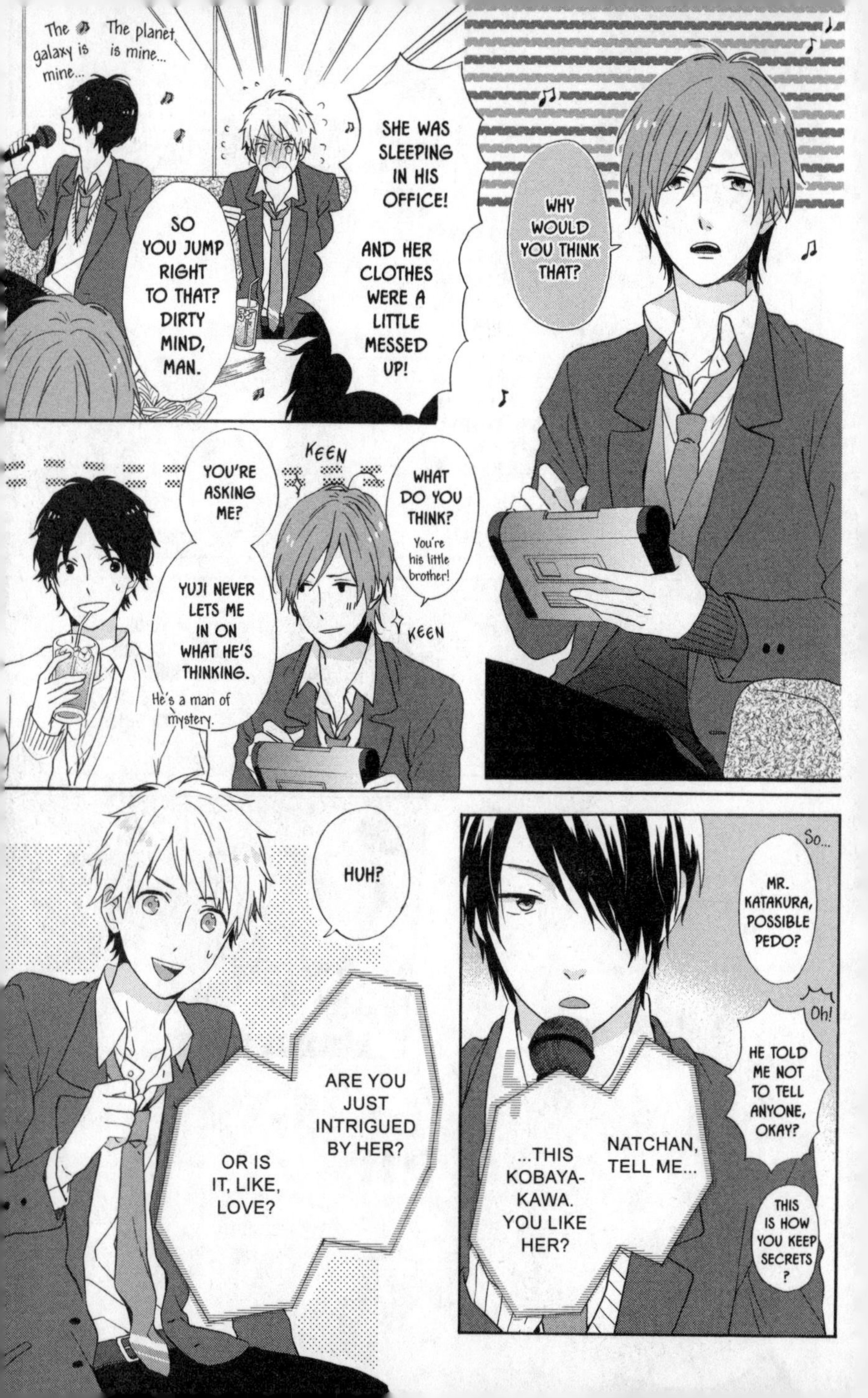
WHY WOULD YOU THINK THAT?
SHE WAS SLEEPING IN HIS OFFICE!
AND HER CLOTHES WERE A LITTLE MESSED UP!
The planet is mine...
The galaxy is mine...
SO YOU JUMP RIGHT TO THAT? DIRTY MIND, MAN.
WHAT DO YOU THINK?
You're his little brother!
KEEN
KEEN
YOU'RE ASKING ME?
YUJI NEVER LETS ME IN ON WHAT HE'S THINKING.
He's a man of mystery.
So...
MR. KATAKURA, POSSIBLE PEDO?
Oh!
HE TOLD ME NOT TO TELL ANYONE, OKAY?
THIS IS HOW YOU KEEP SECRETS?
NATCHAN, TELL ME...
...THIS KOBAYA-KAWA. YOU LIKE HER?
HUH?
ARE YOU JUST INTRIGUED BY HER?
OR IS IT, LIKE, LOVE?

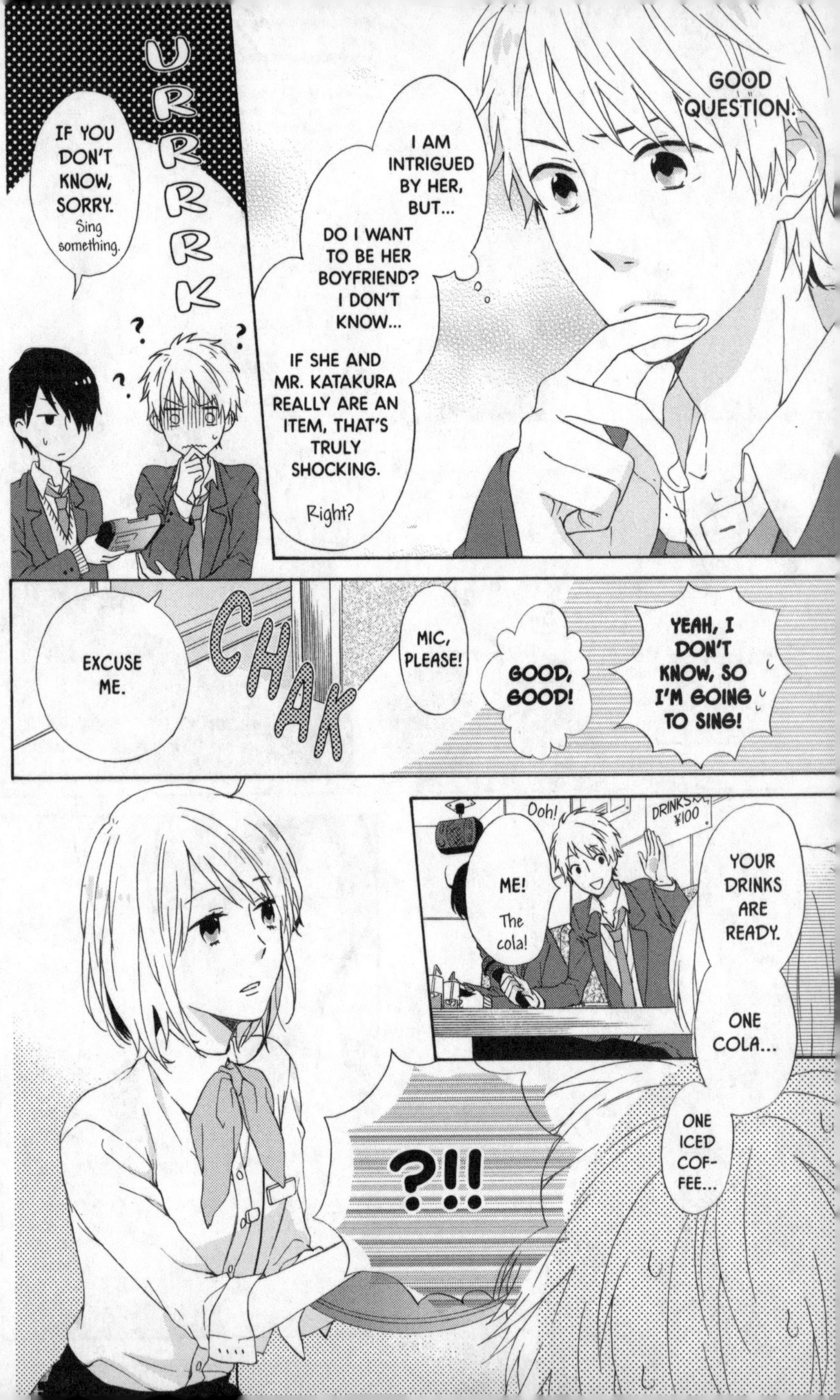
GOOD QUESTION.
I AM INTRIGUED BY HER, BUT...
DO I WANT TO BE HER BOYFRIEND? I DON'T KNOW...
IF SHE AND MR. KATAKURA REALLY ARE AN ITEM, THAT'S TRULY SHOCKING.
Right?
URRRK
IF YOU DON'T KNOW, SORRY.
Sing something.
YEAH, I DON'T KNOW, SO I'M GOING TO SING!
GOOD, GOOD!
MIC, PLEASE!
CHAK
EXCUSE ME.
YOUR DRINKS ARE READY.
ONE COLA...
ONE ICED COF-FEE...
DRINKS ¥100
Ooh!
ME!
The cola!
?!!

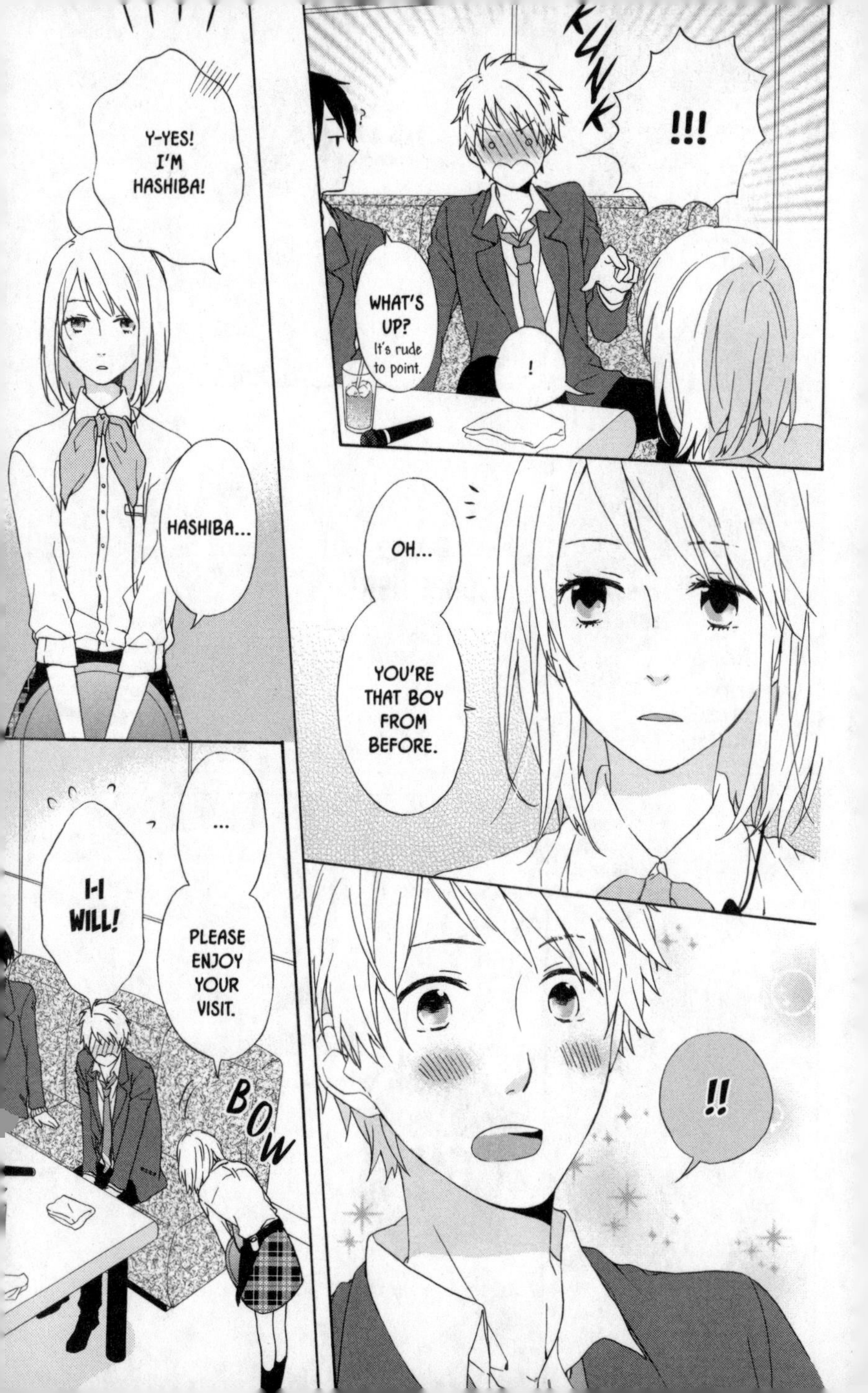
KUNK
!!!
?
WHAT'S UP? It's rude to point.
!
Y-YES! I'M HASHIBA!
HASHIBA...
OH... YOU'RE THAT BOY FROM BEFORE.
!!
... PLEASE ENJOY YOUR VISIT.
I-I WILL!
BOW

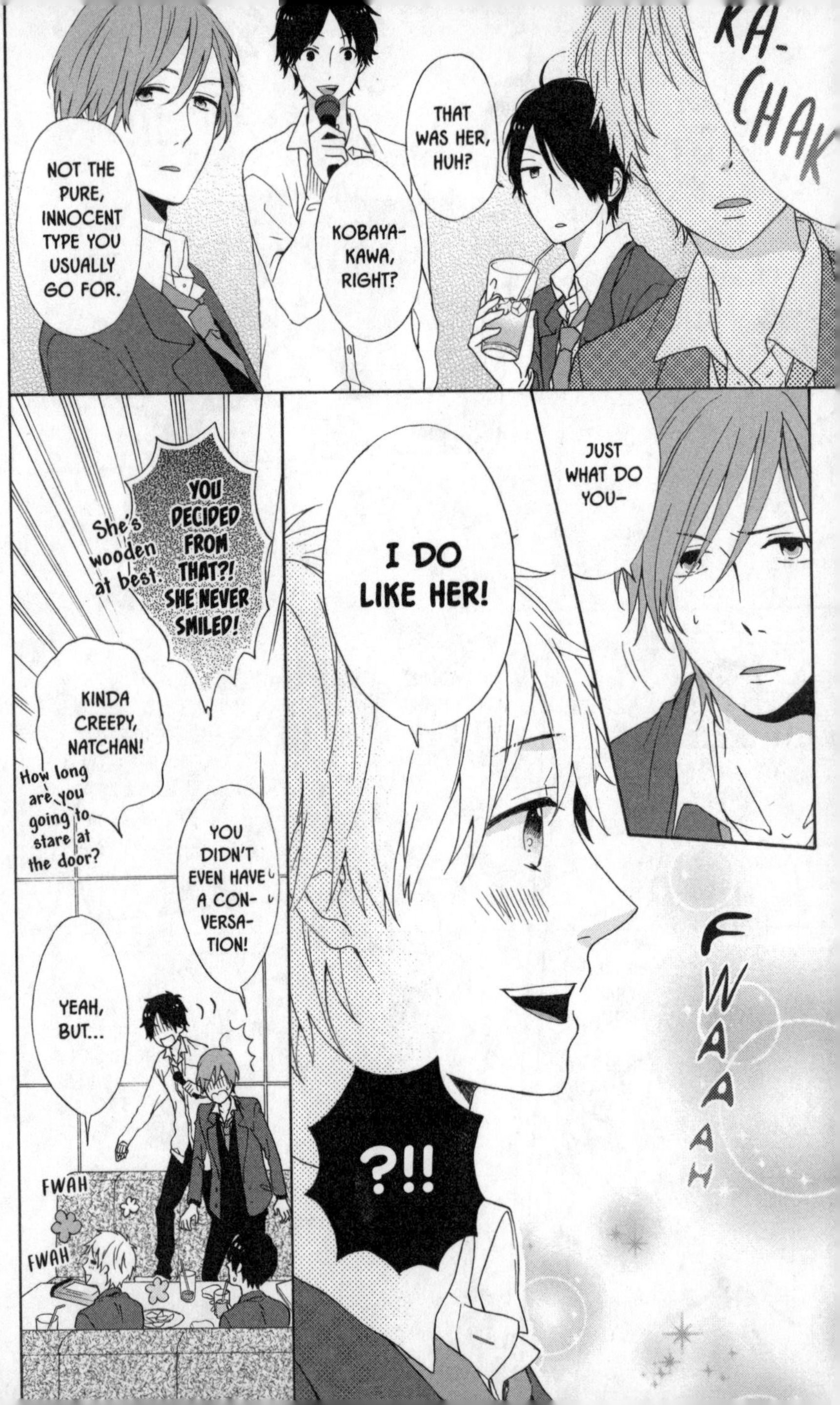
KA-CHAK
THAT WAS HER, HUH?
KOBAYA-KAWA, RIGHT?
NOT THE PURE, INNOCENT TYPE YOU USUALLY GO FOR.
JUST WHAT DO YOU–
I DO LIKE HER!
FWAAAAH
?!!
YOU DECIDED FROM THAT?! SHE NEVER SMILED!
She's wooden at best.
KINDA CREEPY, NATCHAN!
How long are you going to stare at the door?
YOU DIDN'T EVEN HAVE A CON-VERSA-TION!
YEAH, BUT...
FWAH
FWAH

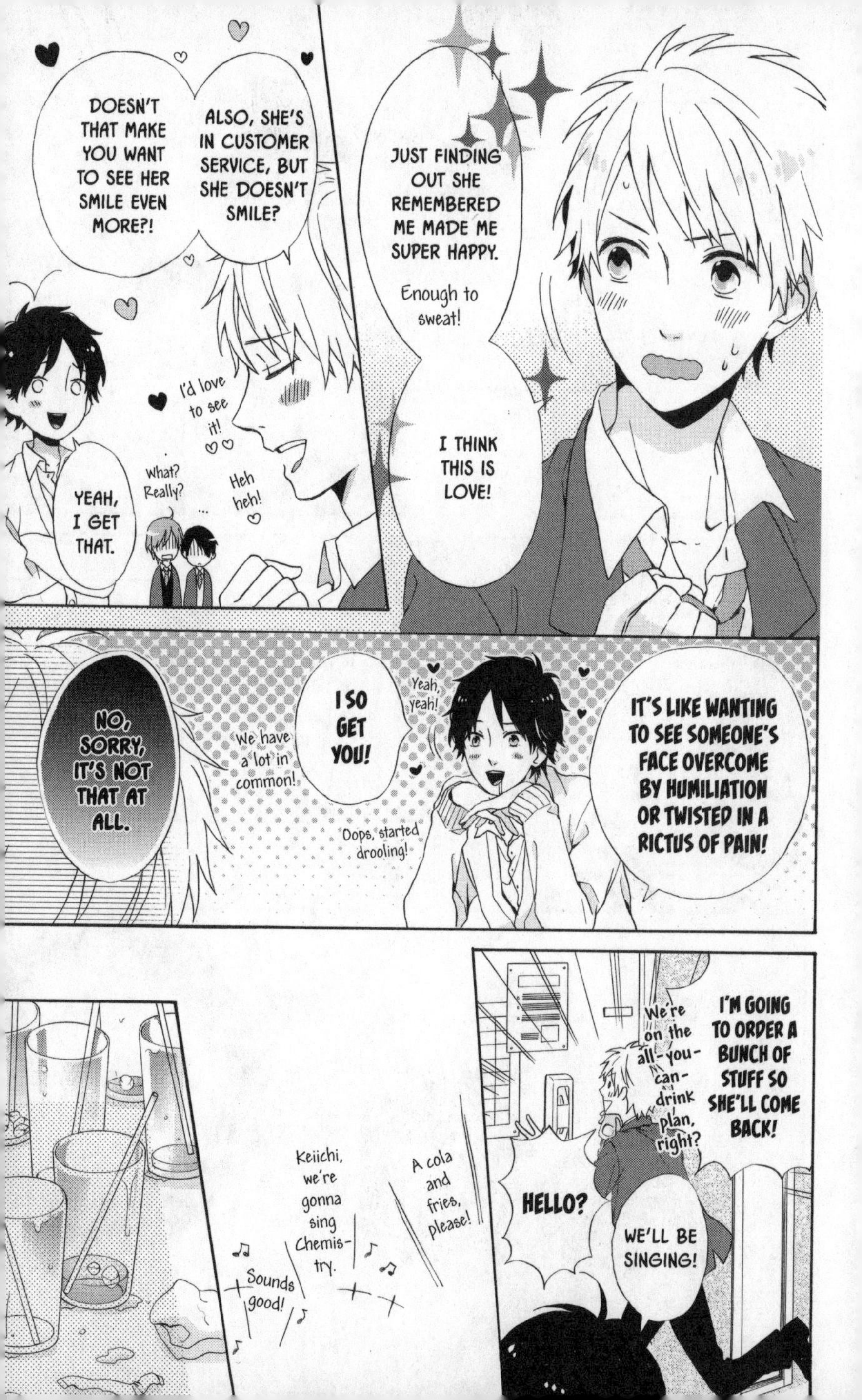
JUST FINDING OUT SHE REMEMBERED ME MADE ME SUPER HAPPY.
Enough to sweat!
I THINK THIS IS LOVE!
ALSO, SHE'S IN CUSTOMER SERVICE, BUT SHE DOESN'T SMILE?
DOESN'T THAT MAKE YOU WANT TO SEE HER SMILE EVEN MORE?!
I'd love to see it!
Heh heh!
What? Really?
...
YEAH, I GET THAT.
IT'S LIKE WANTING TO SEE SOMEONE'S FACE OVERCOME BY HUMILIATION OR TWISTED IN A RICTUS OF PAIN!
Yeah, yeah!
Oops, started drooling!
I SO GET YOU!
We have a lot in common!
NO, SORRY, IT'S NOT THAT AT ALL.
I'M GOING TO ORDER A BUNCH OF STUFF SO SHE'LL COME BACK!
We're on the all-you-can-drink plan, right?
HELLO?
WE'LL BE SINGING!
A cola and fries, please!
Keiichi, we're gonna sing Chemistry.
Sounds good!

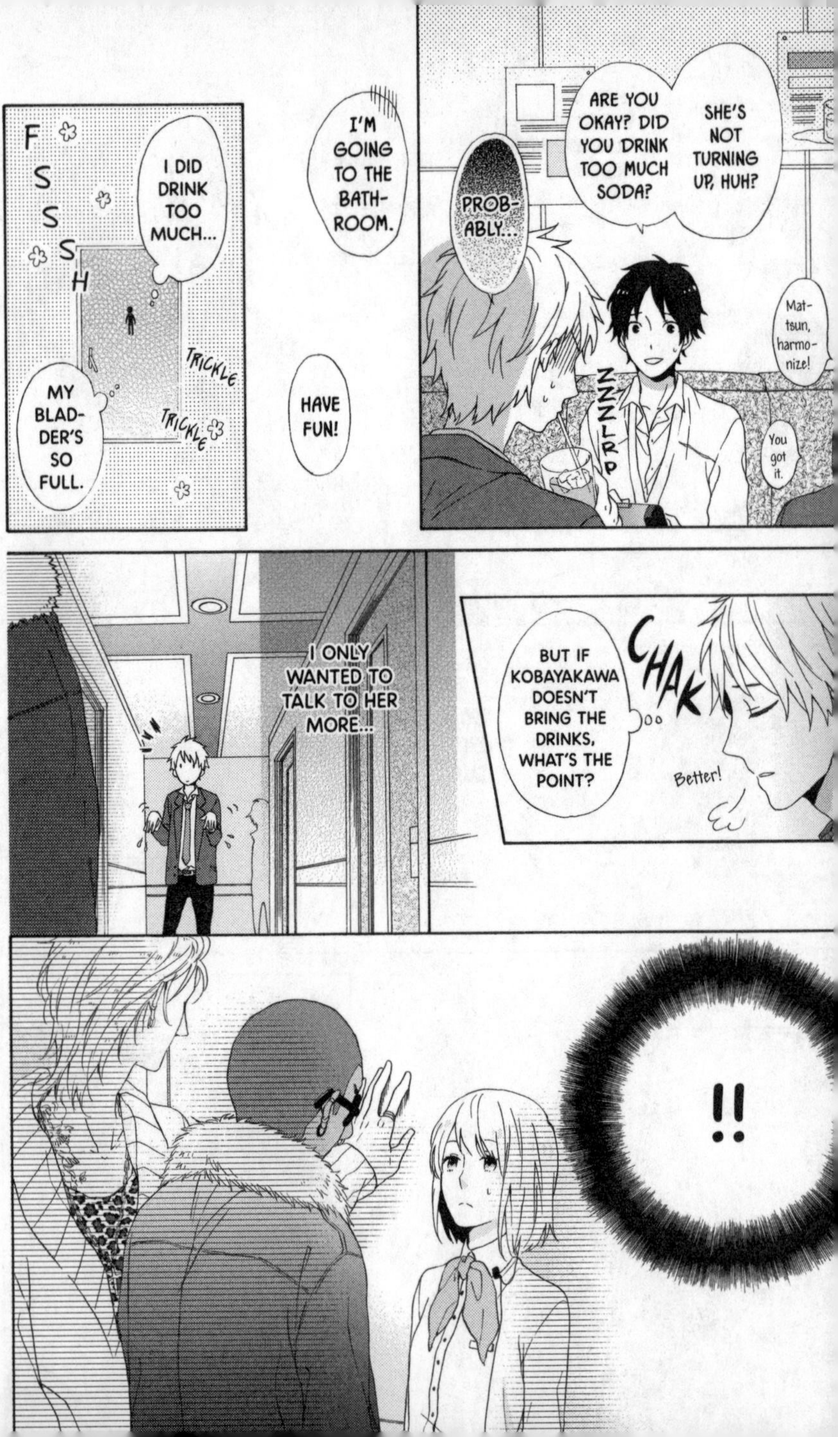
SHE'S NOT TURNING UP, HUH?
ARE YOU OKAY? DID YOU DRINK TOO MUCH SODA?
PROB-ABLY...
Mat-tsun, harmonize!
You got it.
ZZZLRP
I'M GOING TO THE BATH-ROOM.
HAVE FUN!
I DID DRINK TOO MUCH...
FSSSH
MY BLAD-DER'S SO FULL.
TRICKLE
TRICKLE
CHAK
BUT IF KOBAYAKAWA DOESN'T BRING THE DRINKS, WHAT'S THE POINT?
Better!
I ONLY WANTED TO TALK TO HER MORE...
!!

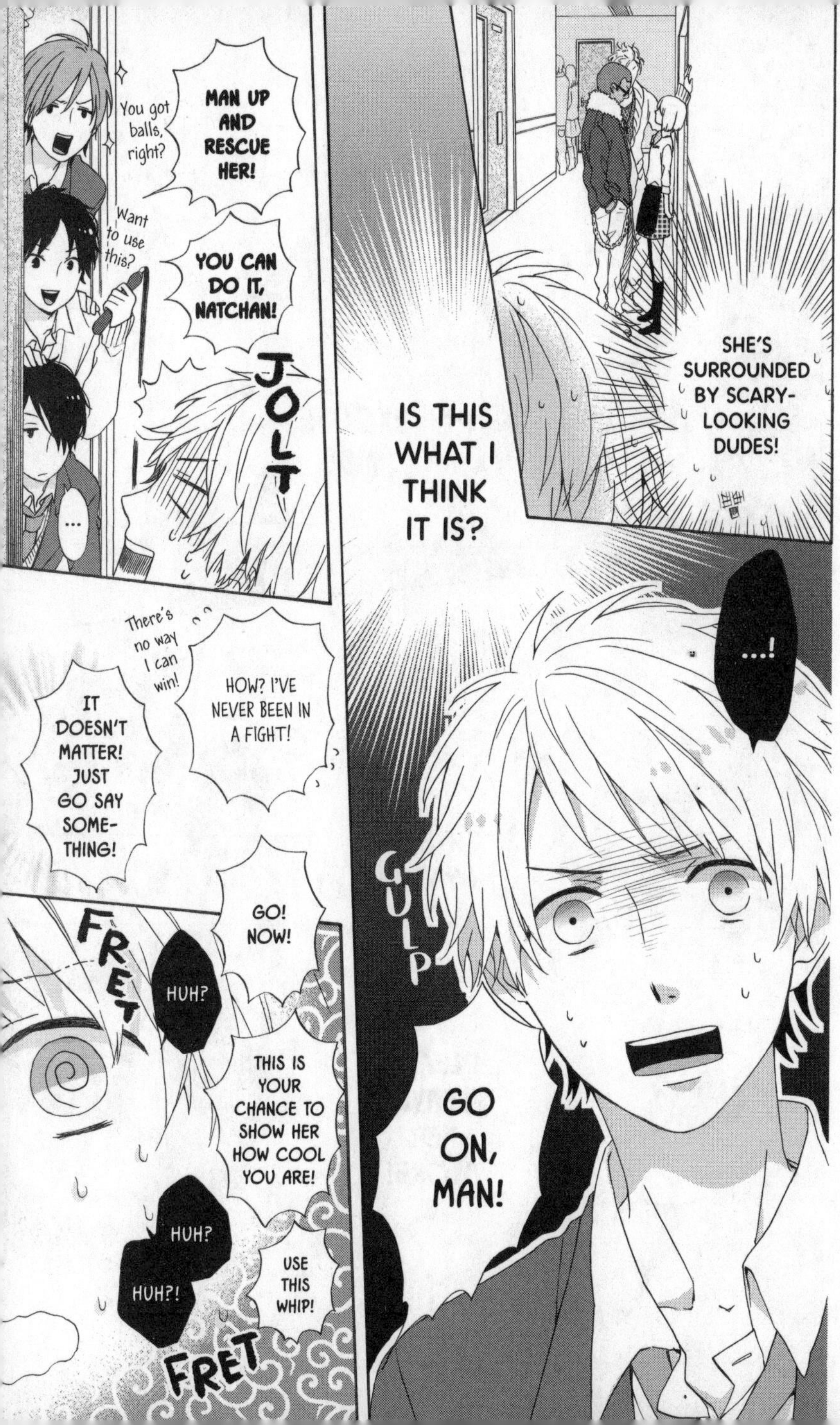
SHE'S SURROUNDED BY SCARY-LOOKING DUDES!
IS THIS WHAT I THINK IT IS?
MAN UP AND RESCUE HER!
You got balls, right?
YOU CAN DO IT, NATCHAN!
Want to use this?
JOLT
...
HOW? I'VE NEVER BEEN IN A FIGHT!
There's no way I can win!
IT DOESN'T MATTER! JUST GO SAY SOME-THING!
GO! NOW!
HUH?
FRET
THIS IS YOUR CHANCE TO SHOW HER HOW COOL YOU ARE!
HUH?
HUH?!
USE THIS WHIP!
FRET
...!
GULP
GO ON, MAN!

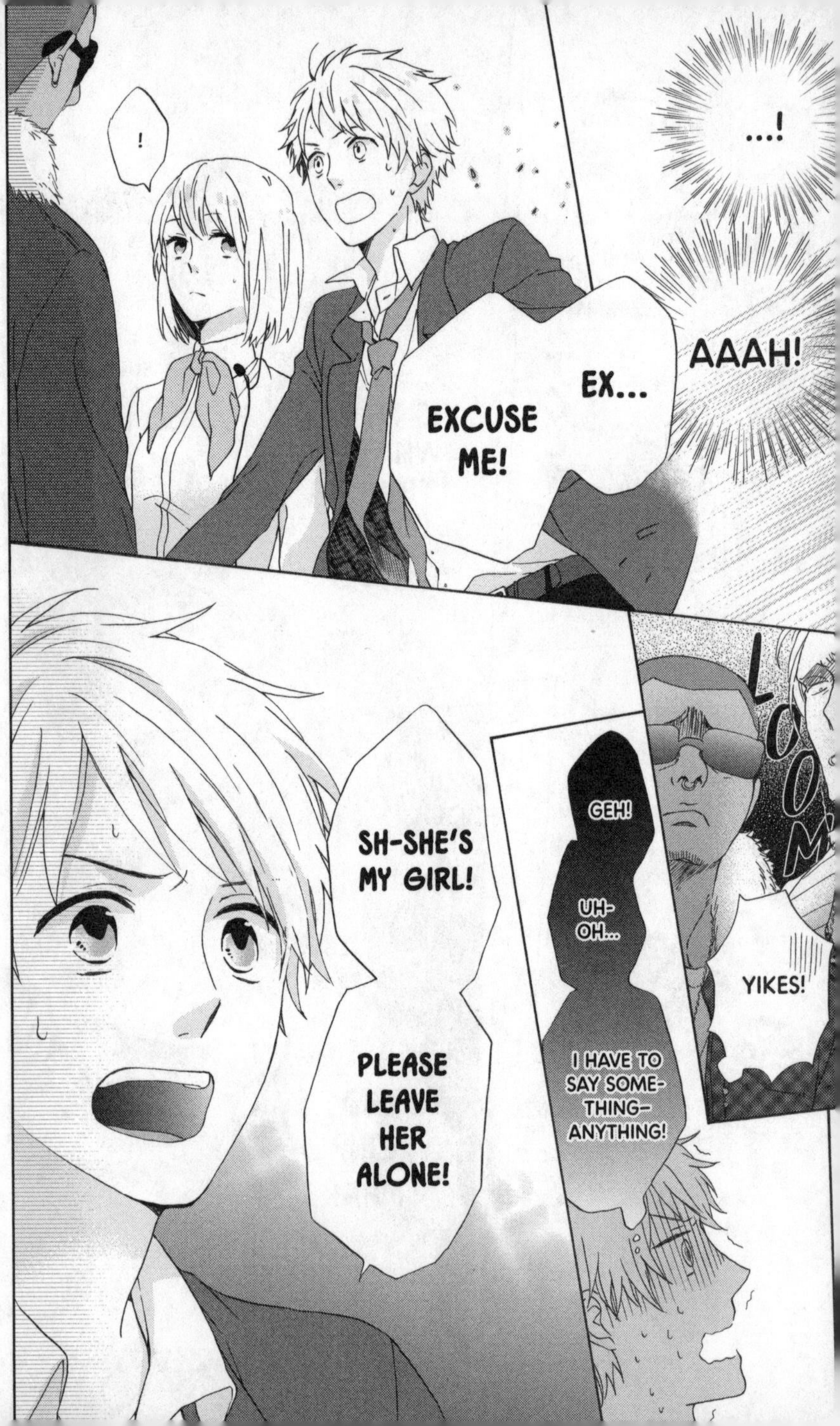
...!
AAAH!
EX...
EXCUSE ME!
!
YIKES!
GEH!
UH-OH...
I HAVE TO SAY SOME-THING—ANYTHING!
SH-SHE'S MY GIRL!
PLEASE LEAVE HER ALONE!

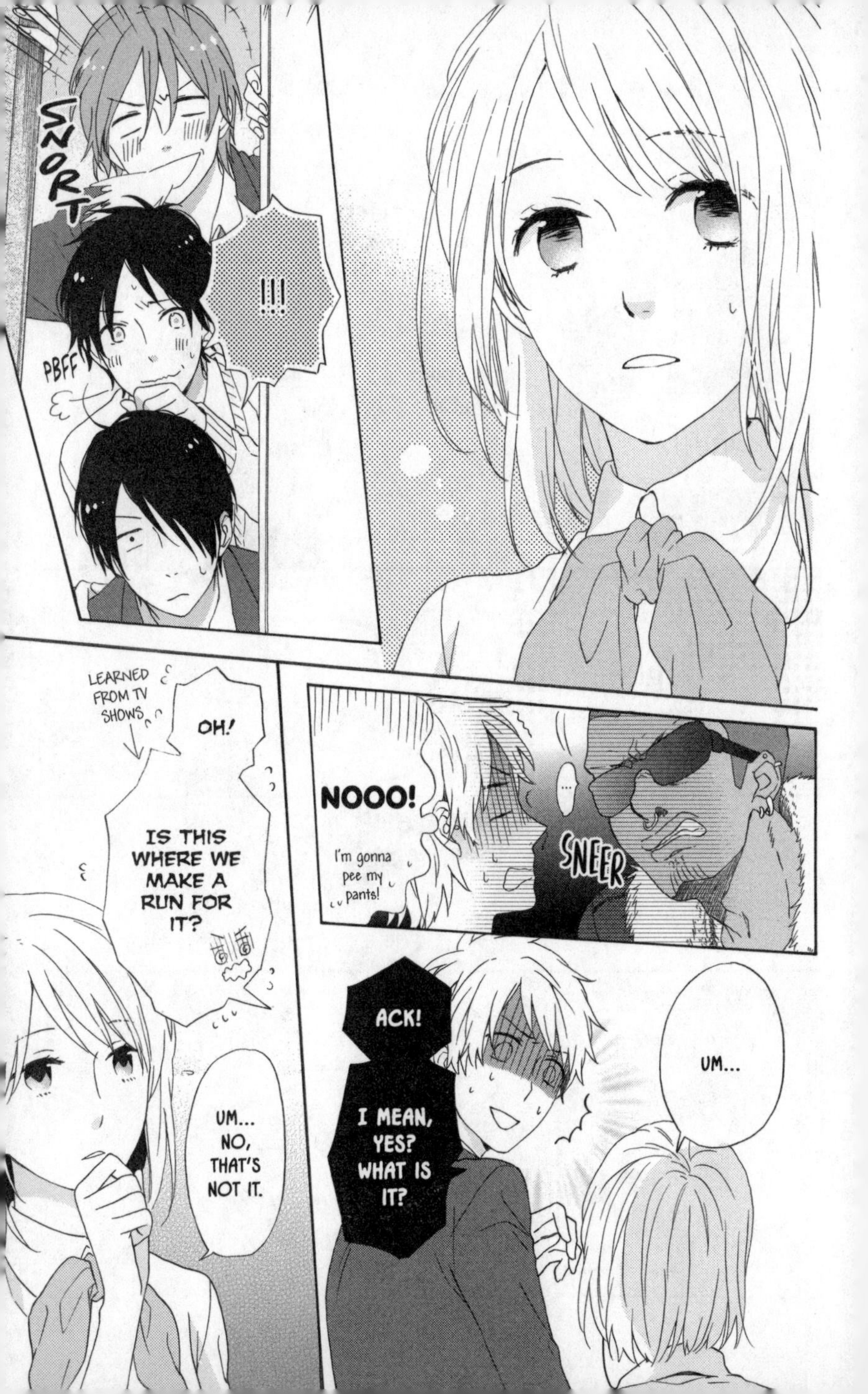
!!!
SNORT
PBFF
...
SNEER
NOOO!
I'm gonna pee my pants!
UM...
ACK!
I MEAN, YES? WHAT IS IT?
OH!
LEARNED FROM TV SHOWS
IS THIS WHERE WE MAKE A RUN FOR IT?
UM... NO, THAT'S NOT IT.

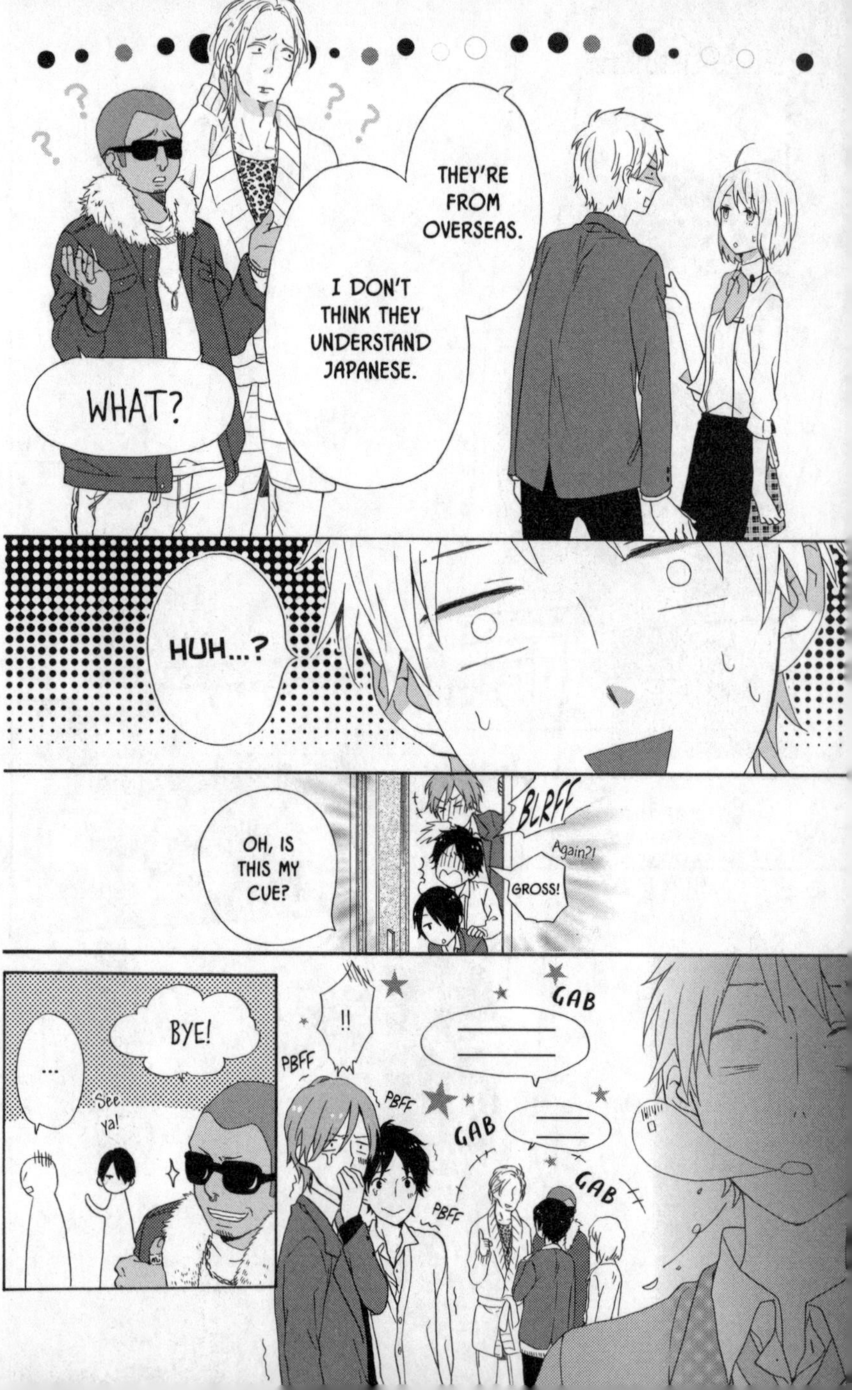
THEY'RE FROM OVERSEAS.
I DON'T THINK THEY UNDERSTAND JAPANESE.
WHAT?
HUH...?
BLRFF
Again?!
GROSS!
OH, IS THIS MY CUE?
GAB
!!
PBFF
PBFF
GAB
GAB
PBFF
BYE!
...
See ya!

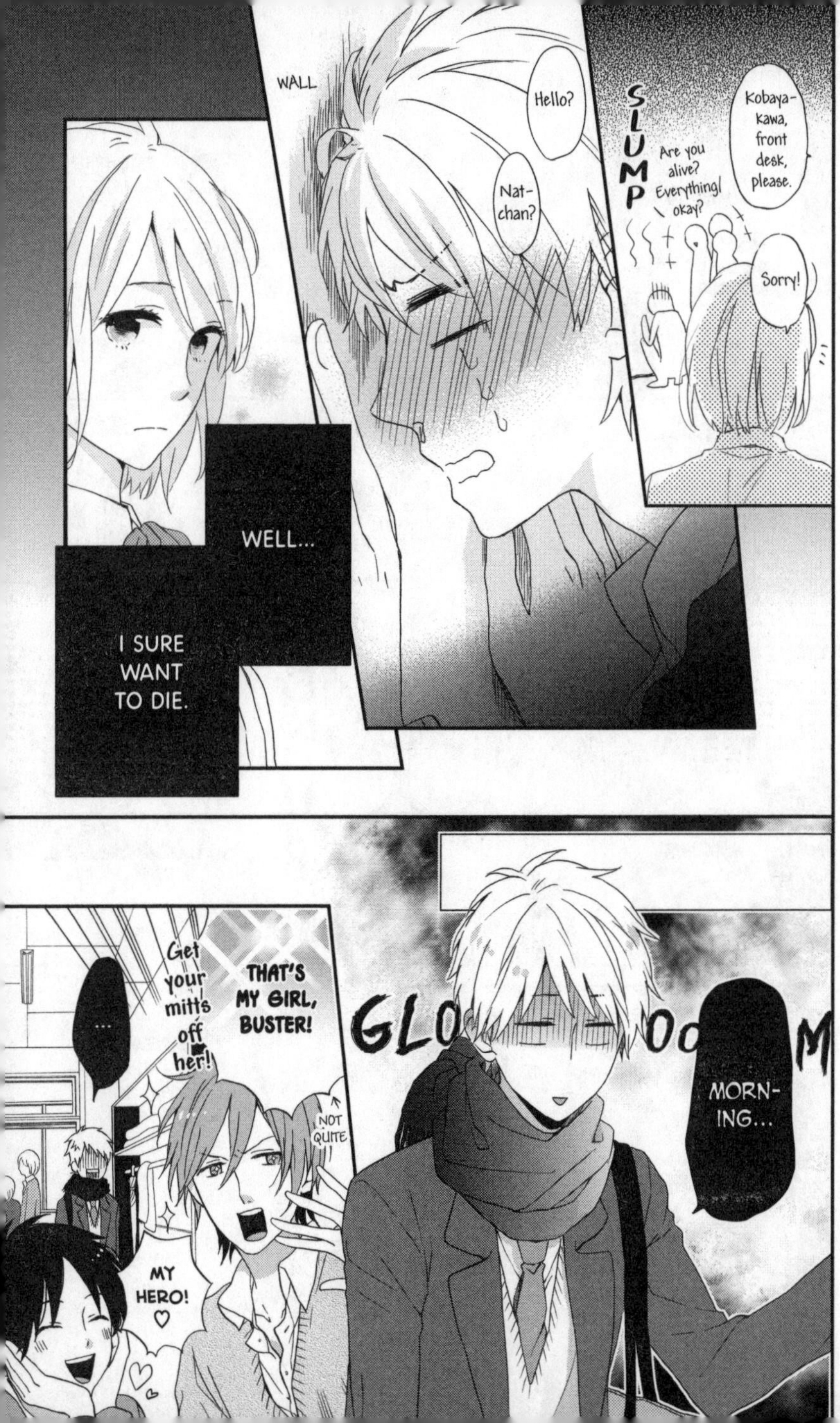
Kobaya-kawa, front desk, please.
Sorry!
Are you alive? Everything okay?
SLUMP
Hello?
Nat-chan?
WALL
WELL...
I SURE WANT TO DIE.
GLOOOM
MORNING...
...
THAT'S MY GIRL, BUSTER!
Get your mitts off her!
NOT QUITE
MY HERO! ♡

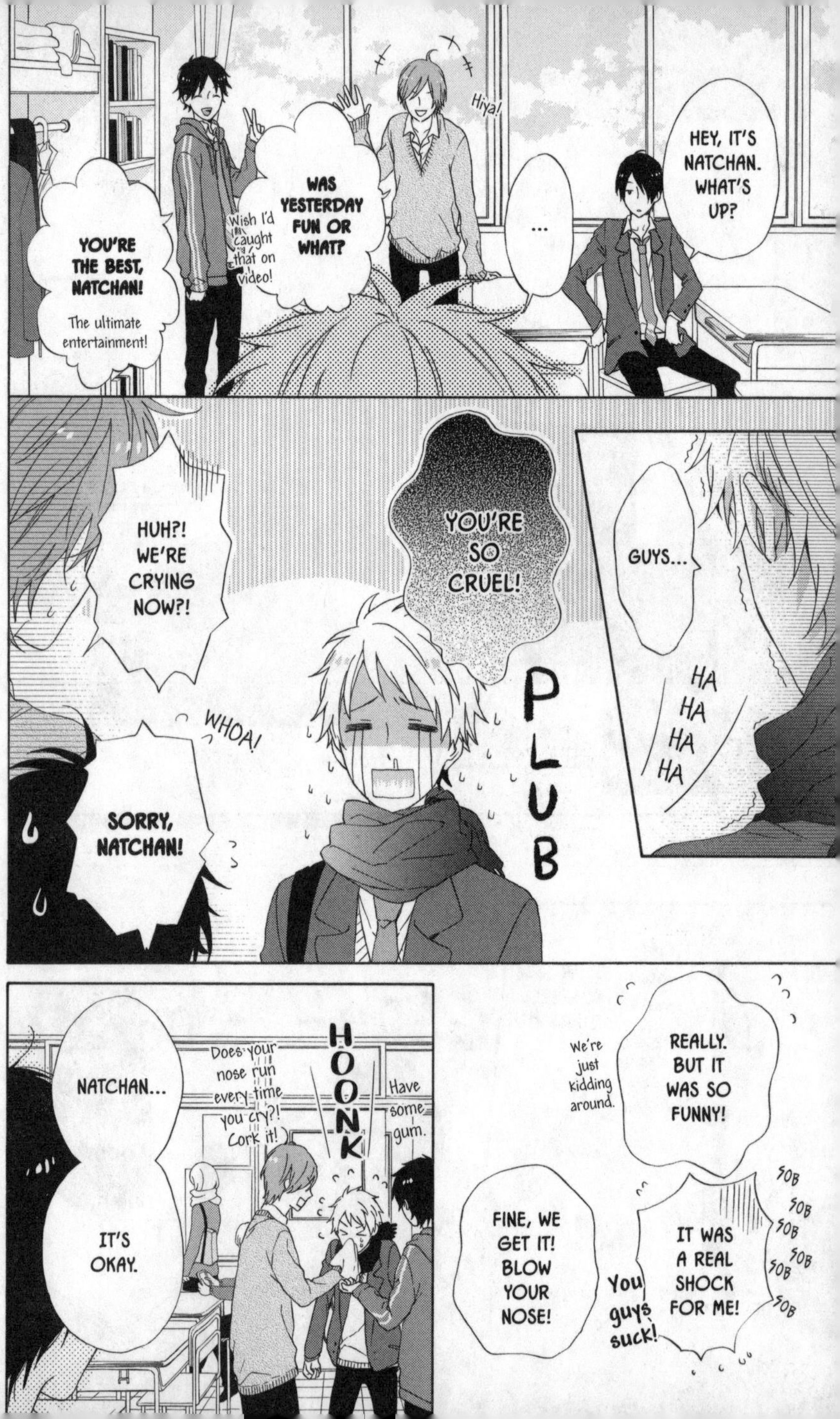
HEY, IT'S NATCHAN. WHAT'S UP?
Hiya!
...
WAS YESTERDAY FUN OR WHAT?
Wish I'd caught that on video!
YOU'RE THE BEST, NATCHAN!
The ultimate entertainment!
GUYS...
HA HA HA HA
YOU'RE SO CRUEL!
PLUB
HUH?! WE'RE CRYING NOW?!
WHOA!
SORRY, NATCHAN!
REALLY. BUT IT WAS SO FUNNY!
We're just kidding around.
IT WAS A REAL SHOCK FOR ME!
SOB SOB SOB SOB SOB SOB
You guys suck!
FINE, WE GET IT! BLOW YOUR NOSE!
NATCHAN...
HOONK
Have some gum.
Does your nose run every time you cry?! Cork it!
IT'S OKAY.

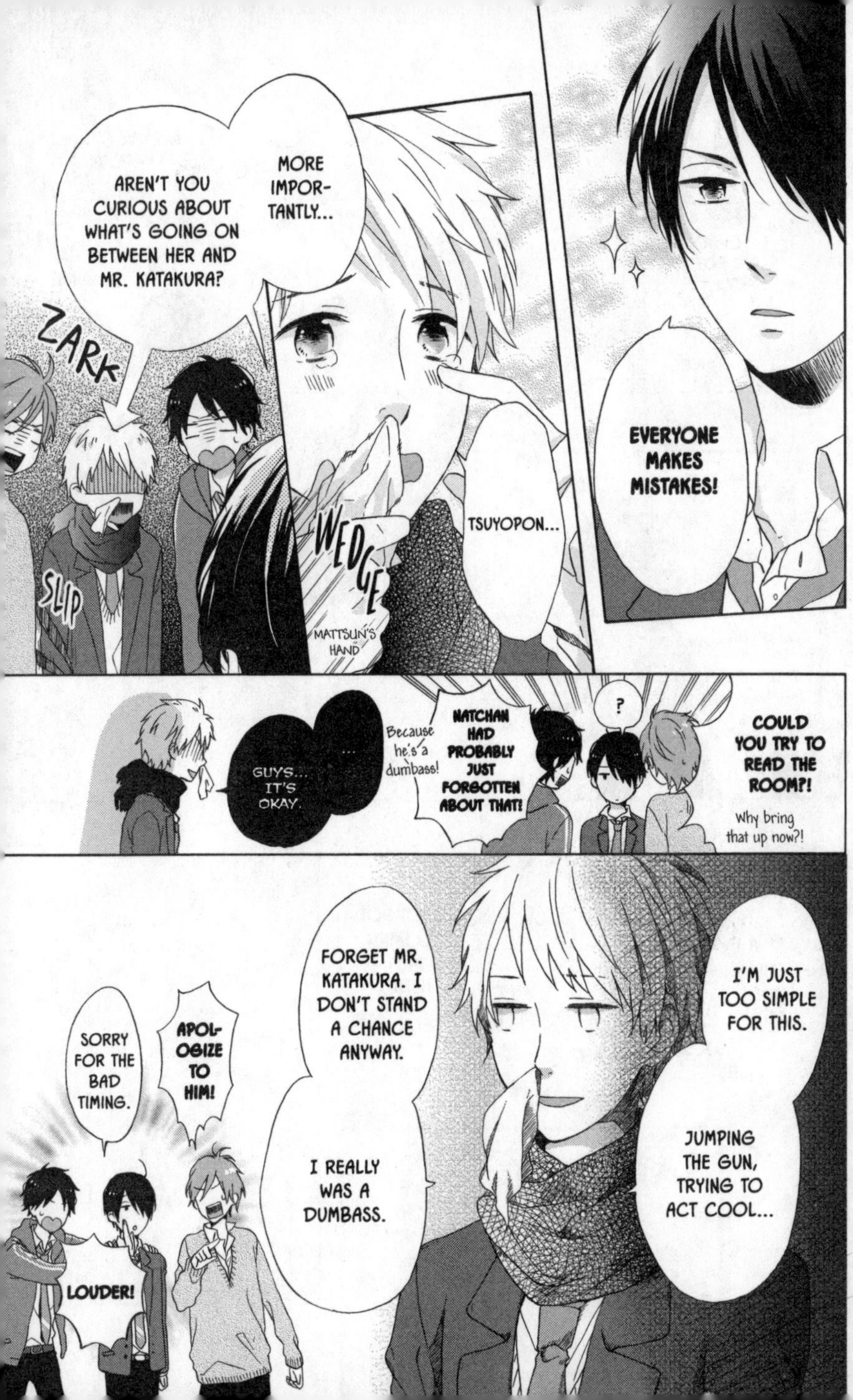
EVERYONE MAKES MISTAKES!
TSUYOPON...
MORE IMPOR-TANTLY...
WEDGE
MATTSUN'S HAND
AREN'T YOU CURIOUS ABOUT WHAT'S GOING ON BETWEEN HER AND MR. KATAKURA?
ZARK
SLIP
COULD YOU TRY TO READ THE ROOM?!
Why bring that up now?!
?
NATCHAN HAD PROBABLY JUST FORGOTTEN ABOUT THAT!
Because he's a dumbass!
...
GUYS... IT'S OKAY.
I'M JUST TOO SIMPLE FOR THIS.
JUMPING THE GUN, TRYING TO ACT COOL...
FORGET MR. KATAKURA. I DON'T STAND A CHANCE ANYWAY.
I REALLY WAS A DUMBASS.
APOL-OGIZE TO HIM!
SORRY FOR THE BAD TIMING.
LOUDER!

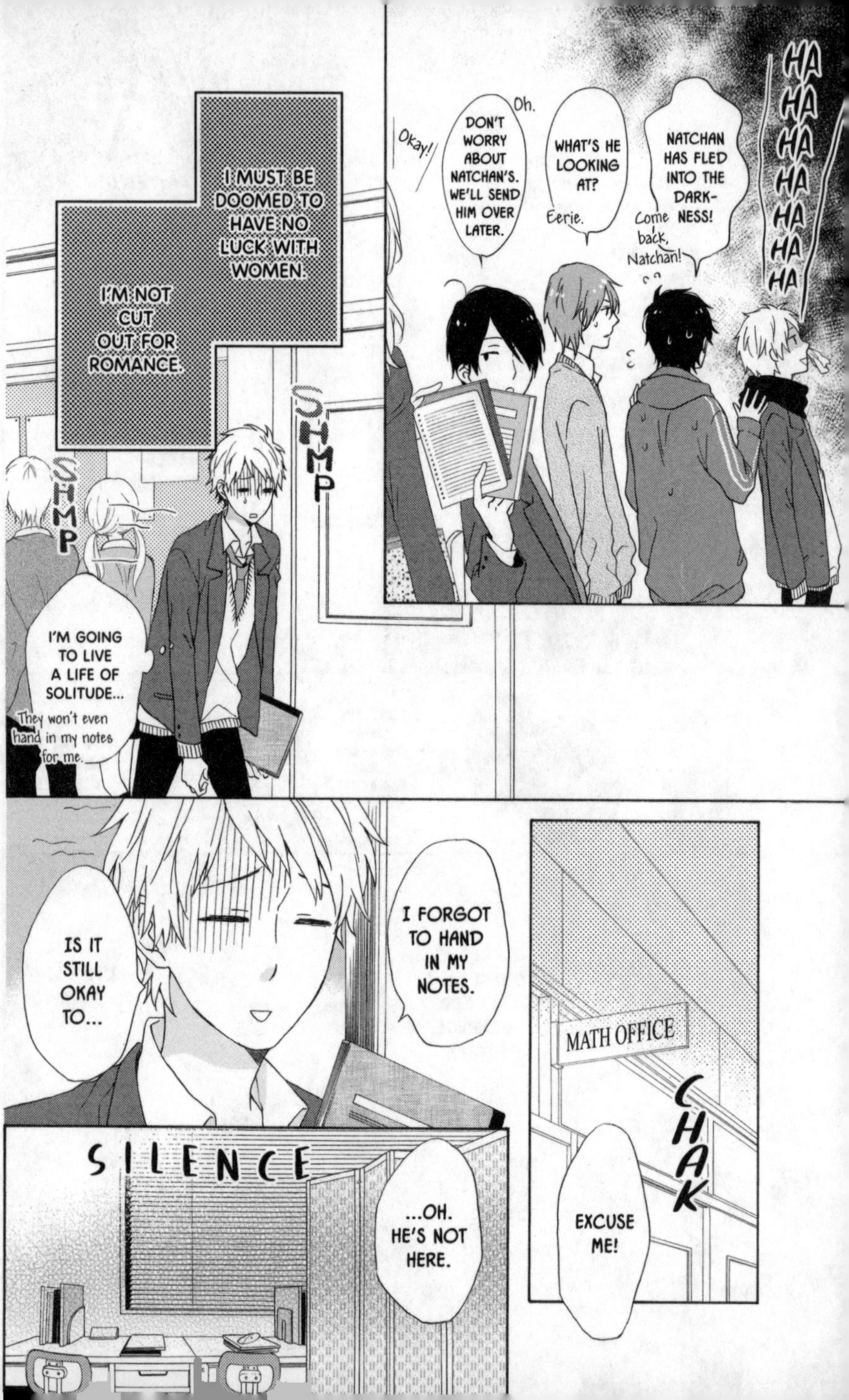
HA HA HA HA HA HA HA
NATCHAN HAS FLED INTO THE DARKNESS!
Come back, Natchan!
WHAT'S HE LOOKING AT?
Eerie.
Oh.
DON'T WORRY ABOUT NATCHAN'S. WE'LL SEND HIM OVER LATER.
Okay!
I MUST BE DOOMED TO HAVE NO LUCK WITH WOMEN.
I'M NOT CUT OUT FOR ROMANCE.
SHMP
SHMP
I'M GOING TO LIVE A LIFE OF SOLITUDE...
They won't even hand in my notes for me.
MATH OFFICE
CHAK
EXCUSE ME!
I FORGOT TO HAND IN MY NOTES.
IS IT STILL OKAY TO...
SILENCE
...OH. HE'S NOT HERE.

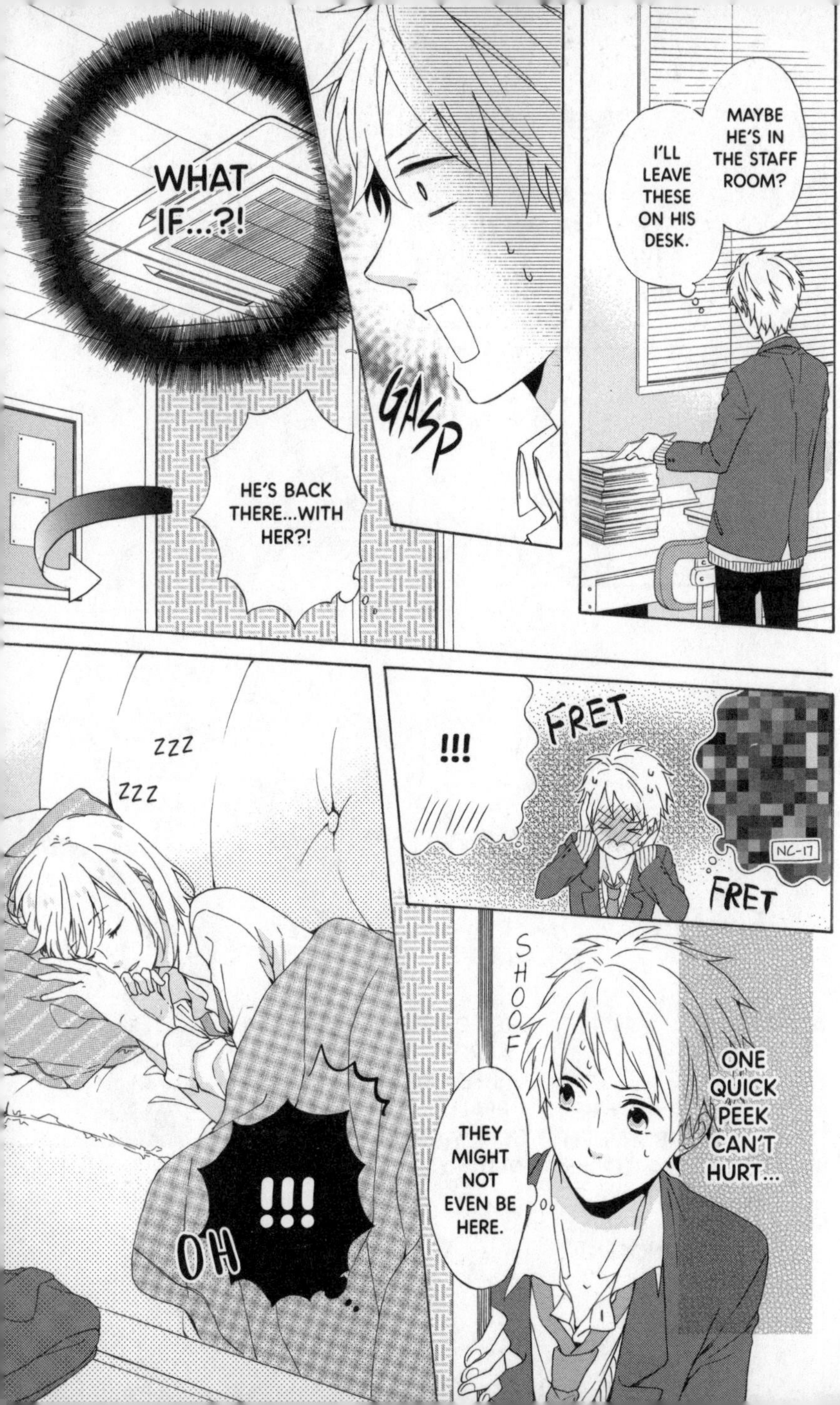
MAYBE HE'S IN THE STAFF ROOM?
I'LL LEAVE THESE ON HIS DESK.
GASP
WHAT IF...?!
HE'S BACK THERE...WITH HER?!
!!!
FRET
NC-17
FRET
SHOOF
ONE QUICK PEEK CAN'T HURT...
THEY MIGHT NOT EVEN BE HERE.
ZZZ
ZZZ
!!!
OH

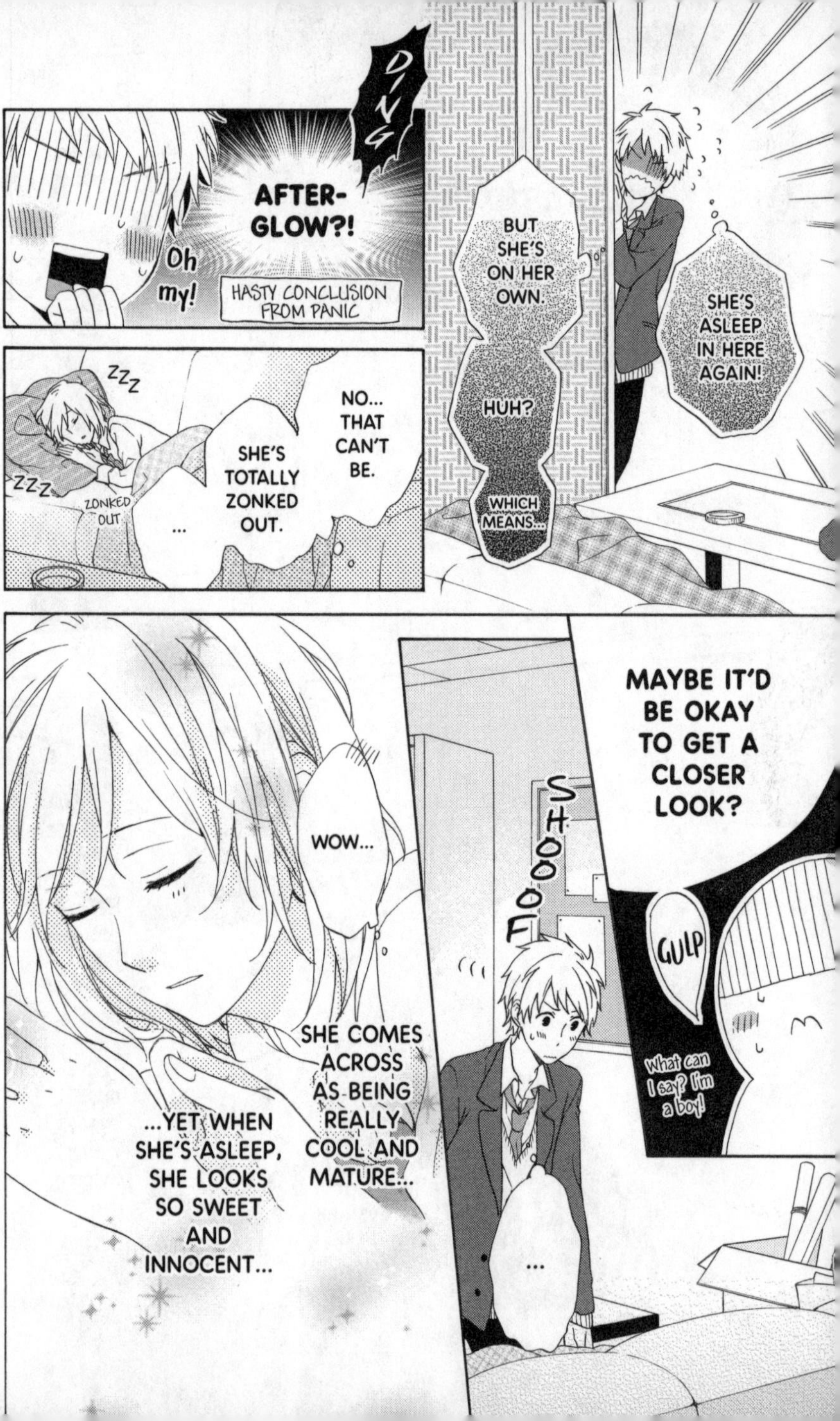
SHE'S ASLEEP IN HERE AGAIN!
BUT SHE'S ON HER OWN.
HUH?
WHICH MEANS...
DING
AFTER-GLOW?!
Oh my!
HASTY CONCLUSION FROM PANIC
NO... THAT CAN'T BE.
SHE'S TOTALLY ZONKED OUT.
...
ZZZ
ZZZ
ZONKED OUT
MAYBE IT'D BE OKAY TO GET A CLOSER LOOK?
GULP
What can I say? I'm a boy!
SHOOOF
...
WOW...
SHE COMES ACROSS AS BEING REALLY COOL AND MATURE...
...YET WHEN SHE'S ASLEEP, SHE LOOKS SO SWEET AND INNOCENT...

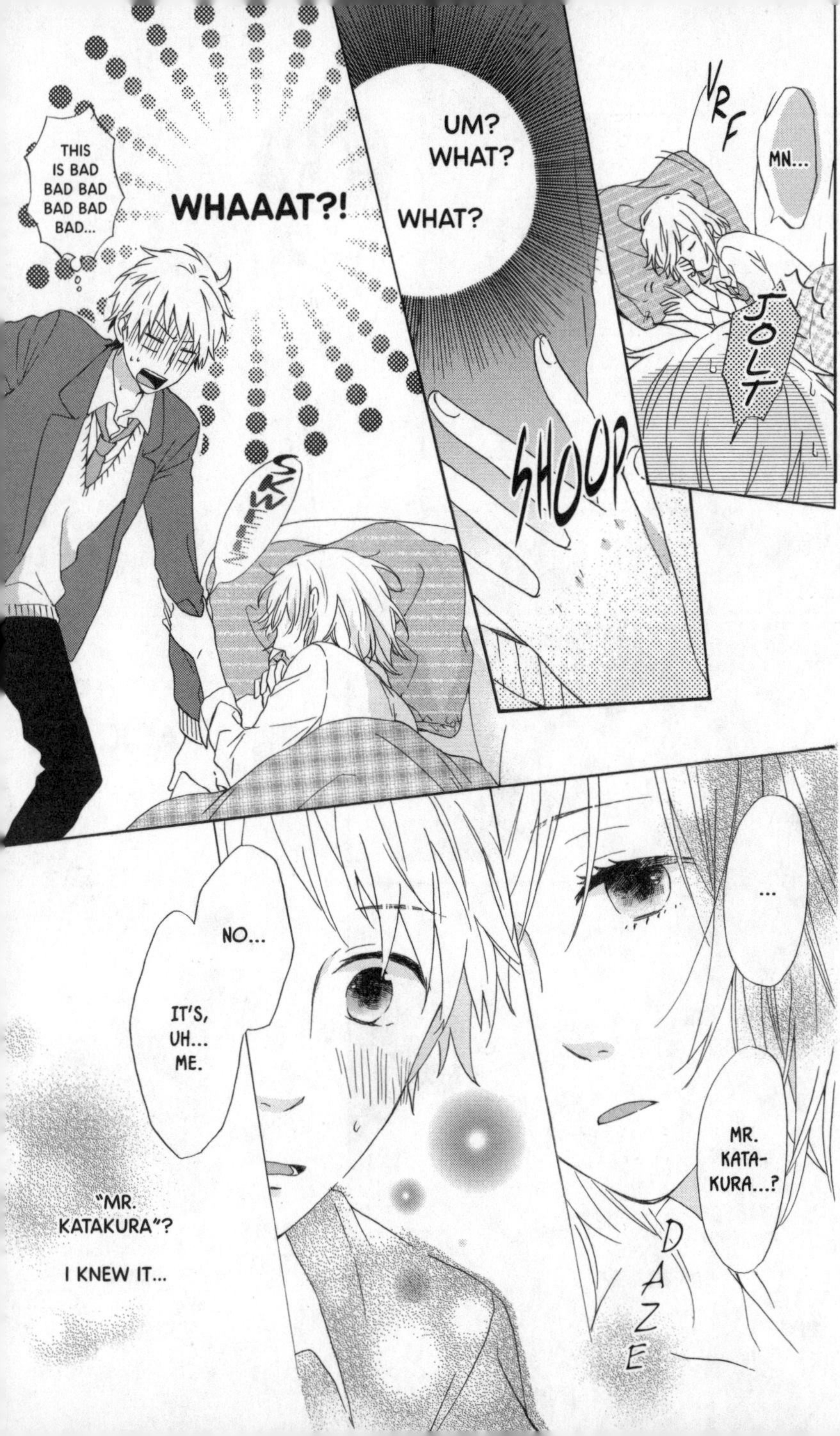
VRF
MN...
JOLT
UM? WHAT?
WHAT?
SHOOP
THIS IS BAD BAD BAD BAD BAD BAD...
WHAAAT?!
SKW
...
MR. KATA-KURA...?
DAZE
NO...
IT'S, UH... ME.
"MR. KATAKURA"?
I KNEW IT...

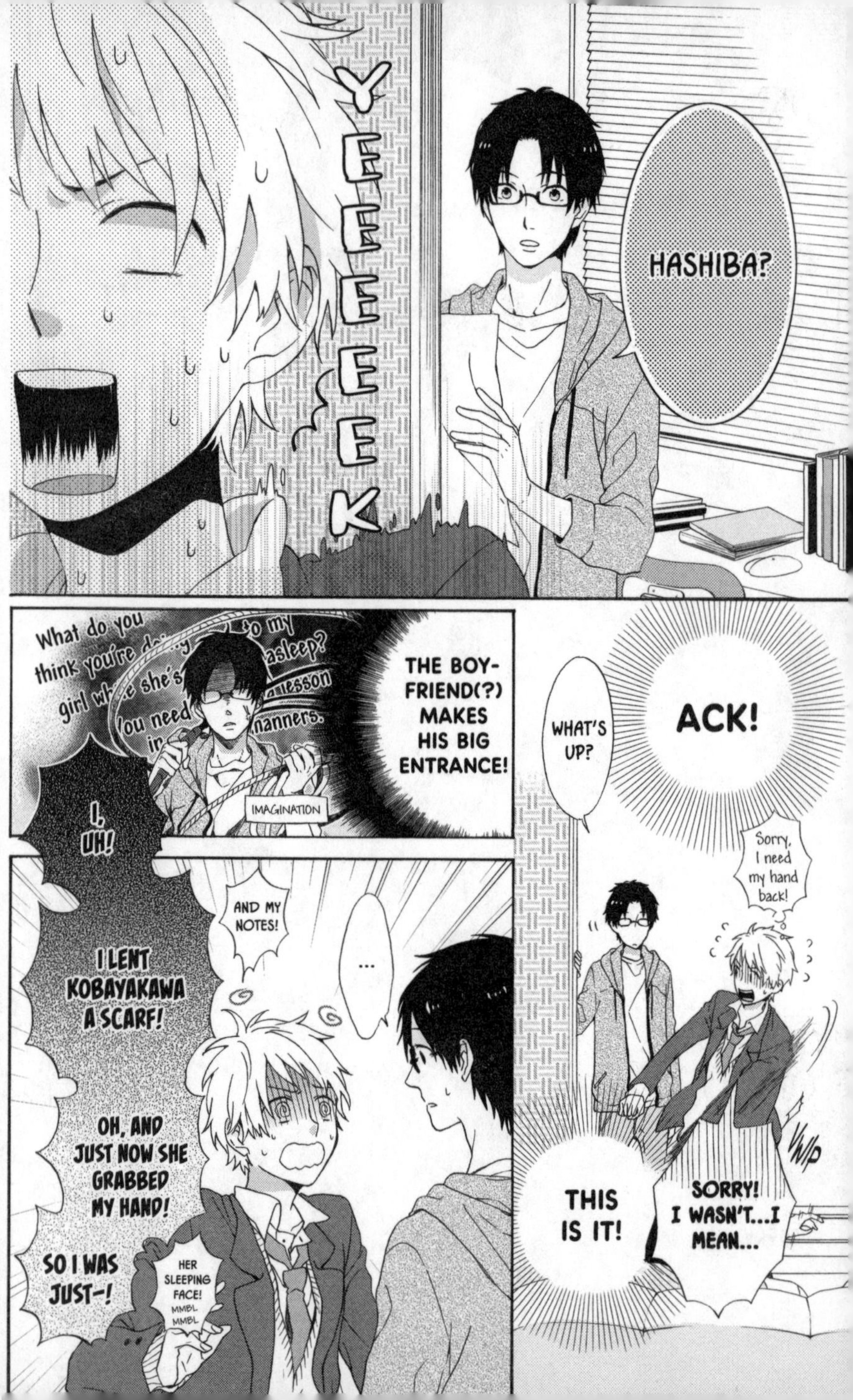
HASHIBA?
YEEEEEK
ACK!
WHAT'S UP?
Sorry, I need my hand back!
SORRY! I WASN'T...I MEAN...
THIS IS IT!
VWIP
THE BOY-FRIEND(?) MAKES HIS BIG ENTRANCE!
What do you think you're do to my girl wh she's asleep? You need a lesson in manners.
IMAGINATION
I, UH!
AND MY NOTES!
...
I LENT KOBAYAKAWA A SCARF!
OH, AND JUST NOW SHE GRABBED MY HAND!
SO I WAS JUST-!
HER SLEEPING FACE! MMBL MMBL

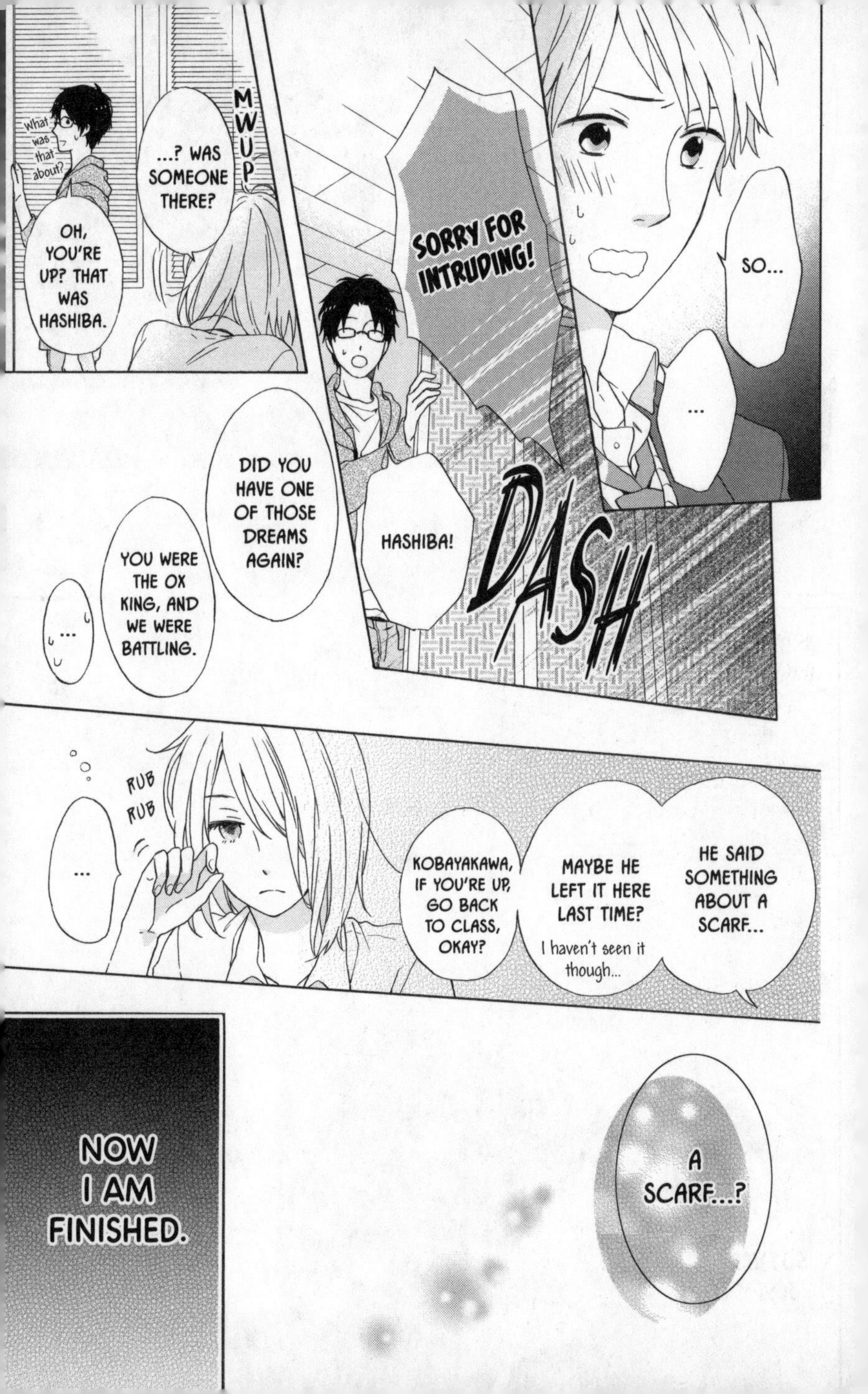
SO...
...
SORRY FOR INTRUDING!
HASHIBA!
DASH
MWUP
...? WAS SOMEONE THERE?
OH, YOU'RE UP? THAT WAS HASHIBA.
What was that about?
DID YOU HAVE ONE OF THOSE DREAMS AGAIN?
YOU WERE THE OX KING, AND WE WERE BATTLING.
...
HE SAID SOMETHING ABOUT A SCARF...
MAYBE HE LEFT IT HERE LAST TIME?
I haven't seen it though...
KOBAYAKAWA, IF YOU'RE UP, GO BACK TO CLASS, OKAY?
RUB RUB
...
A SCARF...?
NOW I AM FINISHED.

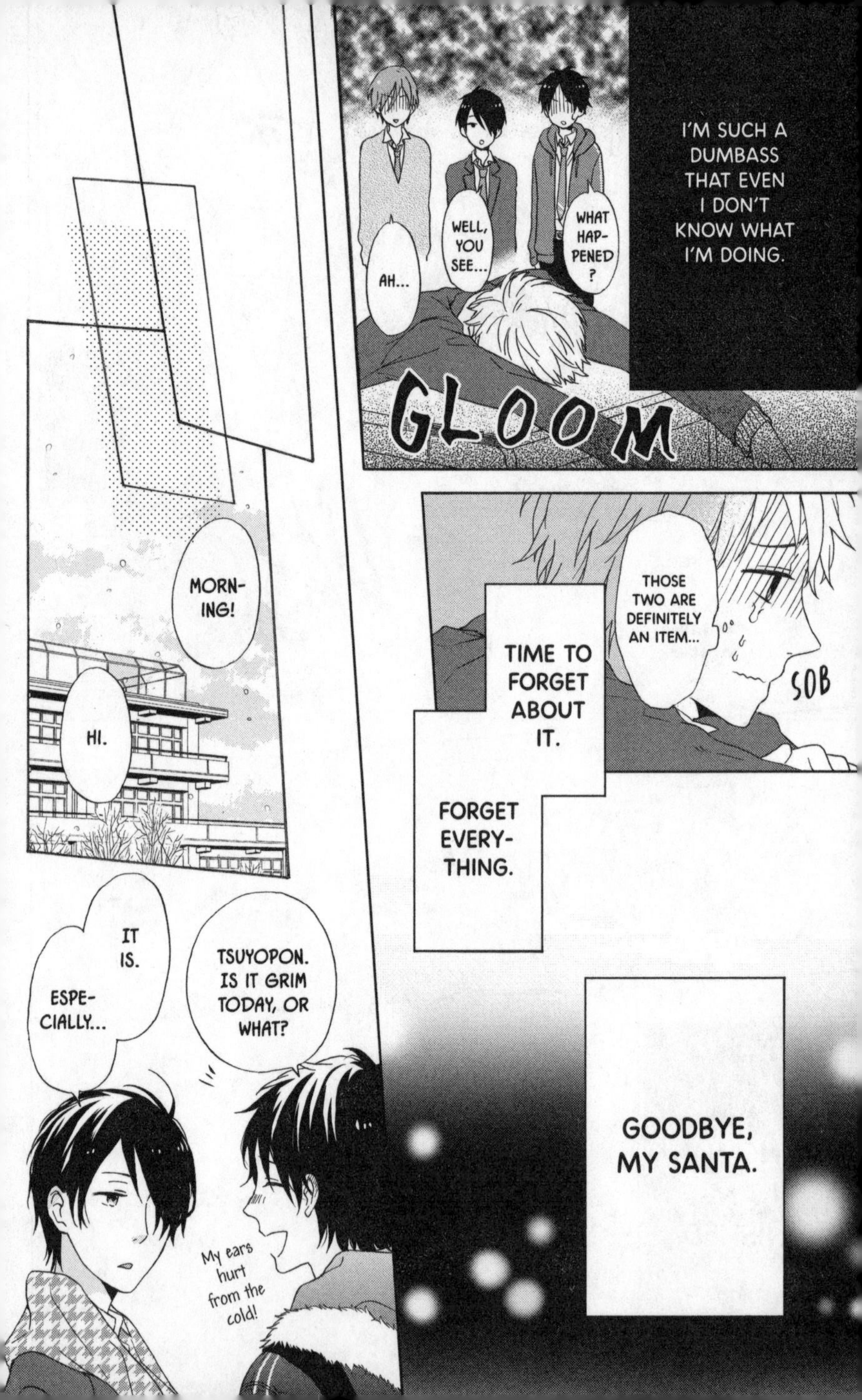
I'M SUCH A DUMBASS THAT EVEN I DON'T KNOW WHAT I'M DOING.
WHAT HAP-PENED?
WELL, YOU SEE...
AH...
GLOOM
THOSE TWO ARE DEFINITELY AN ITEM...
SOB
TIME TO FORGET ABOUT IT.
FORGET EVERY-THING.
GOODBYE, MY SANTA.
MORN-ING!
HI.
TSUYOPON. IS IT GRIM TODAY, OR WHAT?
My ears hurt from the cold!
IT IS.
ESPE-CIALLY...

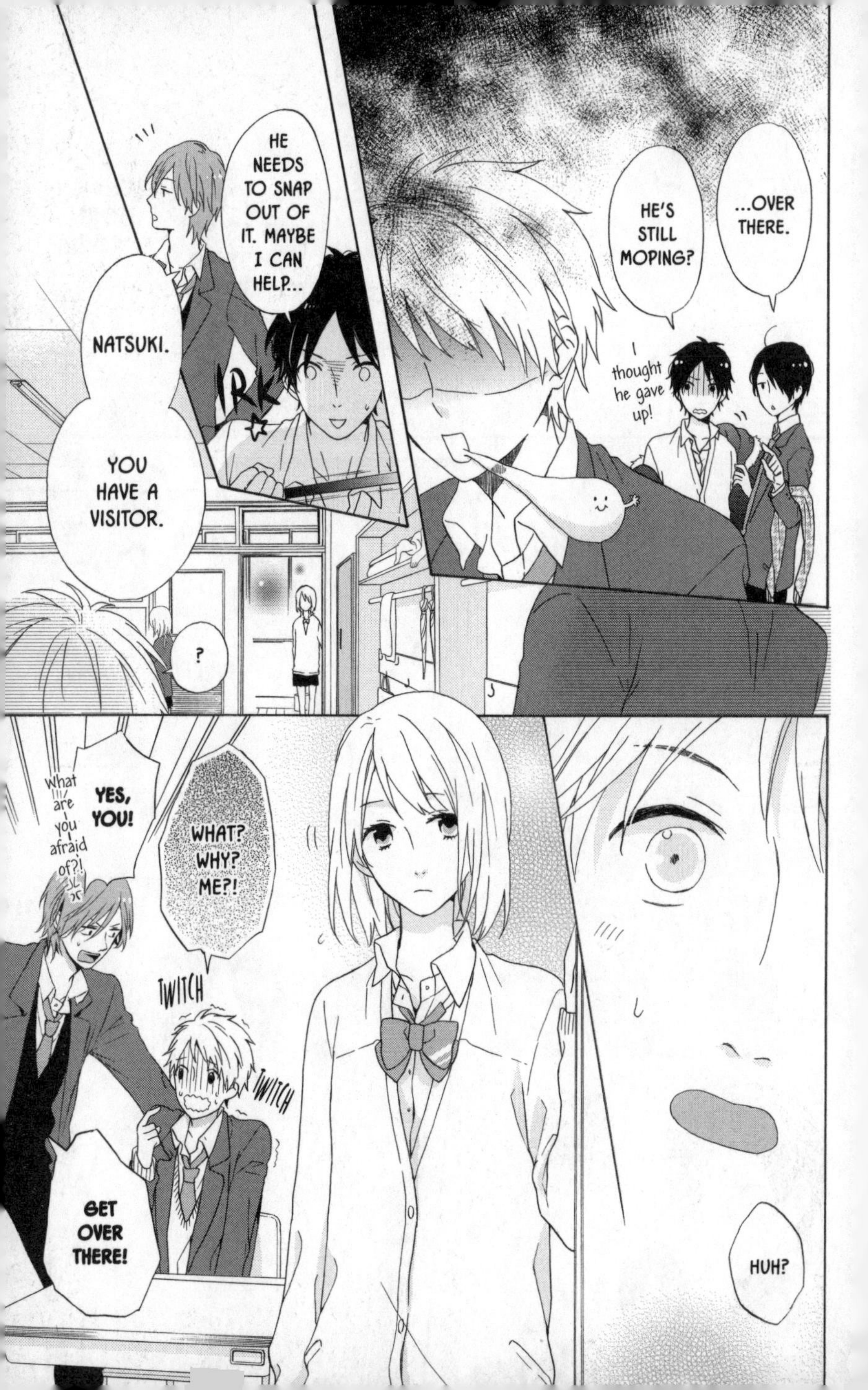
...OVER THERE.
HE'S STILL MOPING?
I thought he gave up!
HE NEEDS TO SNAP OUT OF IT. MAYBE I CAN HELP...
IRK
NATSUKI.
YOU HAVE A VISITOR.
?
HUH?
WHAT? WHY? ME?!
YES, YOU!
What are you afraid of?!
TWITCH
TWITCH
GET OVER THERE!

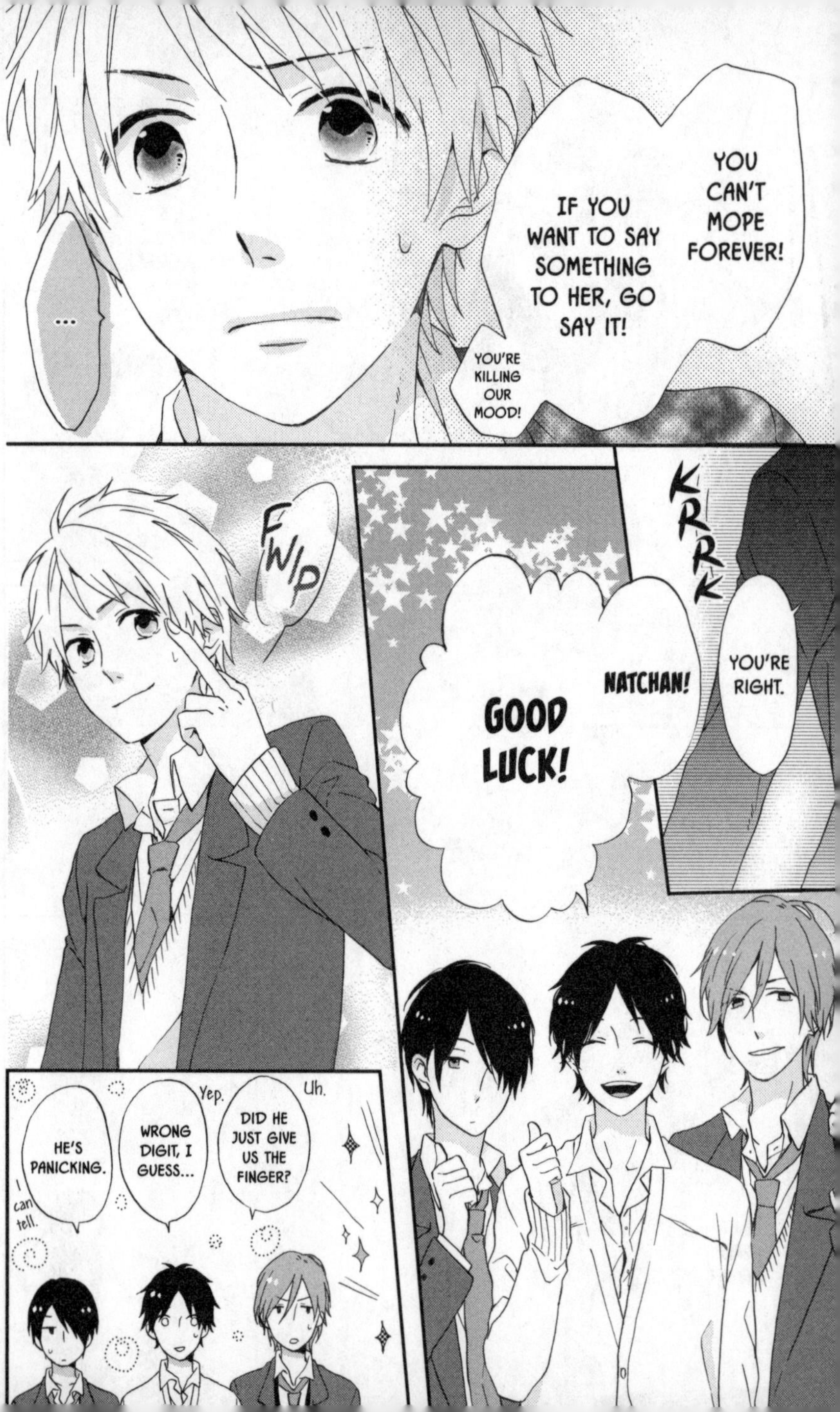
YOU CAN'T MOPE FOREVER!
IF YOU WANT TO SAY SOMETHING TO HER, GO SAY IT!
YOU'RE KILLING OUR MOOD!
...
KRRK
YOU'RE RIGHT.
NATCHAN!
GOOD LUCK!
FWIP
Uh.
DID HE JUST GIVE US THE FINGER?
Yep.
WRONG DIGIT, I GUESS...
HE'S PANICKING.
I can tell.

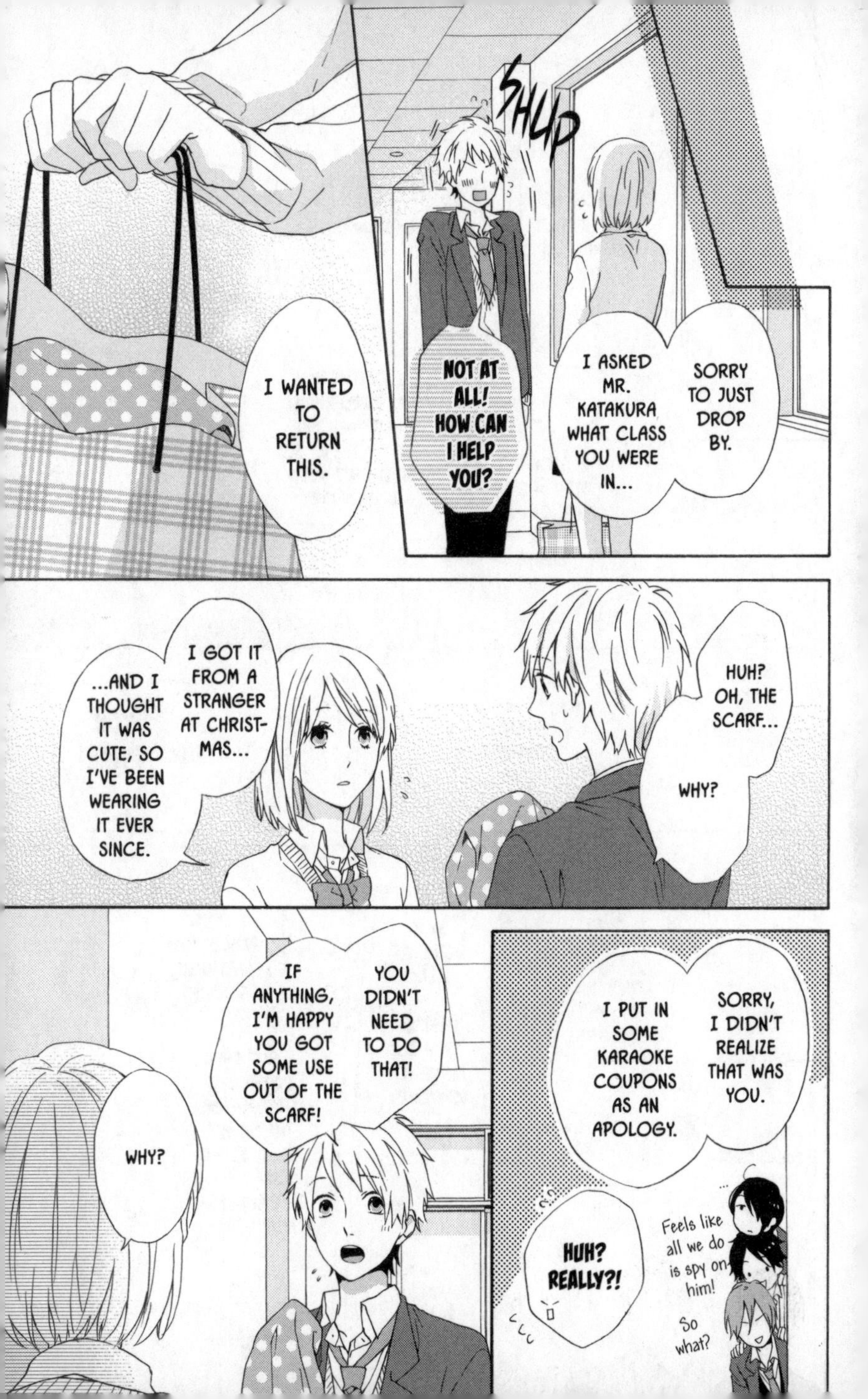
SHUP
SORRY TO JUST DROP BY.
I ASKED MR. KATAKURA WHAT CLASS YOU WERE IN...
NOT AT ALL! HOW CAN I HELP YOU?
I WANTED TO RETURN THIS.
HUH? OH, THE SCARF...
WHY?
I GOT IT FROM A STRANGER AT CHRIST-MAS...
...AND I THOUGHT IT WAS CUTE, SO I'VE BEEN WEARING IT EVER SINCE.
SORRY, I DIDN'T REALIZE THAT WAS YOU.
I PUT IN SOME KARAOKE COUPONS AS AN APOLOGY.
HUH? REALLY?!
Feels like all we do is spy on him!
So what?
YOU DIDN'T NEED TO DO THAT!
IF ANYTHING, I'M HAPPY YOU GOT SOME USE OUT OF THE SCARF!
WHY?

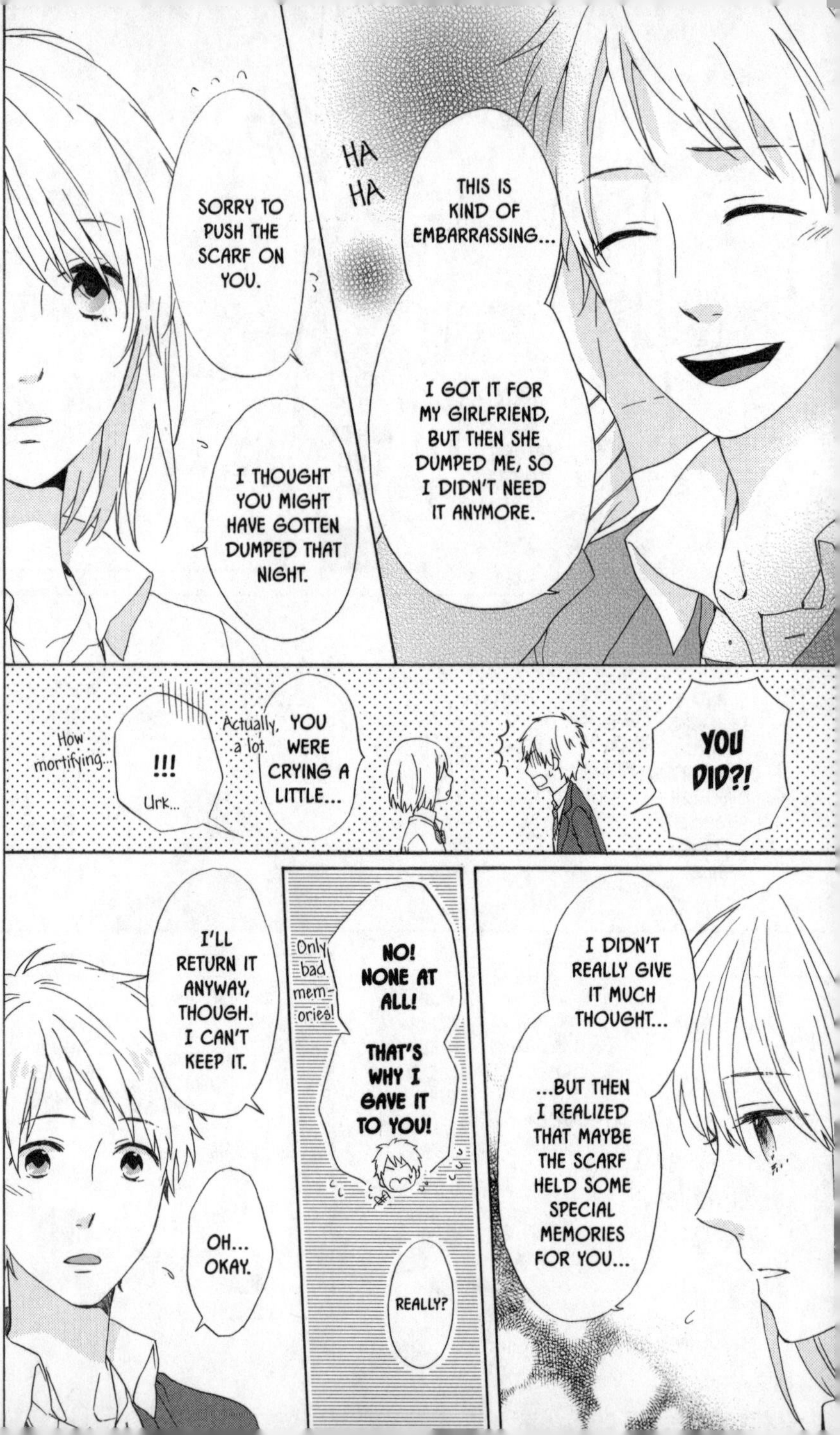
HA HA
THIS IS KIND OF EMBARRASSING...
I GOT IT FOR MY GIRLFRIEND, BUT THEN SHE DUMPED ME, SO I DIDN'T NEED IT ANYMORE.
SORRY TO PUSH THE SCARF ON YOU.
I THOUGHT YOU MIGHT HAVE GOTTEN DUMPED THAT NIGHT.
YOU DID?!
YOU WERE CRYING A LITTLE...
Actually, a lot.
!!!
Urk...
How mortifying...
I DIDN'T REALLY GIVE IT MUCH THOUGHT...
...BUT THEN I REALIZED THAT MAYBE THE SCARF HELD SOME SPECIAL MEMORIES FOR YOU...
NO! NONE AT ALL!
Only bad mem-ories!
THAT'S WHY I GAVE IT TO YOU!
REALLY?
I'LL RETURN IT ANYWAY, THOUGH. I CAN'T KEEP IT.
OH... OKAY.

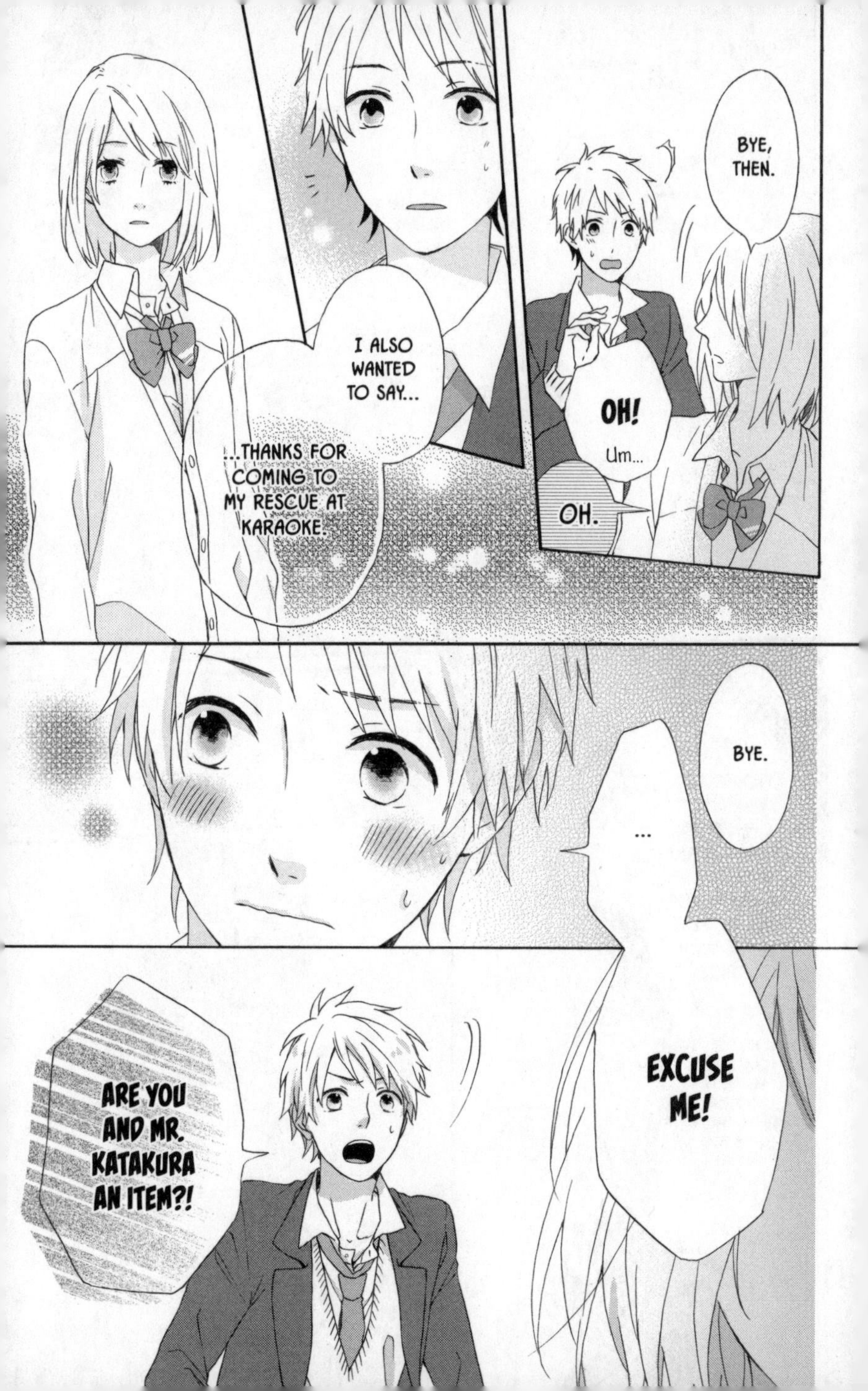
BYE, THEN.
OH!
Um...
OH.
I ALSO WANTED TO SAY...
...THANKS FOR COMING TO MY RESCUE AT KARAOKE.
BYE.
...
EXCUSE ME!
ARE YOU AND MR. KATAKURA AN ITEM?!

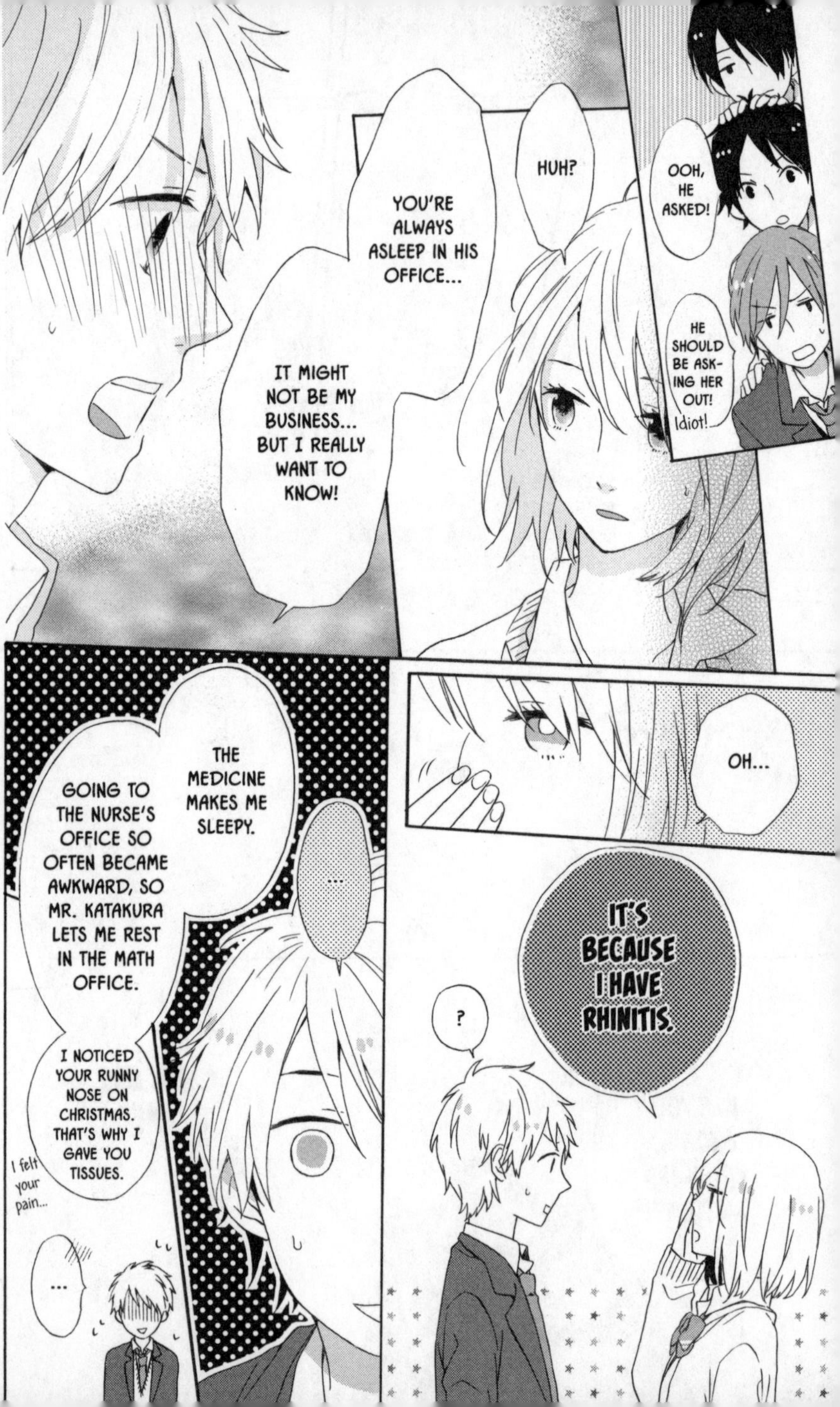
OOH, HE ASKED!
HE SHOULD BE ASKING HER OUT! Idiot!
HUH?
YOU'RE ALWAYS ASLEEP IN HIS OFFICE...
IT MIGHT NOT BE MY BUSINESS... BUT I REALLY WANT TO KNOW!
OH...
IT'S BECAUSE I HAVE RHINITIS.
?
THE MEDICINE MAKES ME SLEEPY.
GOING TO THE NURSE'S OFFICE SO OFTEN BECAME AWKWARD, SO MR. KATAKURA LETS ME REST IN THE MATH OFFICE.
...
I NOTICED YOUR RUNNY NOSE ON CHRISTMAS. THAT'S WHY I GAVE YOU TISSUES.
I felt your pain...
...

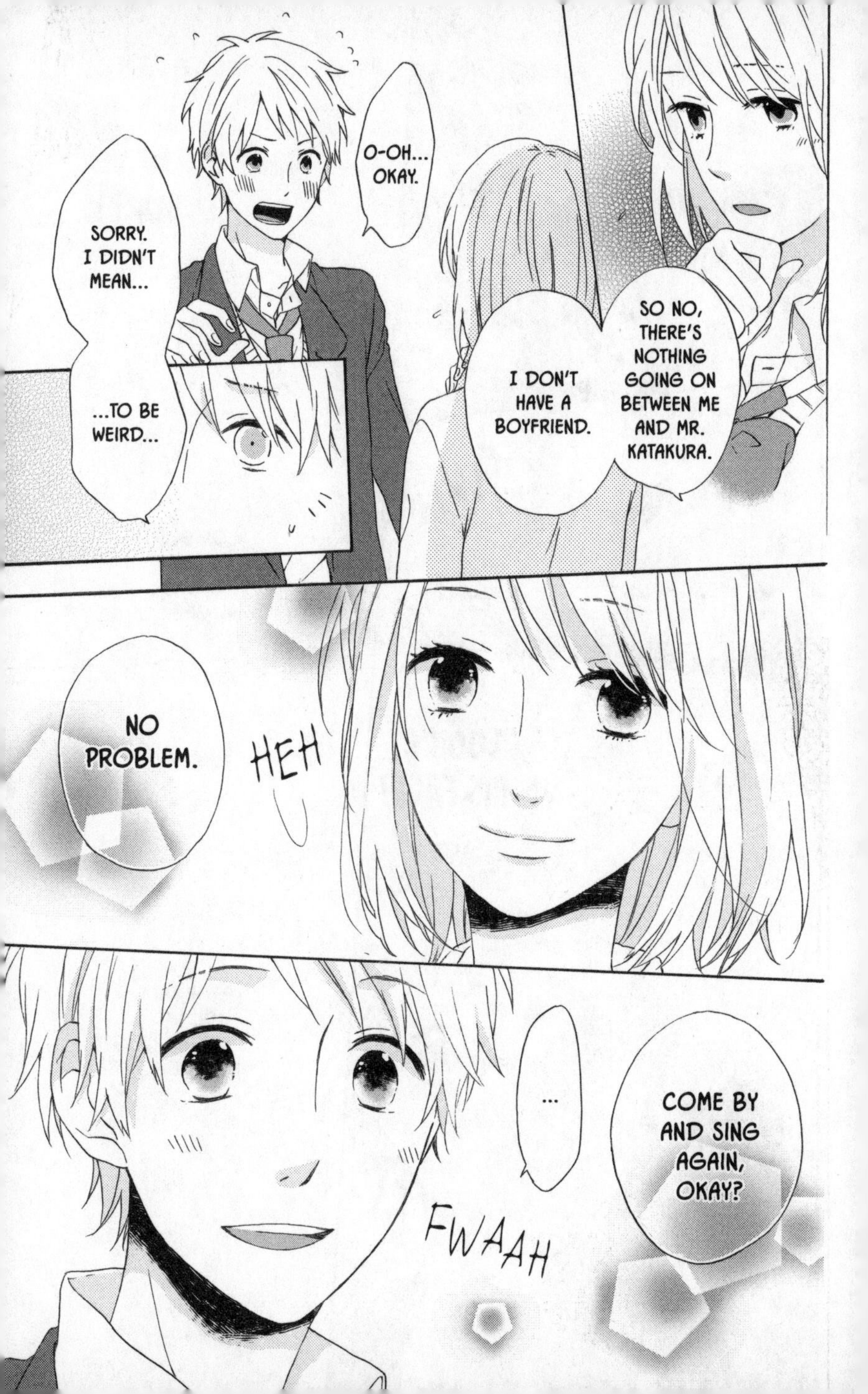
SO NO, THERE'S NOTHING GOING ON BETWEEN ME AND MR. KATAKURA.
I DON'T HAVE A BOYFRIEND.
O-OH... OKAY.
SORRY. I DIDN'T MEAN...
...TO BE WEIRD...
HEH
NO PROBLEM.
COME BY AND SING AGAIN, OKAY?
...
FWAAH

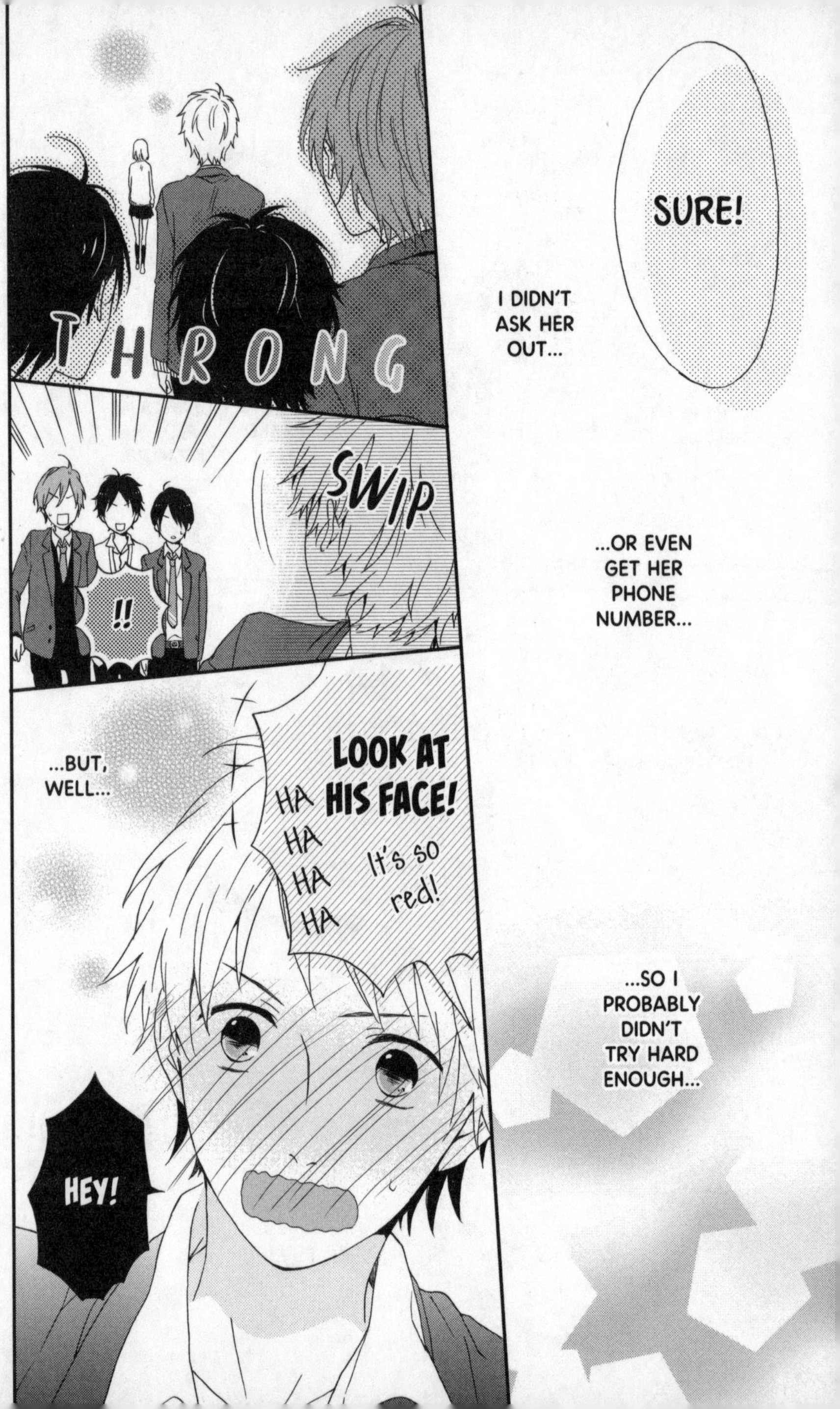

SURE!
I DIDN'T ASK HER OUT...
...OR EVEN GET HER PHONE NUMBER...
...SO I PROBABLY DIDN'T TRY HARD ENOUGH...
THRONG
SWIP
!!
LOOK AT HIS FACE!
HA HA HA HA
It's so red!
...BUT, WELL...
HEY!

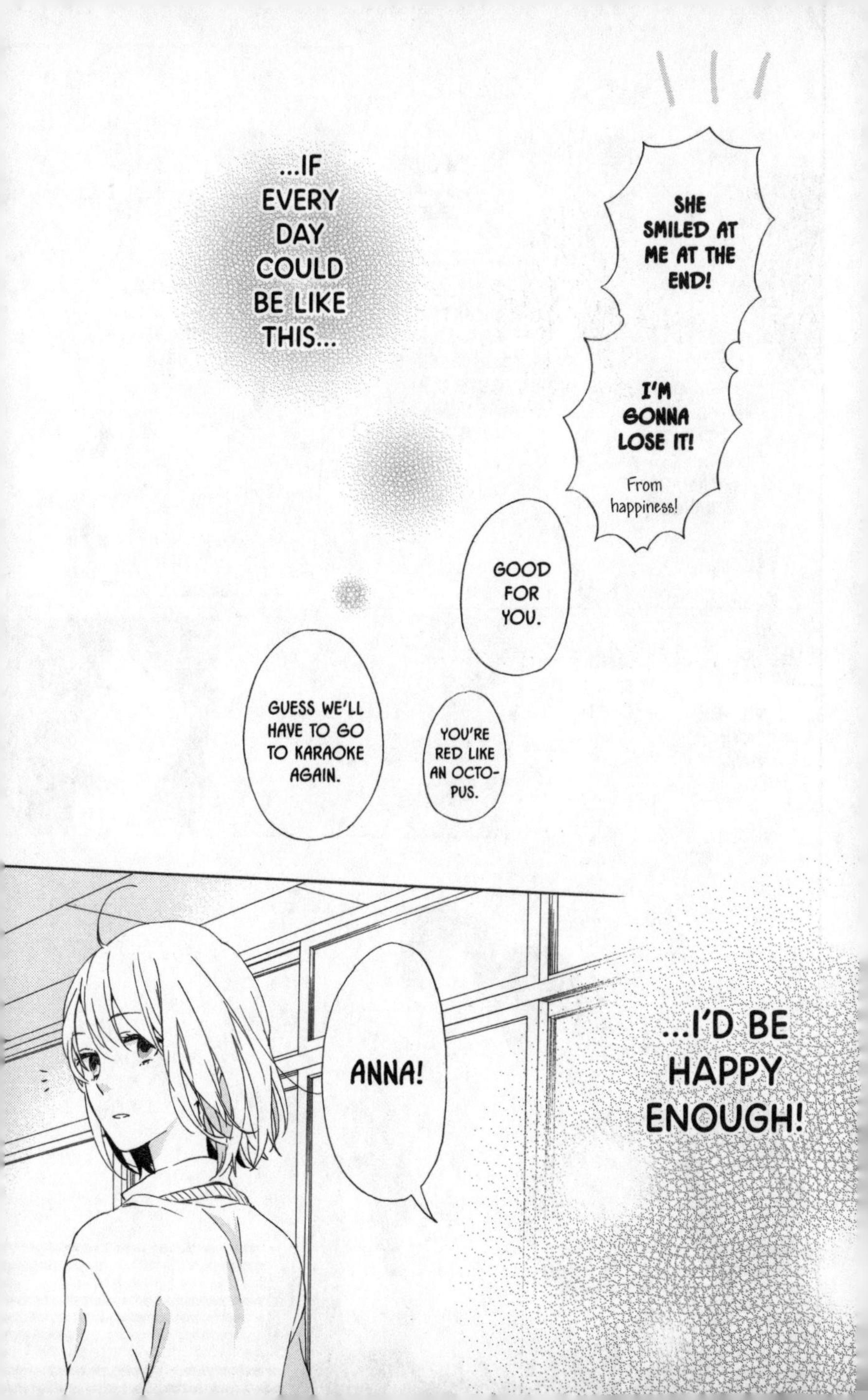
SHE SMILED AT ME AT THE END!
...IF EVERY DAY COULD BE LIKE THIS...
I'M GONNA LOSE IT!
From happiness!
GOOD FOR YOU.
YOU'RE RED LIKE AN OCTO-PUS.
GUESS WE'LL HAVE TO GO TO KARAOKE AGAIN.
...I'D BE HAPPY ENOUGH!
ANNA!

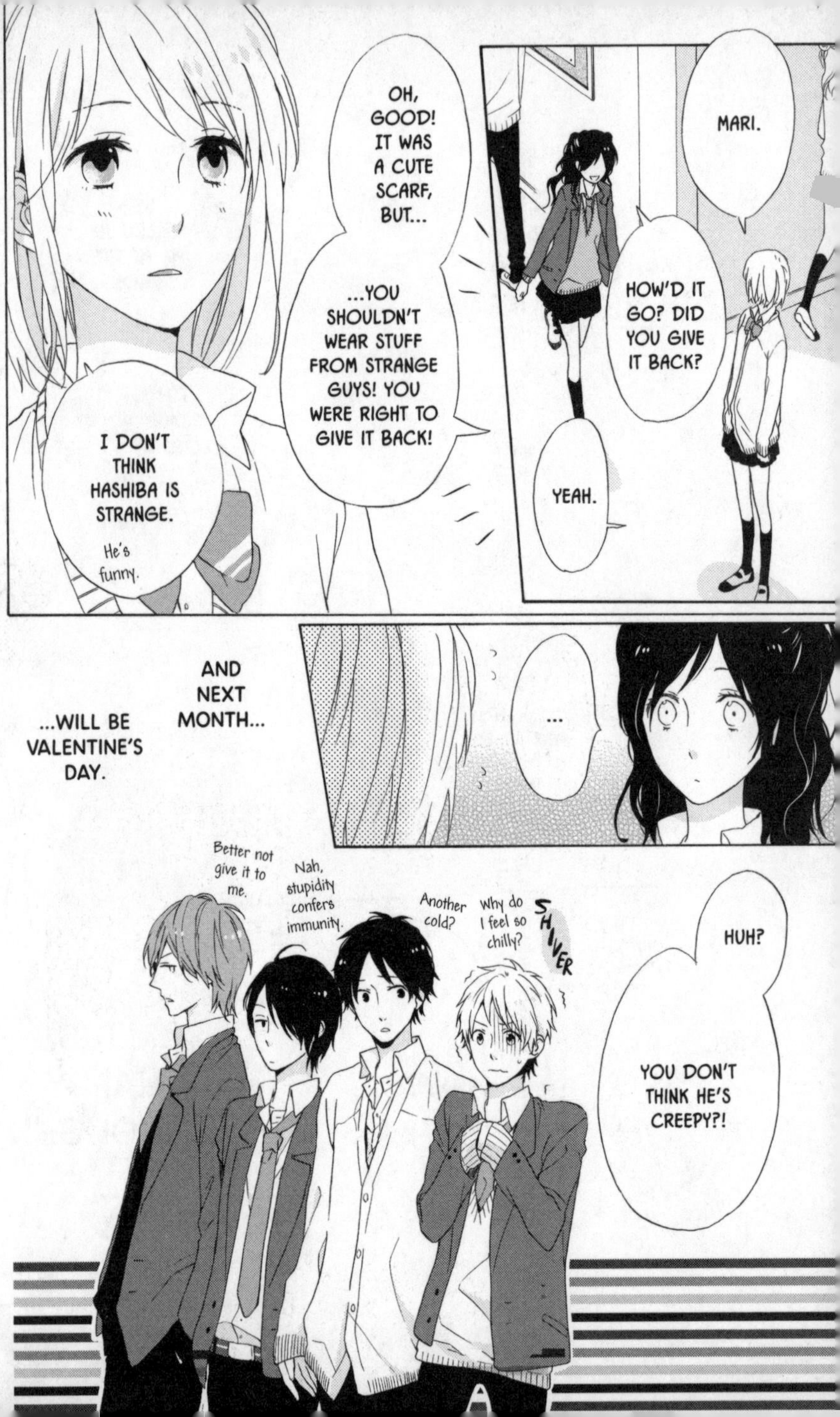

MARI.
HOW'D IT GO? DID YOU GIVE IT BACK?
YEAH.
OH, GOOD! IT WAS A CUTE SCARF, BUT...
...YOU SHOULDN'T WEAR STUFF FROM STRANGE GUYS! YOU WERE RIGHT TO GIVE IT BACK!
I DON'T THINK HASHIBA IS STRANGE.
He's funny.
...
AND NEXT MONTH...
...WILL BE VALENTINE'S DAY.
HUH?
YOU DON'T THINK HE'S CREEPY?!
SHIVER
Why do I feel so chilly?
Another cold?
Nah, stupidity confers immunity.
Better not give it to me.

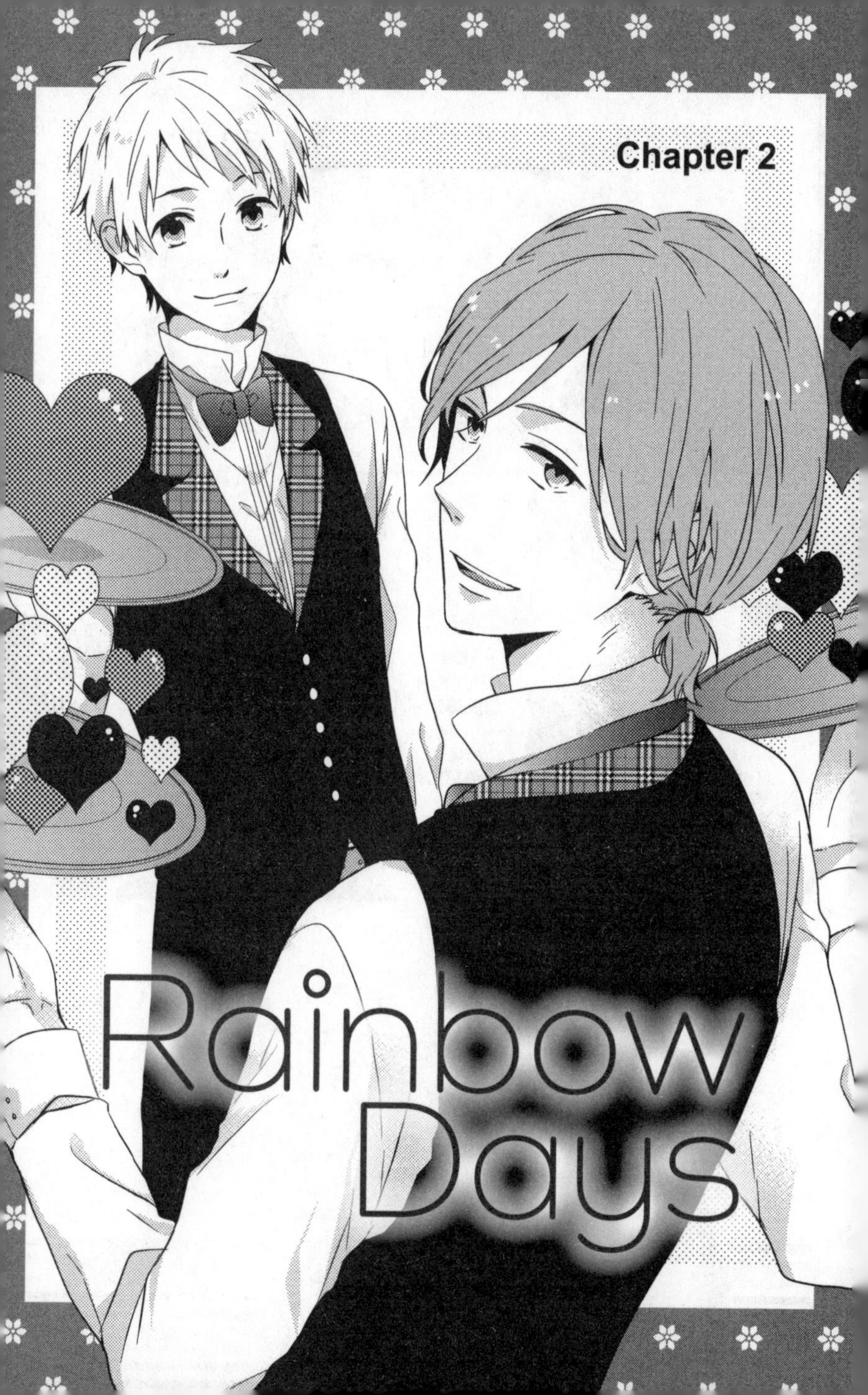
Chapter 2
Rainbow Days

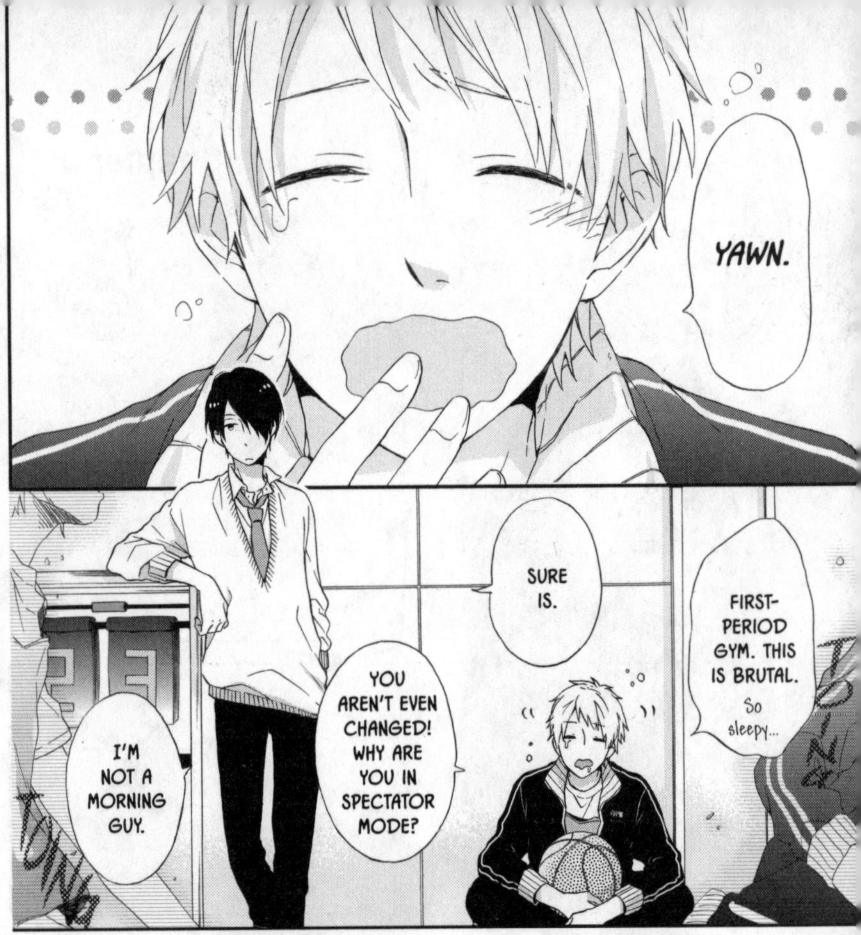
YAWN.
FIRST-PERIOD GYM. THIS IS BRUTAL.
So sleepy...
SURE IS.
YOU AREN'T EVEN CHANGED! WHY ARE YOU IN SPECTATOR MODE?
I'M NOT A MORNING GUY.
TONG

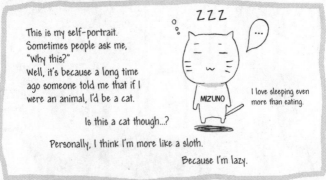

This is my self-portrait.
Sometimes people ask me,
"Why this?"
Well, it's because a long time ago someone told me that if I were an animal, I'd be a cat.

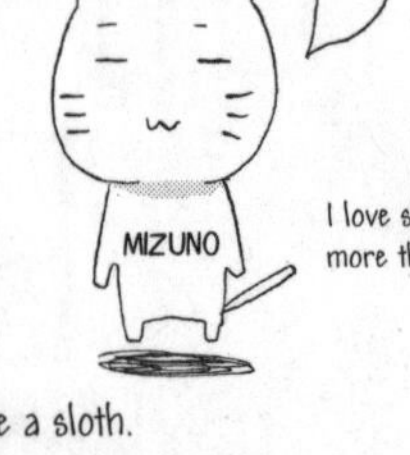
ZZZ
...
MIZUNO

I love sleeping even more than eating.

Is this a cat though...?

Personally, I think I'm more like a sloth.

Because I'm lazy.

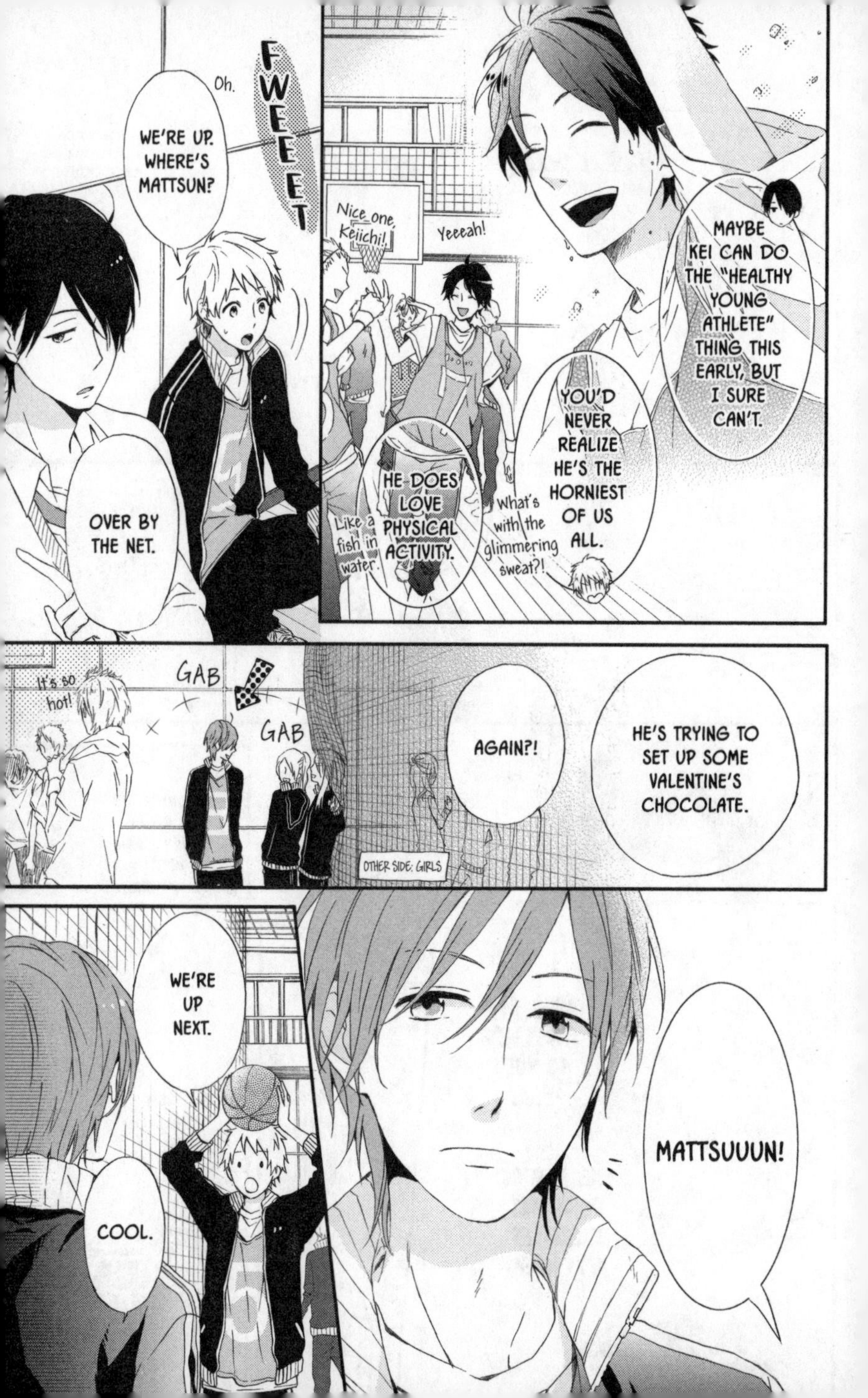
MAYBE KEI CAN DO THE "HEALTHY YOUNG ATHLETE" THING THIS EARLY, BUT I SURE CAN'T.
YOU'D NEVER REALIZE HE'S THE HORNIEST OF US ALL.
What's with the glimmering sweat?!
HE DOES LOVE PHYSICAL ACTIVITY.
Like a fish in water.
Yeeeah!
Nice one, Keiichi!
FWEEET
Oh.
WE'RE UP. WHERE'S MATTSUN?
OVER BY THE NET.
HE'S TRYING TO SET UP SOME VALENTINE'S CHOCOLATE.
AGAIN?!
OTHER SIDE: GIRLS
GAB
GAB
It's so hot!
MATTSUUUN!
WE'RE UP NEXT.
COOL.

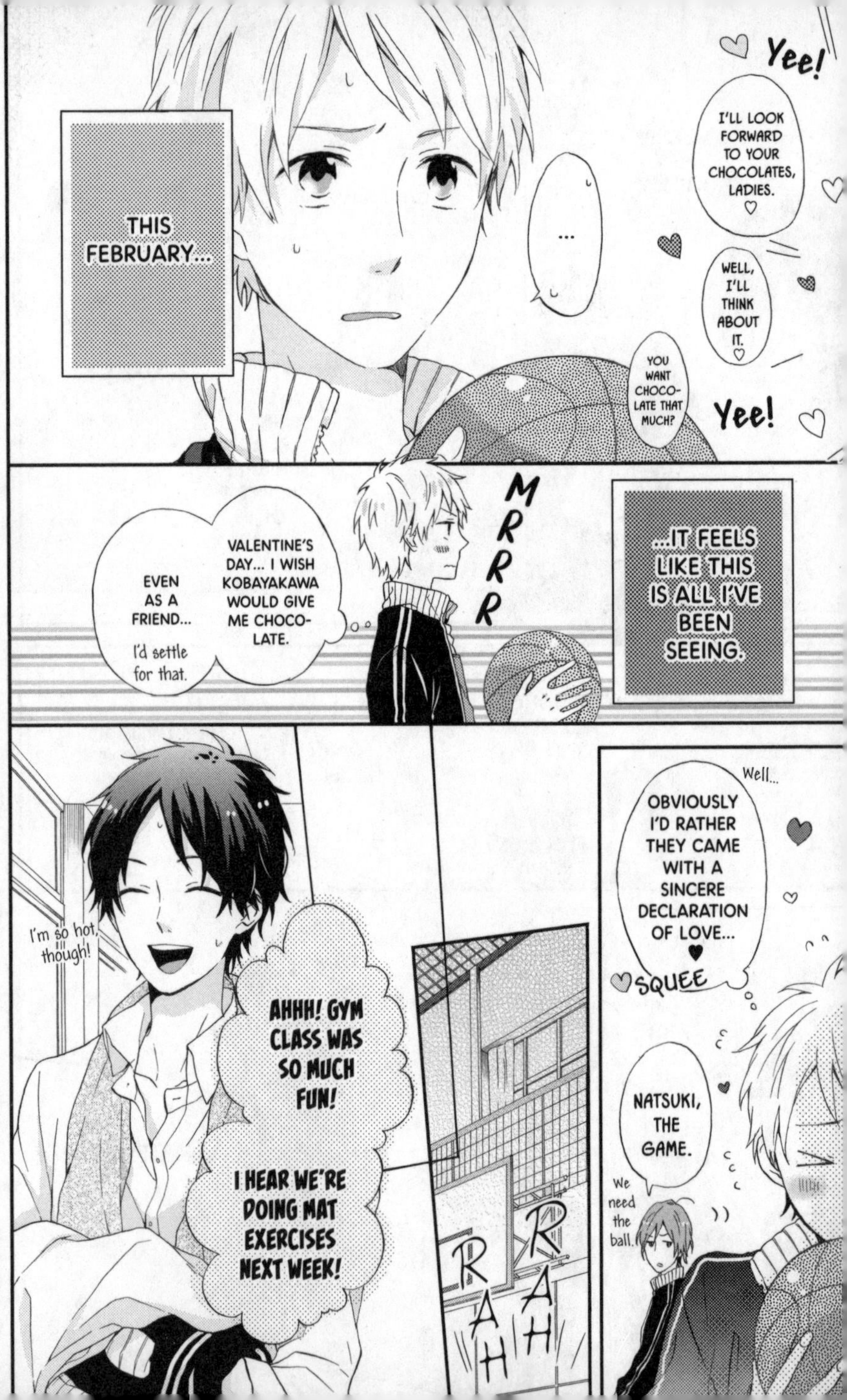
Yee!
I'LL LOOK FORWARD TO YOUR CHOCOLATES, LADIES. ♡
WELL, I'LL THINK ABOUT IT. ♡
YOU WANT CHOCOLATE THAT MUCH?
Yee!
...
THIS FEBRUARY...
...IT FEELS LIKE THIS IS ALL I'VE BEEN SEEING.
MRRRR
VALENTINE'S DAY... I WISH KOBAYAKAWA WOULD GIVE ME CHOCOLATE.
EVEN AS A FRIEND...
I'd settle for that.
Well...
OBVIOUSLY I'D RATHER THEY CAME WITH A SINCERE DECLARATION OF LOVE... ♥
SQUEE
NATSUKI, THE GAME.
We need the ball.
RAH
RAH
AHHH! GYM CLASS WAS SO MUCH FUN!
I HEAR WE'RE DOING MAT EXERCISES NEXT WEEK!
I'm so hot, though!

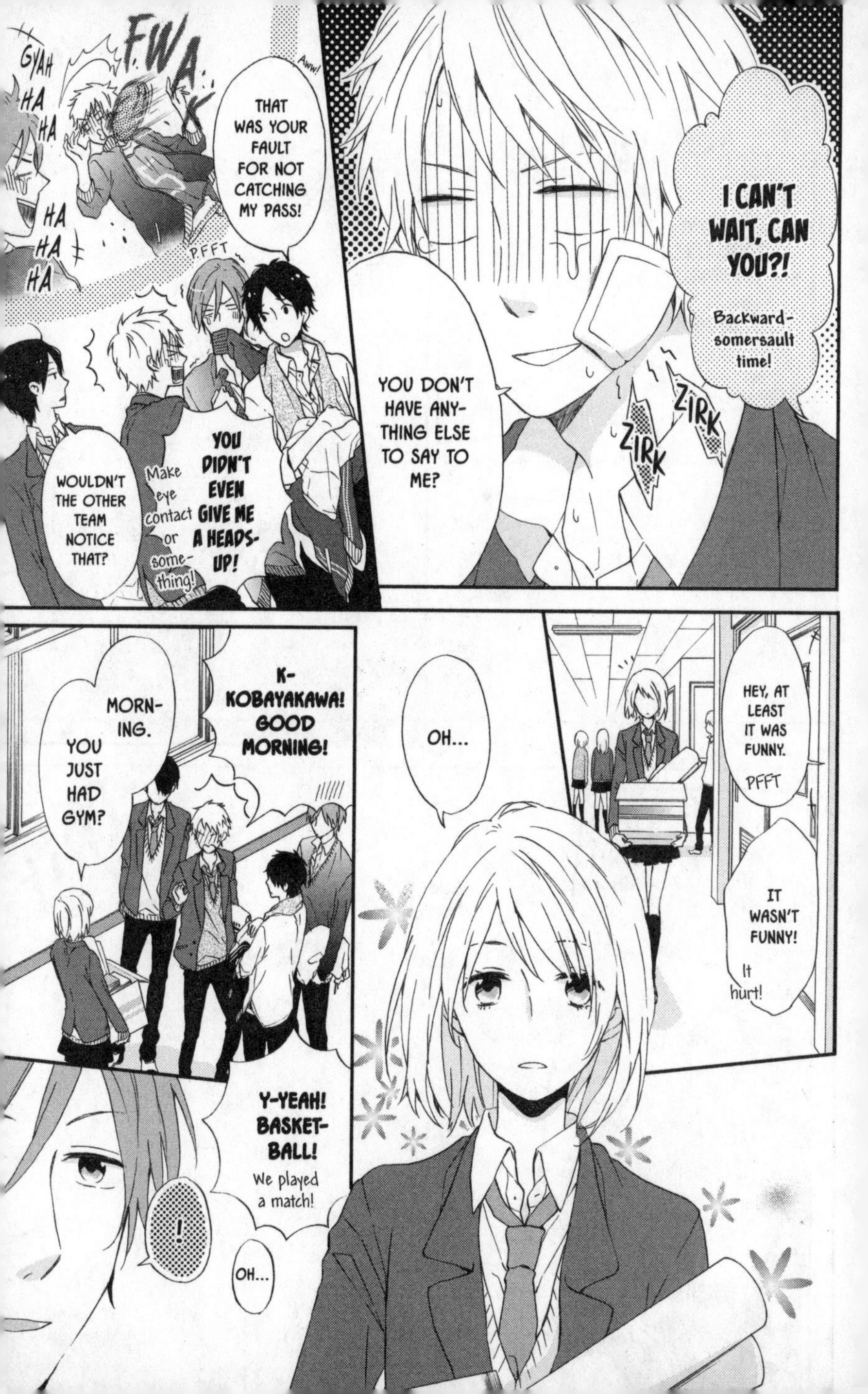
I CAN'T WAIT, CAN YOU?!
Backward-somersault time!
YOU DON'T HAVE ANYTHING ELSE TO SAY TO ME?
ZIRK
ZIRK
FWAK
GYAH HA HA
HA HA HA
Aww!
THAT WAS YOUR FAULT FOR NOT CATCHING MY PASS!
P.FFT
YOU DIDN'T EVEN GIVE ME A HEADS-UP!
Make eye contact or some-thing!
WOULDN'T THE OTHER TEAM NOTICE THAT?
HEY, AT LEAST IT WAS FUNNY.
PFFT
IT WASN'T FUNNY!
It hurt!
OH...
K-KOBAYAKAWA! GOOD MORNING!
MORN-ING. YOU JUST HAD GYM?
Y-YEAH! BASKET-BALL!
We played a match!
!
OH...

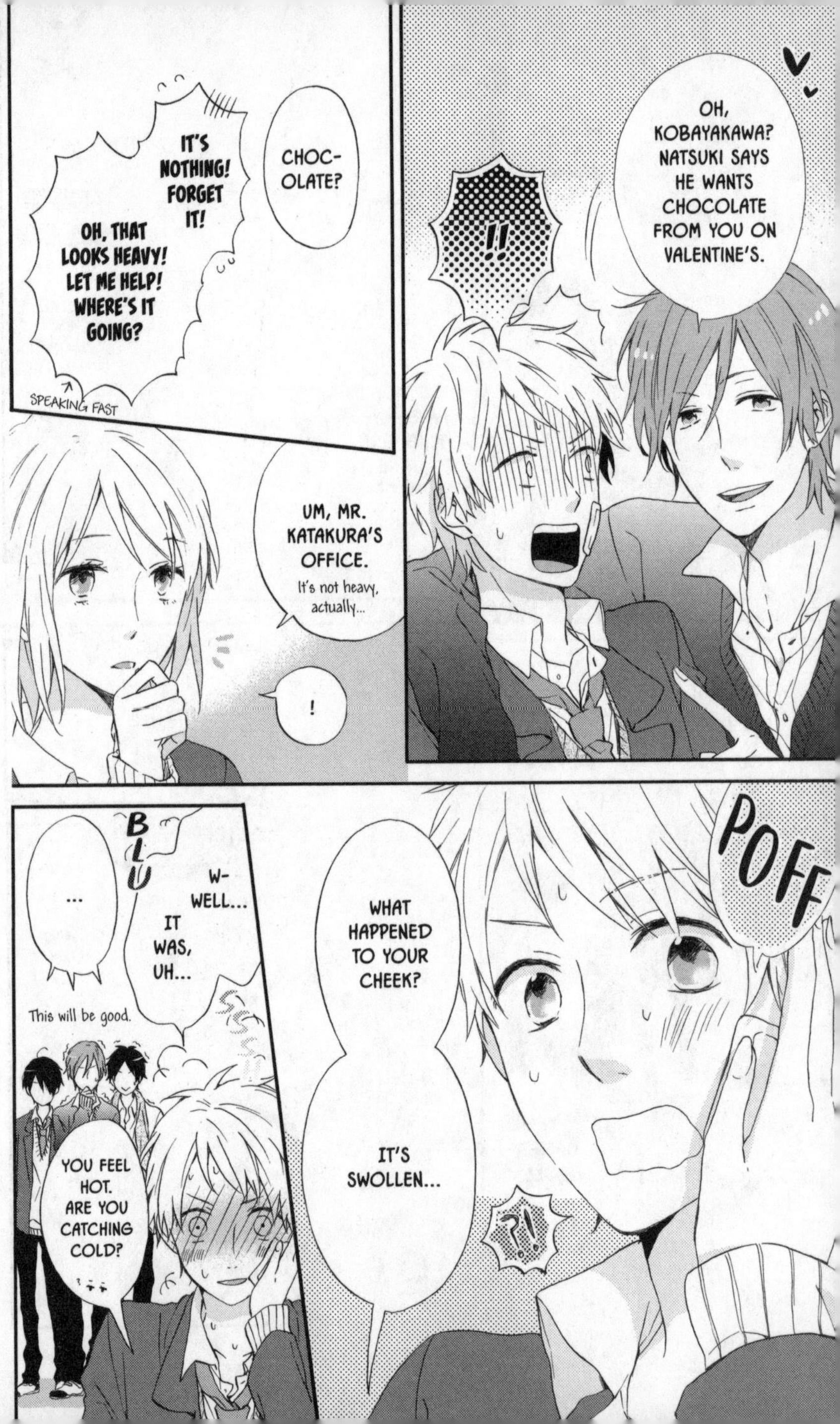
OH, KOBAYAKAWA? NATSUKI SAYS HE WANTS CHOCOLATE FROM YOU ON VALENTINE'S.
!!
CHOC-OLATE?
IT'S NOTHING! FORGET IT!
OH, THAT LOOKS HEAVY! LET ME HELP! WHERE'S IT GOING?
SPEAKING FAST
UM, MR. KATAKURA'S OFFICE.
It's not heavy, actually...
!
POFF
WHAT HAPPENED TO YOUR CHEEK?
IT'S SWOLLEN...
?!
BLU
W-WELL... IT WAS, UH...
...
This will be good.
YOU FEEL HOT. ARE YOU CATCHING COLD?

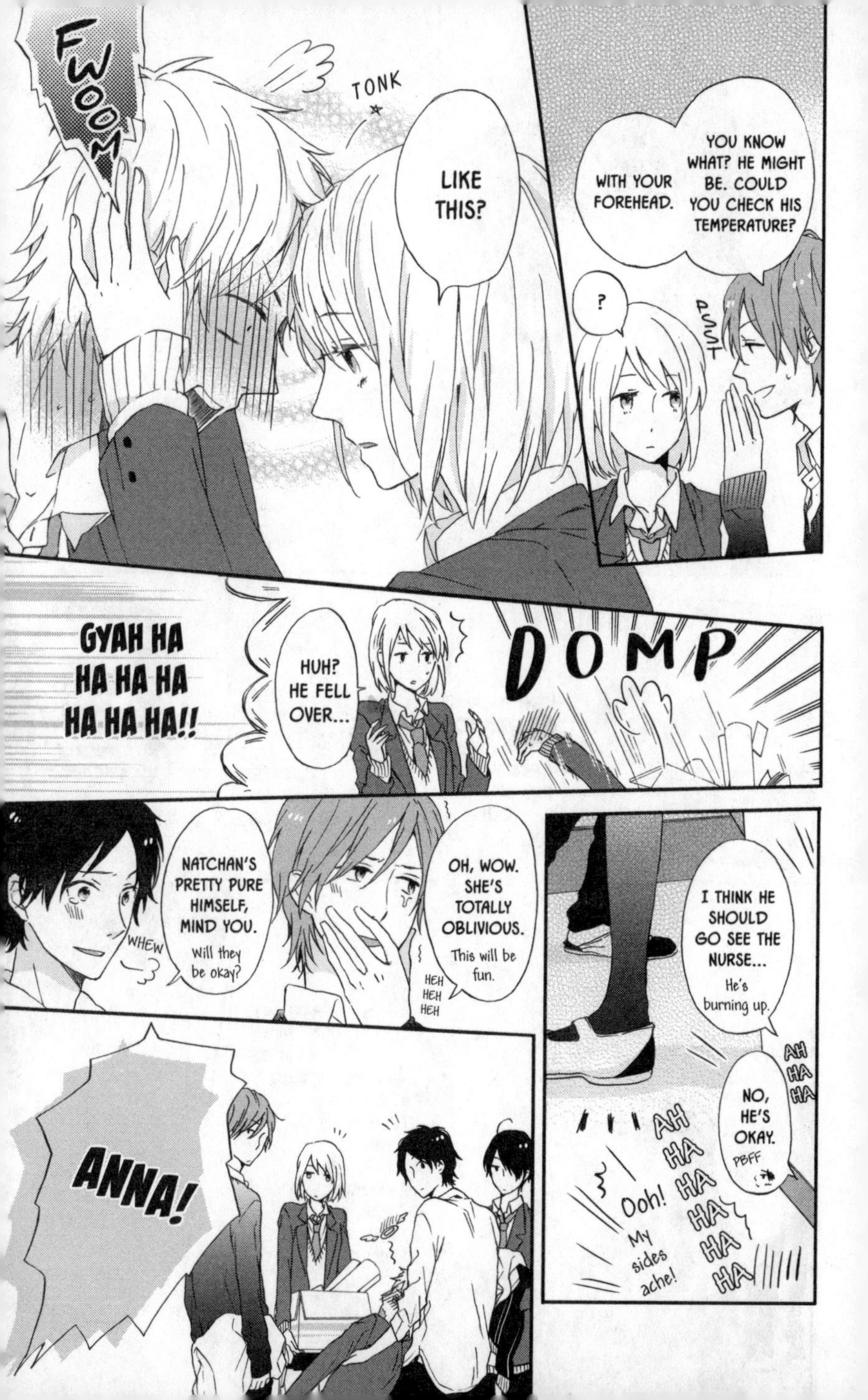
YOU KNOW WHAT? HE MIGHT BE. COULD YOU CHECK HIS TEMPERATURE?
WITH YOUR FOREHEAD.
PSST
?
LIKE THIS?
TONK
FWOOM
DOMP
HUH? HE FELL OVER...
GYAH HA HA HA HA HA HA!!
I THINK HE SHOULD GO SEE THE NURSE... He's burning up.
AH HA HA
NO, HE'S OKAY.
PBFF
AH HA HA HA HA HA HA
Ooh! My sides ache!
OH, WOW. SHE'S TOTALLY OBLIVIOUS. This will be fun.
HEH HEH HEH
NATCHAN'S PRETTY PURE HIMSELF, MIND YOU. Will they be okay?
WHEW
ANNA!

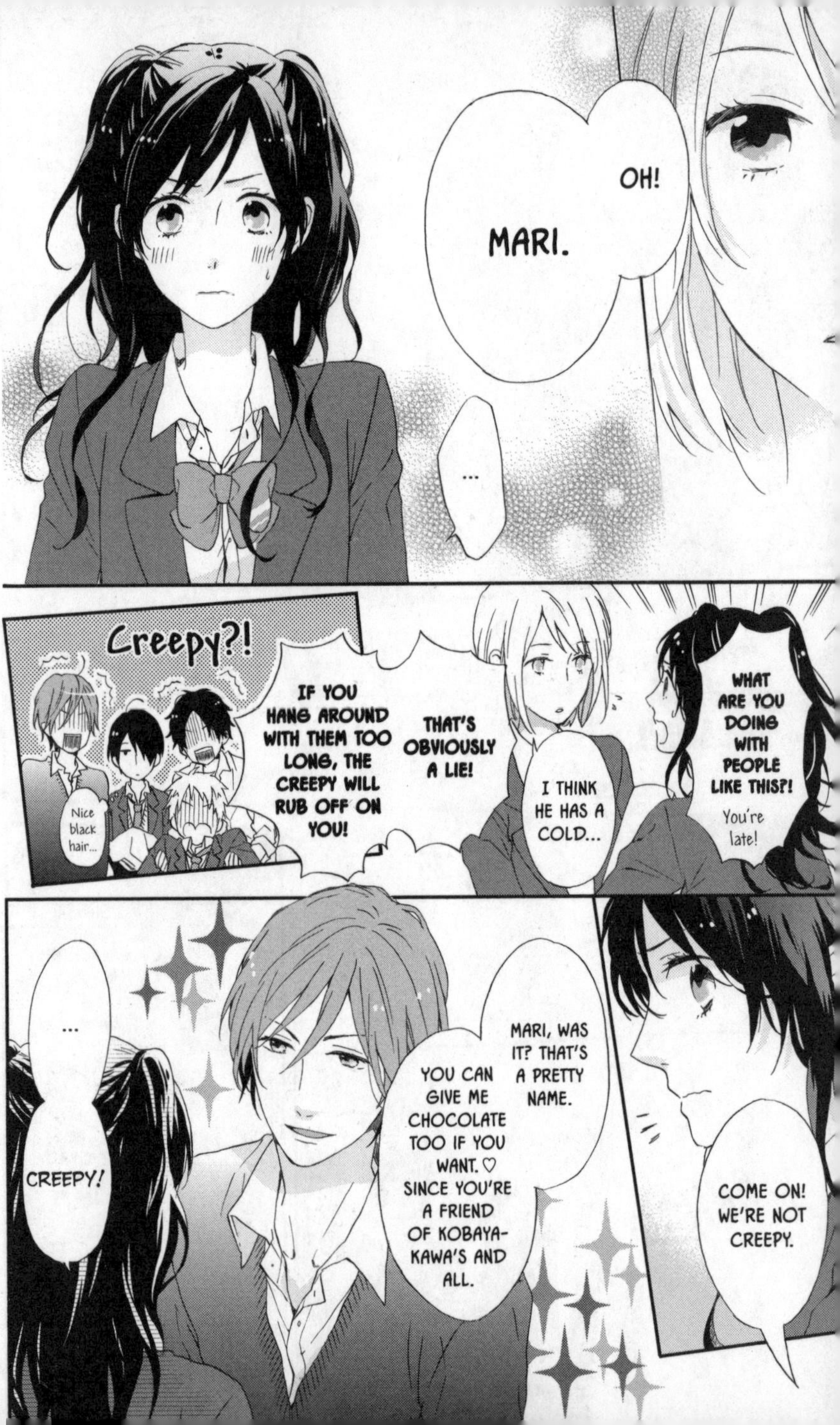
OH! MARI.
...
WHAT ARE YOU DOING WITH PEOPLE LIKE THIS?!
You're late!
I THINK HE HAS A COLD...
THAT'S OBVIOUSLY A LIE!
IF YOU HANG AROUND WITH THEM TOO LONG, THE CREEPY WILL RUB OFF ON YOU!
Creepy?!
Nice black hair...
COME ON! WE'RE NOT CREEPY.
MARI, WAS IT? THAT'S A PRETTY NAME.
YOU CAN GIVE ME CHOCOLATE TOO IF YOU WANT. ♡ SINCE YOU'RE A FRIEND OF KOBAYA-KAWA'S AND ALL.
...
CREEPY!

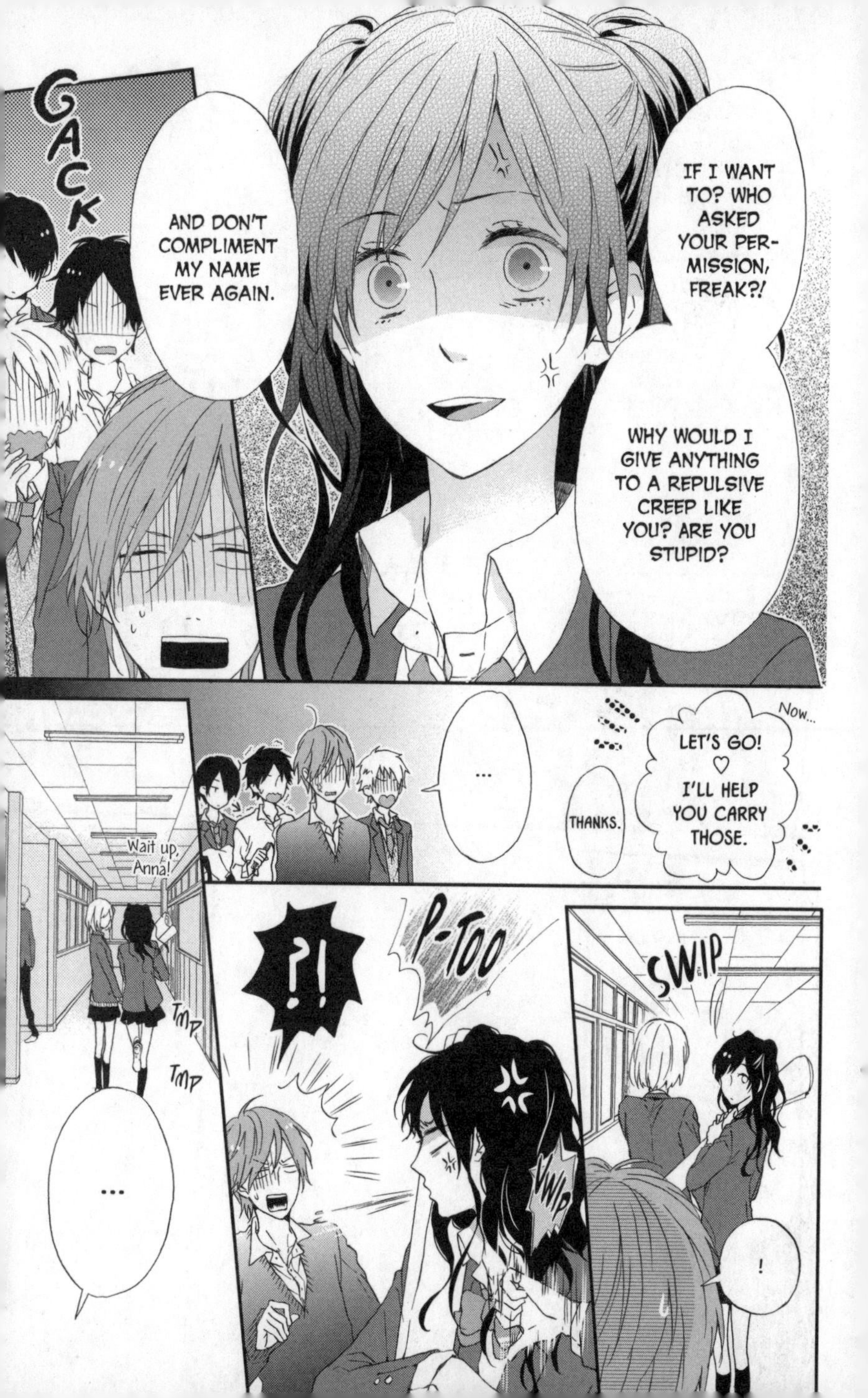
IF I WANT TO? WHO ASKED YOUR PER-MISSION, FREAK?!
WHY WOULD I GIVE ANYTHING TO A REPULSIVE CREEP LIKE YOU? ARE YOU STUPID?
AND DON'T COMPLIMENT MY NAME EVER AGAIN.
GACK
Now...
LET'S GO! ♡ I'LL HELP YOU CARRY THOSE.
THANKS.
...
SWIP
!
P-TOO
?!
SWIP
Wait up, Anna!
TMP
TMP
...

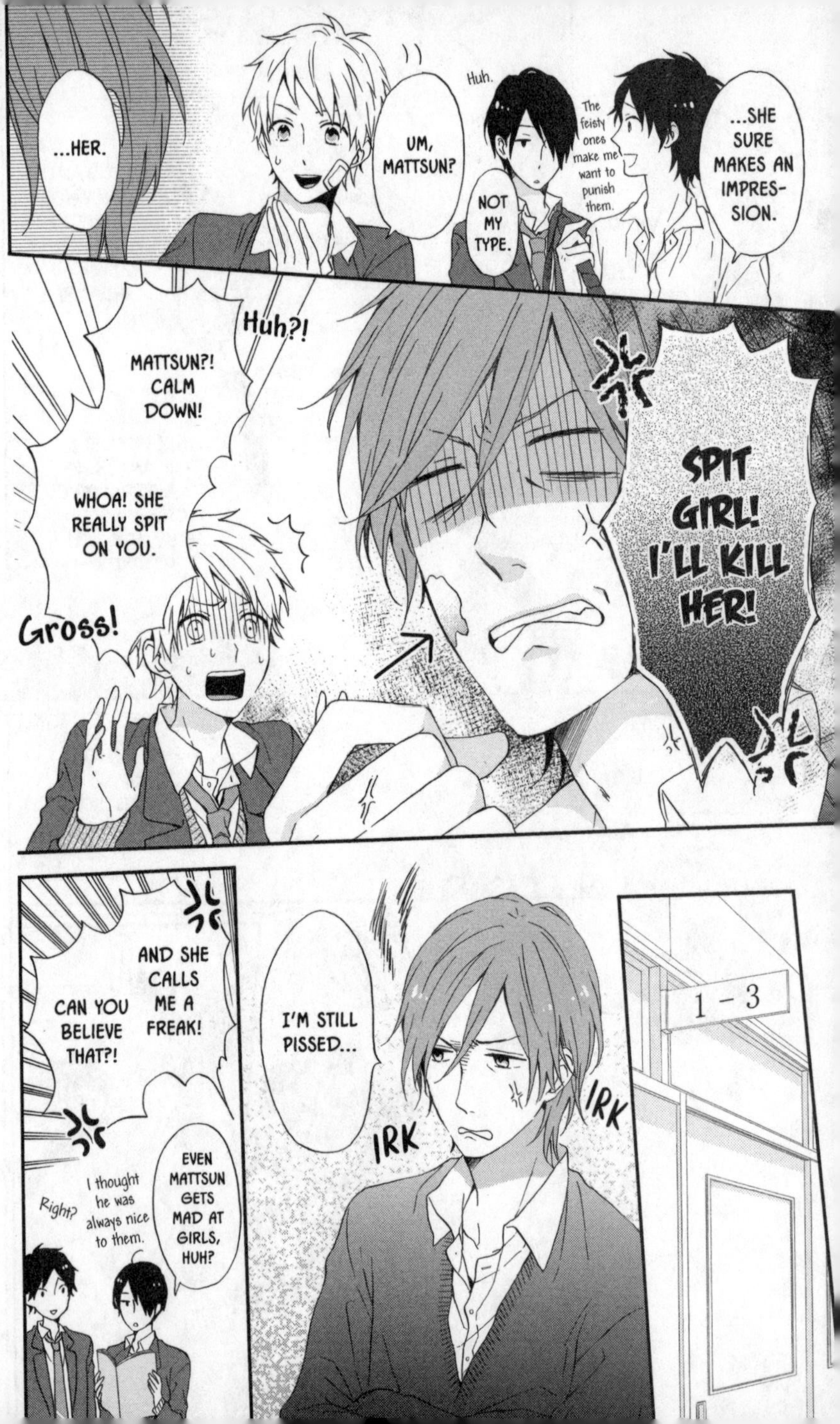
...SHE SURE MAKES AN IMPRES-SION.
The feisty ones make me want to punish them.
Huh.
NOT MY TYPE.
UM, MATTSUN?
...HER.
SPIT GIRL! I'LL KILL HER!
Huh?!
MATTSUN?! CALM DOWN!
WHOA! SHE REALLY SPIT ON YOU.
Gross!
1 – 3
IRK
I'M STILL PISSED...
IRK
AND SHE CALLS ME A FREAK!
CAN YOU BELIEVE THAT?!
EVEN MATTSUN GETS MAD AT GIRLS, HUH?
I thought he was always nice to them.
Right?

2

So, at the end of last year (2011), my assistants and I held a *bonenkai* (forget-the-year party).
There are no regular assistants at my place—the gang is different every time (even now). I get whoever's available to come along.
Some assistants were like, "There are people I always hear about but haven't ever actually met!" I thought, "Well, they're always helping me out, so why not hold a bonenkai? Come on, everyone!"
And it was lots of fun! They're all really great people!!

They understand my baffling way of giving instructions. ("Do the thing here, okay?") What's "the thing"?!
They give me pep talks when I'm sleepy, they make me laugh by being ridiculously goofy, they sing Morning Musume medleys at karaoke with total abandon... And they're really good!
I truly feel like I've met some wonderful people.

A few of those assistants drew some illustrations for me, so I included them in this book.

I love getting illustrations!! I don't normally have many chances to see their art, so whenever I'm working with an assistant for the first time, I'm like, "Gimme a picture!" (*laugh*) Yep, I'm annoying...
But they give them to me! They're all so nice...

Of course I also love getting them from readers too! Please send them in! BAM!

I want to admire them and grin like an idiot! Geh heh heh...

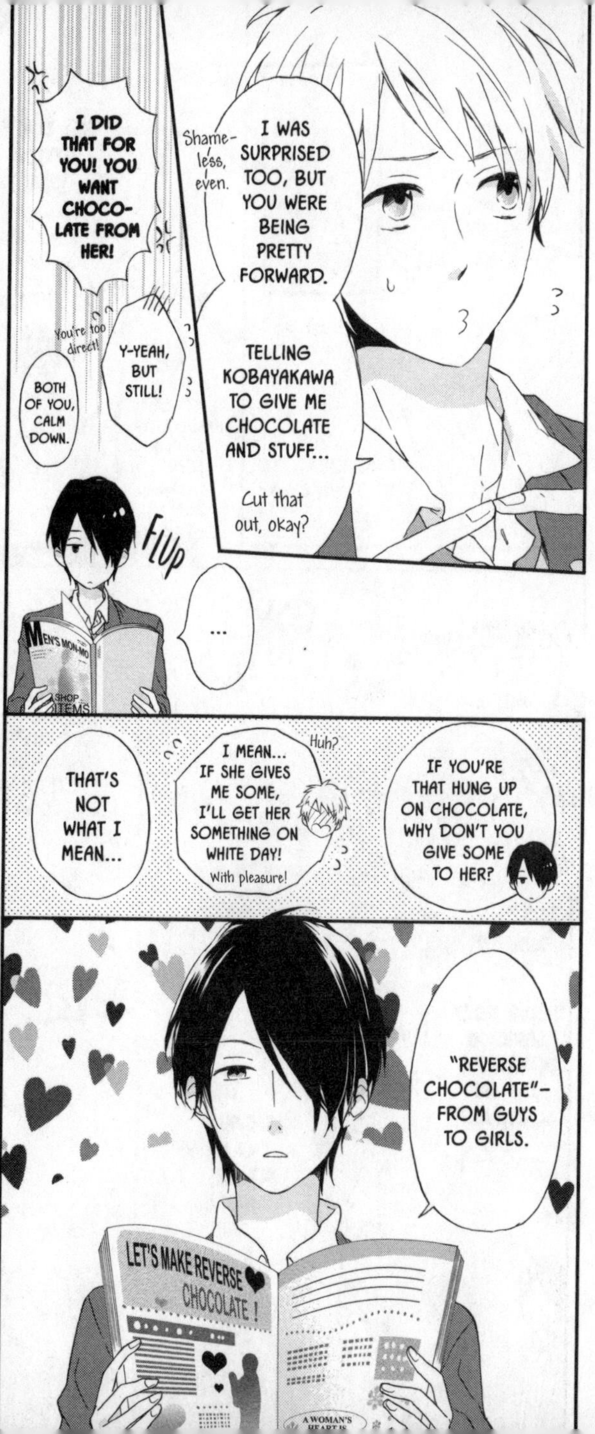

I WAS SURPRISED TOO, BUT YOU WERE BEING PRETTY FORWARD.
Shameless, even.
TELLING KOBAYAKAWA TO GIVE ME CHOCOLATE AND STUFF...
Cut that out, okay?
I DID THAT FOR YOU! YOU WANT CHOCOLATE FROM HER!
Y-YEAH, BUT STILL!
You're too direct!
BOTH OF YOU, CALM DOWN.
FLIP
...
MEN'S MON-MO
SHOP ITEMS
IF YOU'RE THAT HUNG UP ON CHOCOLATE, WHY DON'T YOU GIVE SOME TO HER?
Huh?
I MEAN... IF SHE GIVES ME SOME, I'LL GET HER SOMETHING ON WHITE DAY!
With pleasure!
THAT'S NOT WHAT I MEAN...
"REVERSE CHOCOLATE"—FROM GUYS TO GIRLS.
LET'S MAKE REVERSE CHOCOLATE!
A WOMAN'S HEART IS

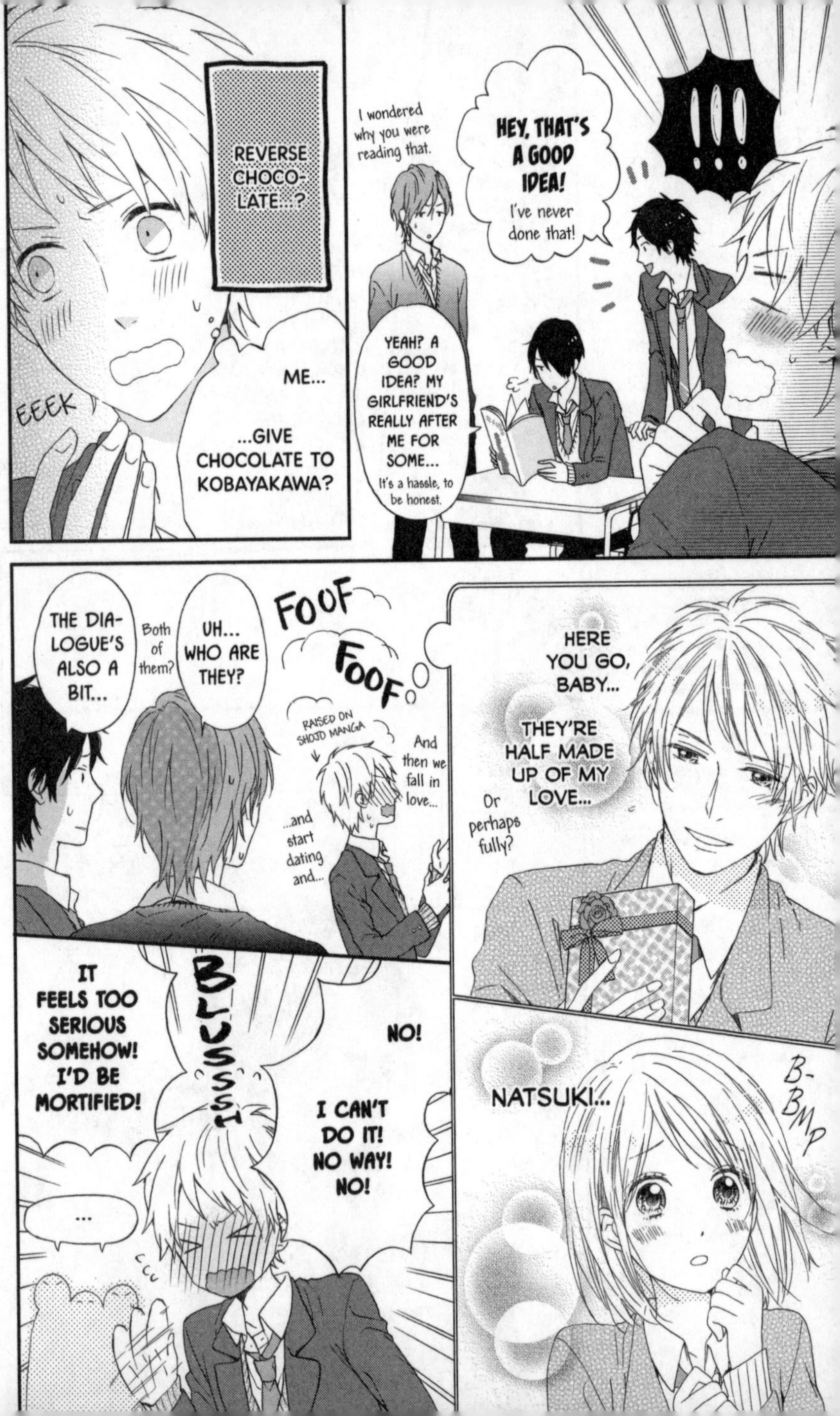
!!!
HEY, THAT'S A GOOD IDEA!
I've never done that!
I wondered why you were reading that.
YEAH? A GOOD IDEA? MY GIRLFRIEND'S REALLY AFTER ME FOR SOME...
It's a hassle, to be honest.
REVERSE CHOCOLATE...?
EEEK
ME...
...GIVE CHOCOLATE TO KOBAYAKAWA?
HERE YOU GO, BABY...
THEY'RE HALF MADE UP OF MY LOVE...
Or perhaps fully?
B-BMP
NATSUKI...
FOOF
FOOF
RAISED ON SHOJO MANGA
And then we fall in love...
...and start dating and...
UH... WHO ARE THEY?
Both of them?
THE DIALOGUE'S ALSO A BIT...
NO!
I CAN'T DO IT! NO WAY! NO!
BLUSSSH
IT FEELS TOO SERIOUS SOMEHOW! I'D BE MORTIFIED!
...

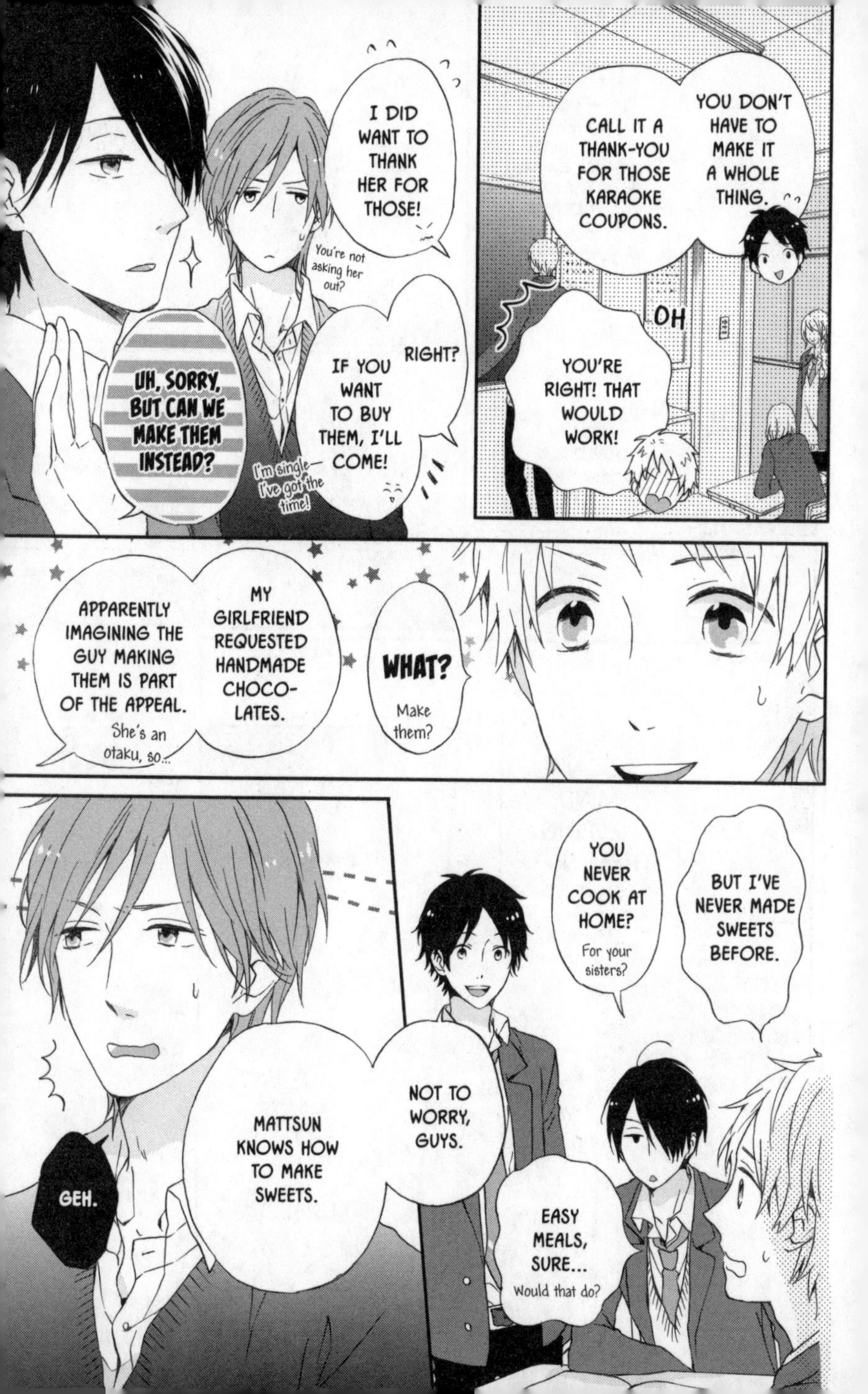
YOU DON'T HAVE TO MAKE IT A WHOLE THING.
CALL IT A THANK-YOU FOR THOSE KARAOKE COUPONS.
OH
YOU'RE RIGHT! THAT WOULD WORK!
I DID WANT TO THANK HER FOR THOSE!
You're not asking her out?
RIGHT?
IF YOU WANT TO BUY THEM, I'LL COME!
I'm single—I've got the time!
UH, SORRY, BUT CAN WE MAKE THEM INSTEAD?
WHAT?
Make them?
MY GIRLFRIEND REQUESTED HANDMADE CHOCO-LATES.
APPARENTLY IMAGINING THE GUY MAKING THEM IS PART OF THE APPEAL.
She's an otaku, so...
BUT I'VE NEVER MADE SWEETS BEFORE.
YOU NEVER COOK AT HOME?
For your sisters?
NOT TO WORRY, GUYS.
MATTSUN KNOWS HOW TO MAKE SWEETS.
EASY MEALS, SURE...
Would that do?
GEH.

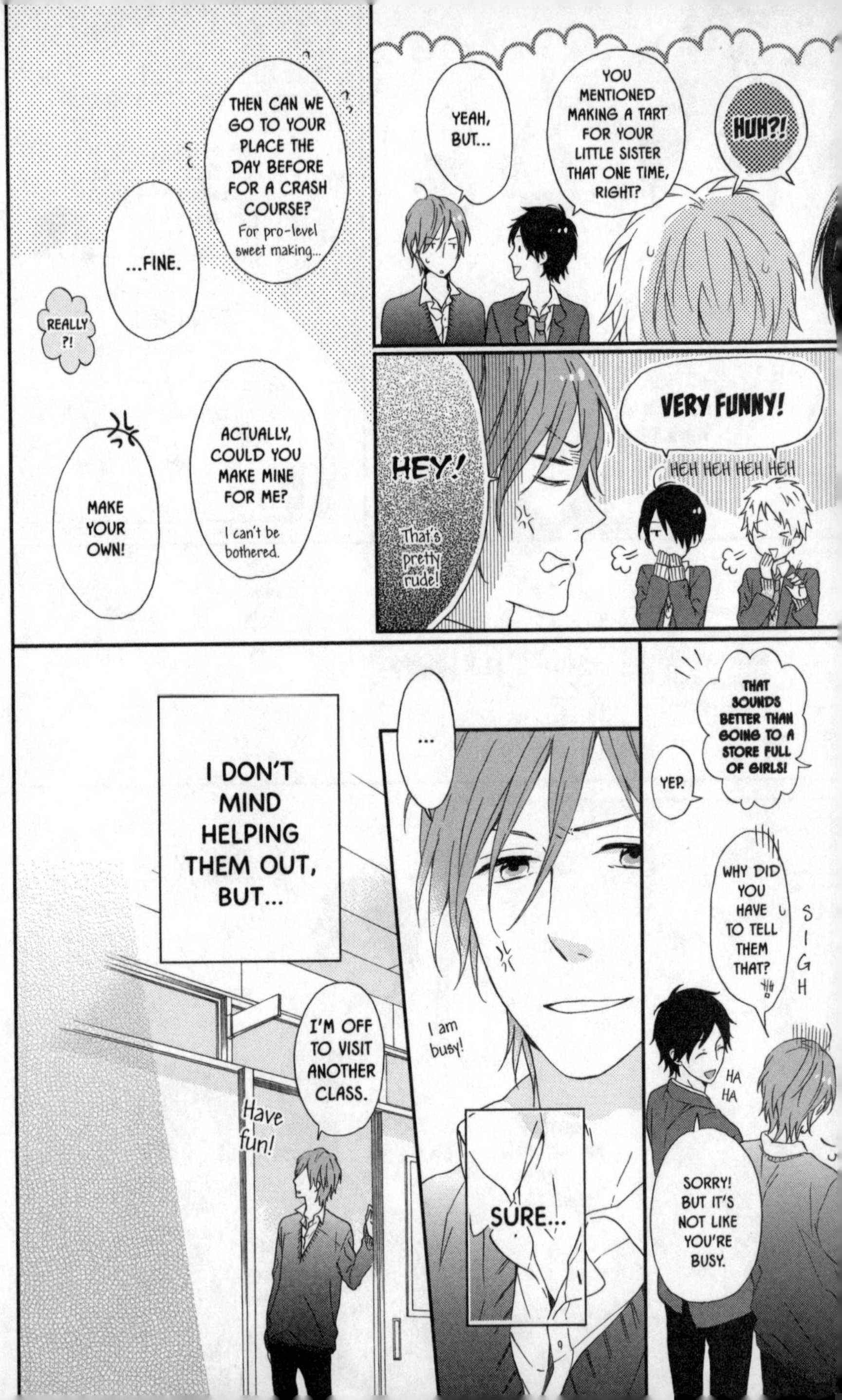
HUH?!
YOU MENTIONED MAKING A TART FOR YOUR LITTLE SISTER THAT ONE TIME, RIGHT?
YEAH, BUT...
VERY FUNNY!
HEH HEH HEH HEH
HEY!
That's pretty rude!
THEN CAN WE GO TO YOUR PLACE THE DAY BEFORE FOR A CRASH COURSE?
For pro-level sweet making...
...FINE.
REALLY?!
ACTUALLY, COULD YOU MAKE MINE FOR ME?
I can't be bothered.
MAKE YOUR OWN!
THAT SOUNDS BETTER THAN GOING TO A STORE FULL OF GIRLS!
YEP.
WHY DID YOU HAVE TO TELL THEM THAT?
SIGH
HA HA
SORRY! BUT IT'S NOT LIKE YOU'RE BUSY.
...
I am busy!
SURE...
I DON'T MIND HELPING THEM OUT, BUT...
I'M OFF TO VISIT ANOTHER CLASS.
Have fun!

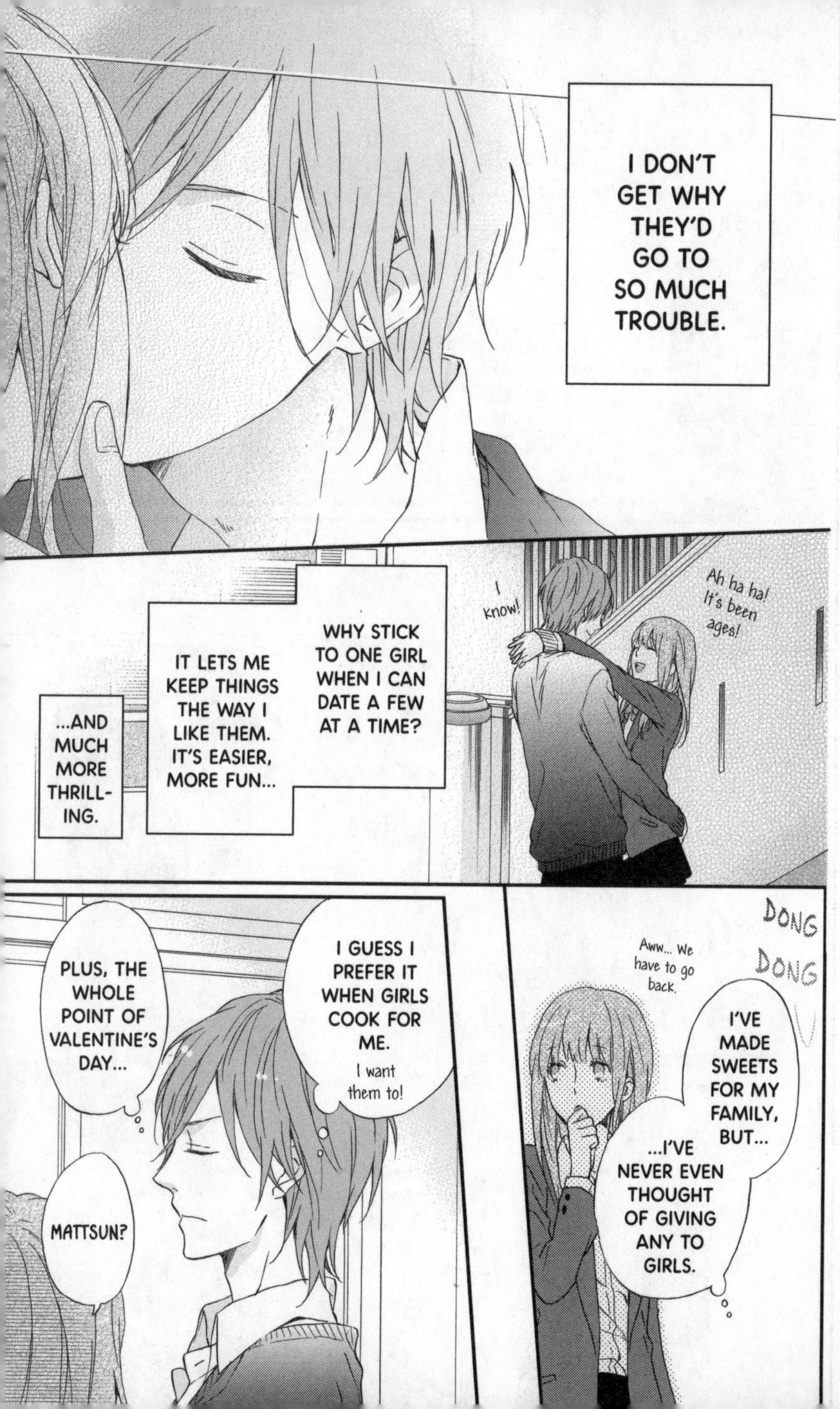
I DON'T GET WHY THEY'D GO TO SO MUCH TROUBLE.
Ah ha ha! It's been ages!
I know!
WHY STICK TO ONE GIRL WHEN I CAN DATE A FEW AT A TIME?
IT LETS ME KEEP THINGS THE WAY I LIKE THEM. IT'S EASIER, MORE FUN...
...AND MUCH MORE THRILL-ING.
DONG DONG
Aww... We have to go back.
I'VE MADE SWEETS FOR MY FAMILY, BUT...
...I'VE NEVER EVEN THOUGHT OF GIVING ANY TO GIRLS.
I GUESS I PREFER IT WHEN GIRLS COOK FOR ME.
I want them to!
PLUS, THE WHOLE POINT OF VALENTINE'S DAY...
MATTSUN?

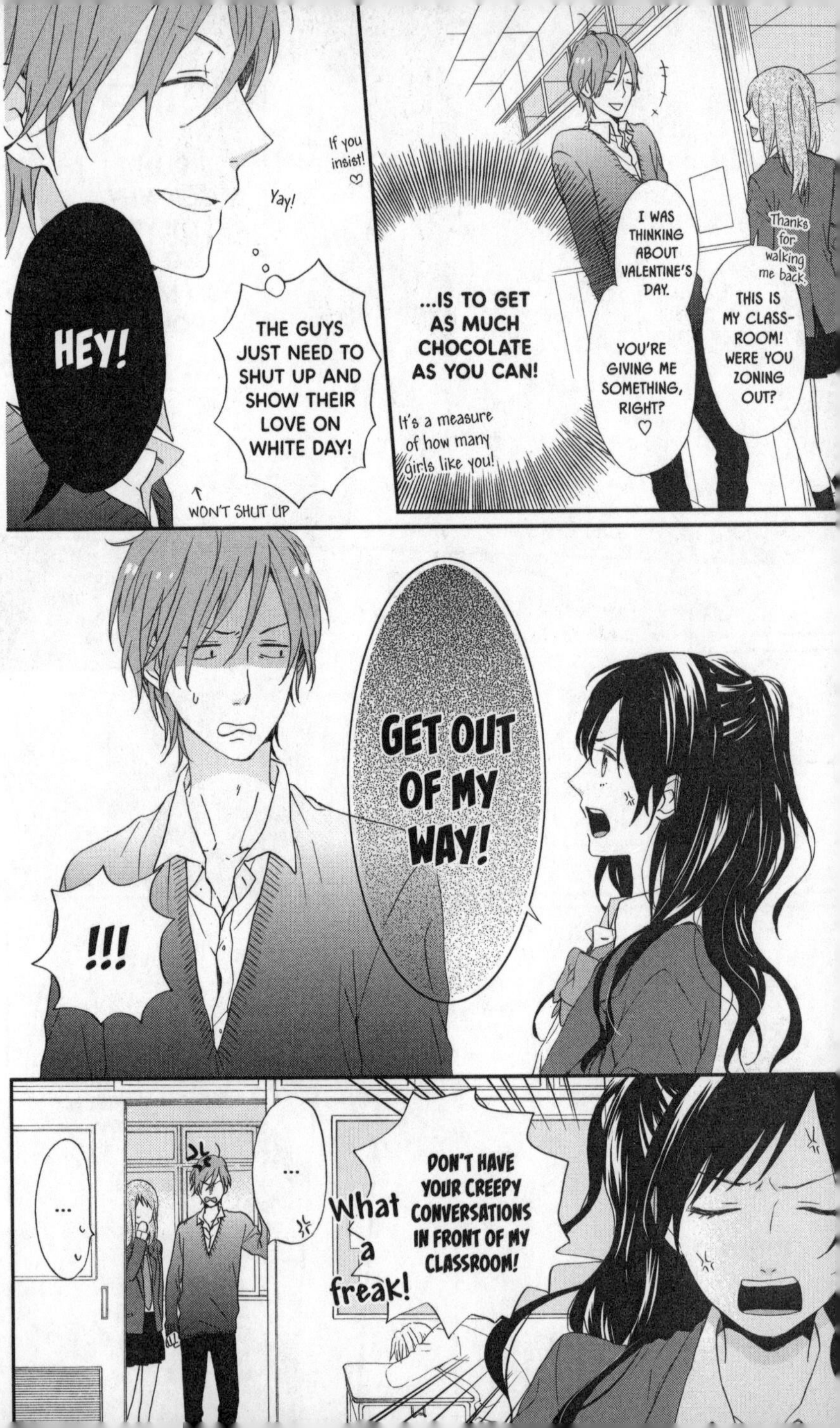
Thanks for walking me back.
THIS IS MY CLASSROOM! WERE YOU ZONING OUT?
I WAS THINKING ABOUT VALENTINE'S DAY.
YOU'RE GIVING ME SOMETHING, RIGHT? ♡
...IS TO GET AS MUCH CHOCOLATE AS YOU CAN!
It's a measure of how many girls like you!
If you insist! ♡
Yay!
THE GUYS JUST NEED TO SHUT UP AND SHOW THEIR LOVE ON WHITE DAY!
WON'T SHUT UP
HEY!
GET OUT OF MY WAY!
!!!
DON'T HAVE YOUR CREEPY CONVERSATIONS IN FRONT OF MY CLASSROOM!
What a freak!
...
...

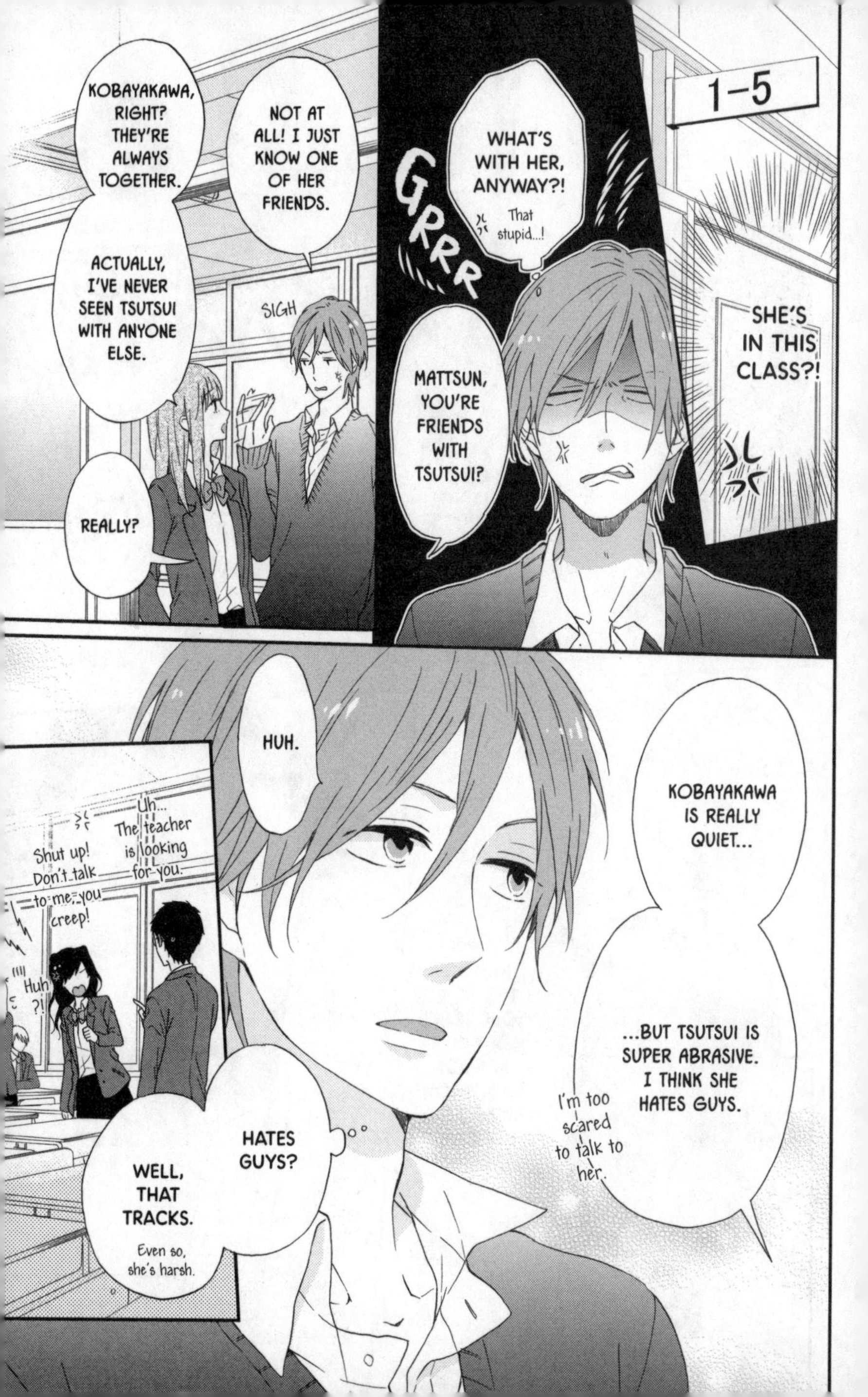
1-5
SHE'S IN THIS CLASS?!
WHAT'S WITH HER, ANYWAY?!
That stupid...!
GRRR
MATTSUN, YOU'RE FRIENDS WITH TSUTSUI?
NOT AT ALL! I JUST KNOW ONE OF HER FRIENDS.
SIGH
KOBAYAKAWA, RIGHT? THEY'RE ALWAYS TOGETHER.
ACTUALLY, I'VE NEVER SEEN TSUTSUI WITH ANYONE ELSE.
REALLY?
HUH.
KOBAYAKAWA IS REALLY QUIET...
...BUT TSUTSUI IS SUPER ABRASIVE. I THINK SHE HATES GUYS.
I'm too scared to talk to her.
HATES GUYS?
Uh... The teacher is looking for you.
Shut up! Don't talk to me, you creep!
Huh ?!
WELL, THAT TRACKS.
Even so, she's harsh.

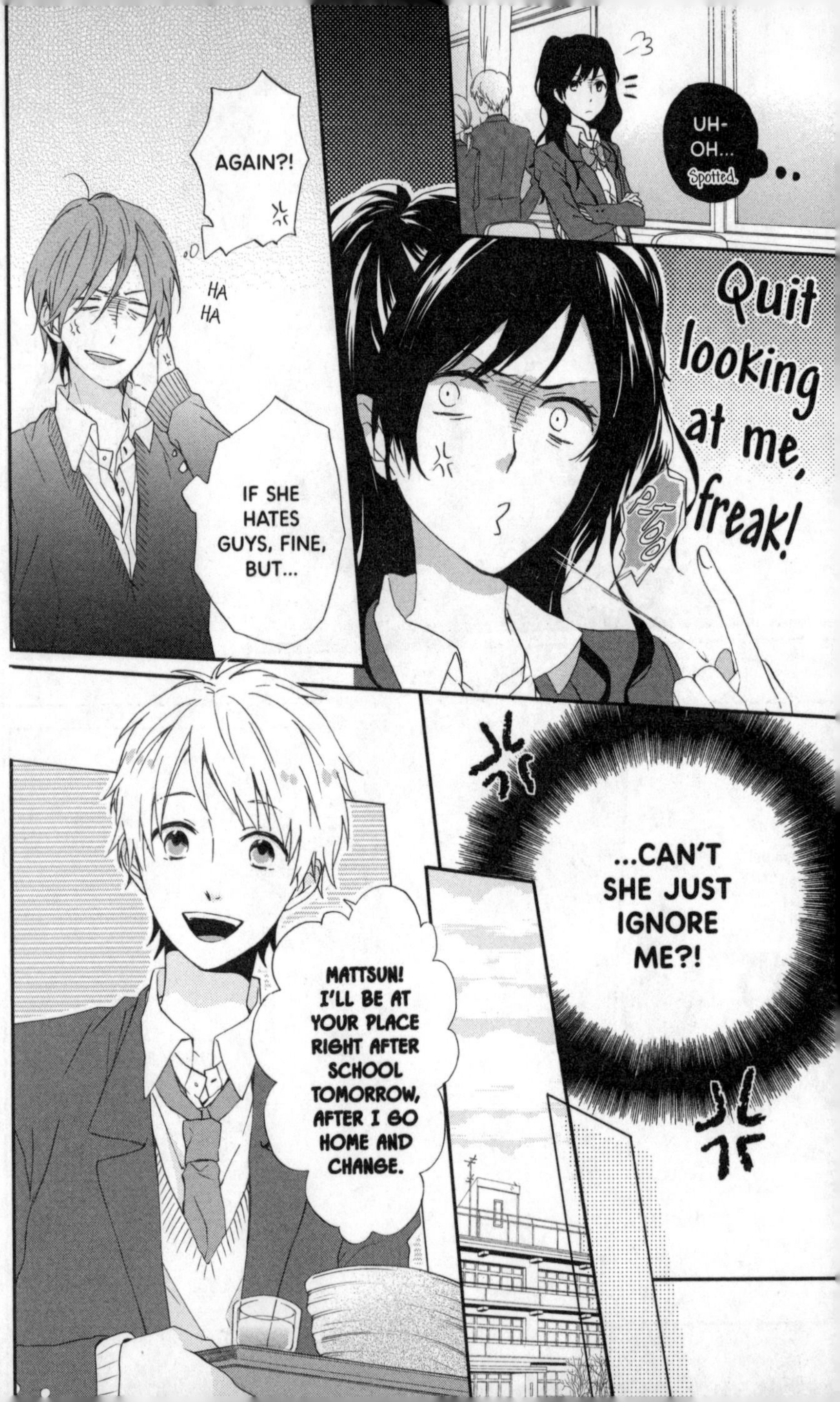
UH-OH...
Spotted.
Quit looking at me, freak!
P-TOO
AGAIN?!
HA HA
IF SHE HATES GUYS, FINE, BUT...
...CAN'T SHE JUST IGNORE ME?!
MATTSUN! I'LL BE AT YOUR PLACE RIGHT AFTER SCHOOL TOMORROW, AFTER I GO HOME AND CHANGE.

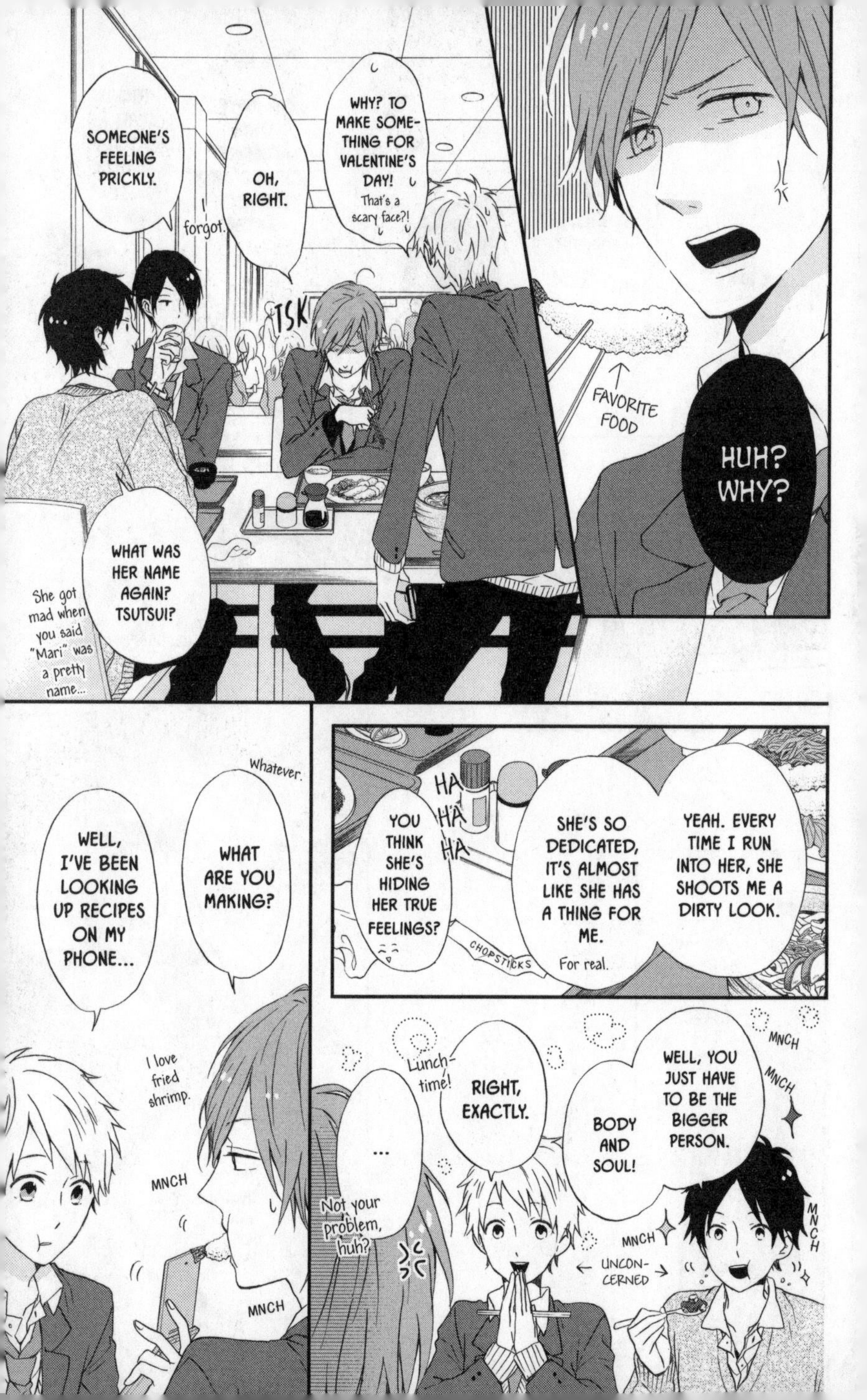
HUH? WHY?
FAVORITE FOOD
WHY? TO MAKE SOME-THING FOR VALENTINE'S DAY!
That's a scary face?!
OH, RIGHT.
I forgot.
SOMEONE'S FEELING PRICKLY.
TSK
WHAT WAS HER NAME AGAIN? TSUTSUI?
She got mad when you said "Mari" was a pretty name...
YEAH. EVERY TIME I RUN INTO HER, SHE SHOOTS ME A DIRTY LOOK.
SHE'S SO DEDICATED, IT'S ALMOST LIKE SHE HAS A THING FOR ME.
For real.
HA HA HA
YOU THINK SHE'S HIDING HER TRUE FEELINGS?
CHOPSTICKS
WELL, YOU JUST HAVE TO BE THE BIGGER PERSON.
MNCH
MNCH
BODY AND SOUL!
RIGHT, EXACTLY.
Lunch-time!
...
Not your problem, huh?
MNCH
MNCH
← UNCON-CERNED →
WHAT ARE YOU MAKING?
Whatever.
WELL, I'VE BEEN LOOKING UP RECIPES ON MY PHONE...
I love fried shrimp.
MNCH
MNCH

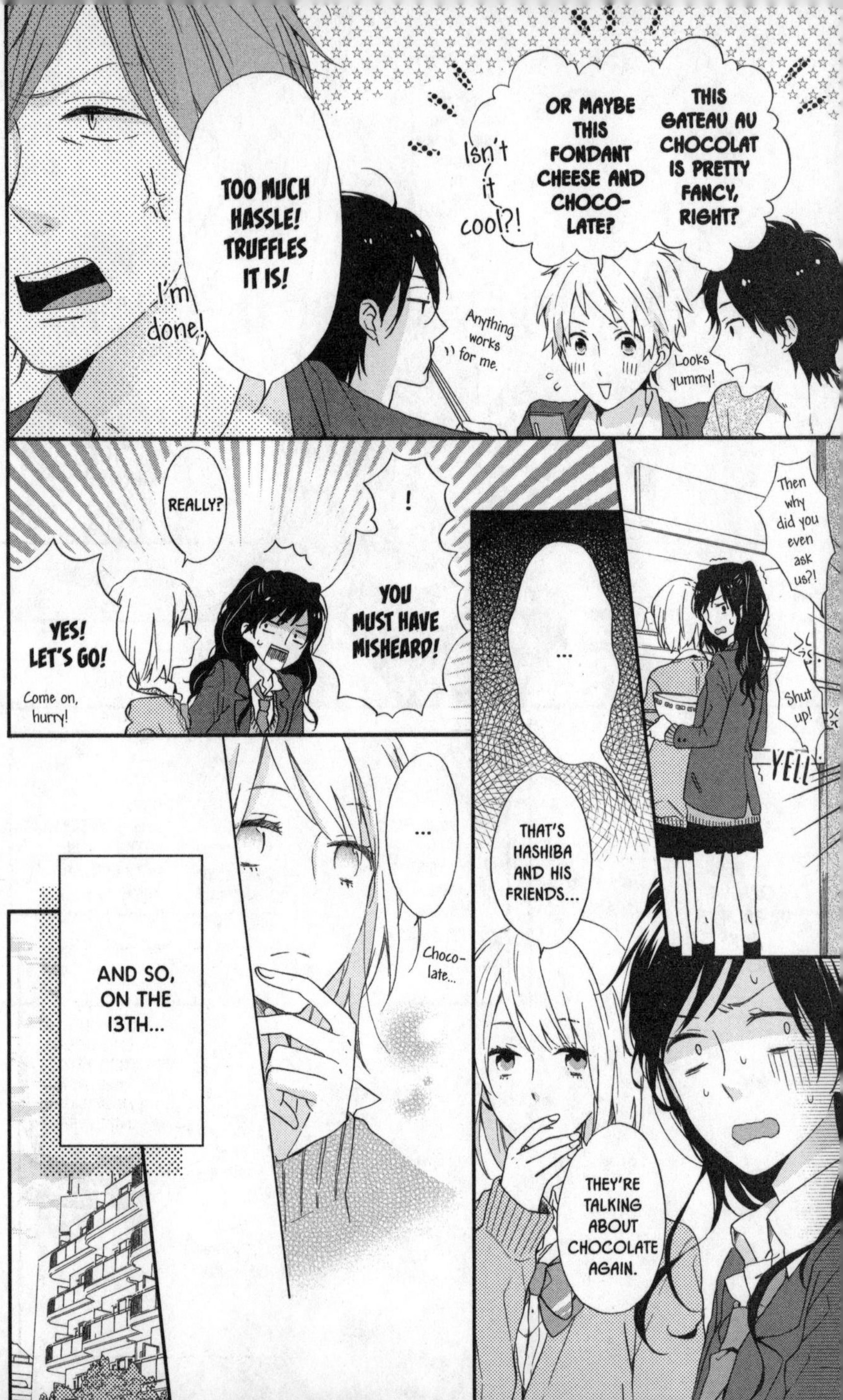
THIS GATEAU AU CHOCOLAT IS PRETTY FANCY, RIGHT?
Looks yummy!
OR MAYBE THIS FONDANT CHEESE AND CHOCO-LATE?
Isn't it cool?!
Anything works for me.
TOO MUCH HASSLE! TRUFFLES IT IS!
I'm done!
Then why did you even ask us?!
Shut up!
YELL
REALLY?
!
YOU MUST HAVE MISHEARD!
YES! LET'S GO!
Come on, hurry!
...
THAT'S HASHIBA AND HIS FRIENDS...
THEY'RE TALKING ABOUT CHOCOLATE AGAIN.
...
Choco-late...
AND SO, ON THE 13TH...

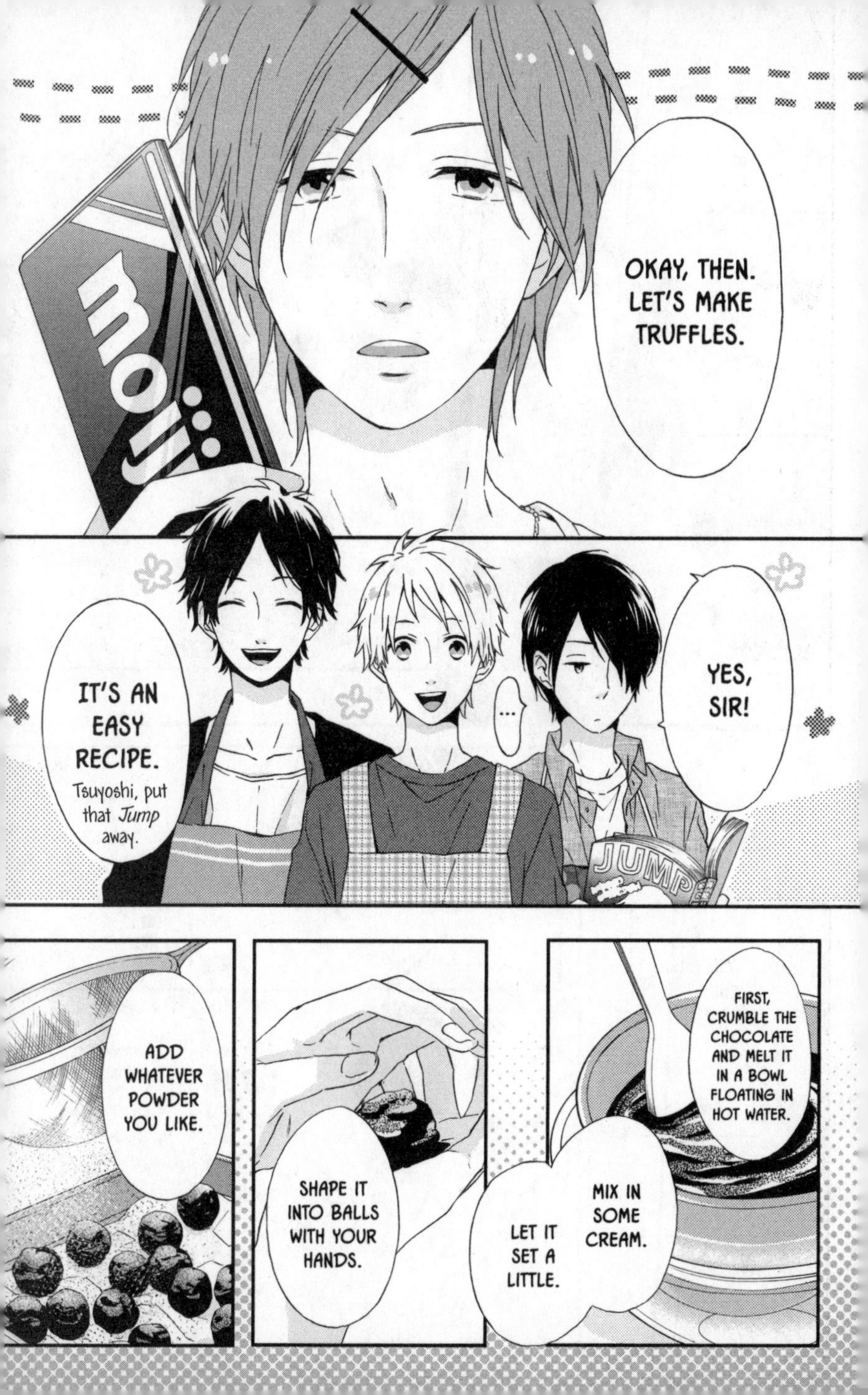
OKAY, THEN. LET'S MAKE TRUFFLES.
YES, SIR!
...
IT'S AN EASY RECIPE.
Tsuyoshi, put that *Jump* away.
JUMP
FIRST, CRUMBLE THE CHOCOLATE AND MELT IT IN A BOWL FLOATING IN HOT WATER.
MIX IN SOME CREAM.
LET IT SET A LITTLE.
SHAPE IT INTO BALLS WITH YOUR HANDS.
ADD WHATEVER POWDER YOU LIKE.

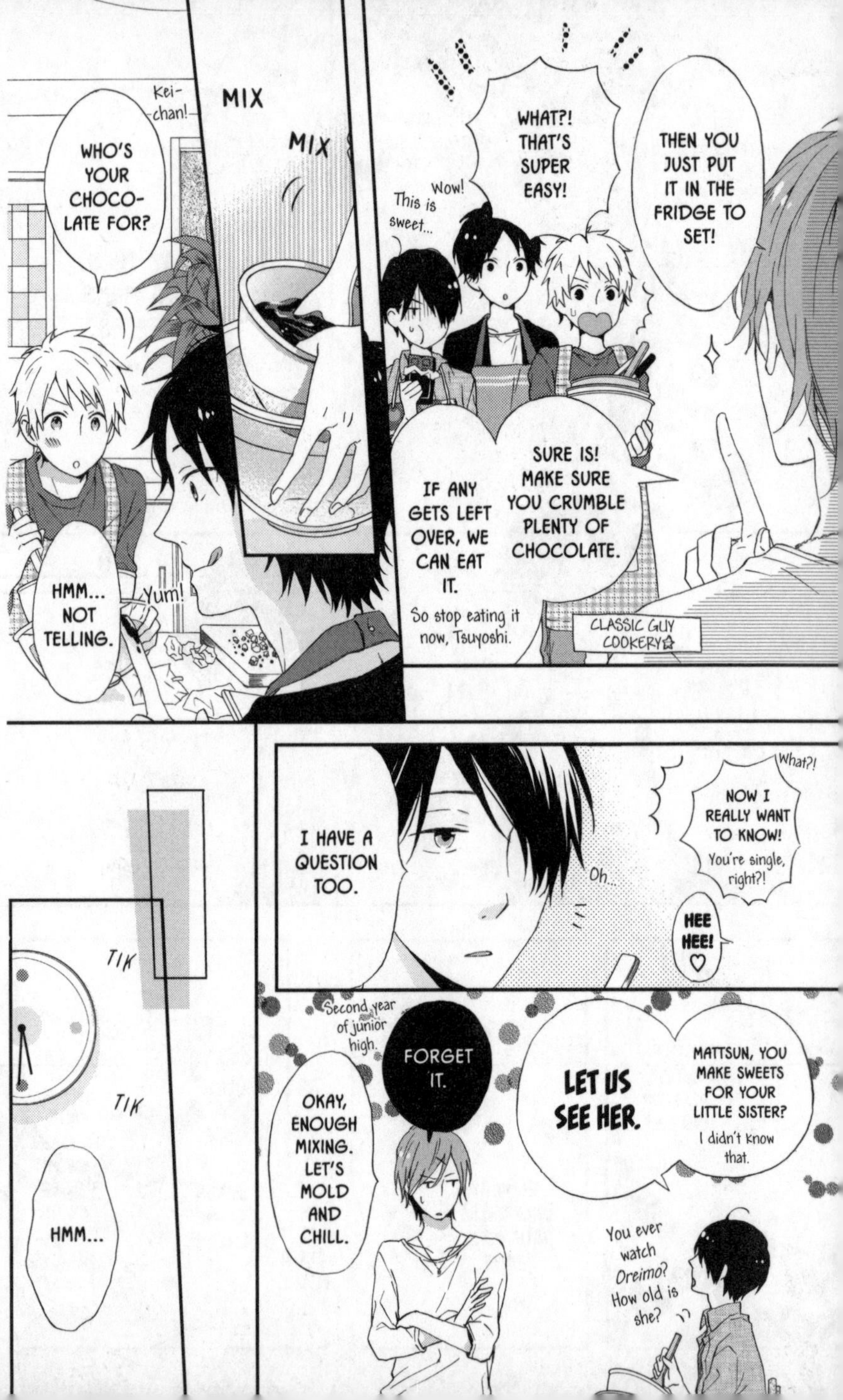

THEN YOU JUST PUT IT IN THE FRIDGE TO SET!
WHAT?! THAT'S SUPER EASY!
Wow! This is sweet...
SURE IS! MAKE SURE YOU CRUMBLE PLENTY OF CHOCOLATE.
IF ANY GETS LEFT OVER, WE CAN EAT IT.
So stop eating it now, Tsuyoshi.
CLASSIC GUY COOKERY☆
MIX
MIX
Kei-chan!
WHO'S YOUR CHOCO-LATE FOR?
HMM... NOT TELLING.
Yum!
What?!
NOW I REALLY WANT TO KNOW!
You're single, right?!
HEE HEE! ♡
Oh...
I HAVE A QUESTION TOO.
MATTSUN, YOU MAKE SWEETS FOR YOUR LITTLE SISTER?
I didn't know that.
LET US SEE HER.
You ever watch Oreimo? How old is she?
Second year of junior high.
FORGET IT.
OKAY, ENOUGH MIXING. LET'S MOLD AND CHILL.
TIK
TIK
HMM...

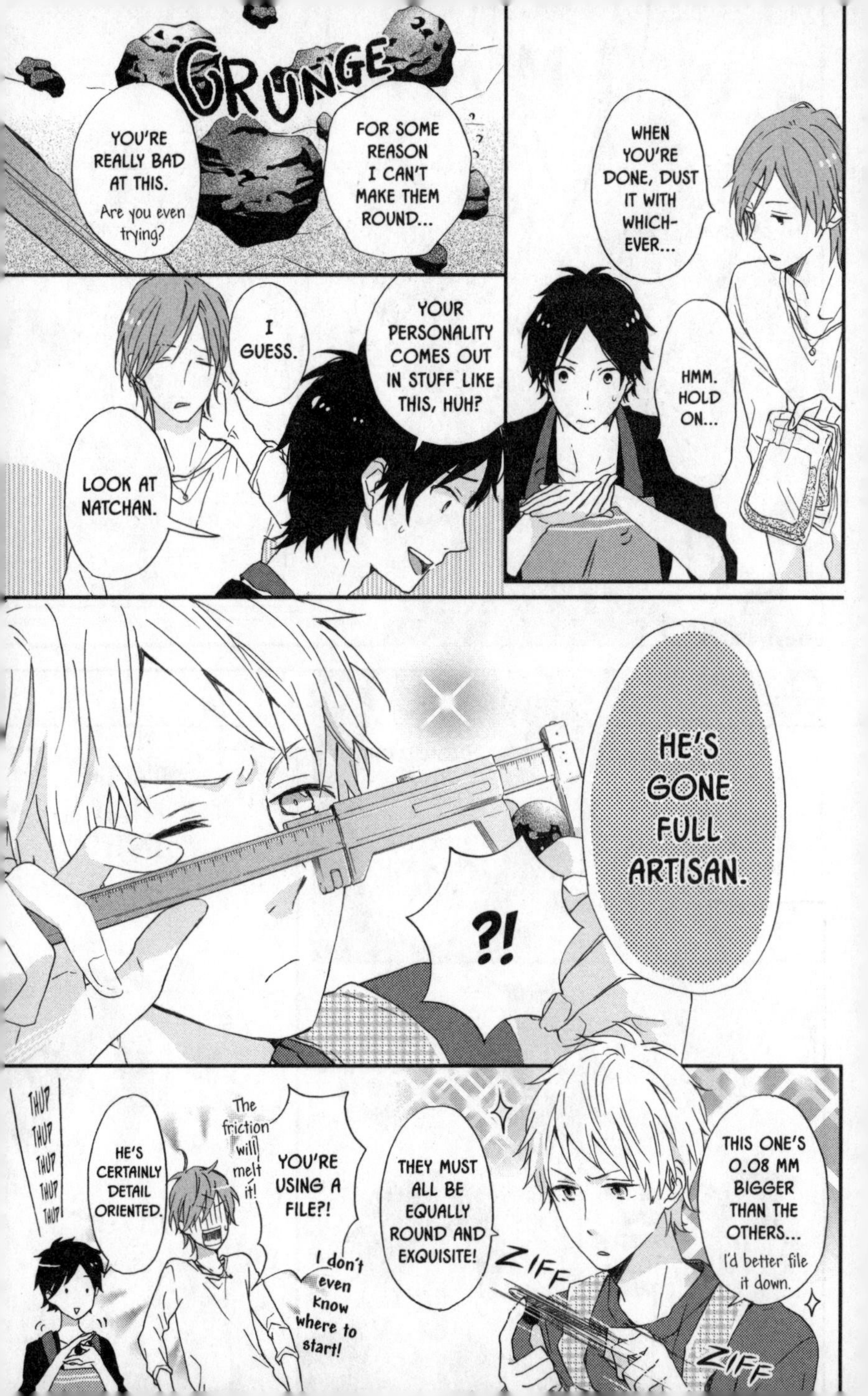

WHEN YOU'RE DONE, DUST IT WITH WHICH-EVER...
HMM. HOLD ON...
GRUNGE
FOR SOME REASON I CAN'T MAKE THEM ROUND...
YOU'RE REALLY BAD AT THIS.
Are you even trying?
YOUR PERSONALITY COMES OUT IN STUFF LIKE THIS, HUH?
I GUESS.
LOOK AT NATCHAN.
HE'S GONE FULL ARTISAN.
?!
THIS ONE'S 0.08 MM BIGGER THAN THE OTHERS...
I'd better file it down.
ZIFF
ZIFF
THEY MUST ALL BE EQUALLY ROUND AND EXQUISITE!
YOU'RE USING A FILE?!
The friction will melt it!
I don't even know where to start!
HE'S CERTAINLY DETAIL ORIENTED.
THUP THUP THUP THUP THUP

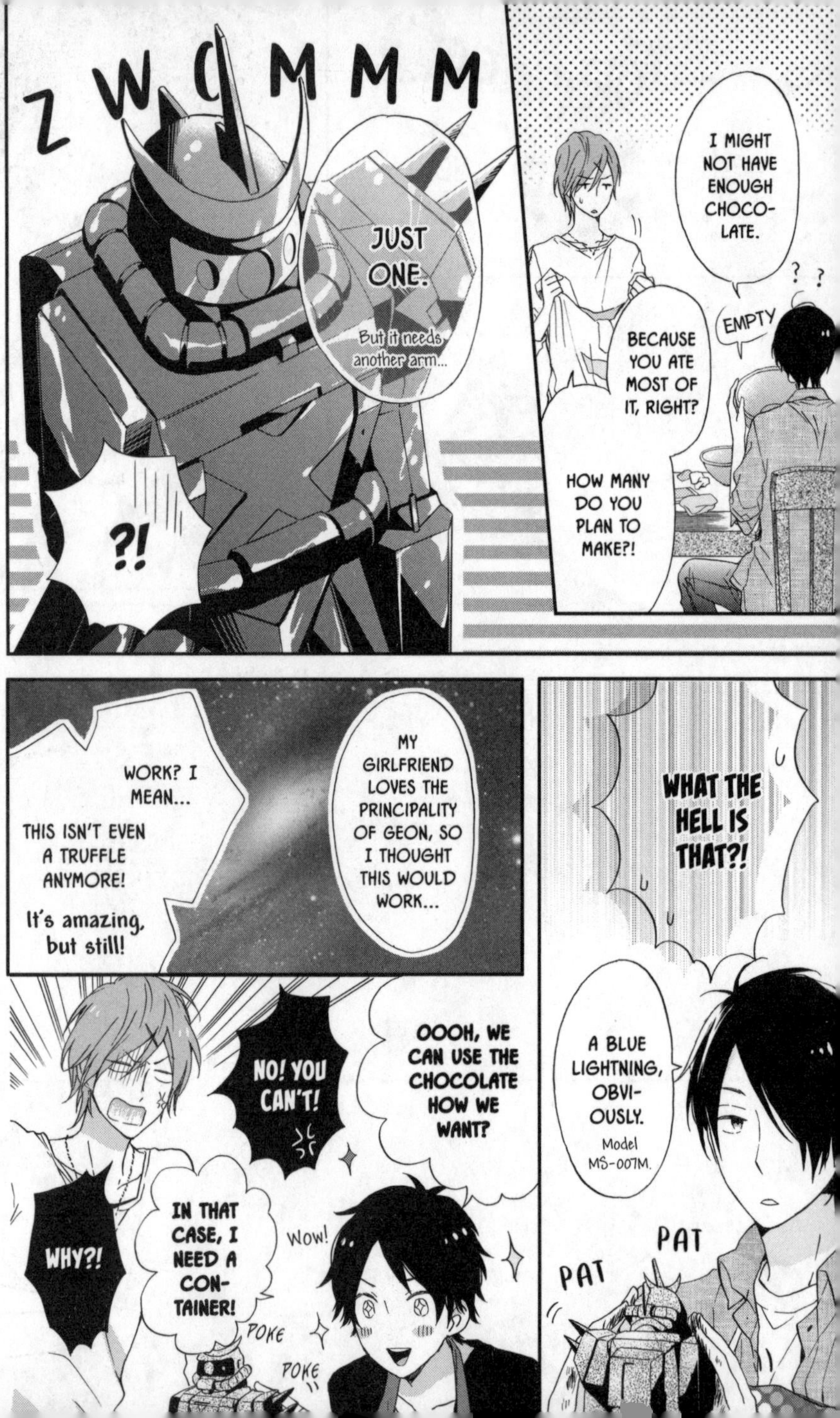
I MIGHT NOT HAVE ENOUGH CHOCO-LATE.
? ?
EMPTY
BECAUSE YOU ATE MOST OF IT, RIGHT?
HOW MANY DO YOU PLAN TO MAKE?!
ZWOMMM
JUST ONE.
But it needs another arm...
?!
WHAT THE HELL IS THAT?!
A BLUE LIGHTNING, OBVI-OUSLY.
Model MS-007M.
PAT
PAT
MY GIRLFRIEND LOVES THE PRINCIPALITY OF GEON, SO I THOUGHT THIS WOULD WORK...
WORK? I MEAN...
THIS ISN'T EVEN A TRUFFLE ANYMORE!
It's amazing, but still!
OOOH, WE CAN USE THE CHOCOLATE HOW WE WANT?
NO! YOU CAN'T!
IN THAT CASE, I NEED A CON-TAINER!
Wow!
WHY?!
POKE
POKE

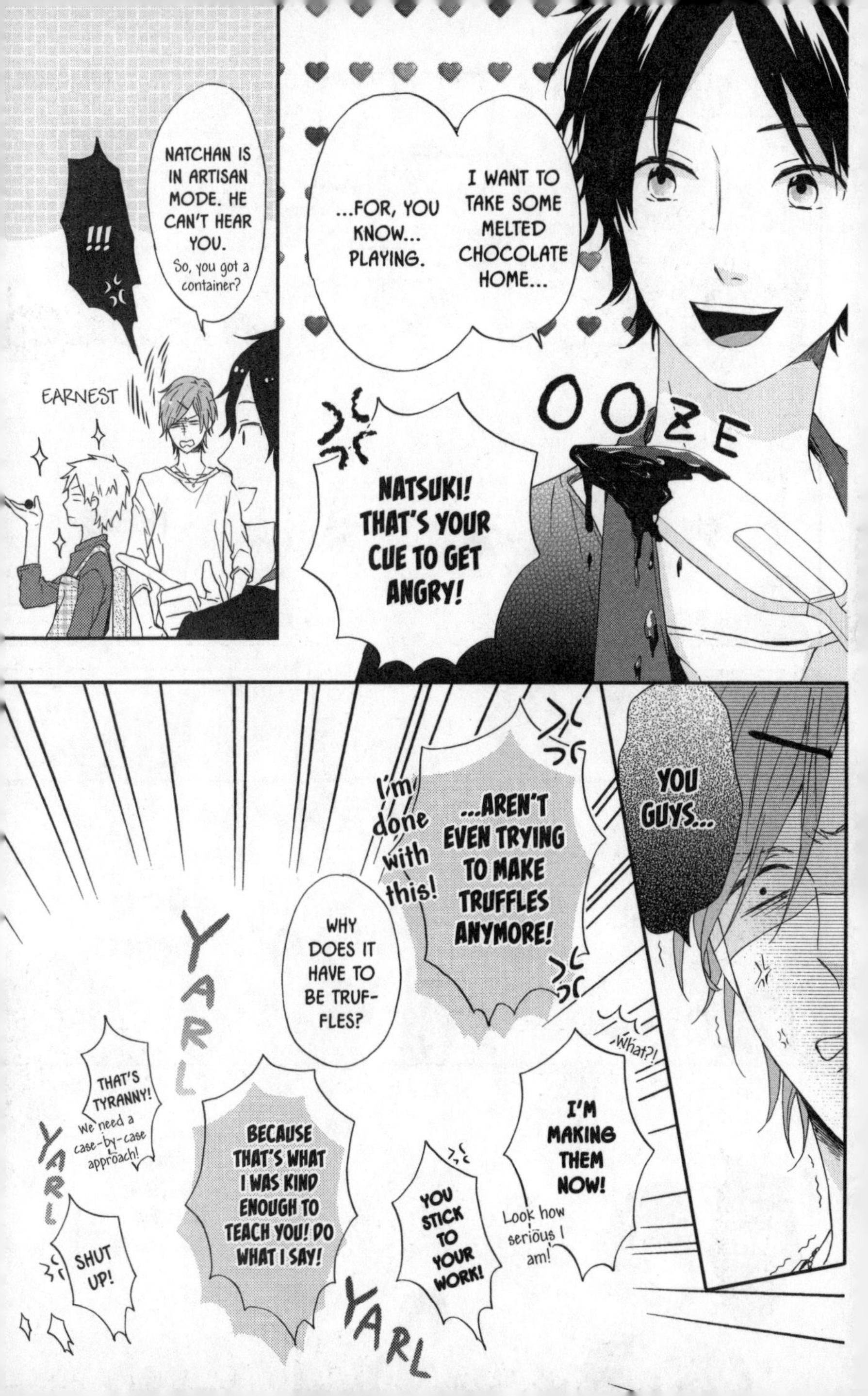
I WANT TO TAKE SOME MELTED CHOCOLATE HOME...
...FOR, YOU KNOW... PLAYING.
OOZE
NATSUKI! THAT'S YOUR CUE TO GET ANGRY!
NATCHAN IS IN ARTISAN MODE. HE CAN'T HEAR YOU.
So, you got a container?
!!!
EARNEST
YOU GUYS...
...AREN'T EVEN TRYING TO MAKE TRUFFLES ANYMORE!
I'm done with this!
What?!
I'M MAKING THEM NOW!
Look how serious I am!
WHY DOES IT HAVE TO BE TRUFFLES?
YOU STICK TO YOUR WORK!
BECAUSE THAT'S WHAT I WAS KIND ENOUGH TO TEACH YOU! DO WHAT I SAY!
YARL
YARL
THAT'S TYRANNY!
We need a case-by-case approach!
YARL
SHUT UP!

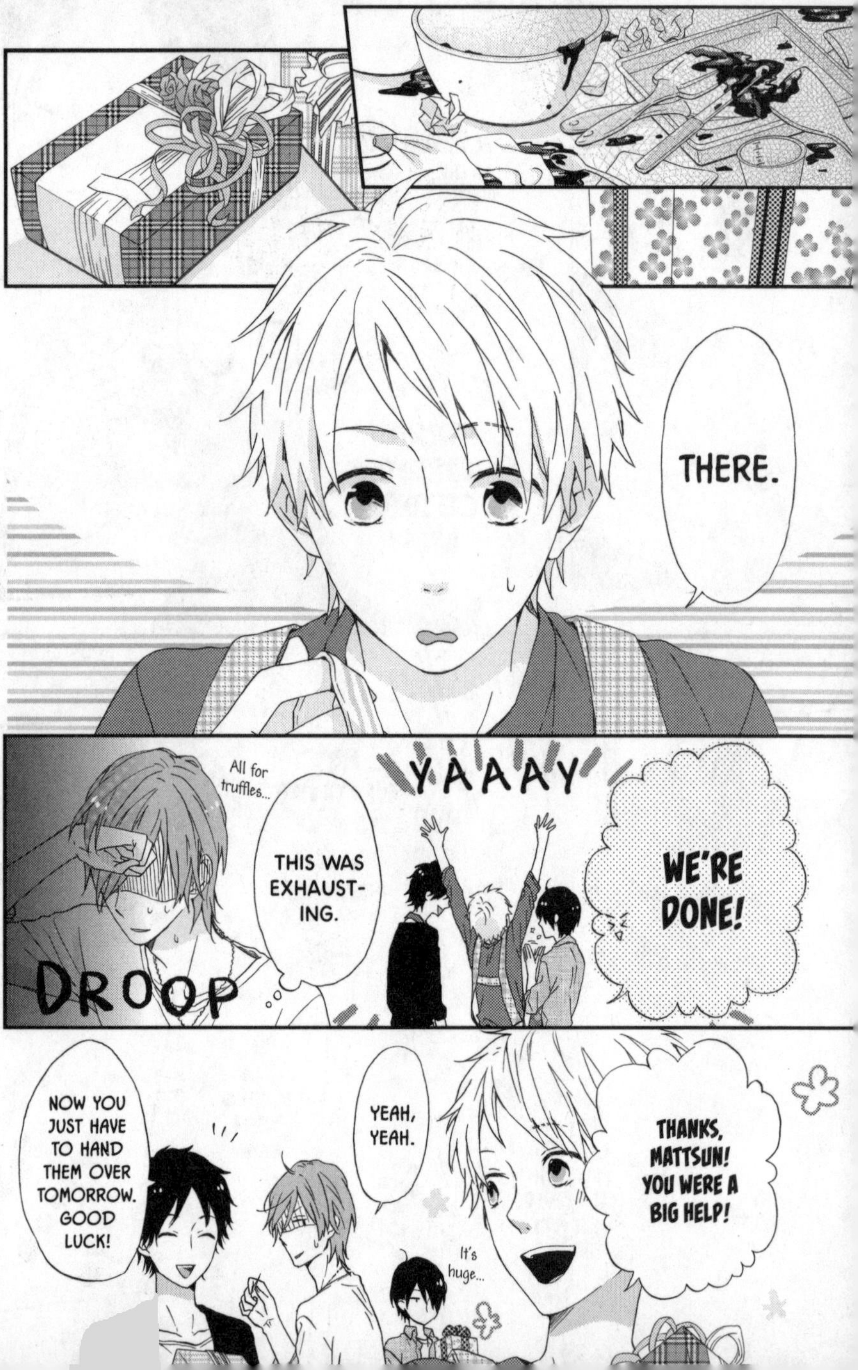
THERE.
WE'RE DONE!
YAAAY
THIS WAS EXHAUST-ING.
All for truffles...
DROOP
THANKS, MATTSUN! YOU WERE A BIG HELP!
YEAH, YEAH.
It's huge...
NOW YOU JUST HAVE TO HAND THEM OVER TOMORROW. GOOD LUCK!

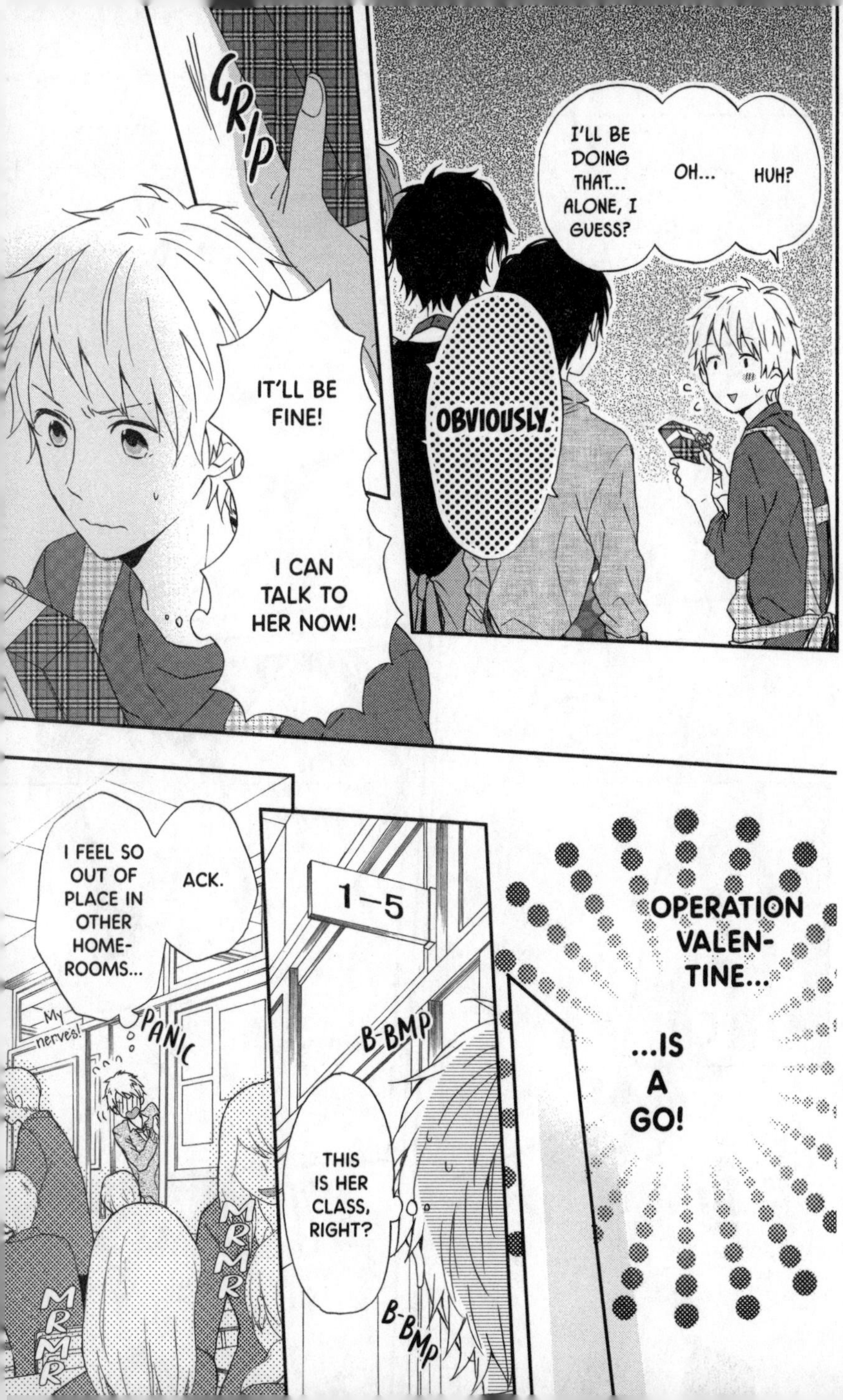
HUH?
OH...
I'LL BE DOING THAT... ALONE, I GUESS?
OBVIOUSLY.
GRIP
IT'LL BE FINE!
I CAN TALK TO HER NOW!
OPERATION VALENTINE...
...IS A GO!
1–5
B-BMP
THIS IS HER CLASS, RIGHT?
B-BMP
ACK.
I FEEL SO OUT OF PLACE IN OTHER HOME-ROOMS...
PANIC
My nerves!
MRMR
MRMR

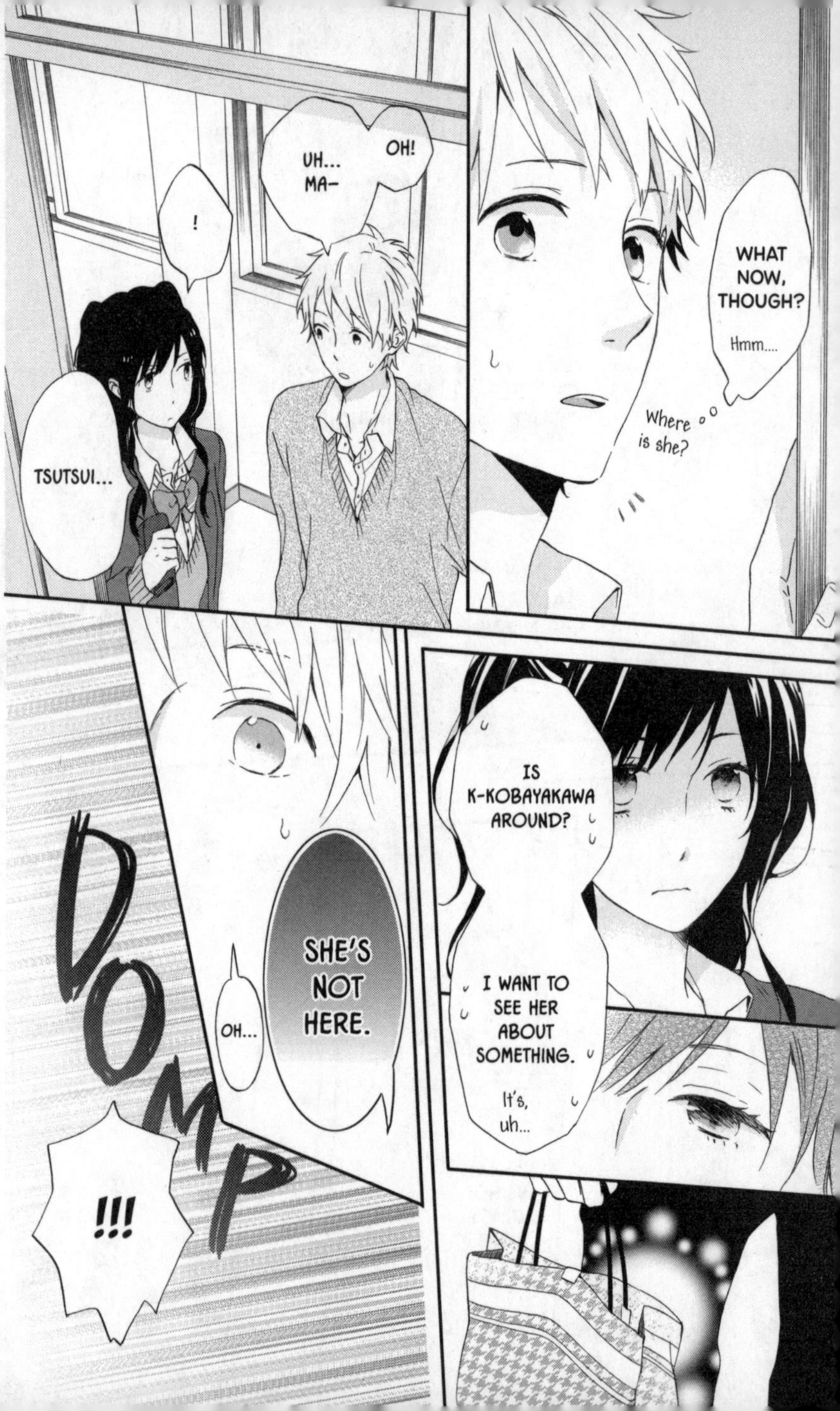
WHAT NOW, THOUGH?
Hmm....
Where is she?
OH!
UH... MA–
!
TSUTSUI...
IS K-KOBAYAKAWA AROUND?
I WANT TO SEE HER ABOUT SOMETHING.
It's, uh...
SHE'S NOT HERE.
OH...
DOMP
!!!

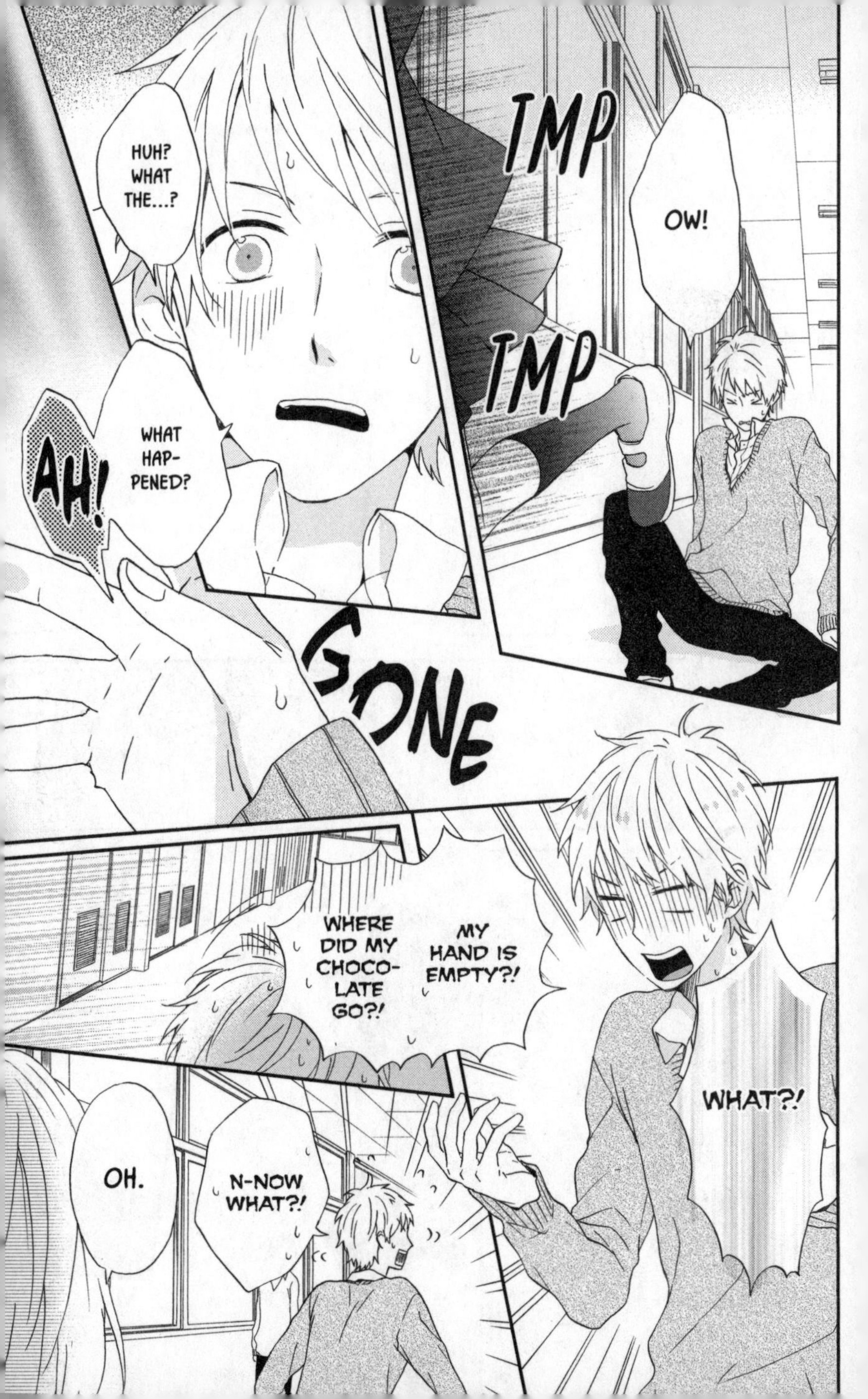
TMP
TMP
OW!
HUH? WHAT THE...?
WHAT HAP-PENED?
AH!
GONE
WHAT?!
MY HAND IS EMPTY?!
WHERE DID MY CHOCO-LATE GO?!
N-NOW WHAT?!
OH.

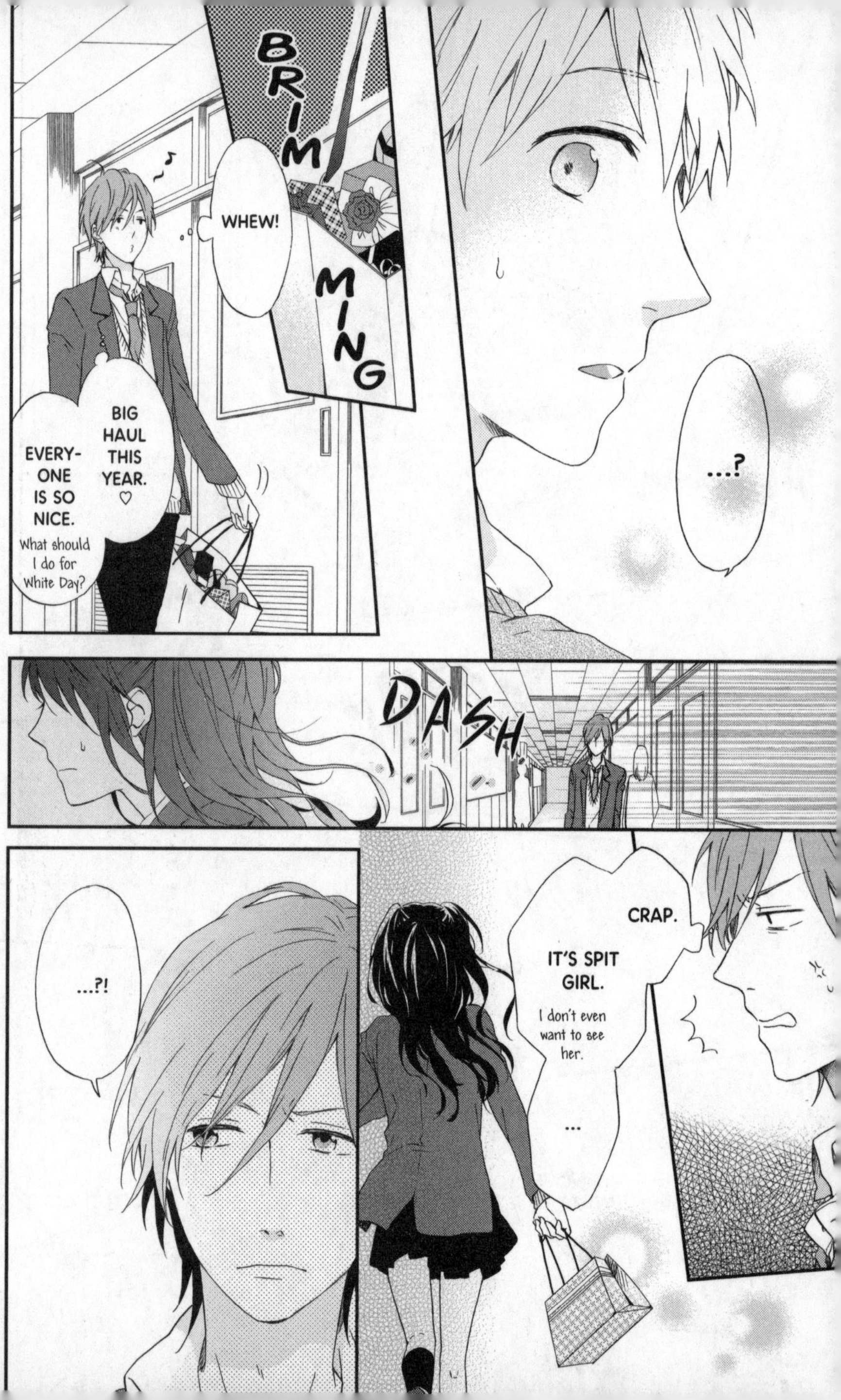
...?
BRIM MING
WHEW!
BIG HAUL THIS YEAR. ♡
EVERY-ONE IS SO NICE.
What should I do for White Day?
DASH
CRAP.
IT'S SPIT GIRL.
I don't even want to see her.
...
...?!

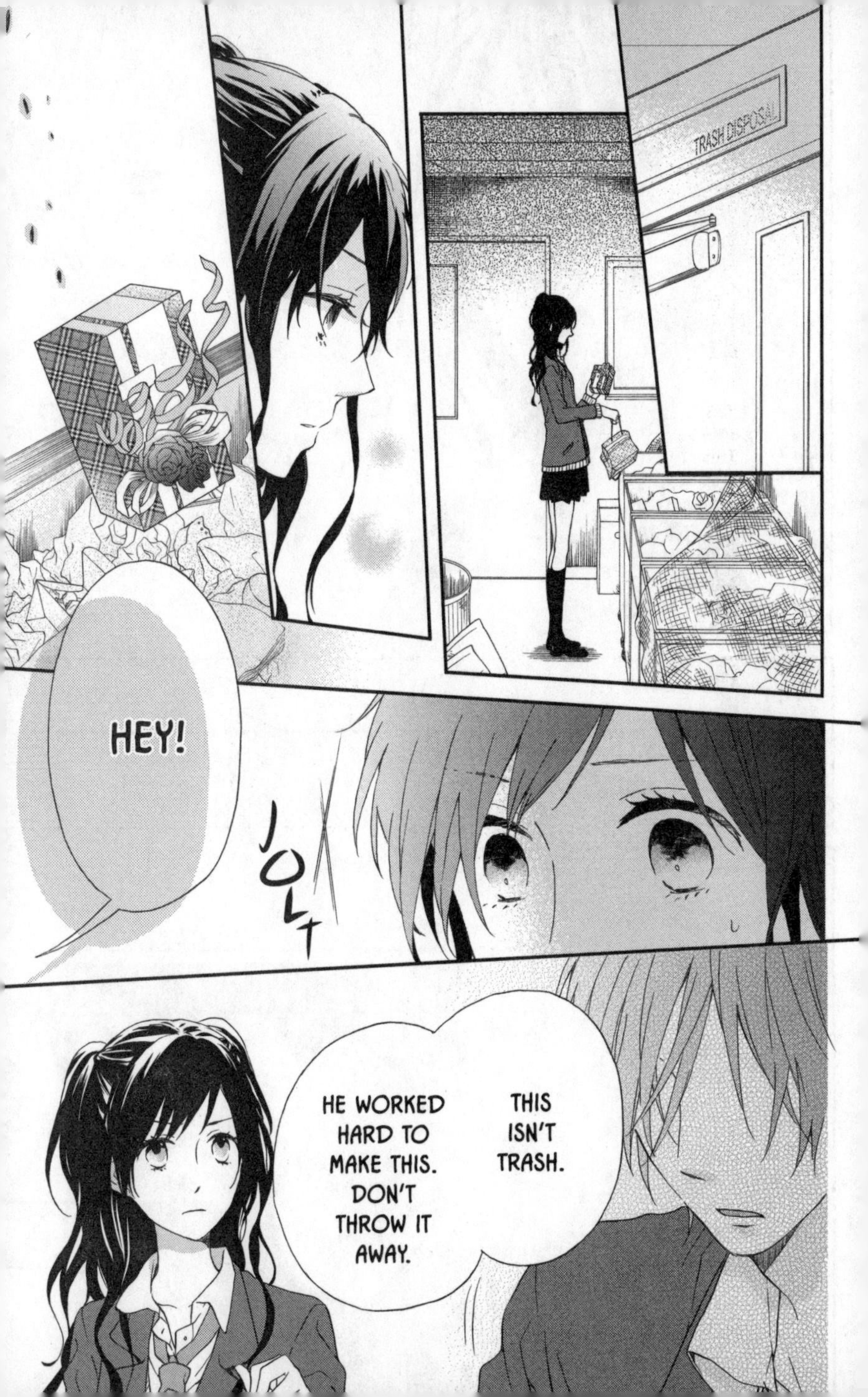
TRASH DISPOSAL
HEY!
JOLT
THIS ISN'T TRASH.
HE WORKED HARD TO MAKE THIS. DON'T THROW IT AWAY.

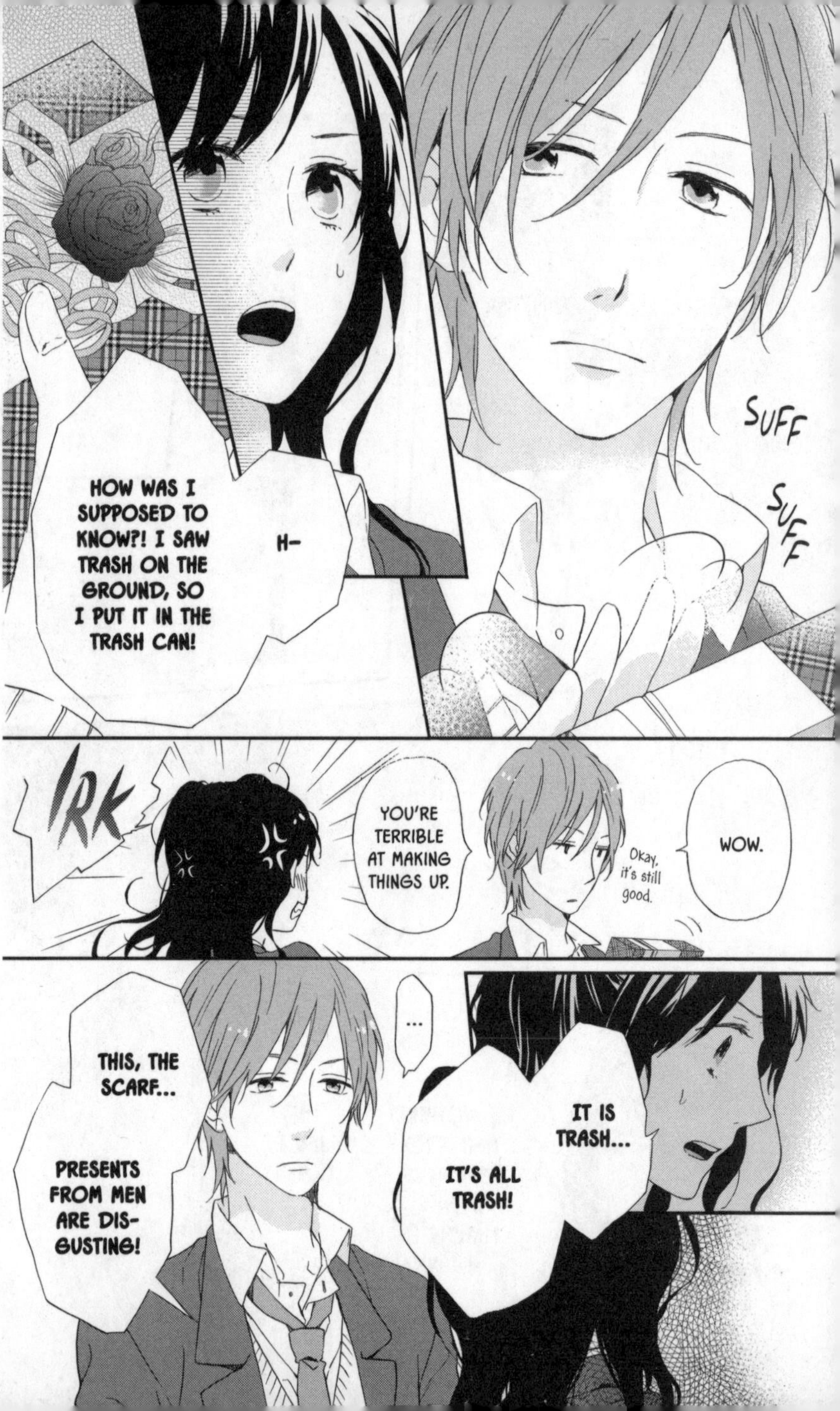
SUFF
SUFF
H-
HOW WAS I SUPPOSED TO KNOW?! I SAW TRASH ON THE GROUND, SO I PUT IT IN THE TRASH CAN!
WOW.
Okay, it's still good.
YOU'RE TERRIBLE AT MAKING THINGS UP.
IRK
IT IS TRASH...
IT'S ALL TRASH!
...
THIS, THE SCARF...
PRESENTS FROM MEN ARE DIS-GUSTING!

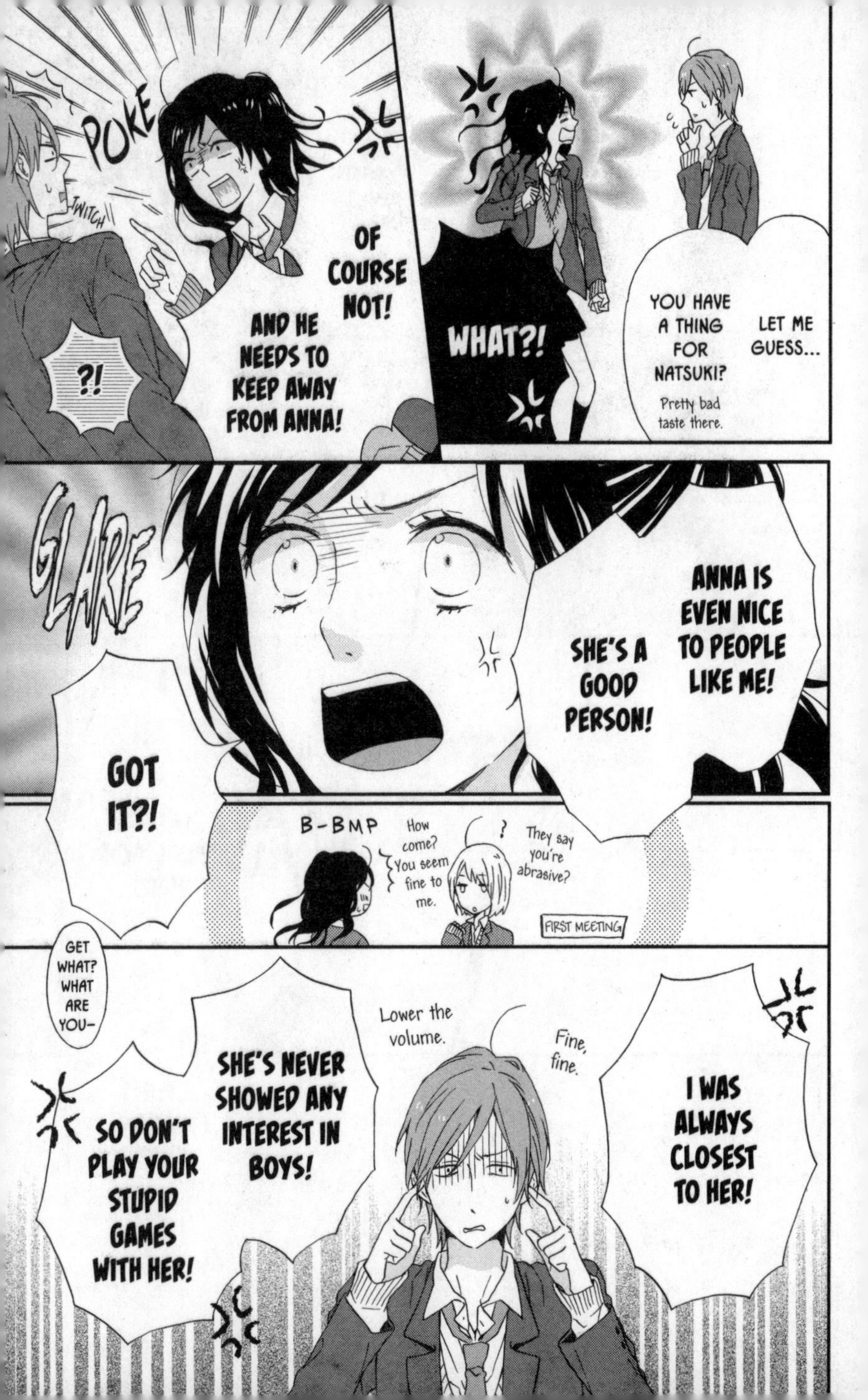
LET ME GUESS...
YOU HAVE A THING FOR NATSUKI?
Pretty bad taste there.
WHAT?!
OF COURSE NOT!
AND HE NEEDS TO KEEP AWAY FROM ANNA!
POKE
TWITCH
?!
GLARE
ANNA IS EVEN NICE TO PEOPLE LIKE ME!
SHE'S A GOOD PERSON!
GOT IT?!
They say you're abrasive?
How come? You seem fine to me.
B-BMP
FIRST MEETING
GET WHAT? WHAT ARE YOU-
I WAS ALWAYS CLOSEST TO HER!
Fine, fine.
Lower the volume.
SHE'S NEVER SHOWED ANY INTEREST IN BOYS!
SO DON'T PLAY YOUR STUPID GAMES WITH HER!

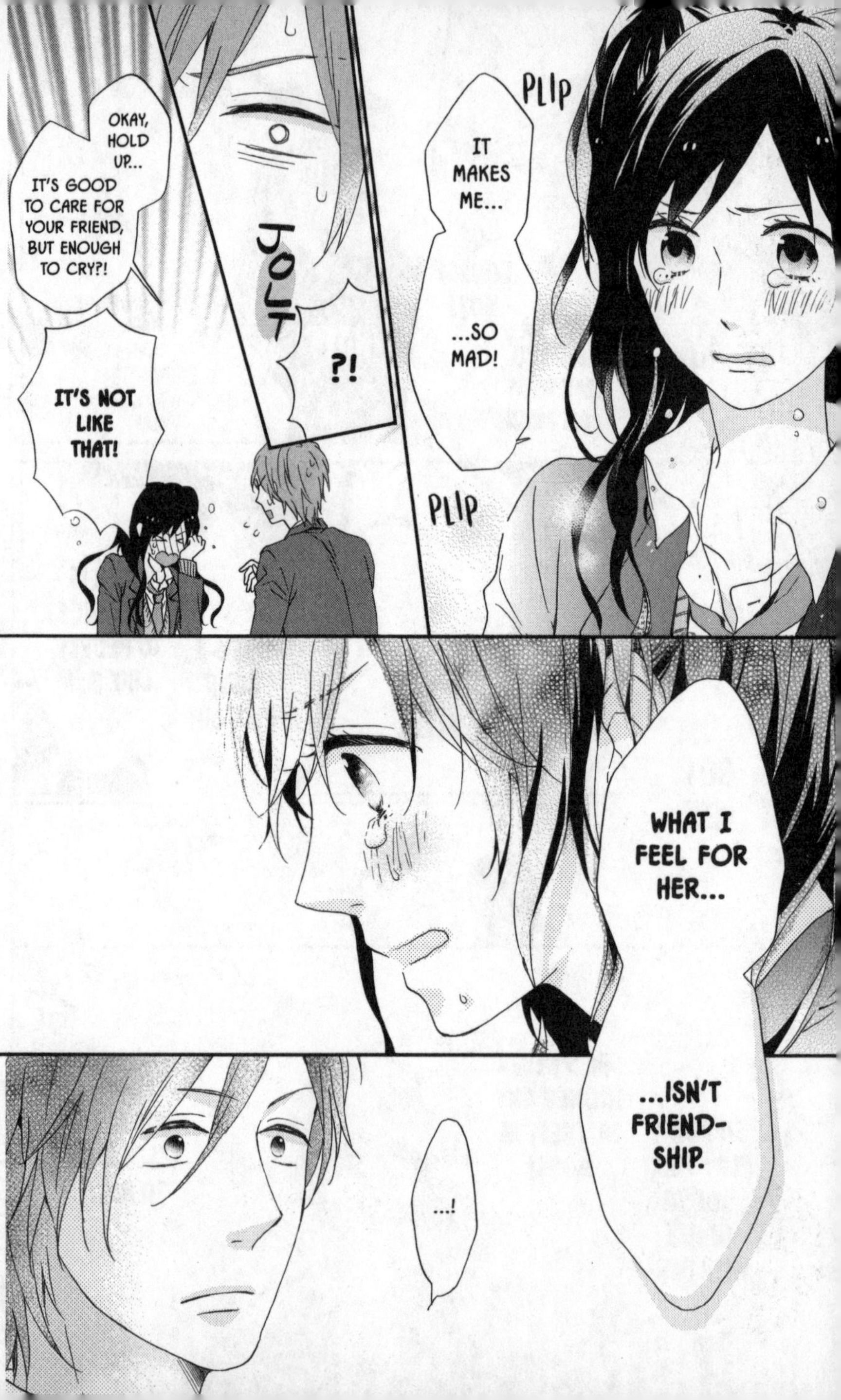
PLIP
IT MAKES ME...
...SO MAD!
PLIP
JOLT
?!
OKAY, HOLD UP... IT'S GOOD TO CARE FOR YOUR FRIEND, BUT ENOUGH TO CRY?!
IT'S NOT LIKE THAT!
WHAT I FEEL FOR HER...
...ISN'T FRIENDSHIP.
...!

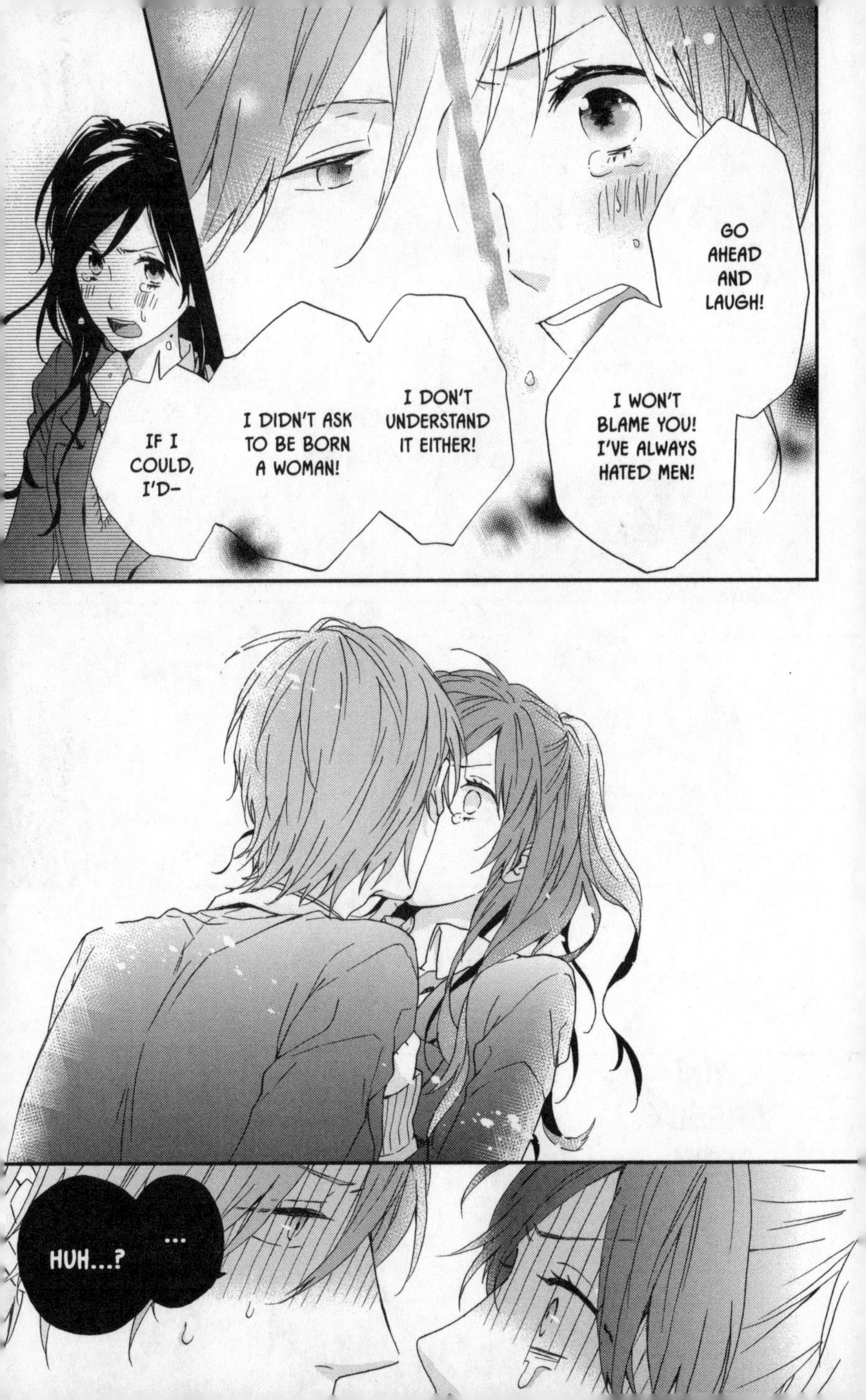
GO AHEAD AND LAUGH!
I WON'T BLAME YOU! I'VE ALWAYS HATED MEN!
I DON'T UNDERSTAND IT EITHER!
I DIDN'T ASK TO BE BORN A WOMAN!
IF I COULD, I'D-
...
HUH...?

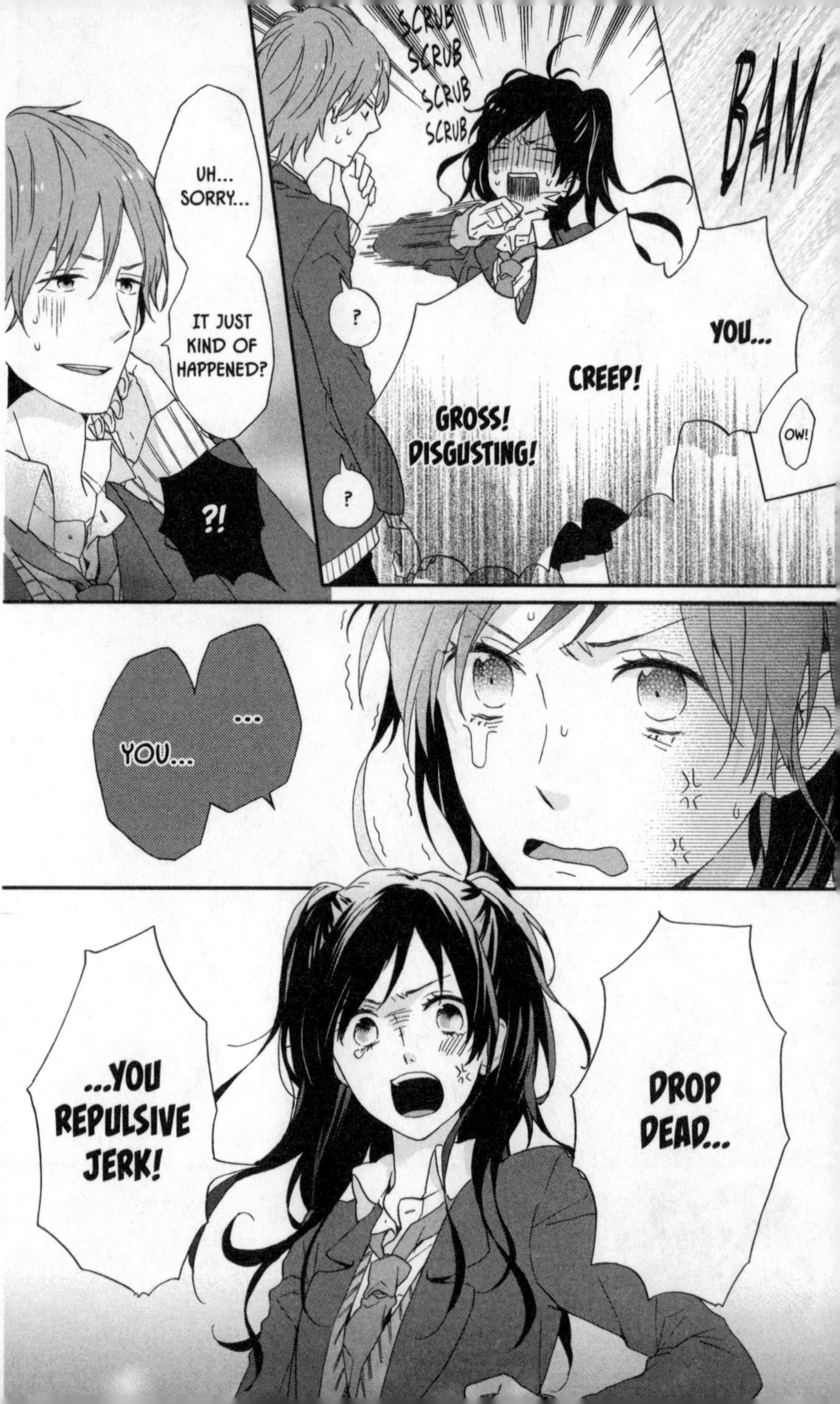
BAM
SCRUB SCRUB SCRUB SCRUB
YOU...
CREEP!
OW!
?
GROSS! DISGUSTING!
?
UH... SORRY...
IT JUST KIND OF HAPPENED?
?!
...
YOU...
DROP DEAD...
...YOU REPULSIVE JERK!

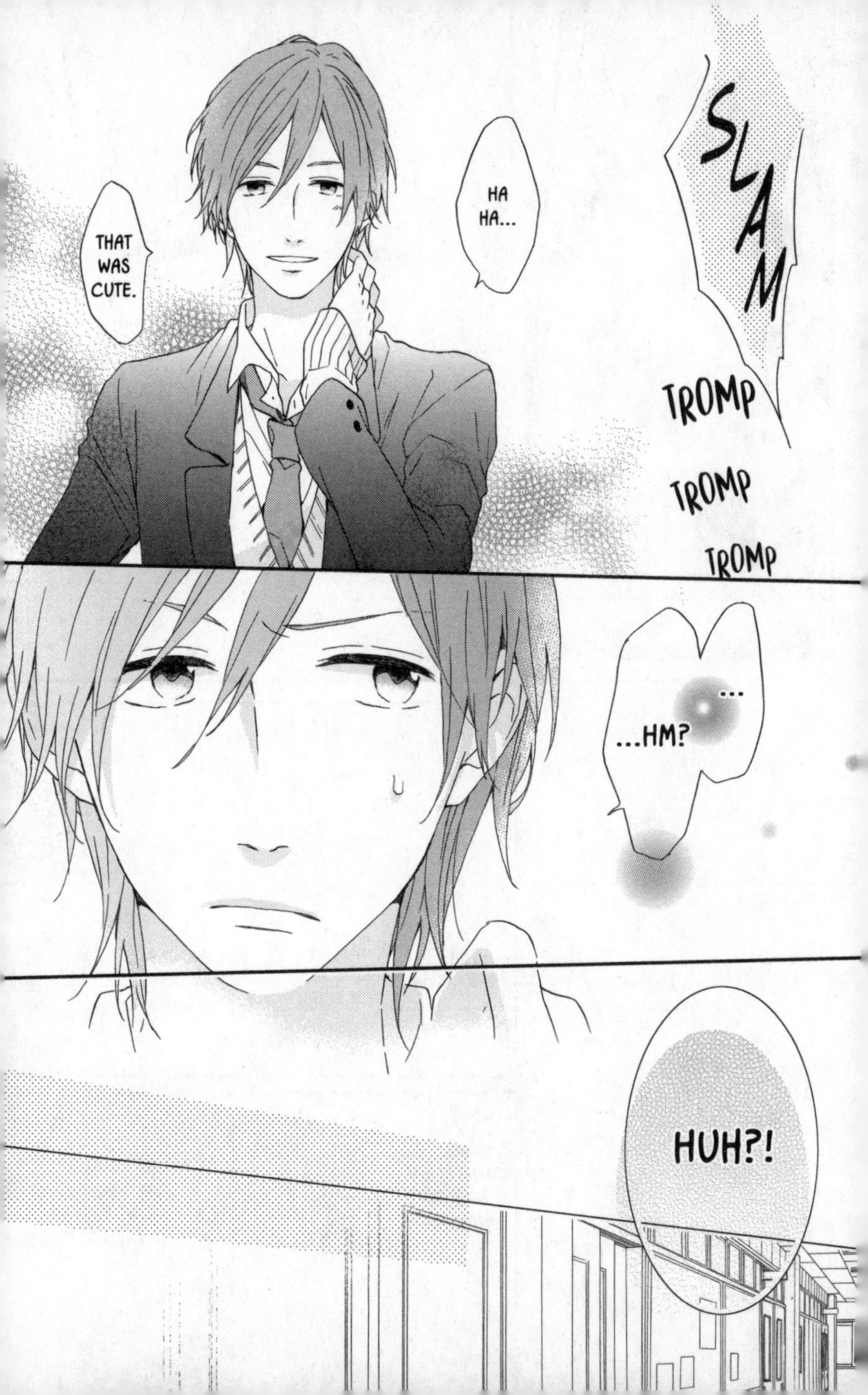
SLAM
TROMP
TROMP
TROMP
HA HA...
THAT WAS CUTE.
...
...HM?
HUH?!

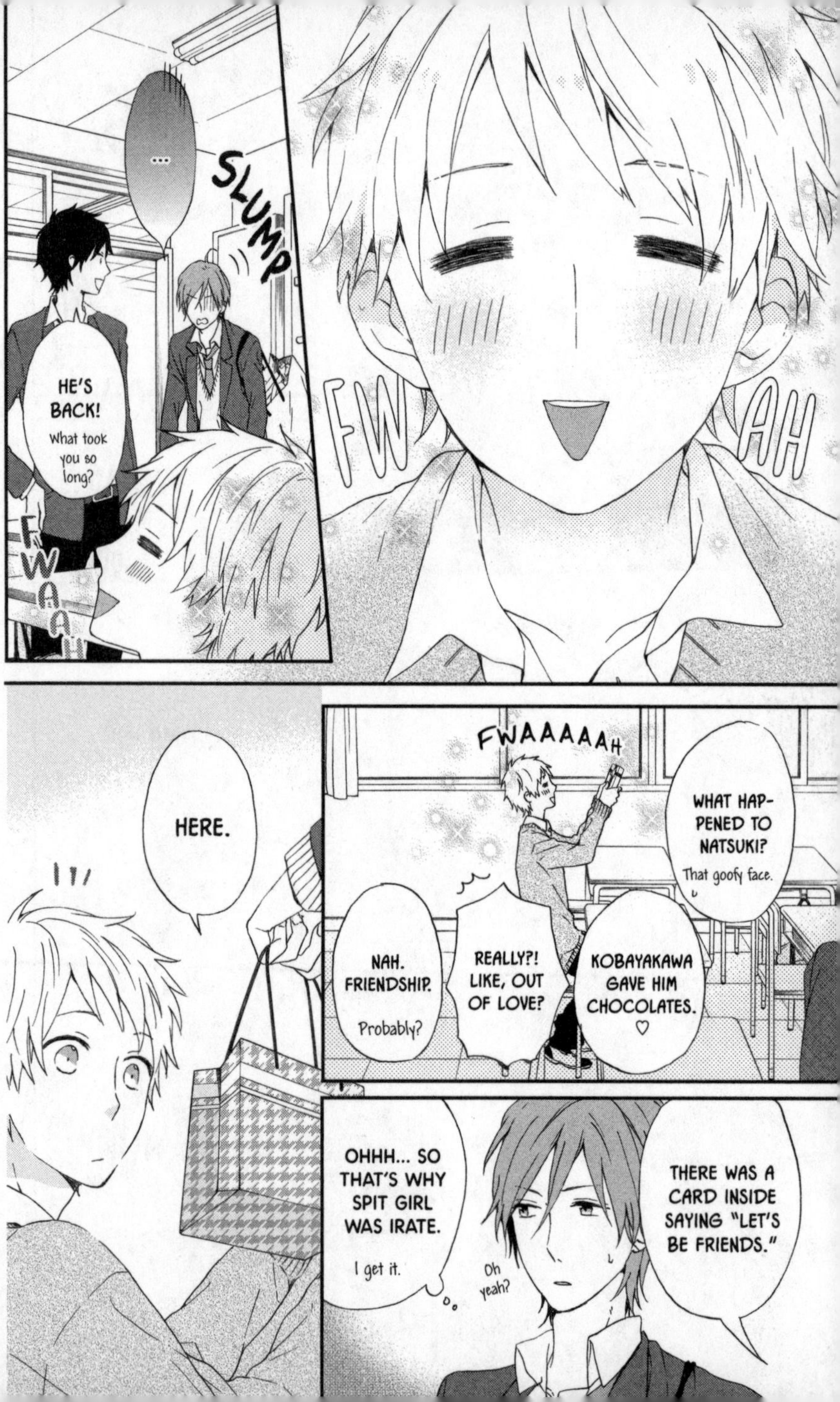
FW AH
SLUMP
...
HE'S BACK! What took you so long?
FWAAAH
FWAAAAAH
WHAT HAP-PENED TO NATSUKI? That goofy face.
KOBAYAKAWA GAVE HIM CHOCOLATES. ♡
REALLY?! LIKE, OUT OF LOVE?
NAH. FRIENDSHIP. Probably?
THERE WAS A CARD INSIDE SAYING "LET'S BE FRIENDS."
Oh yeah?
OHHH... SO THAT'S WHY SPIT GIRL WAS IRATE.
I get it.
HERE.

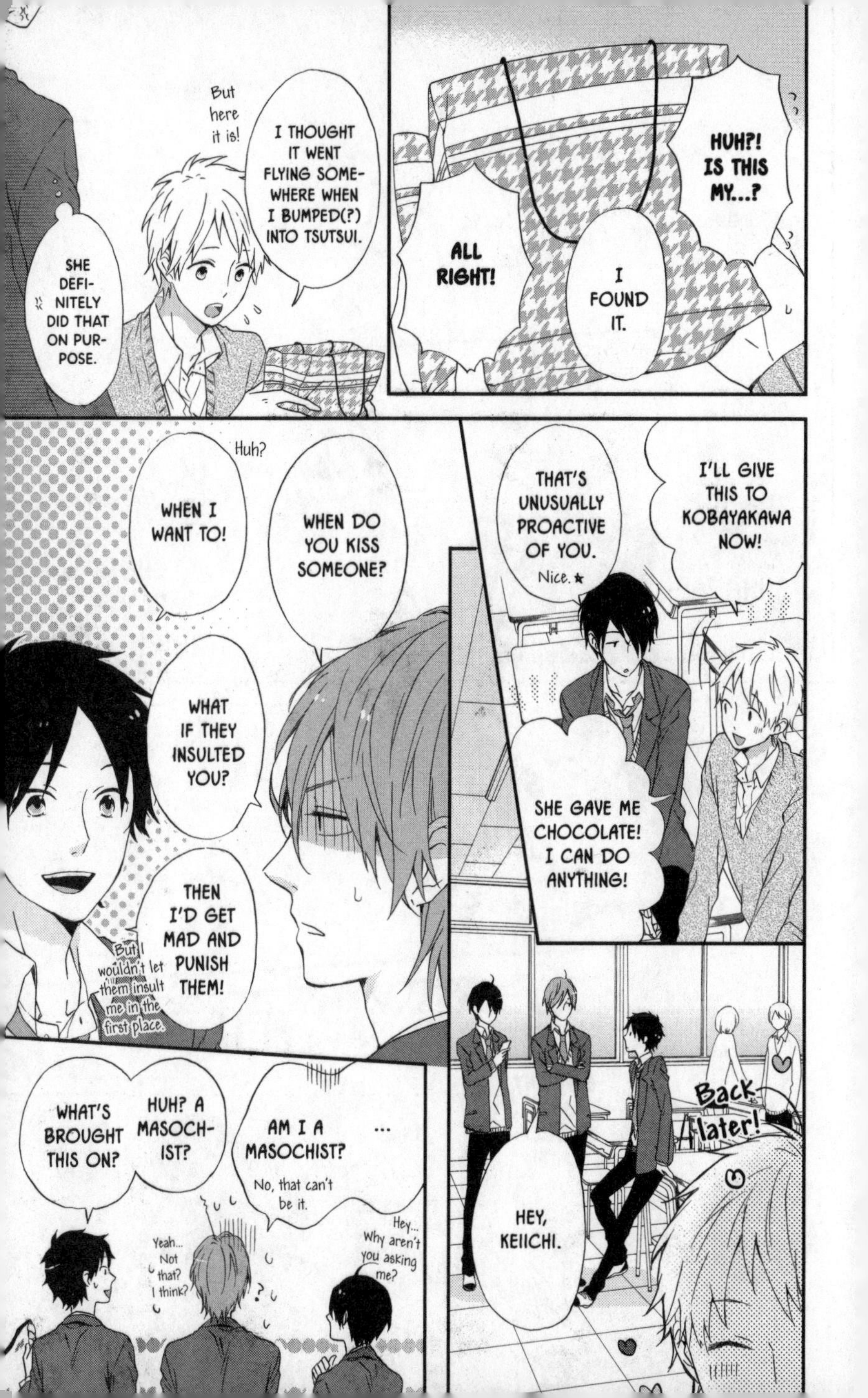
HUH?! IS THIS MY...?
I FOUND IT.
ALL RIGHT!
I THOUGHT IT WENT FLYING SOME-WHERE WHEN I BUMPED(?) INTO TSUTSUI.
But here it is!
SHE DEFI-NITELY DID THAT ON PUR-POSE.
I'LL GIVE THIS TO KOBAYAKAWA NOW!
THAT'S UNUSUALLY PROACTIVE OF YOU.
Nice. ★
SHE GAVE ME CHOCOLATE! I CAN DO ANYTHING!
Back later!
HEY, KEIICHI.
WHEN DO YOU KISS SOMEONE?
Huh?
WHEN I WANT TO!
WHAT IF THEY INSULTED YOU?
THEN I'D GET MAD AND PUNISH THEM!
But I wouldn't let them insult me in the first place.
...
AM I A MASOCHIST?
No, that can't be it.
HUH? A MASOCH-IST?
WHAT'S BROUGHT THIS ON?
Hey... Why aren't you asking me?
Yeah... Not that? I think?

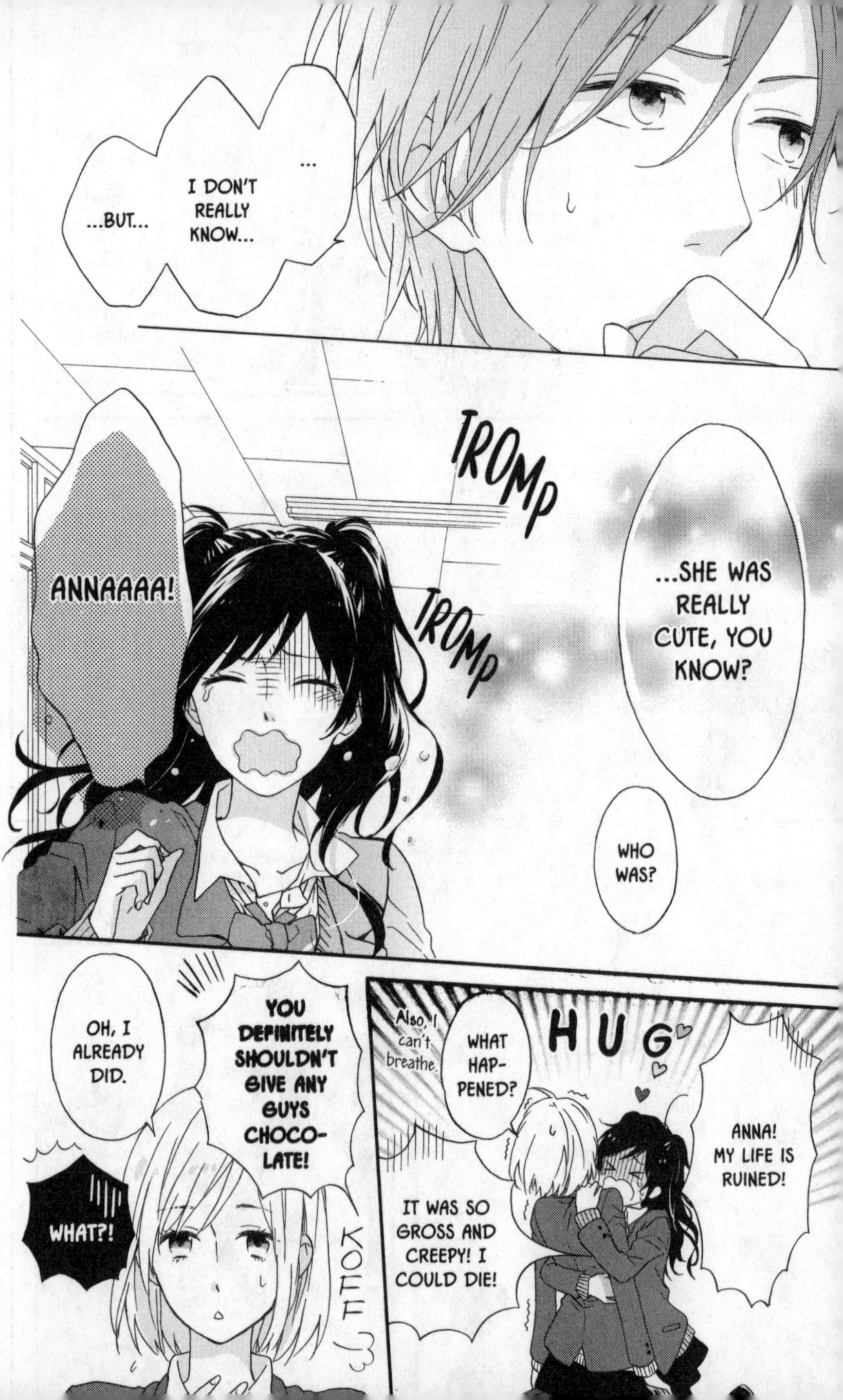
...
I DON'T REALLY KNOW...
...BUT...
...SHE WAS REALLY CUTE, YOU KNOW?
WHO WAS?
TROMP
TROMP
ANNAAAA!
ANNA! MY LIFE IS RUINED!
HUG
WHAT HAP-PENED?
Also, I can't breathe.
IT WAS SO GROSS AND CREEPY! I COULD DIE!
YOU DEFINITELY SHOULDN'T GIVE ANY GUYS CHOCO-LATE!
OH, I ALREADY DID.
KOFF
WHAT?!

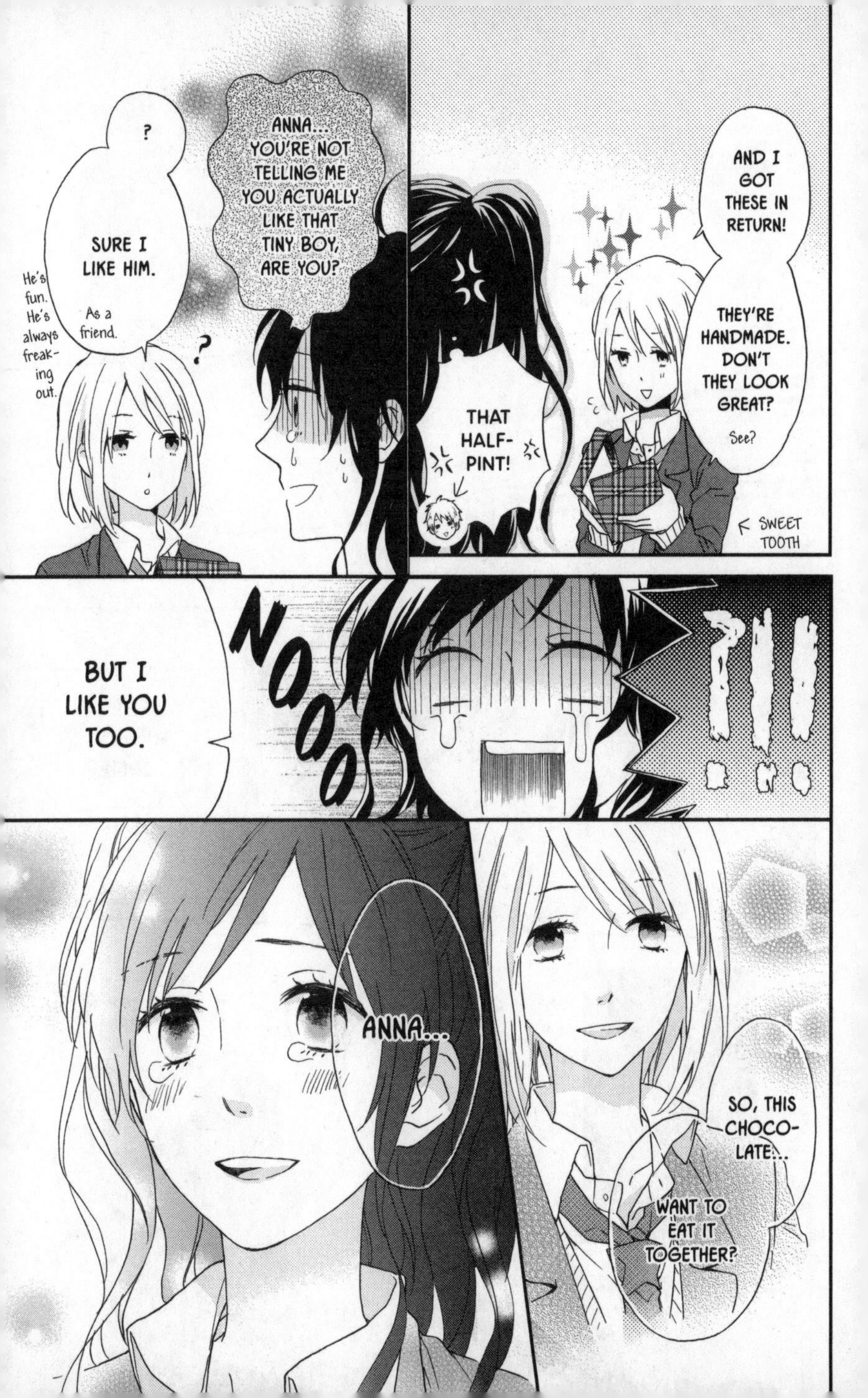
AND I GOT THESE IN RETURN!
THEY'RE HANDMADE. DON'T THEY LOOK GREAT?
See?
SWEET TOOTH
THAT HALF-PINT!
ANNA... YOU'RE NOT TELLING ME YOU ACTUALLY LIKE THAT TINY BOY, ARE YOU?
?
SURE I LIKE HIM.
As a friend.
He's fun. He's always freak-ing out.
?
NOOOO
BUT I LIKE YOU TOO.
SO, THIS CHOCO-LATE...
WANT TO EAT IT TOGETHER?
ANNA...

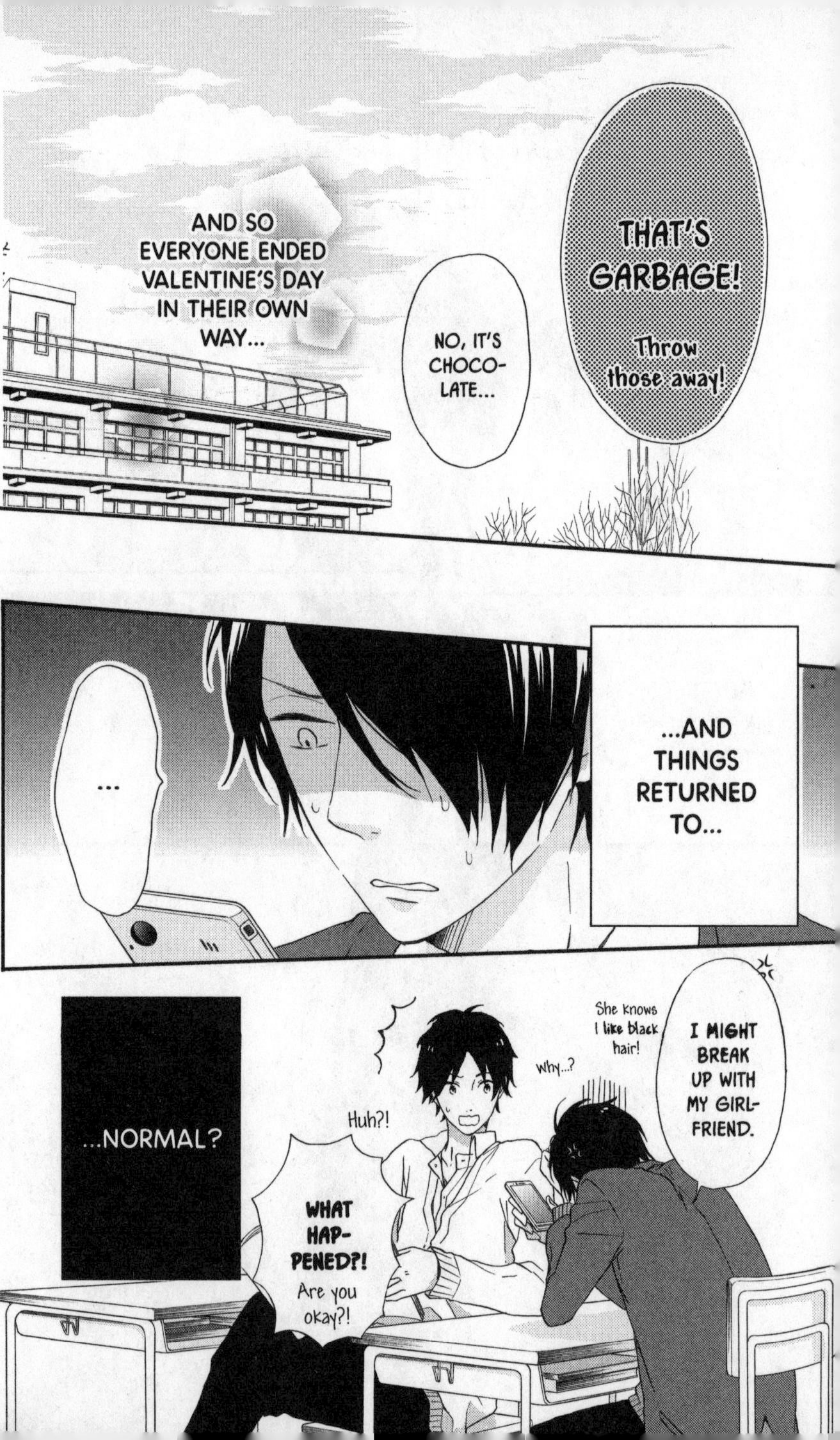
THAT'S GARBAGE!
Throw those away!
NO, IT'S CHOCO-LATE...
AND SO EVERYONE ENDED VALENTINE'S DAY IN THEIR OWN WAY...
...AND THINGS RETURNED TO...
...
I MIGHT BREAK UP WITH MY GIRL-FRIEND.
She knows I like black hair!
Why...?
...NORMAL?
Huh?!
WHAT HAP-PENED?!
Are you okay?!

Rainbow Days

Chapter 3

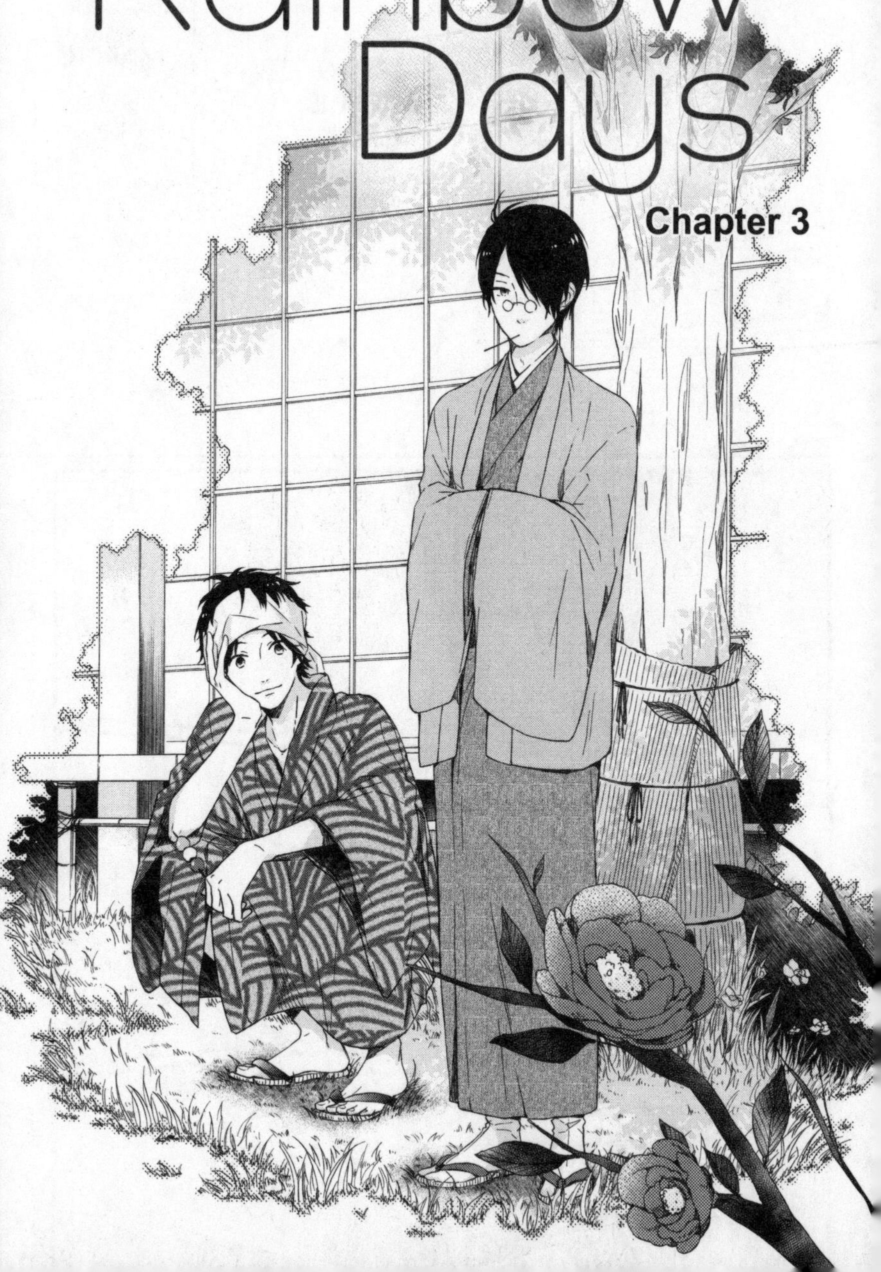

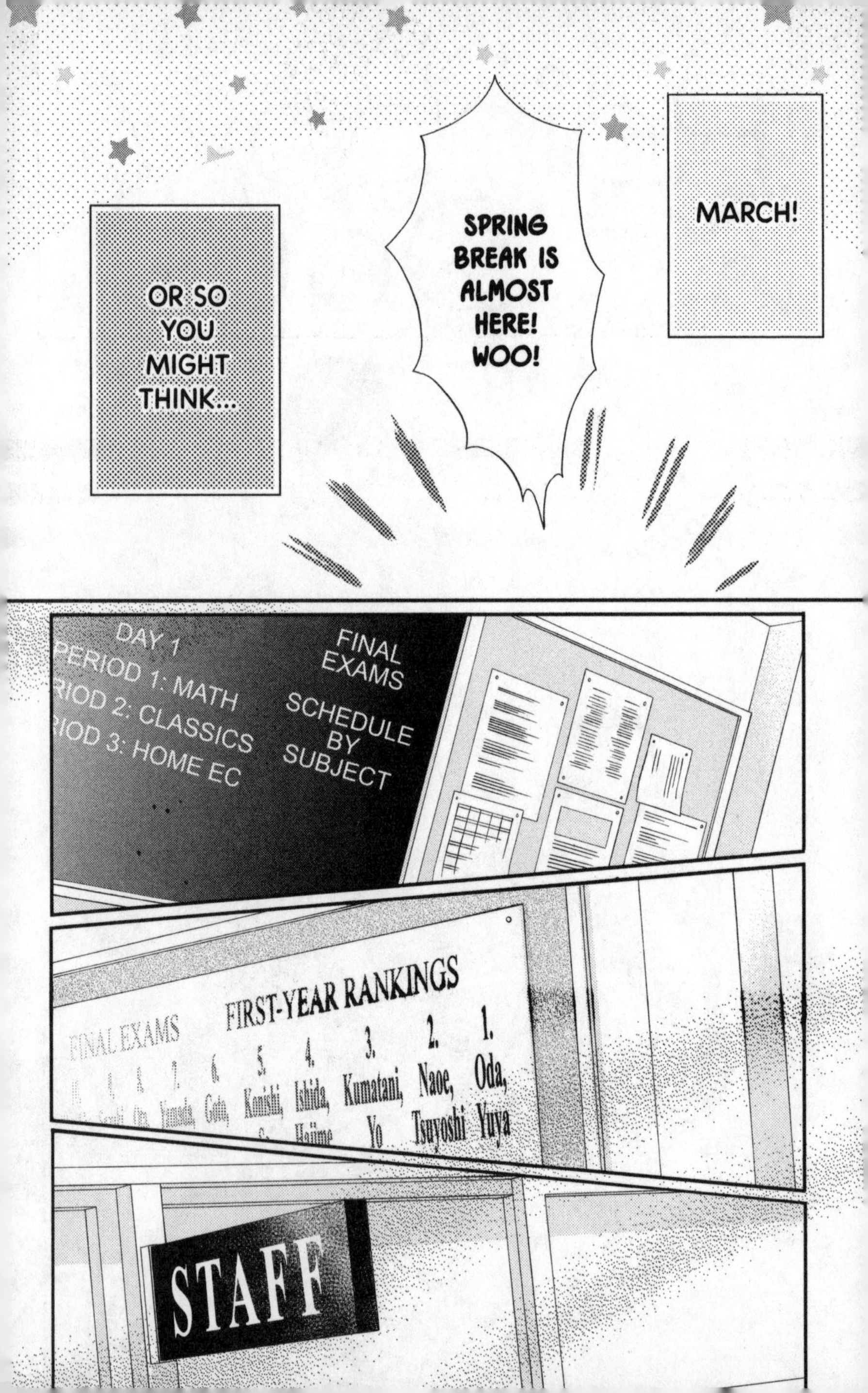
MARCH!
SPRING BREAK IS ALMOST HERE! WOO!
OR SO YOU MIGHT THINK...
FINAL EXAMS
SCHEDULE BY SUBJECT
DAY 1
PERIOD 1: MATH
RIOD 2: CLASSICS
RIOD 3: HOME EC
FIRST-YEAR RANKINGS
FINAL EXAMS
1. Oda, Yuya
2. Naoe, Tsuyoshi
3. Kumatani, Yo
4. Ishida, Hajime
5. Konishi,
6. Goto,
7. Yamada
STAFF

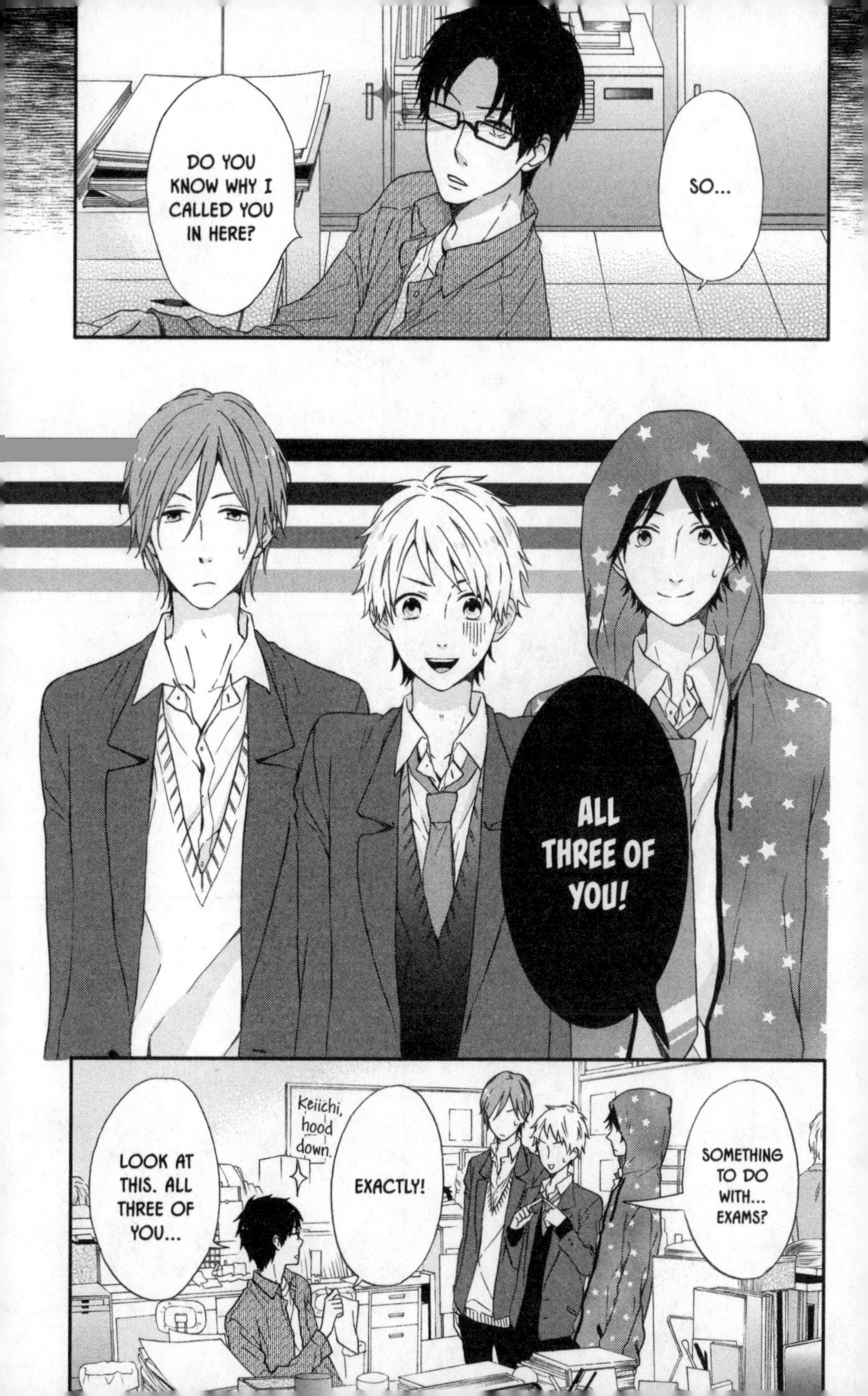
SO...
DO YOU KNOW WHY I CALLED YOU IN HERE?
ALL THREE OF YOU!
SOMETHING TO DO WITH... EXAMS?
EXACTLY!
Keiichi, hood down.
LOOK AT THIS. ALL THREE OF YOU...

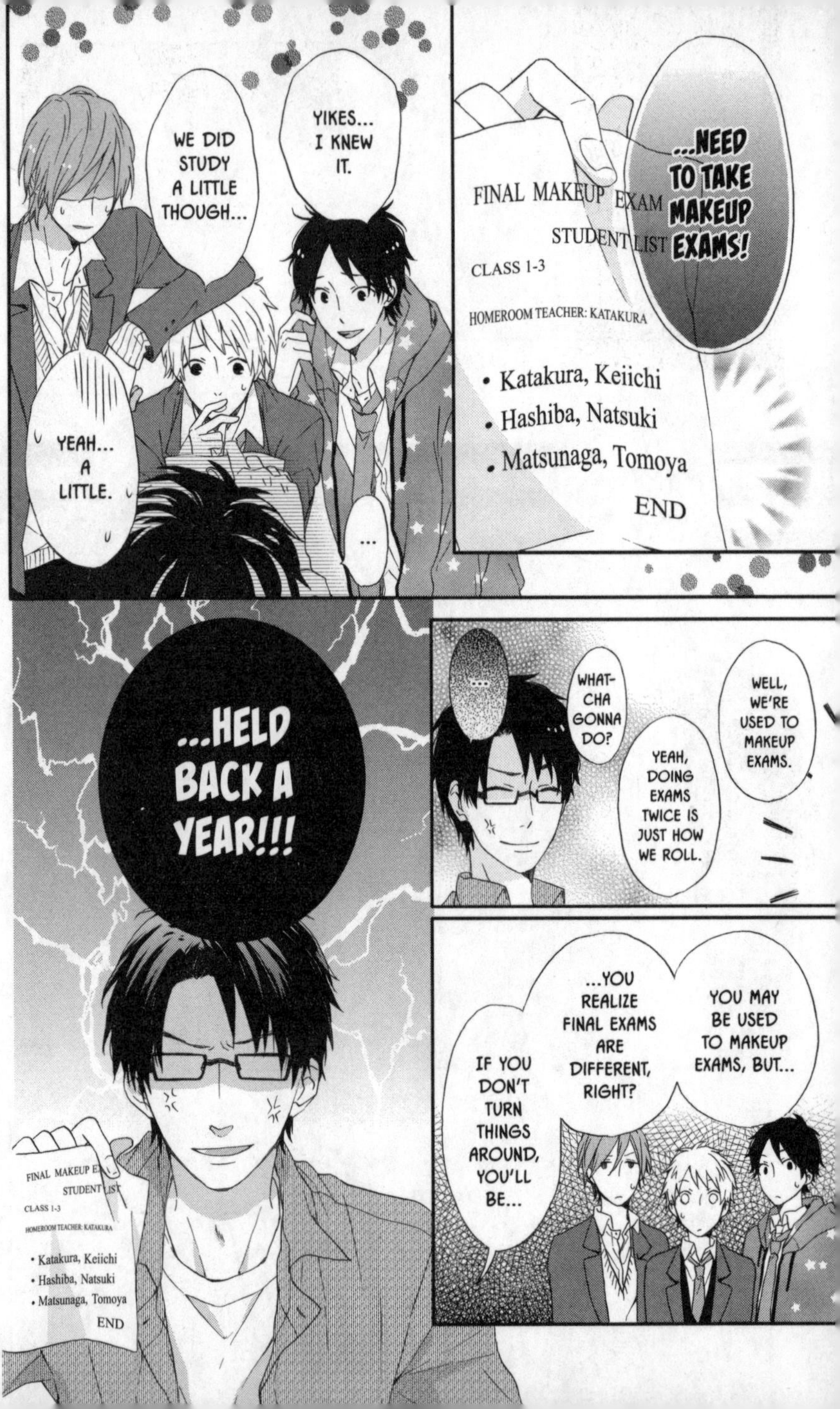
FINAL MAKEUP EXAM
STUDENT LIST
CLASS 1-3
HOMEROOM TEACHER: KATAKURA
• Katakura, Keiichi
• Hashiba, Natsuki
• Matsunaga, Tomoya
END
...NEED TO TAKE MAKEUP EXAMS!
YIKES... I KNEW IT.
WE DID STUDY A LITTLE THOUGH...
...
YEAH... A LITTLE.
WELL, WE'RE USED TO MAKEUP EXAMS.
YEAH, DOING EXAMS TWICE IS JUST HOW WE ROLL.
WHAT-CHA GONNA DO?
...
YOU MAY BE USED TO MAKEUP EXAMS, BUT...
...YOU REALIZE FINAL EXAMS ARE DIFFERENT, RIGHT?
IF YOU DON'T TURN THINGS AROUND, YOU'LL BE...
...HELD BACK A YEAR!!!
FINAL MAKEUP EX
STUDENT LIST
CLASS 1-3
HOMEROOM TEACHER: KATAKURA
• Katakura, Keiichi
• Hashiba, Natsuki
• Matsunaga, Tomoya
END

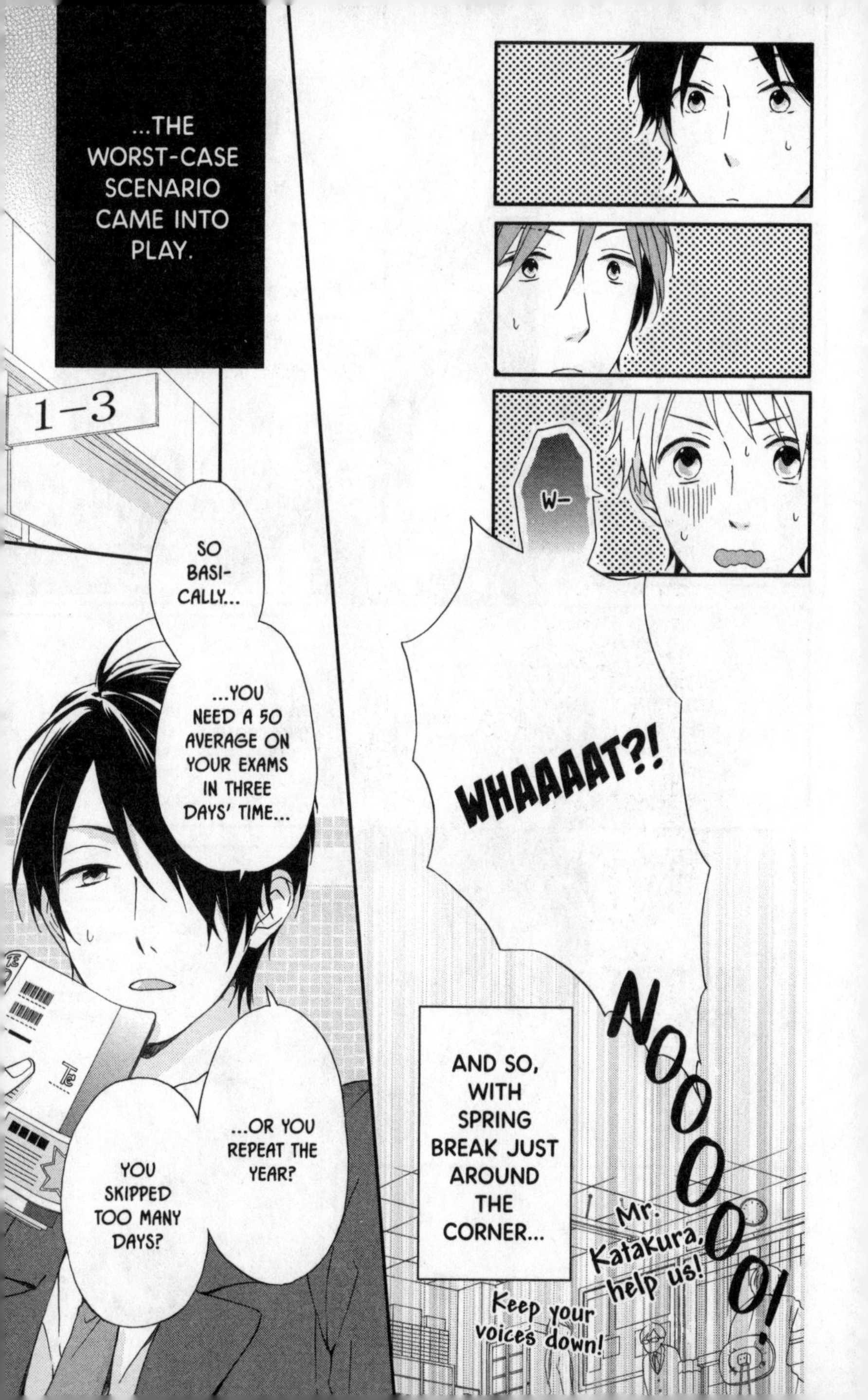
W-
WHAAAAT?!
NOOOOOO!
AND SO, WITH SPRING BREAK JUST AROUND THE CORNER...
Mr. Katakura, help us!
Keep your voices down!
...THE WORST-CASE SCENARIO CAME INTO PLAY.
1-3
SO BASICALLY...
...YOU NEED A 50 AVERAGE ON YOUR EXAMS IN THREE DAYS' TIME...
...OR YOU REPEAT THE YEAR?
YOU SKIPPED TOO MANY DAYS?

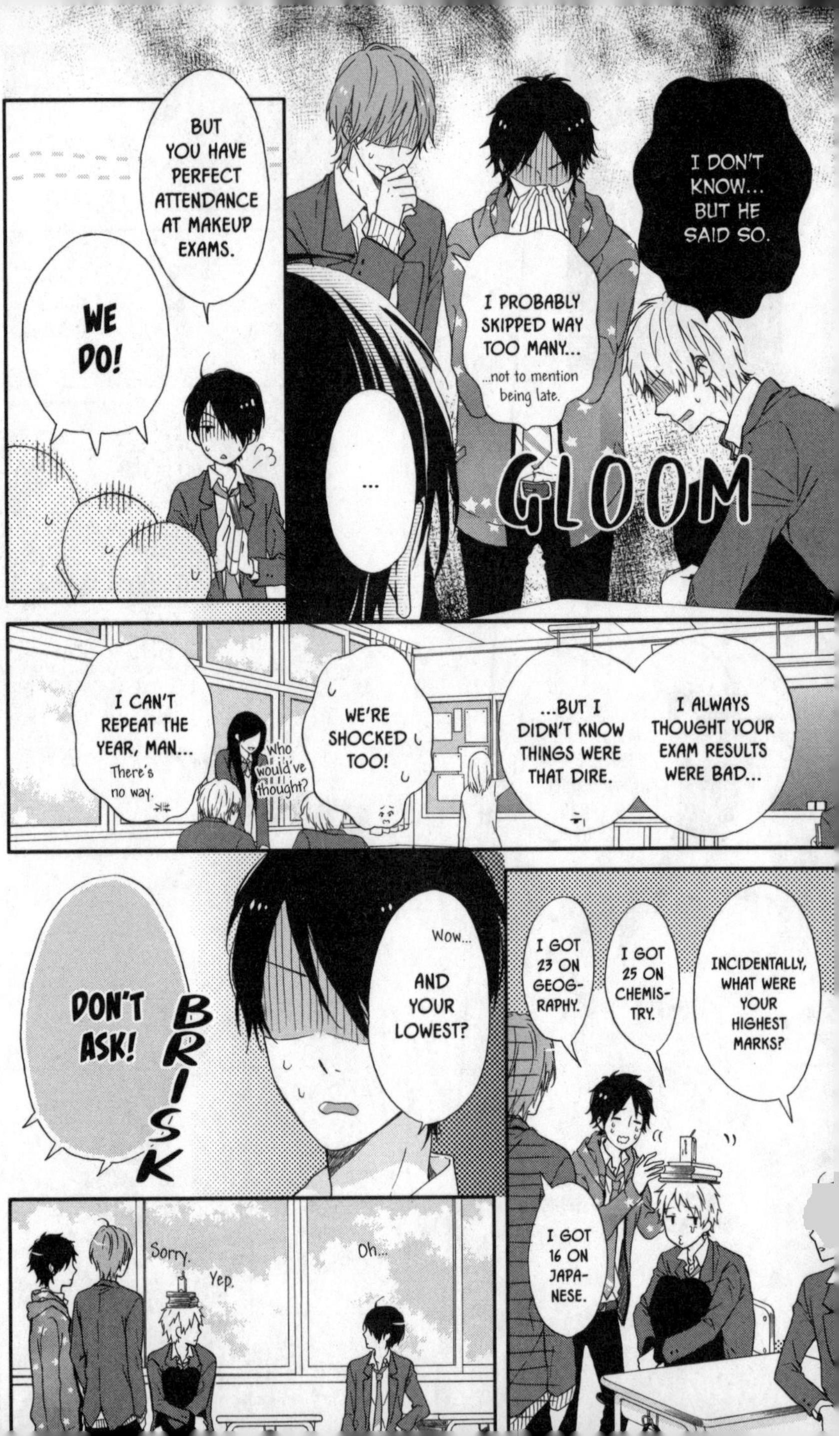
I DON'T KNOW... BUT HE SAID SO.
I PROBABLY SKIPPED WAY TOO MANY...
...not to mention being late.
GLOOM
...
BUT YOU HAVE PERFECT ATTENDANCE AT MAKEUP EXAMS.
WE DO!
I ALWAYS THOUGHT YOUR EXAM RESULTS WERE BAD...
...BUT I DIDN'T KNOW THINGS WERE THAT DIRE.
WE'RE SHOCKED TOO!
Who would've thought?
I CAN'T REPEAT THE YEAR, MAN...
There's no way.
INCIDENTALLY, WHAT WERE YOUR HIGHEST MARKS?
I GOT 25 ON CHEMISTRY.
I GOT 23 ON GEOGRAPHY.
I GOT 16 ON JAPANESE.
Wow...
AND YOUR LOWEST?
DON'T ASK!
BRISK
Oh...
Yep.
Sorry.

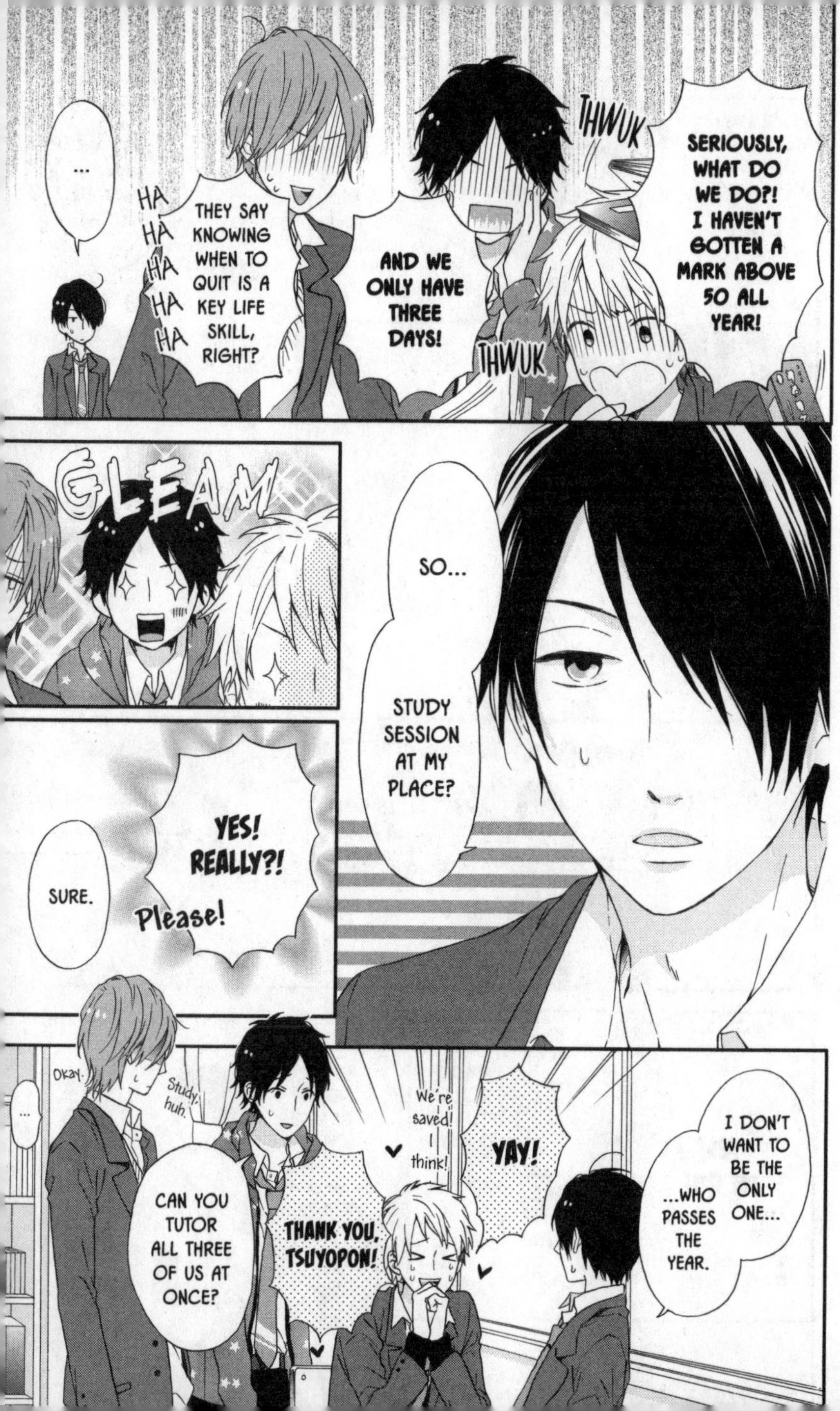
SERIOUSLY, WHAT DO WE DO?! I HAVEN'T GOTTEN A MARK ABOVE 50 ALL YEAR!
THWUK
AND WE ONLY HAVE THREE DAYS!
THWUK
THEY SAY KNOWING WHEN TO QUIT IS A KEY LIFE SKILL, RIGHT?
HA HA HA HA HA
...
SO...
STUDY SESSION AT MY PLACE?
GLEAM
YES! REALLY?!
Please!
SURE.
I DON'T WANT TO BE THE ONLY ONE...
...WHO PASSES THE YEAR.
YAY!
We're saved! I think!
THANK YOU, TSUYOPON!
CAN YOU TUTOR ALL THREE OF US AT ONCE?
Study, huh.
Okay.
...

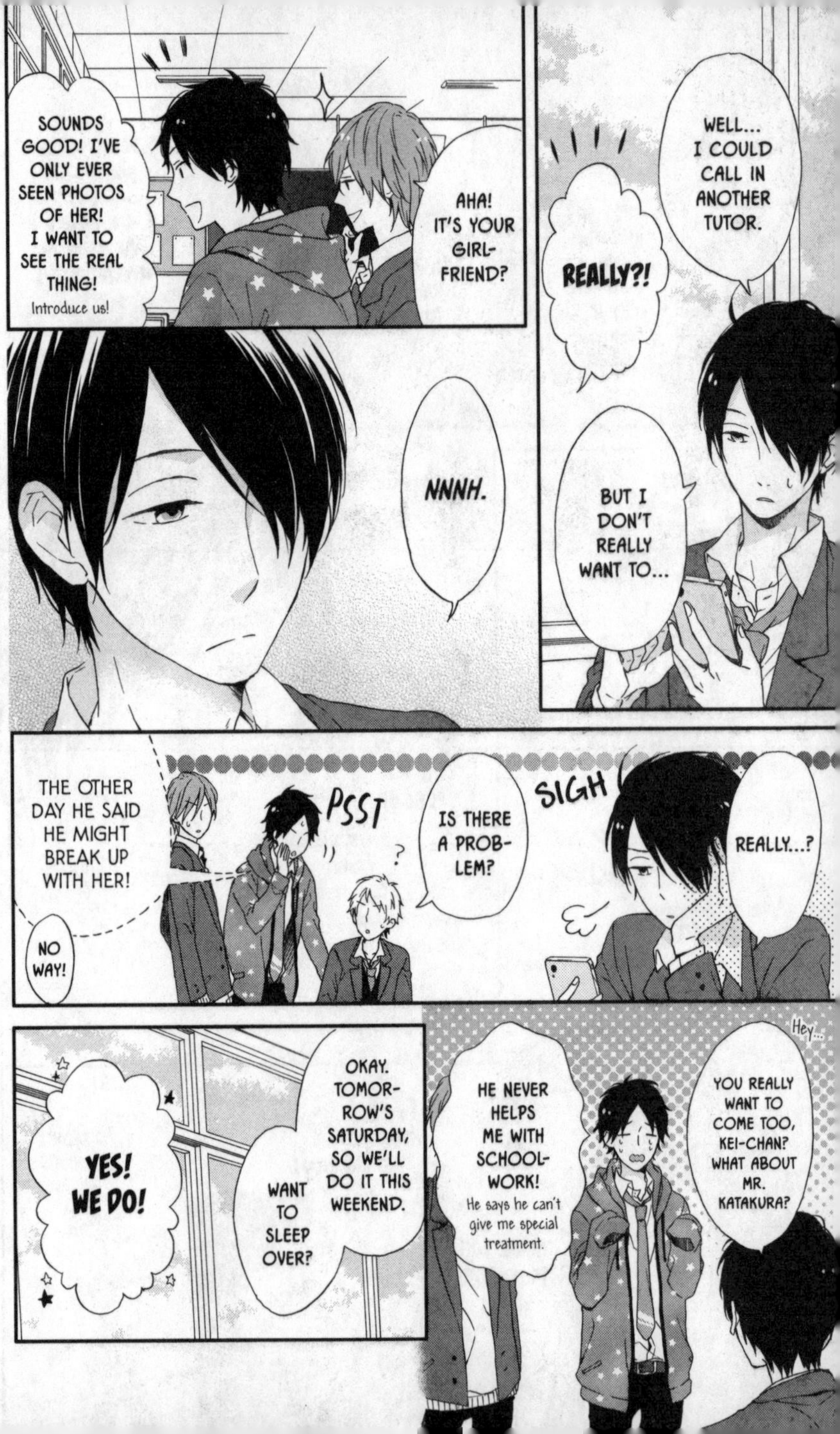
WELL... I COULD CALL IN ANOTHER TUTOR.
REALLY?!
BUT I DON'T REALLY WANT TO...
AHA! IT'S YOUR GIRL-FRIEND?
SOUNDS GOOD! I'VE ONLY EVER SEEN PHOTOS OF HER! I WANT TO SEE THE REAL THING!
Introduce us!
NNNH.
REALLY...?
SIGH
IS THERE A PROB-LEM?
PSST
THE OTHER DAY HE SAID HE MIGHT BREAK UP WITH HER!
NO WAY!
Hey...
YOU REALLY WANT TO COME TOO, KEI-CHAN? WHAT ABOUT MR. KATAKURA?
HE NEVER HELPS ME WITH SCHOOL-WORK!
He says he can't give me special treatment.
OKAY. TOMOR-ROW'S SATURDAY, SO WE'LL DO IT THIS WEEKEND.
WANT TO SLEEP OVER?
YES! WE DO!

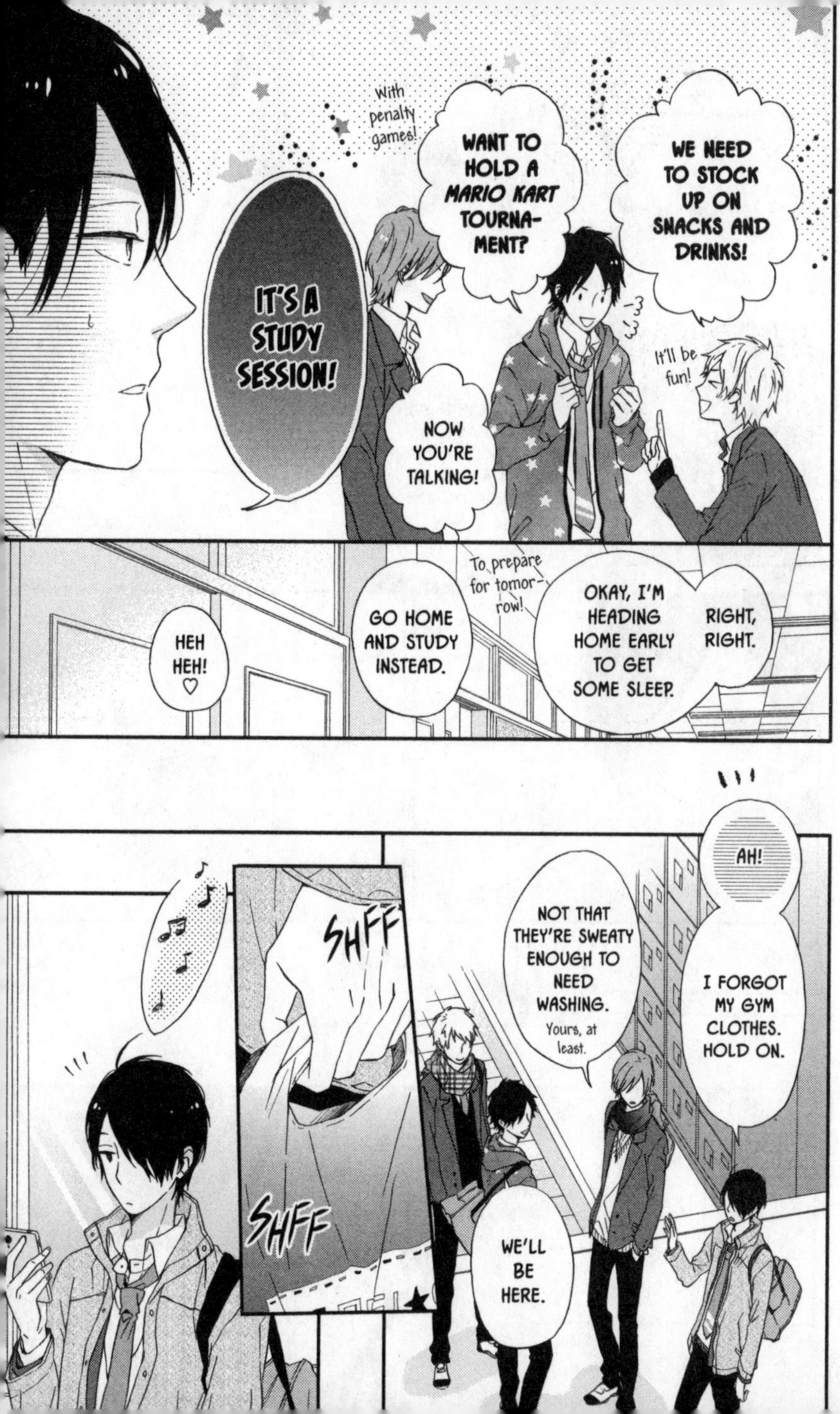
WE NEED TO STOCK UP ON SNACKS AND DRINKS!
It'll be fun!
WANT TO HOLD A MARIO KART TOURNAMENT?
With penalty games!
NOW YOU'RE TALKING!
IT'S A STUDY SESSION!
RIGHT, RIGHT.
OKAY, I'M HEADING HOME EARLY TO GET SOME SLEEP.
To prepare for tomorrow!
GO HOME AND STUDY INSTEAD.
HEH HEH! ♡
AH!
I FORGOT MY GYM CLOTHES. HOLD ON.
NOT THAT THEY'RE SWEATY ENOUGH TO NEED WASHING.
Yours, at least.
WE'LL BE HERE.
SHFF
SHFF

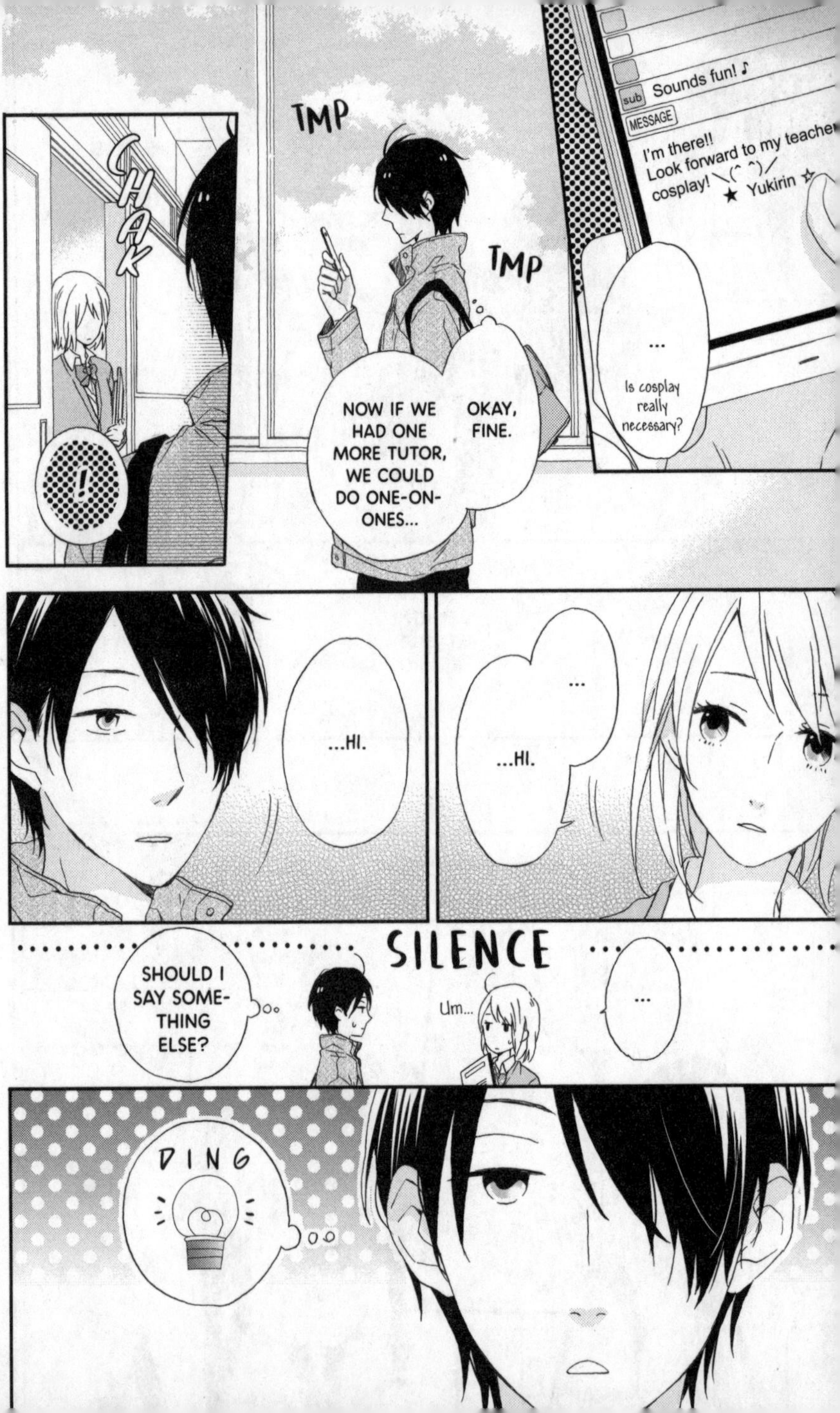

sub
Sounds fun! ♪
MESSAGE
I'm there!! Look forward to my teache cosplay! \(^ ^)/ ★ Yukirin ☆
...
Is cosplay really necessary?
TMP
TMP
OKAY, FINE.
NOW IF WE HAD ONE MORE TUTOR, WE COULD DO ONE-ON-ONES...
CHAK
!
...
...HI.
...HI.
SILENCE
...
Um...
SHOULD I SAY SOME-THING ELSE?
DING

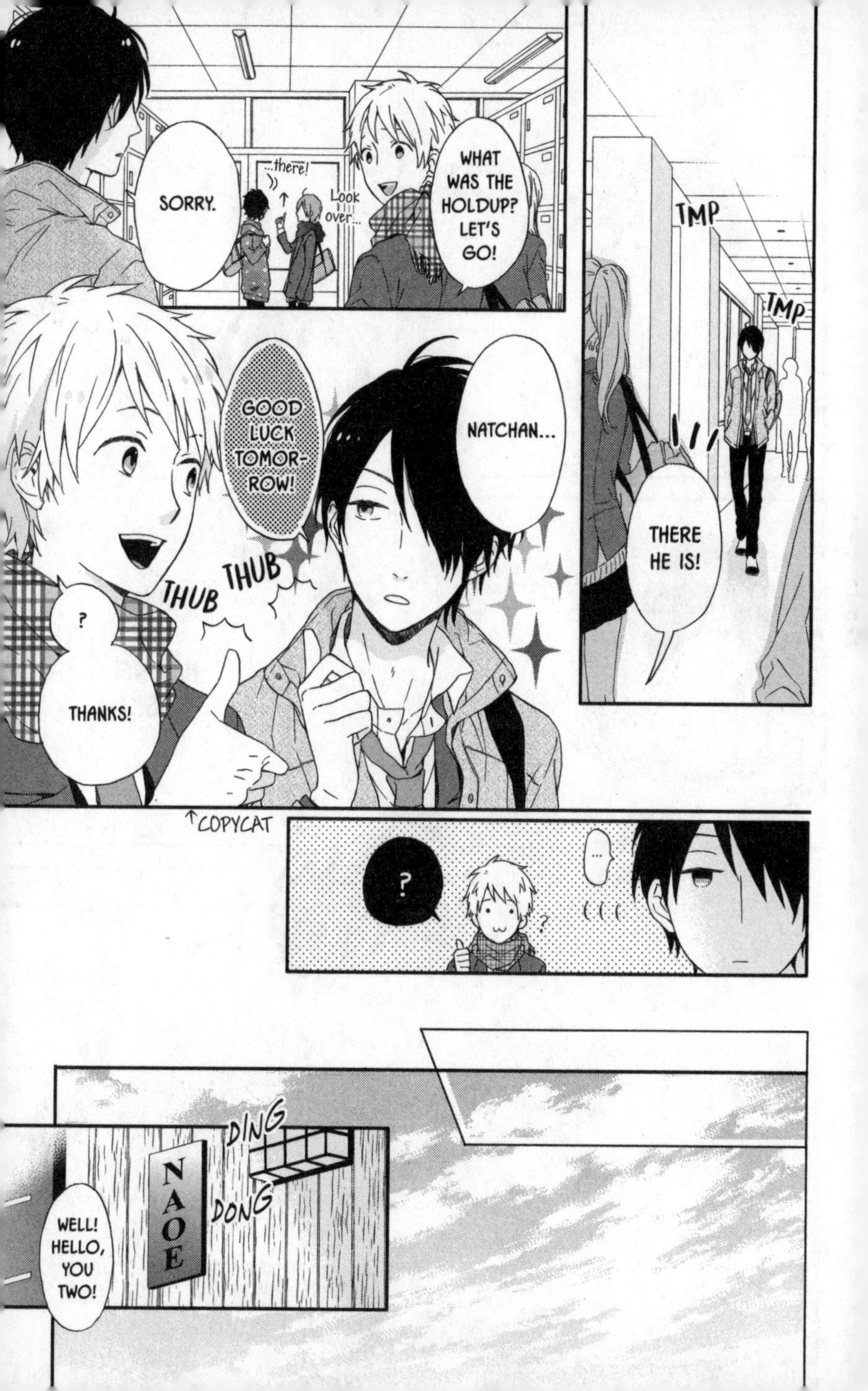
TMP
TMP
THERE HE IS!
WHAT WAS THE HOLDUP? LET'S GO!
Look over...
...there!
SORRY.
NATCHAN...
GOOD LUCK TOMORROW!
THUB
THUB
?
THANKS!
COPYCAT
...
?
DING
DONG
NAOE
WELL! HELLO, YOU TWO!

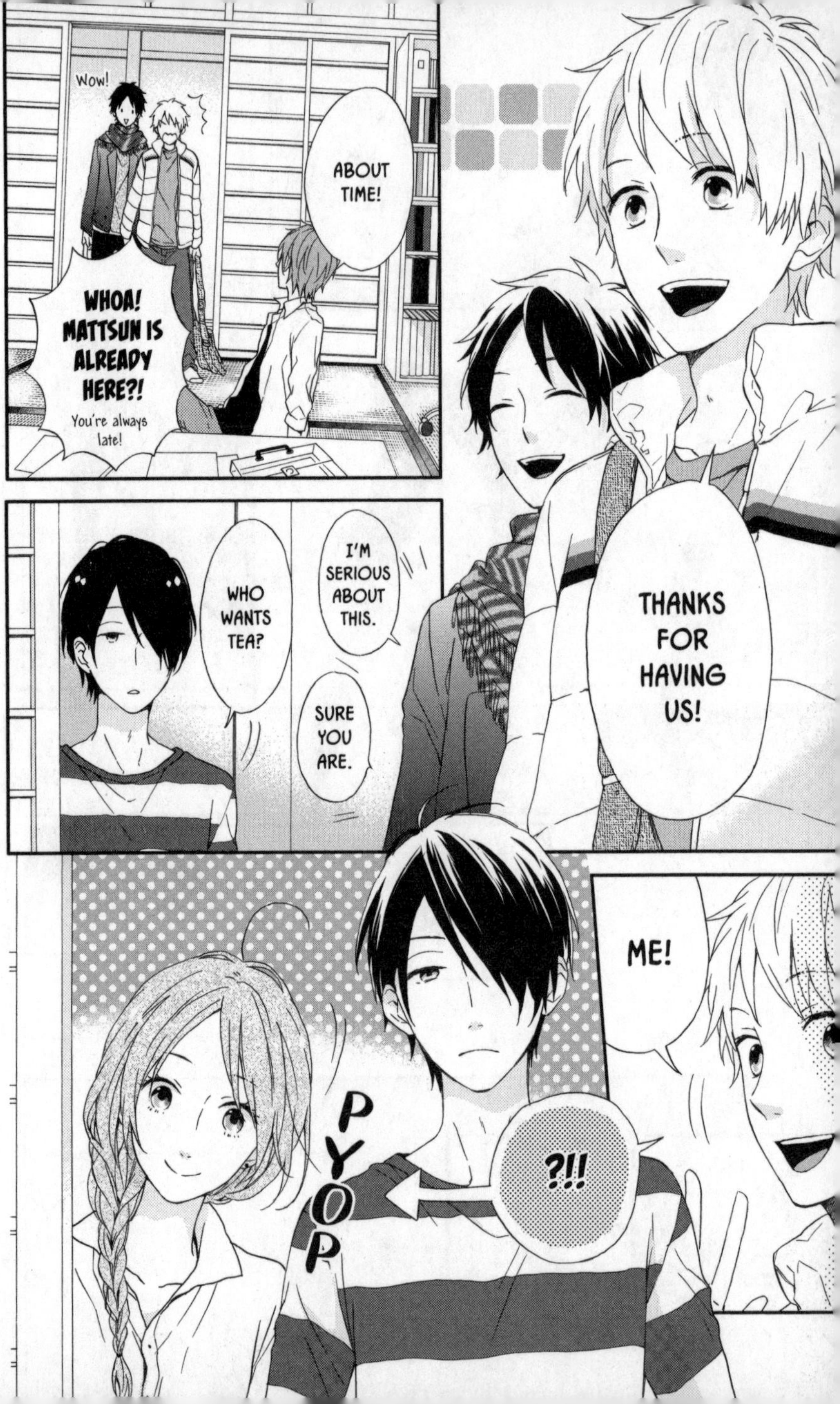
THANKS FOR HAVING US!
ABOUT TIME!
Wow!
WHOA! MATTSUN IS ALREADY HERE?!
You're always late!
I'M SERIOUS ABOUT THIS.
WHO WANTS TEA?
SURE YOU ARE.
ME!
?!!
PYOP

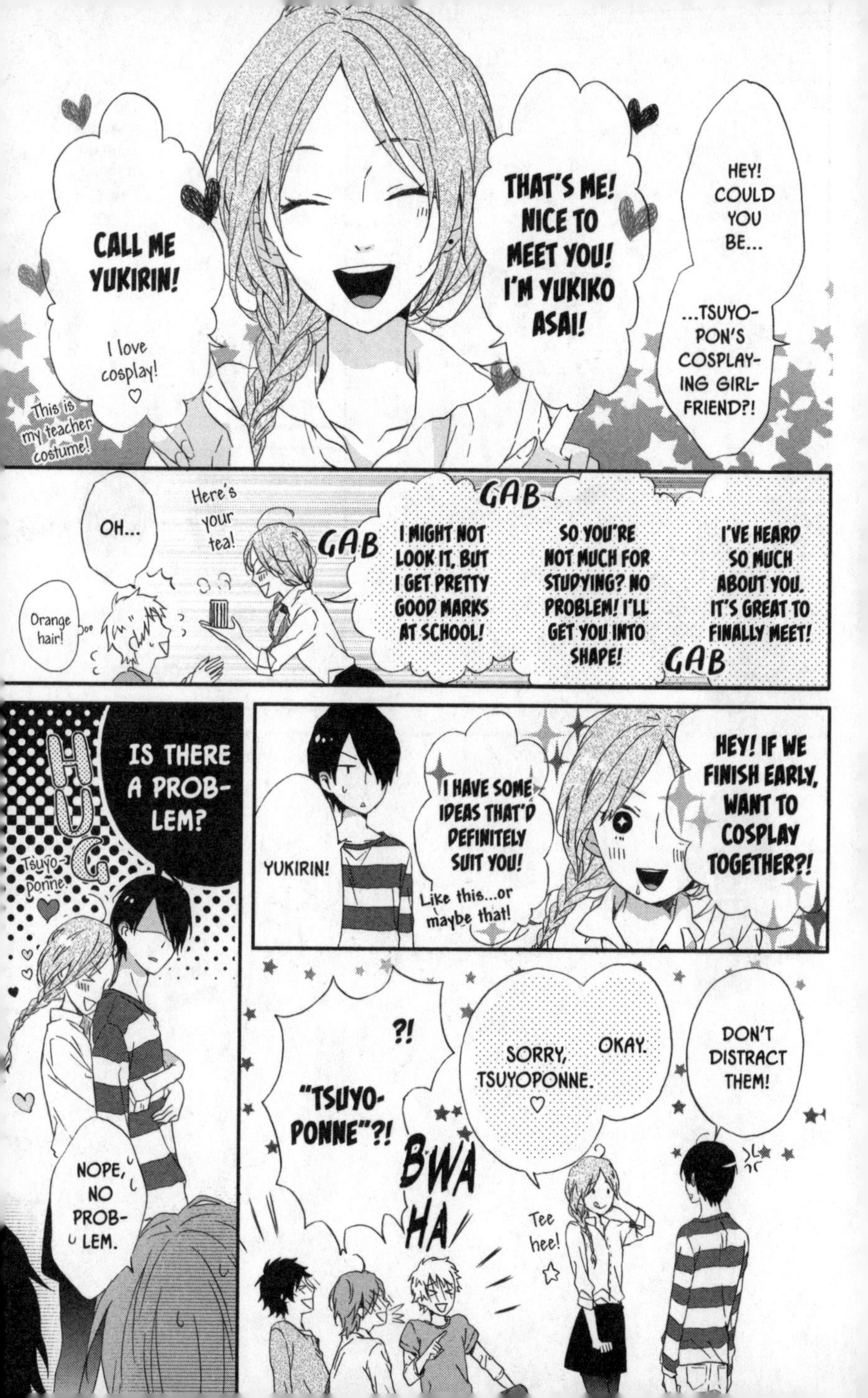
HEY! COULD YOU BE...
...TSUYO-PON'S COSPLAYING GIRLFRIEND?!
THAT'S ME! NICE TO MEET YOU! I'M YUKIKO ASAI!
CALL ME YUKIRIN!
I love cosplay! ♡
This is my teacher costume!
GAB
I'VE HEARD SO MUCH ABOUT YOU. IT'S GREAT TO FINALLY MEET!
GAB
SO YOU'RE NOT MUCH FOR STUDYING? NO PROBLEM! I'LL GET YOU INTO SHAPE!
I MIGHT NOT LOOK IT, BUT I GET PRETTY GOOD MARKS AT SCHOOL!
GAB
Here's your tea!
OH...
Orange hair!
HEY! IF WE FINISH EARLY, WANT TO COSPLAY TOGETHER?!
I HAVE SOME IDEAS THAT'D DEFINITELY SUIT YOU!
Like this...or maybe that!
YUKIRIN!
DON'T DISTRACT THEM!
OKAY.
SORRY, TSUYOPONNE. ♡
Tee hee!
?!
"TSUYO-PONNE"?!
BWA HA
HUG
IS THERE A PROBLEM?
Tsuyo-ponne ♥
NOPE, NO PROBLEM.

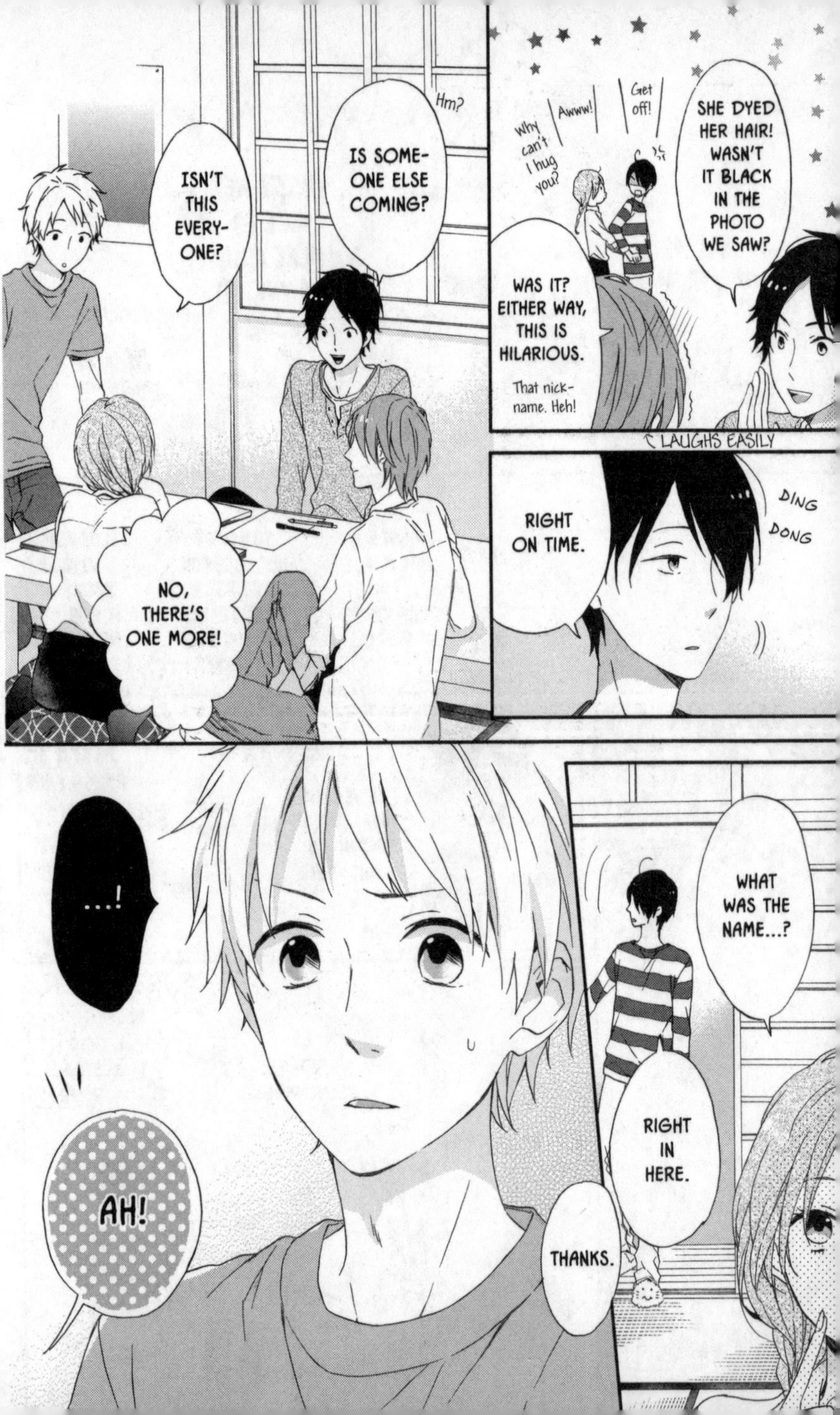
SHE DYED HER HAIR! WASN'T IT BLACK IN THE PHOTO WE SAW?
Get off!
Awww!
Why can't I hug you?
WAS IT? EITHER WAY, THIS IS HILARIOUS.
That nick-name. Heh!
LAUGHS EASILY
DING DONG
RIGHT ON TIME.
Hm?
IS SOME-ONE ELSE COMING?
ISN'T THIS EVERY-ONE?
NO, THERE'S ONE MORE!
WHAT WAS THE NAME...?
RIGHT IN HERE.
THANKS.
...!
AH!

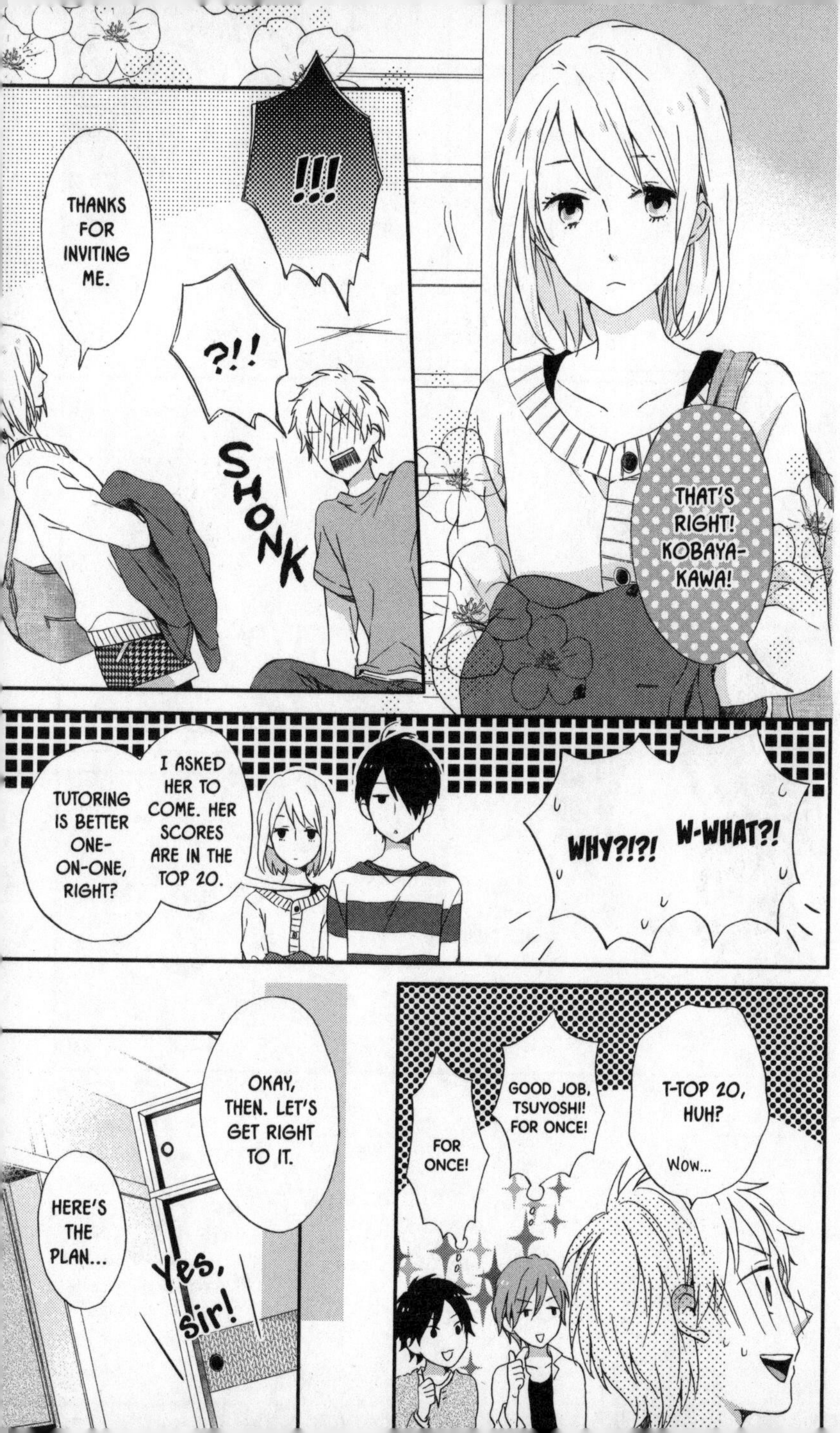
THAT'S RIGHT! KOBAYA-KAWA!
!!!
THANKS FOR INVITING ME.
?!!
SHONK
W-WHAT?!
WHY?!?!
I ASKED HER TO COME. HER SCORES ARE IN THE TOP 20.
TUTORING IS BETTER ONE-ON-ONE, RIGHT?
T-TOP 20, HUH?
Wow...
GOOD JOB, TSUYOSHI! FOR ONCE!
FOR ONCE!
OKAY, THEN. LET'S GET RIGHT TO IT.
HERE'S THE PLAN...
Yes, sir!

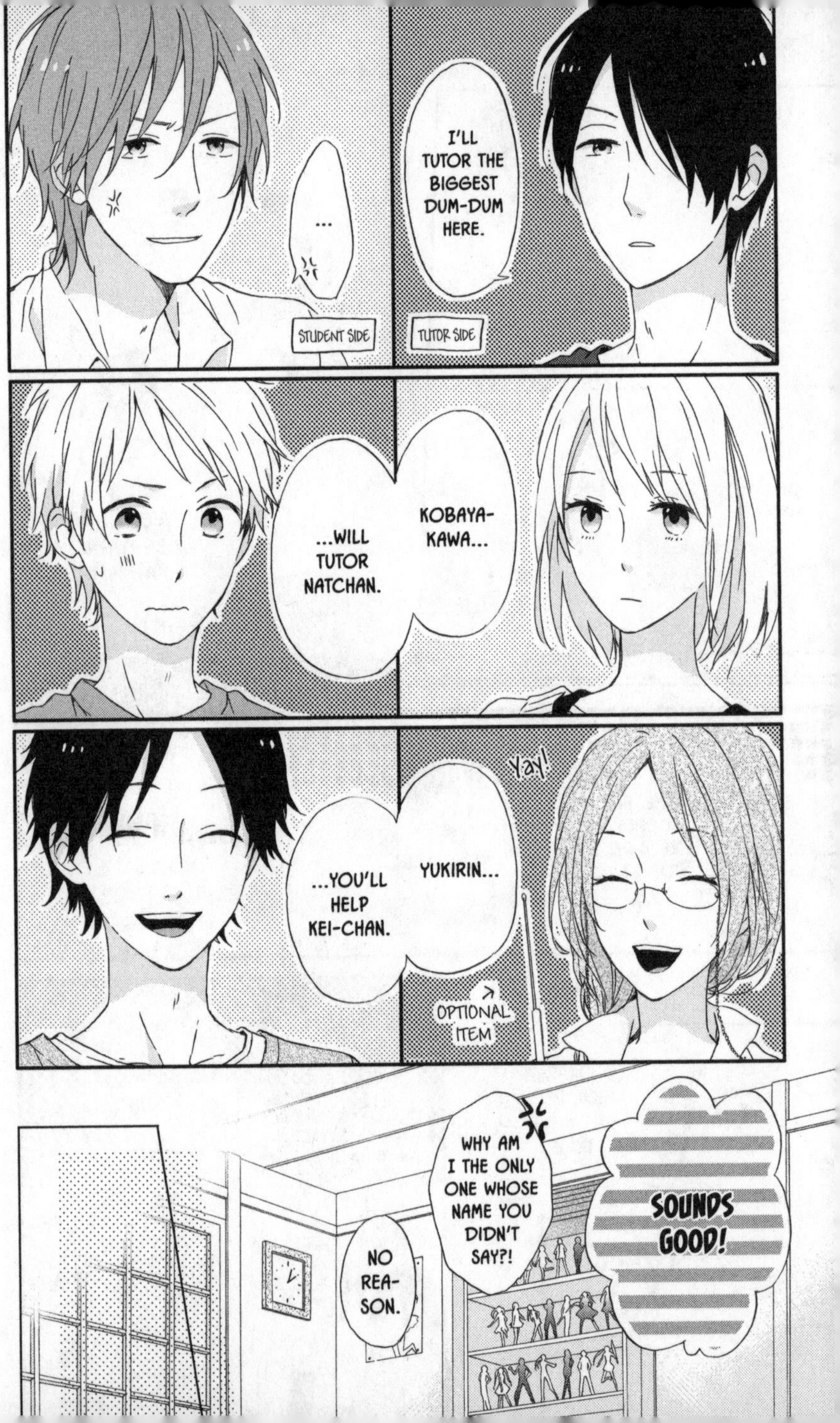
TUTOR SIDE
I'LL TUTOR THE BIGGEST DUM-DUM HERE.
...
STUDENT SIDE
KOBAYA-KAWA...
...WILL TUTOR NATCHAN.
Yay!
YUKIRIN...
OPTIONAL ITEM
...YOU'LL HELP KEI-CHAN.
SOUNDS GOOD!
WHY AM I THE ONLY ONE WHOSE NAME YOU DIDN'T SAY?!
NO REA-SON.

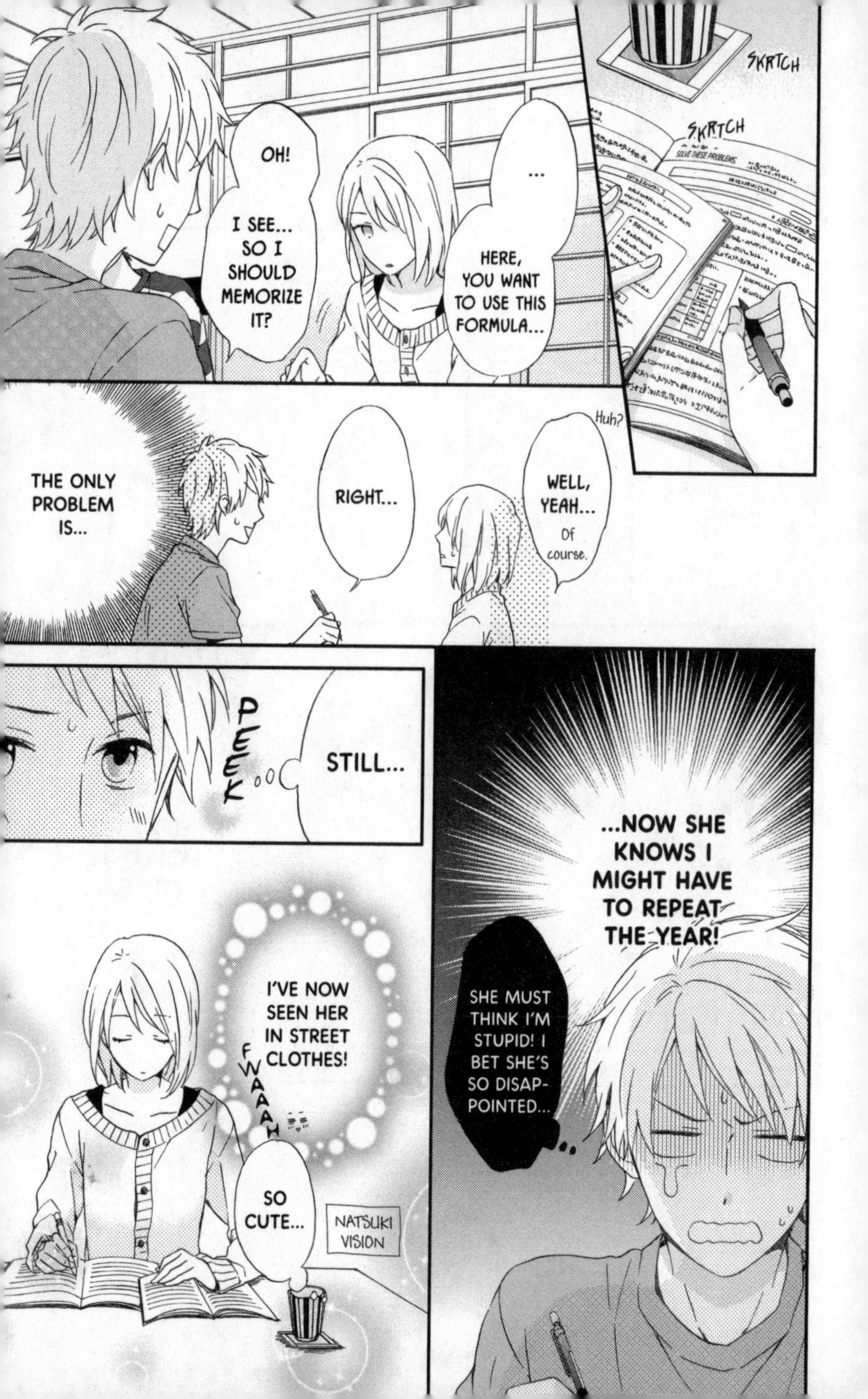
SKRTCH
SKRTCH
SOLVE THESE PROBLEMS
...
HERE, YOU WANT TO USE THIS FORMULA...
OH!
I SEE... SO I SHOULD MEMORIZE IT?
Huh?
WELL, YEAH...
Of course.
RIGHT...
THE ONLY PROBLEM IS...
...NOW SHE KNOWS I MIGHT HAVE TO REPEAT THE YEAR!
SHE MUST THINK I'M STUPID! I BET SHE'S SO DISAP-POINTED...
STILL...
PEEK
I'VE NOW SEEN HER IN STREET CLOTHES!
FWAAAH
SO CUTE...
NATSUKI VISION

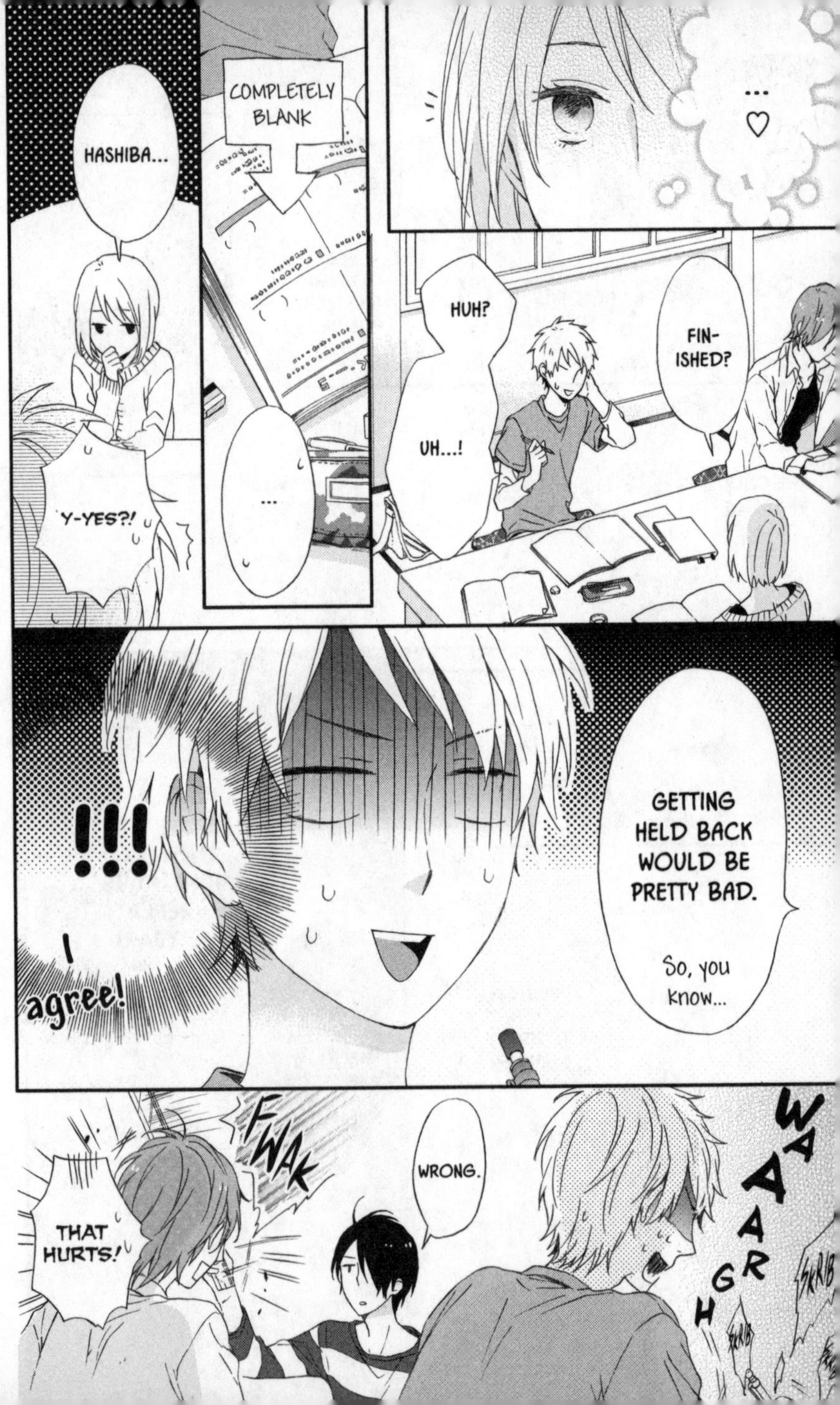
...
♡
FIN-ISHED?
HUH?
UH...!
COMPLETELY BLANK
...
HASHIBA...
Y-YES?!
GETTING HELD BACK WOULD BE PRETTY BAD.
So, you know...
!!!
I agree!
WAAARGH
SKRIB
WRONG.
FWAK
THAT HURTS!

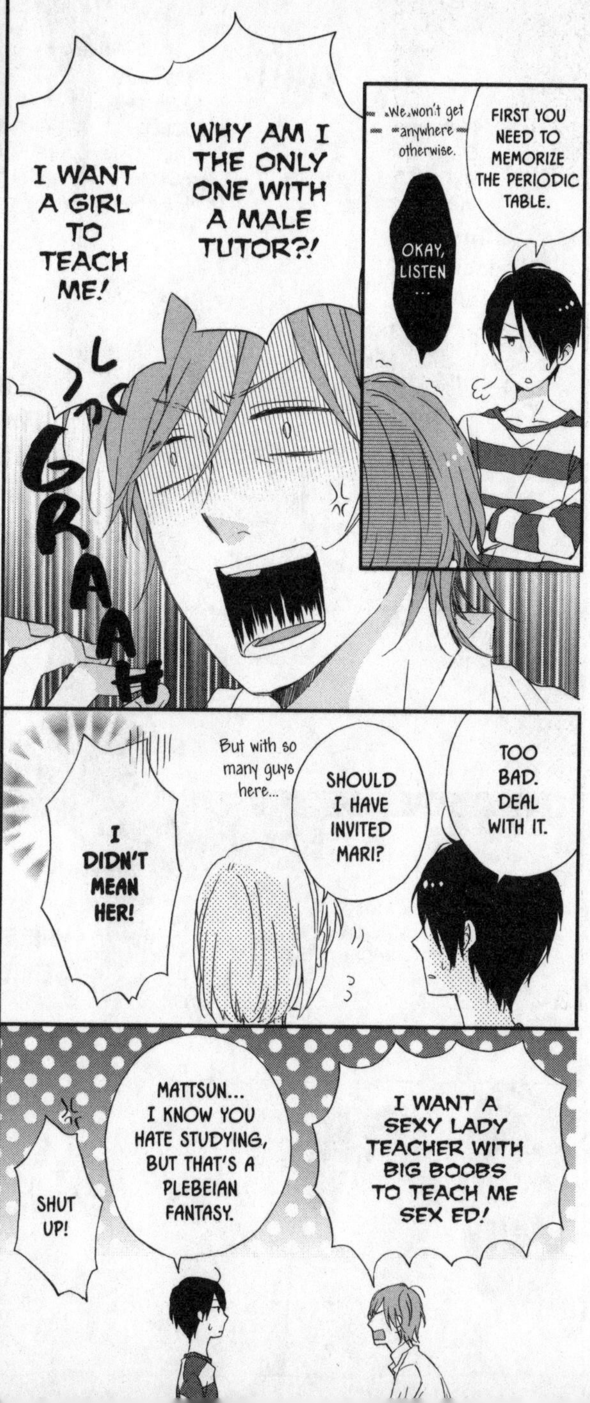
FIRST YOU NEED TO MEMORIZE THE PERIODIC TABLE.
We won't get anywhere otherwise.
OKAY, LISTEN...
WHY AM I THE ONLY ONE WITH A MALE TUTOR?!
I WANT A GIRL TO TEACH ME!
GRAAH
TOO BAD. DEAL WITH IT.
SHOULD I HAVE INVITED MARI?
But with so many guys here...
I DIDN'T MEAN HER!
I WANT A SEXY LADY TEACHER WITH BIG BOOBS TO TEACH ME SEX ED!
MATTSUN... I KNOW YOU HATE STUDYING, BUT THAT'S A PLEBEIAN FANTASY.
SHUT UP!

Special Thanks

- Hiromi Okawa-sama
- Nanami Koyama-sama
- Noriko Shinoda-sama
- Sei Suzuki-sama
- Hiromi Seki-sama
- Rui Hase-sama
- Konomi Moriwaki-sama

♥

- kgr-sama
- nao-sama
- sanarin-sama

♥

- Ayaka T.-sama

♥

My editor: Yabu-sama
Designer: Kawatani-sama

Everyone involved in publishing this book

♥

Friends and family

And everyone reading this ♡

Thank you very much! ♡

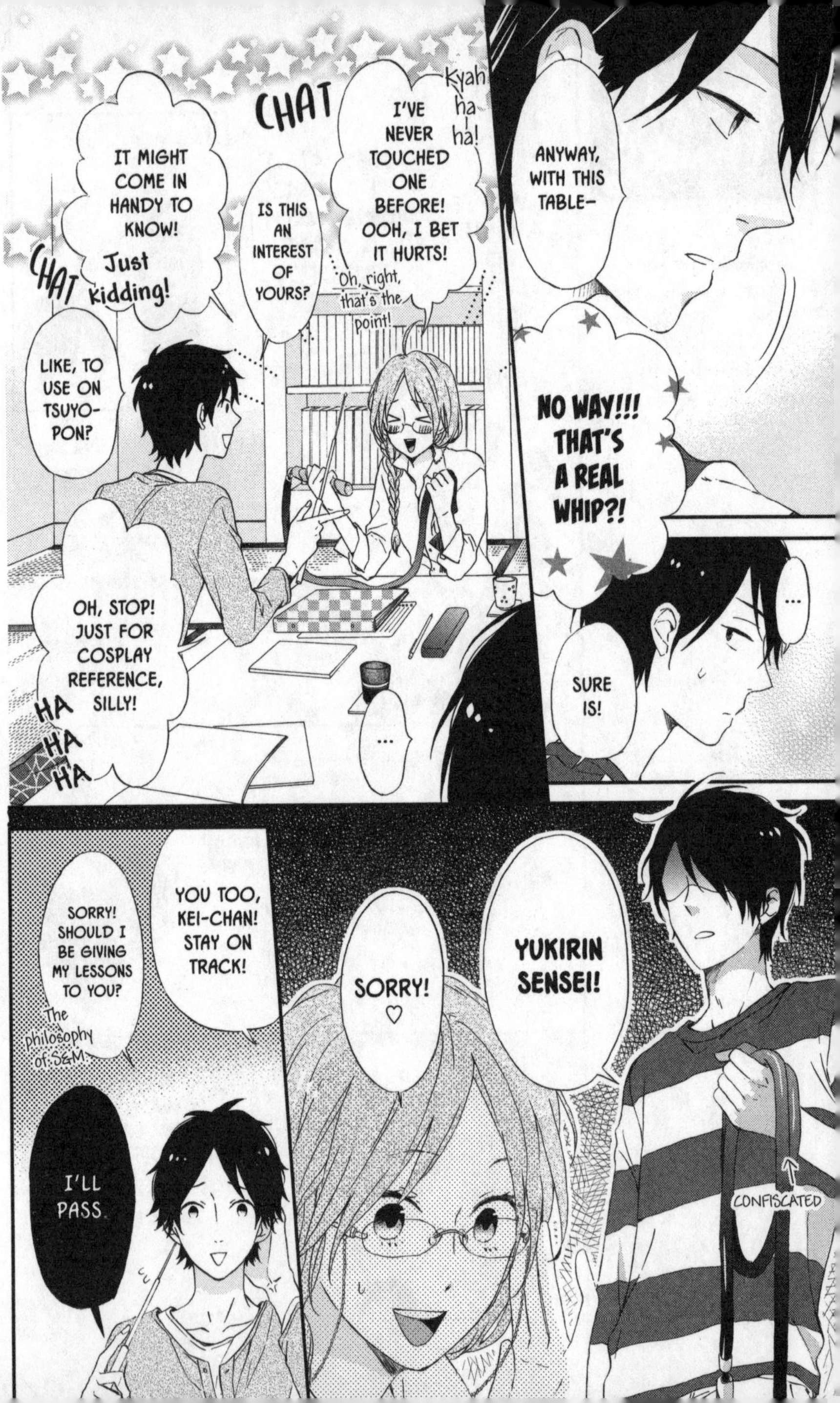
ANYWAY, WITH THIS TABLE–
NO WAY!!! THAT'S A REAL WHIP?!
...
SURE IS!
Kyah ha ha!
I'VE NEVER TOUCHED ONE BEFORE! OOH, I BET IT HURTS!
CHAT
IS THIS AN INTEREST OF YOURS?
Oh, right, that's the point!
IT MIGHT COME IN HANDY TO KNOW! Just kidding!
CHAT
LIKE, TO USE ON TSUYO-PON?
OH, STOP! JUST FOR COSPLAY REFERENCE, SILLY!
HA HA HA
...
YUKIRIN SENSEI!
CONFISCATED
SORRY! ♡
YOU TOO, KEI-CHAN! STAY ON TRACK!
SORRY! SHOULD I BE GIVING MY LESSONS TO YOU?
The philosophy of S&M.
I'LL PASS.

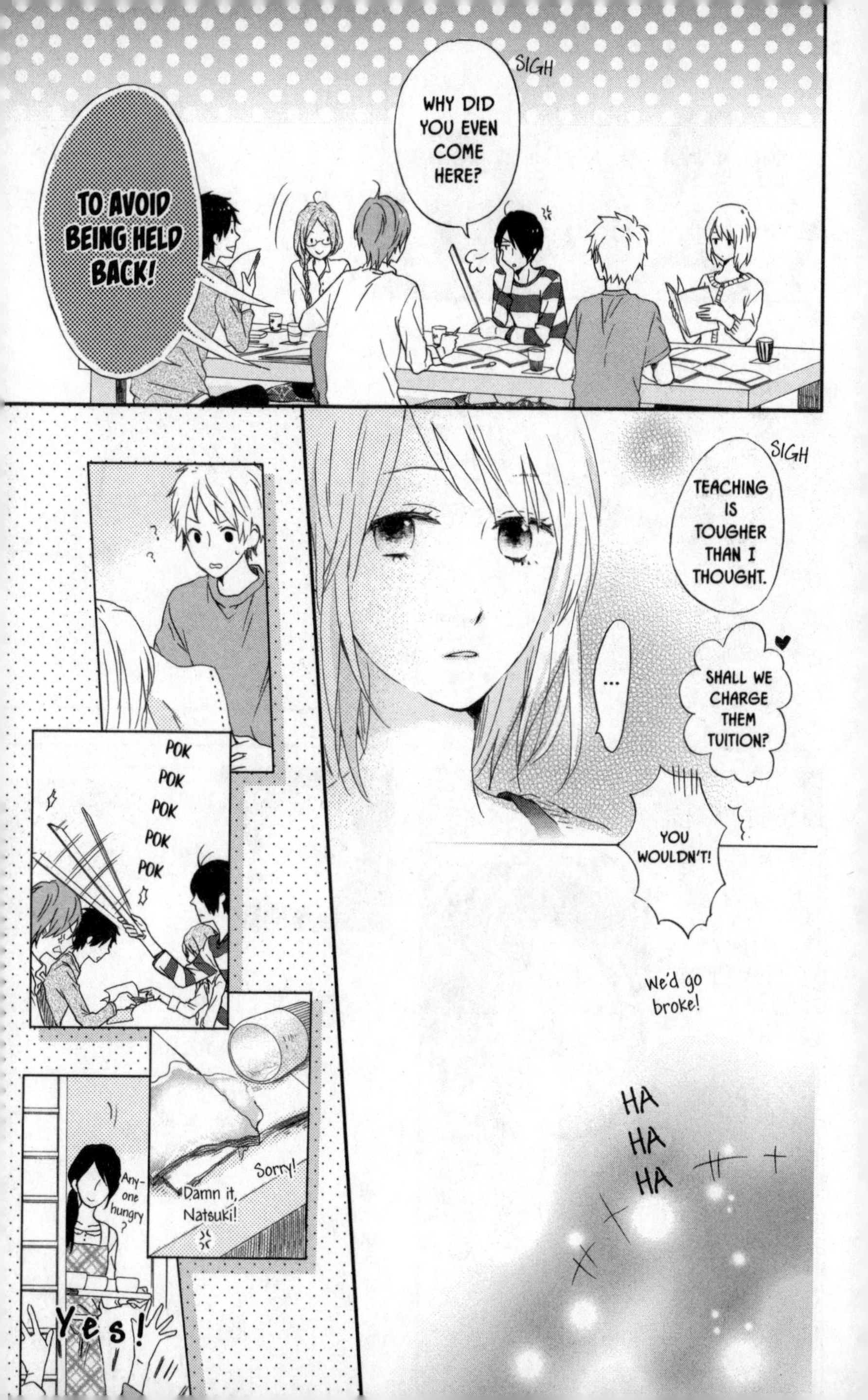
SIGH
WHY DID YOU EVEN COME HERE?
TO AVOID BEING HELD BACK!
SIGH
TEACHING IS TOUGHER THAN I THOUGHT.
...
SHALL WE CHARGE THEM TUITION?
YOU WOULDN'T!
We'd go broke!
HA HA HA
POK POK POK POK POK
Sorry!
Damn it, Natsuki!
Any-one hungry?
Yes!

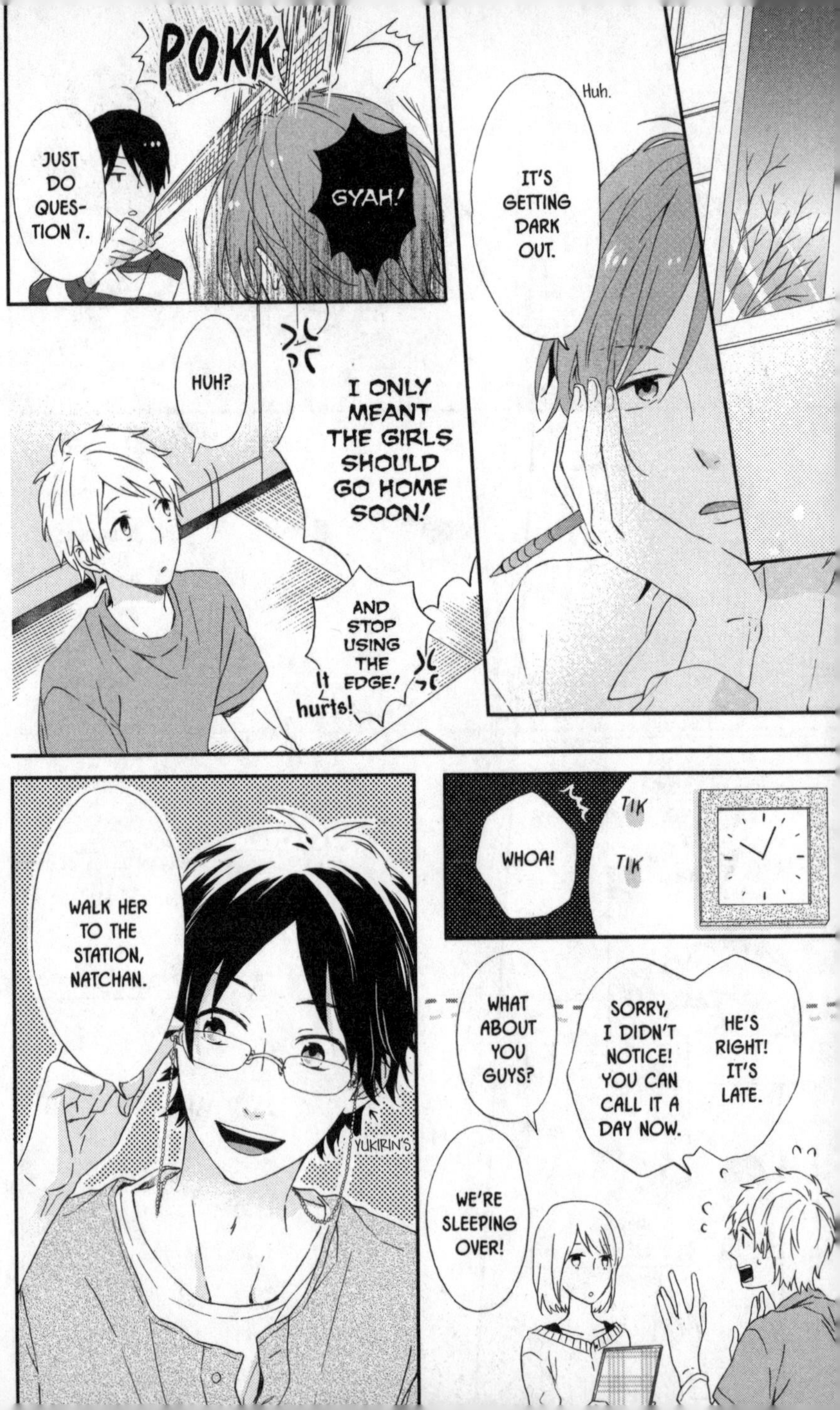
Huh.
IT'S GETTING DARK OUT.
POKK
GYAH!
JUST DO QUES-TION 7.
I ONLY MEANT THE GIRLS SHOULD GO HOME SOON!
HUH?
AND STOP USING THE EDGE!
It hurts!
WHOA!
TIK
TIK
HE'S RIGHT! IT'S LATE.
SORRY, I DIDN'T NOTICE! YOU CAN CALL IT A DAY NOW.
WHAT ABOUT YOU GUYS?
WE'RE SLEEPING OVER!
WALK HER TO THE STATION, NATCHAN.
YUKIRIN'S

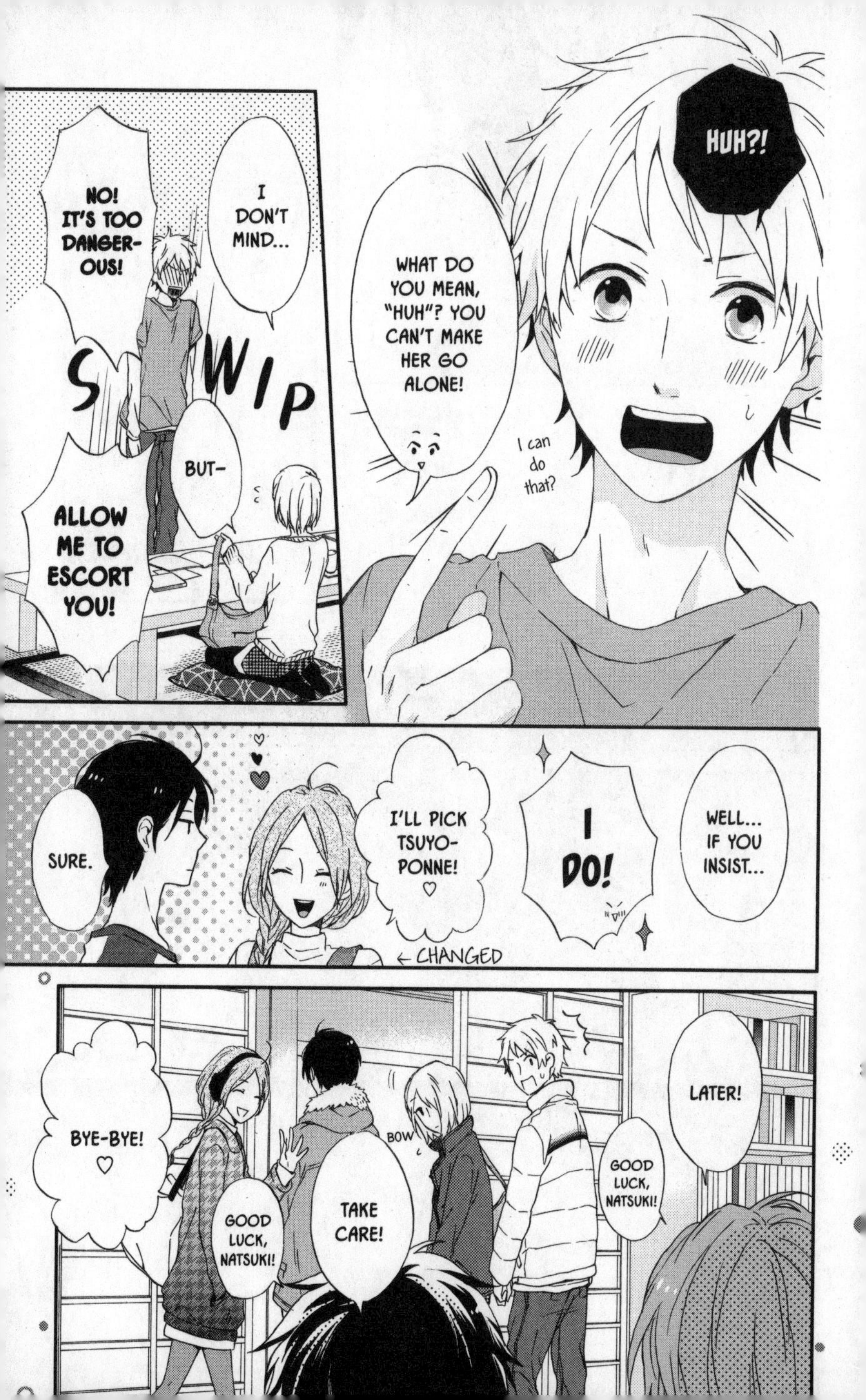
HUH?!
WHAT DO YOU MEAN, "HUH"? YOU CAN'T MAKE HER GO ALONE!
I can do that?
I DON'T MIND...
NO! IT'S TOO DANGER-OUS!
SWIP
BUT-
ALLOW ME TO ESCORT YOU!
WELL... IF YOU INSIST...
I DO!
I'LL PICK TSUYO-PONNE! ♡
← CHANGED
SURE.
LATER!
GOOD LUCK, NATSUKI!
BOW
TAKE CARE!
GOOD LUCK, NATSUKI!
BYE-BYE! ♡

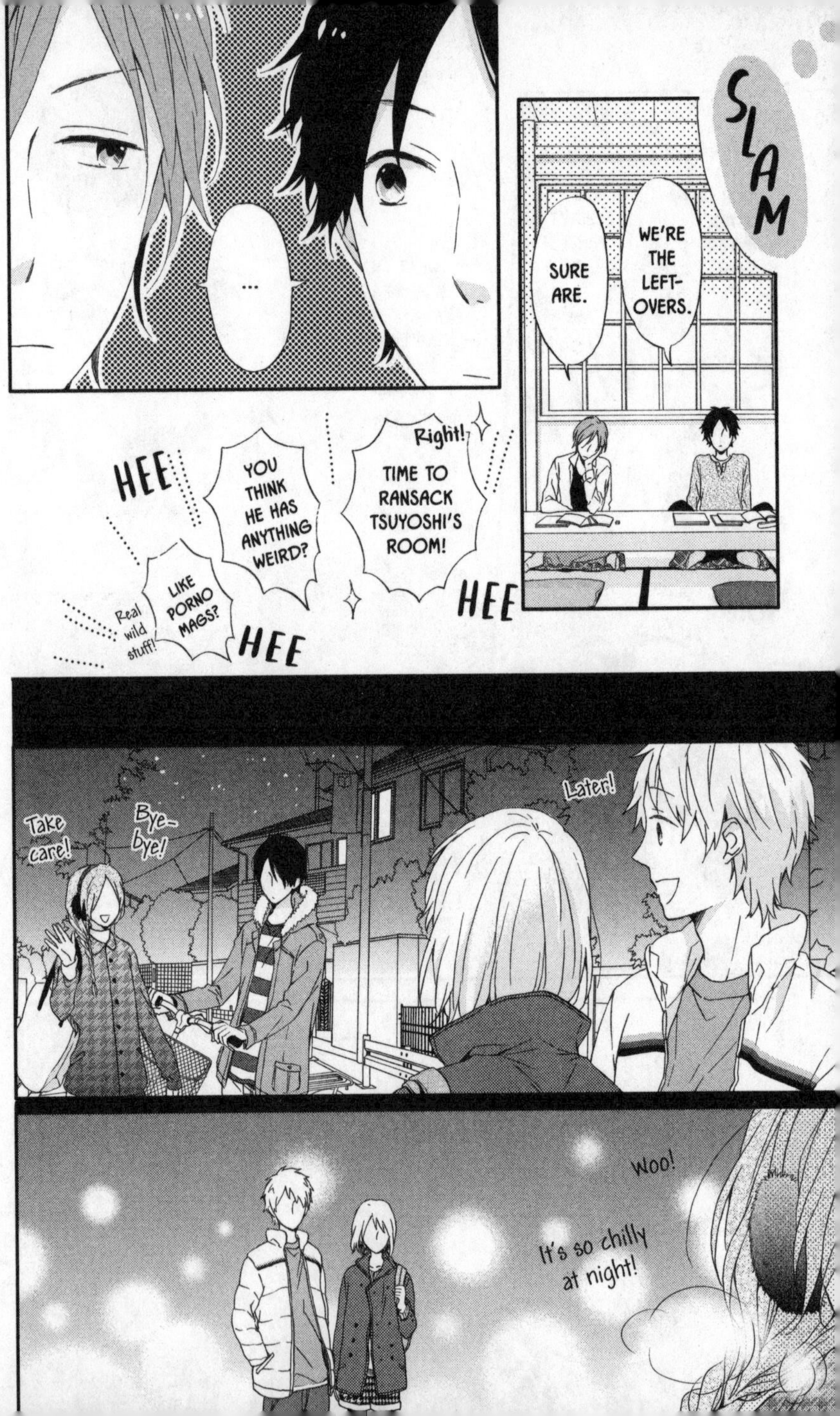
SLAM
WE'RE THE LEFT-OVERS.
SURE ARE.
...
Right!
TIME TO RANSACK TSUYOSHI'S ROOM!
HEE
YOU THINK HE HAS ANYTHING WEIRD?
HEE
LIKE PORNO MAGS?
Real wild stuff!
HEE
Later!
Bye-bye!
Take care!
Woo!
It's so chilly at night!

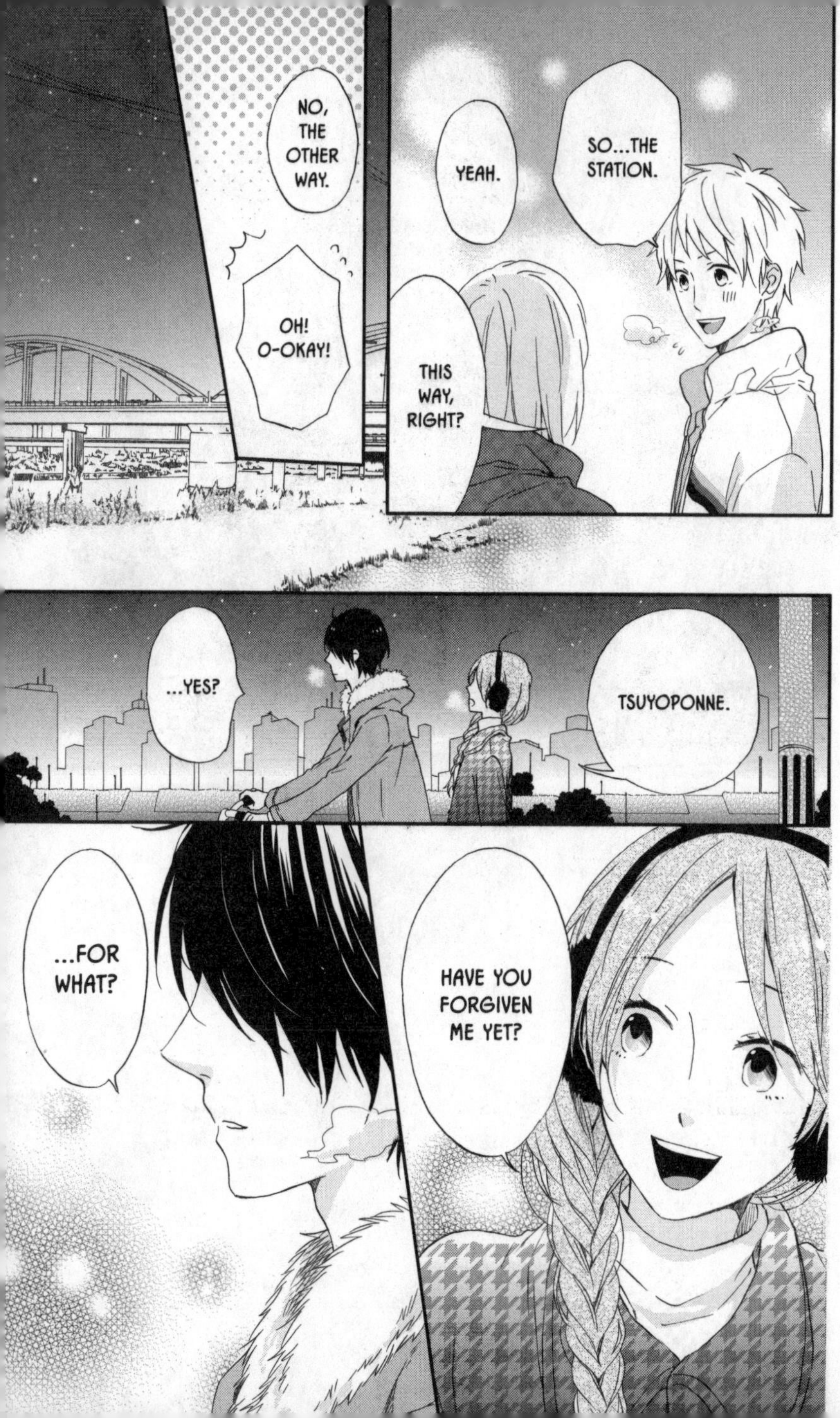
SO...THE STATION.
YEAH.
THIS WAY, RIGHT?
NO, THE OTHER WAY.
OH! O-OKAY!
TSUYOPONNE.
...YES?
HAVE YOU FORGIVEN ME YET?
...FOR WHAT?

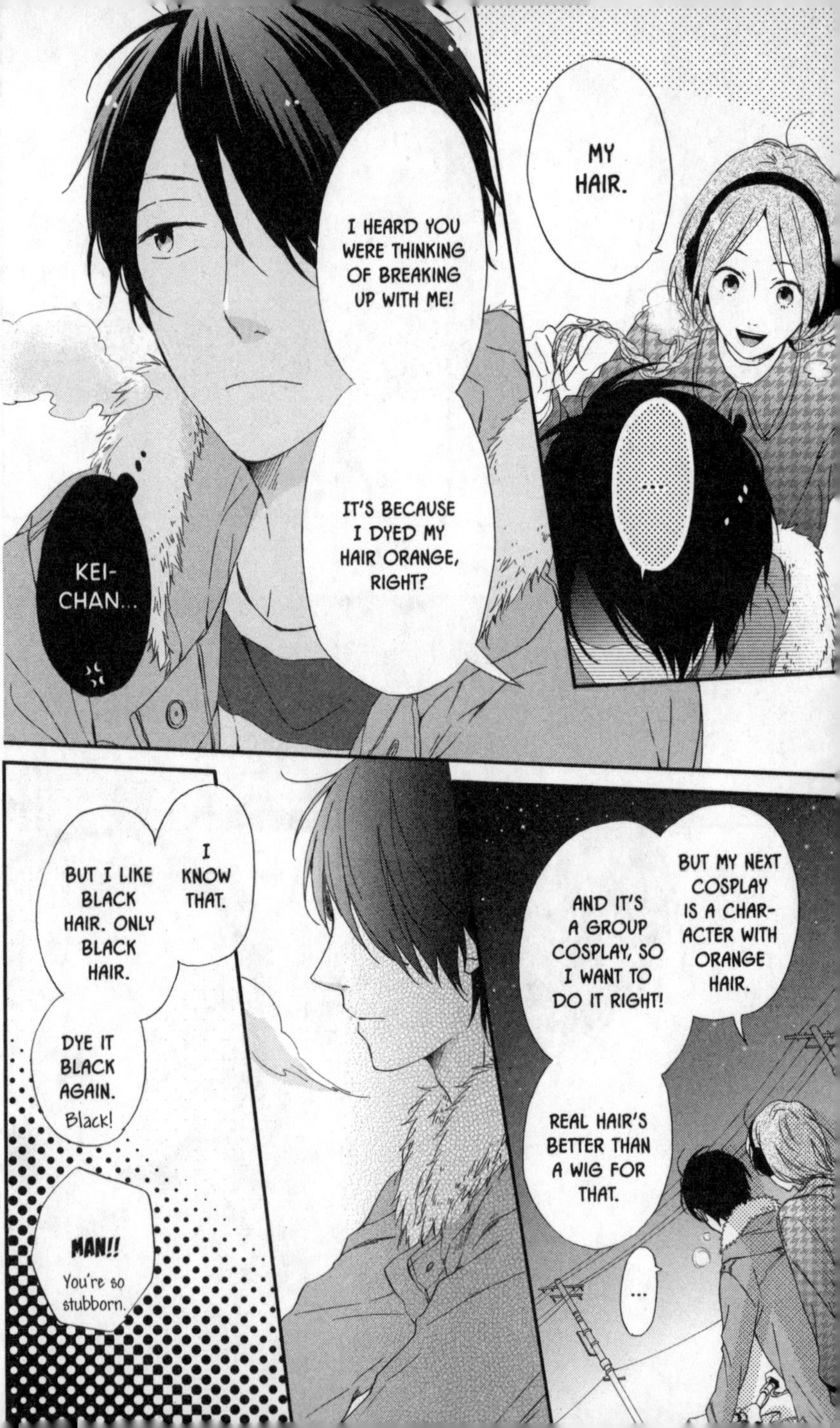
MY HAIR.
...
I HEARD YOU WERE THINKING OF BREAKING UP WITH ME!
IT'S BECAUSE I DYED MY HAIR ORANGE, RIGHT?
KEI-CHAN...
BUT MY NEXT COSPLAY IS A CHAR-ACTER WITH ORANGE HAIR.
AND IT'S A GROUP COSPLAY, SO I WANT TO DO IT RIGHT!
REAL HAIR'S BETTER THAN A WIG FOR THAT.
...
I KNOW THAT.
BUT I LIKE BLACK HAIR. ONLY BLACK HAIR.
DYE IT BLACK AGAIN. Black!
MAN!! You're so stubborn.

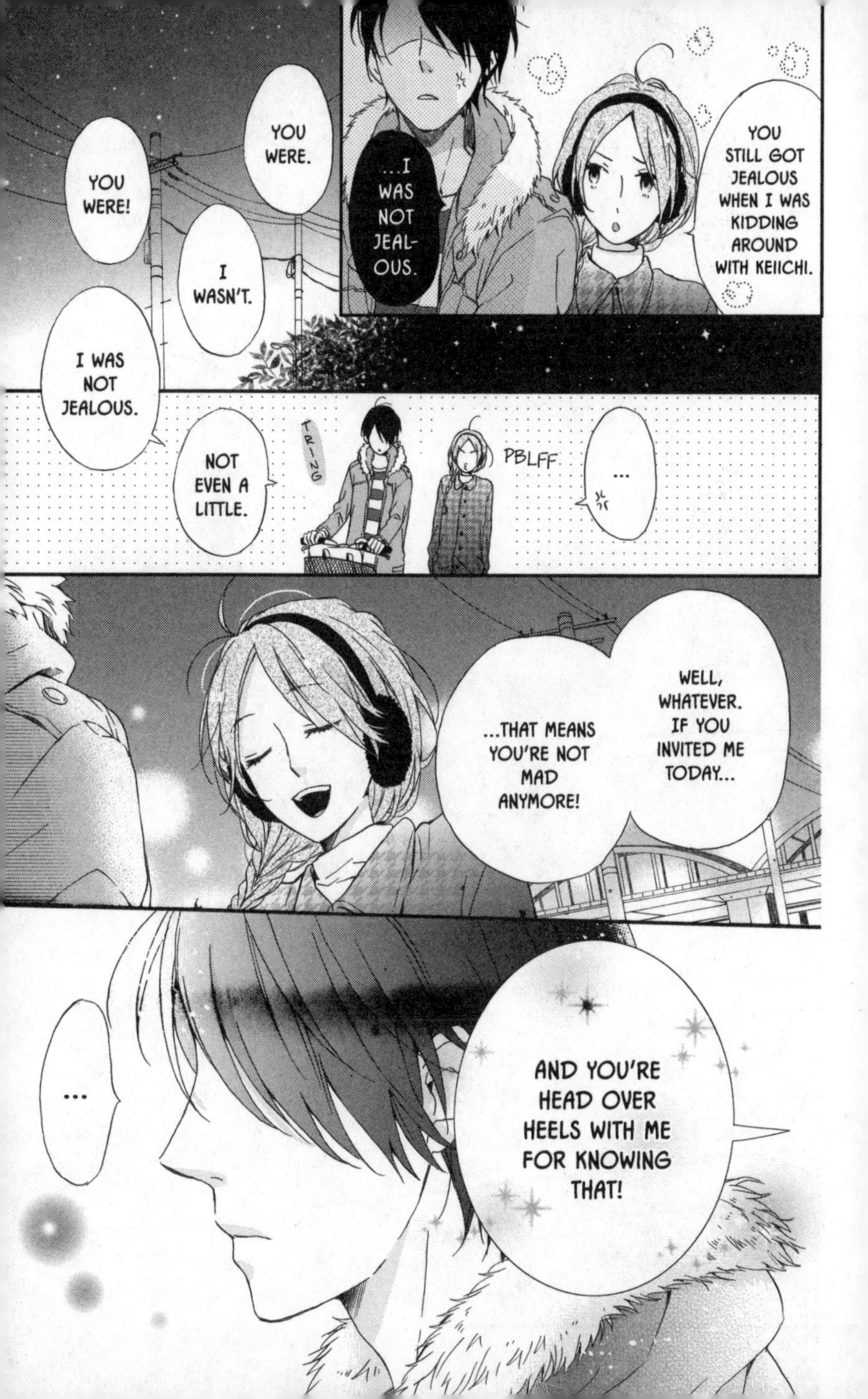
YOU STILL GOT JEALOUS WHEN I WAS KIDDING AROUND WITH KEIICHI.
...I WAS NOT JEALOUS.
YOU WERE.
I WASN'T.
YOU WERE!
I WAS NOT JEALOUS.
...
PBLFF
TRING
NOT EVEN A LITTLE.
WELL, WHATEVER. IF YOU INVITED ME TODAY...
...THAT MEANS YOU'RE NOT MAD ANYMORE!
AND YOU'RE HEAD OVER HEELS WITH ME FOR KNOWING THAT!
...

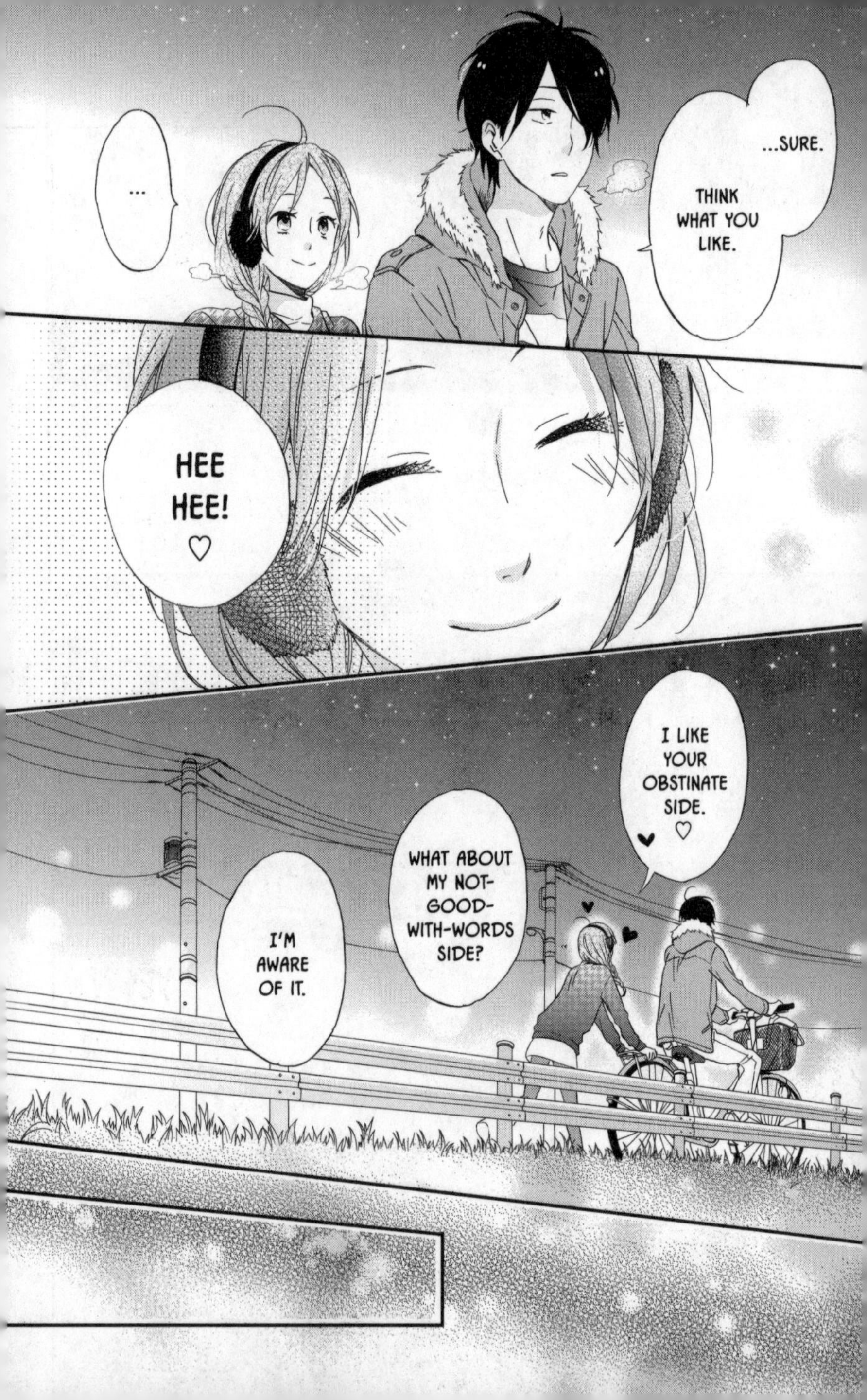
...SURE.
THINK WHAT YOU LIKE.
...
HEE HEE! ♡
I LIKE YOUR OBSTINATE SIDE. ♡
WHAT ABOUT MY NOT-GOOD-WITH-WORDS SIDE?
I'M AWARE OF IT.

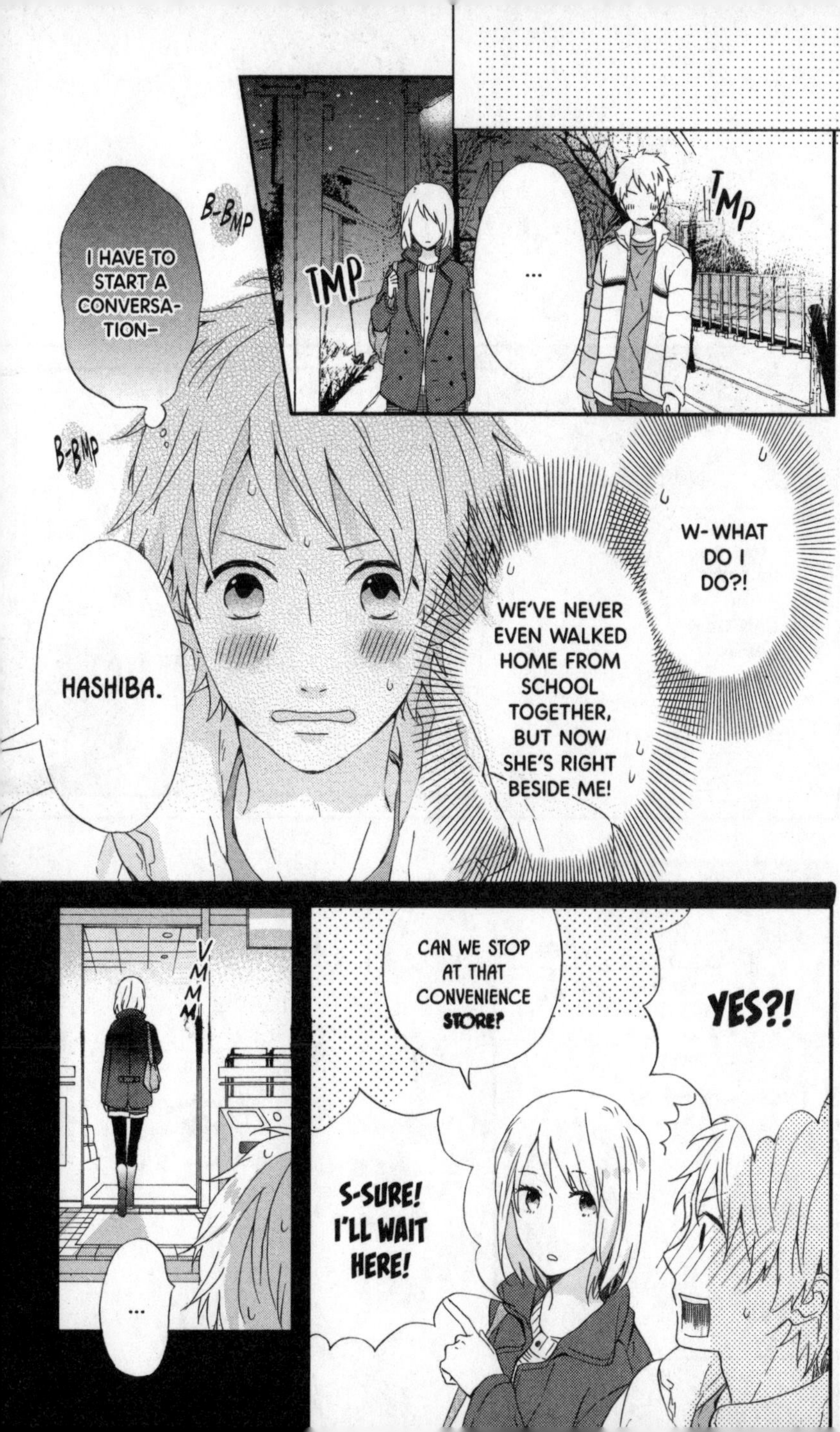
TMP
...
TMP
B-BMP
W-WHAT DO I DO?!
WE'VE NEVER EVEN WALKED HOME FROM SCHOOL TOGETHER, BUT NOW SHE'S RIGHT BESIDE ME!
I HAVE TO START A CONVERSATION-
B-BMP
HASHIBA.
CAN WE STOP AT THAT CONVENIENCE STORE?
YES?!
S-SURE! I'LL WAIT HERE!
VMMM
...

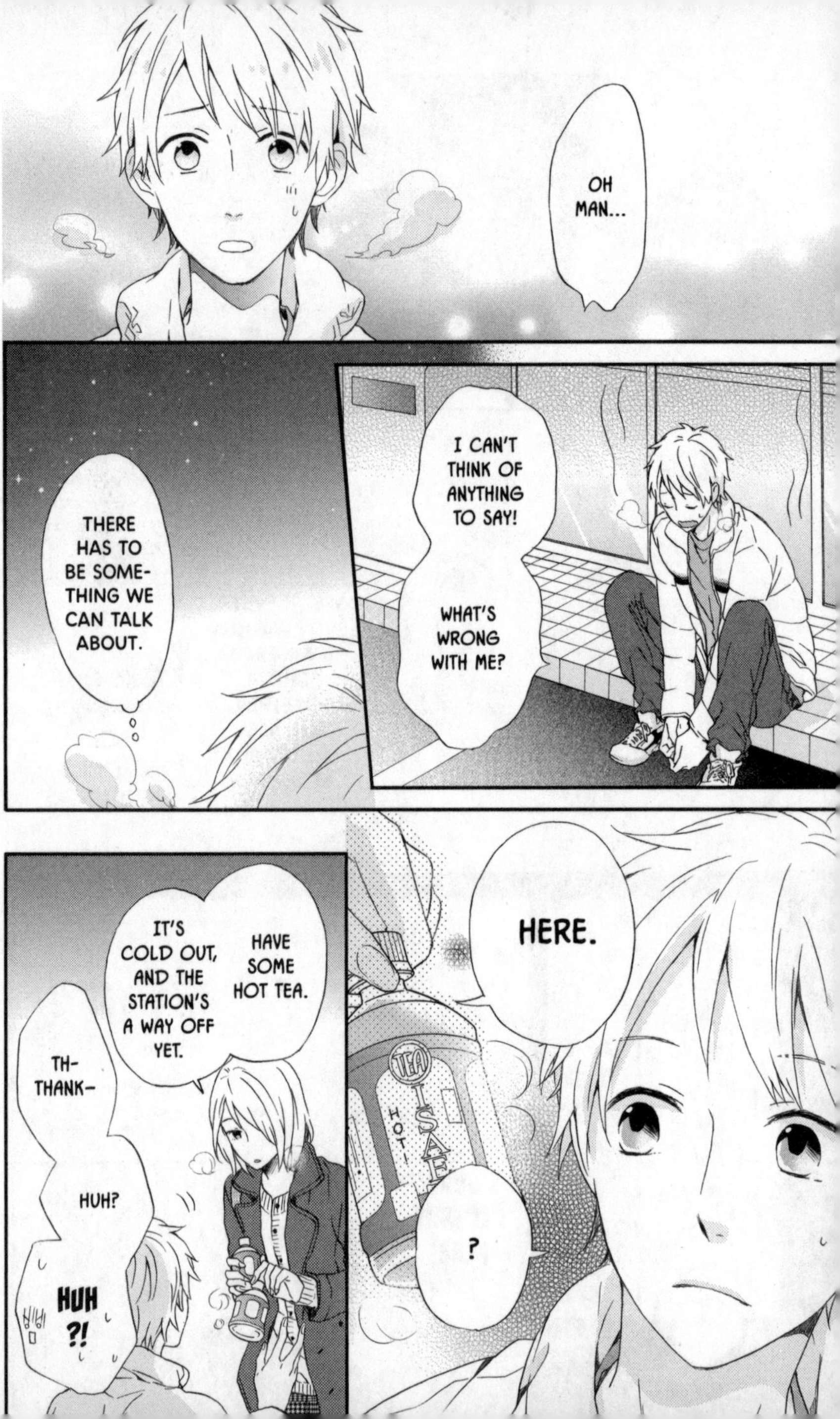
OH MAN...
I CAN'T THINK OF ANYTHING TO SAY!
WHAT'S WRONG WITH ME?
THERE HAS TO BE SOME-THING WE CAN TALK ABOUT.
HERE.
?
HAVE SOME HOT TEA.
IT'S COLD OUT, AND THE STATION'S A WAY OFF YET.
TH- THANK-
HUH?
HUH ?!

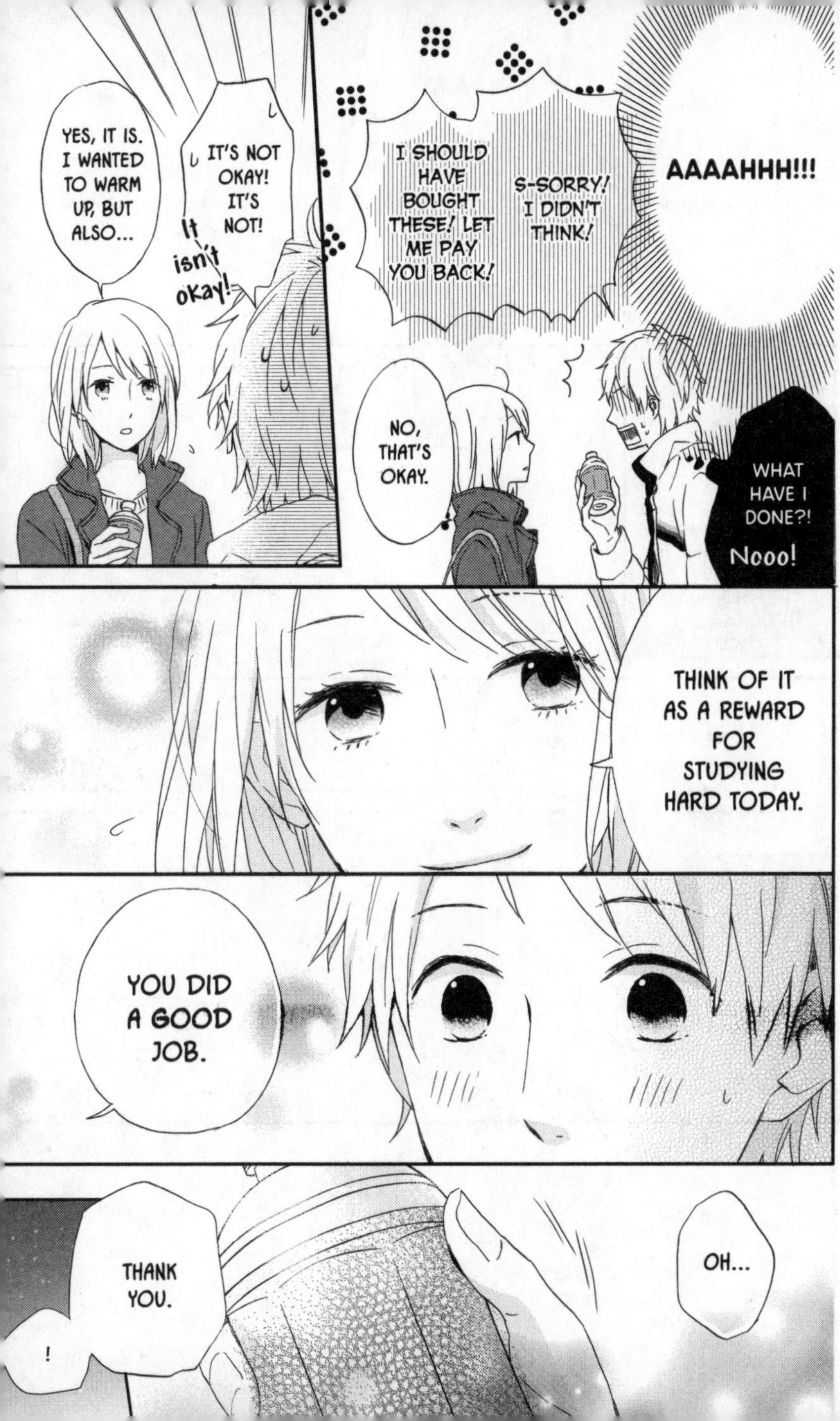

AAAAHHH!!!
S-SORRY! I DIDN'T THINK!
I SHOULD HAVE BOUGHT THESE! LET ME PAY YOU BACK!
WHAT HAVE I DONE?!
Nooo!
NO, THAT'S OKAY.
IT'S NOT OKAY! IT'S NOT!
It isn't okay!
YES, IT IS. I WANTED TO WARM UP, BUT ALSO...
THINK OF IT AS A REWARD FOR STUDYING HARD TODAY.
YOU DID A GOOD JOB.
OH...
THANK YOU.
!

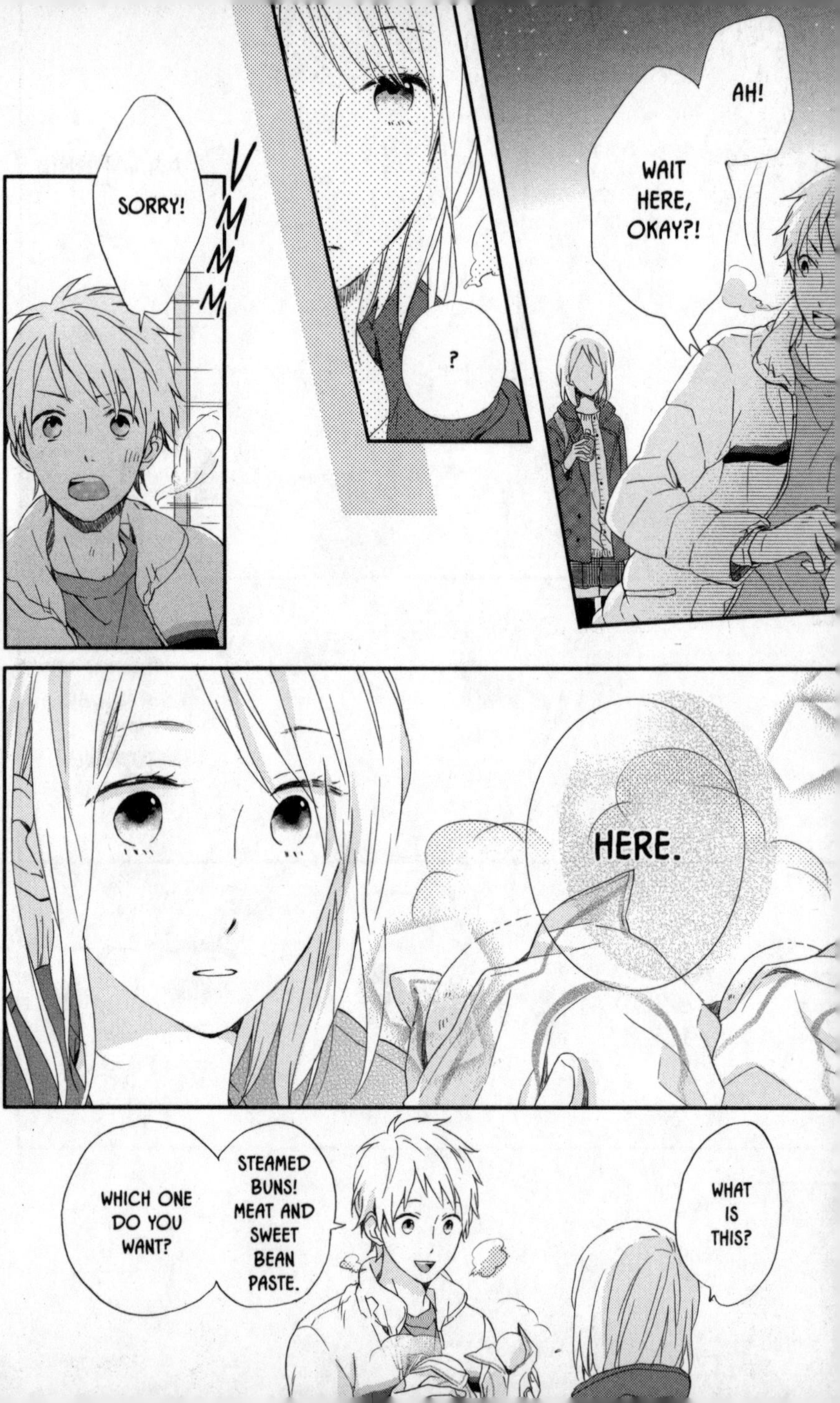
AH!
WAIT HERE, OKAY?!
?
SORRY!
VMMMM
HERE.
WHAT IS THIS?
STEAMED BUNS! MEAT AND SWEET BEAN PASTE.
WHICH ONE DO YOU WANT?

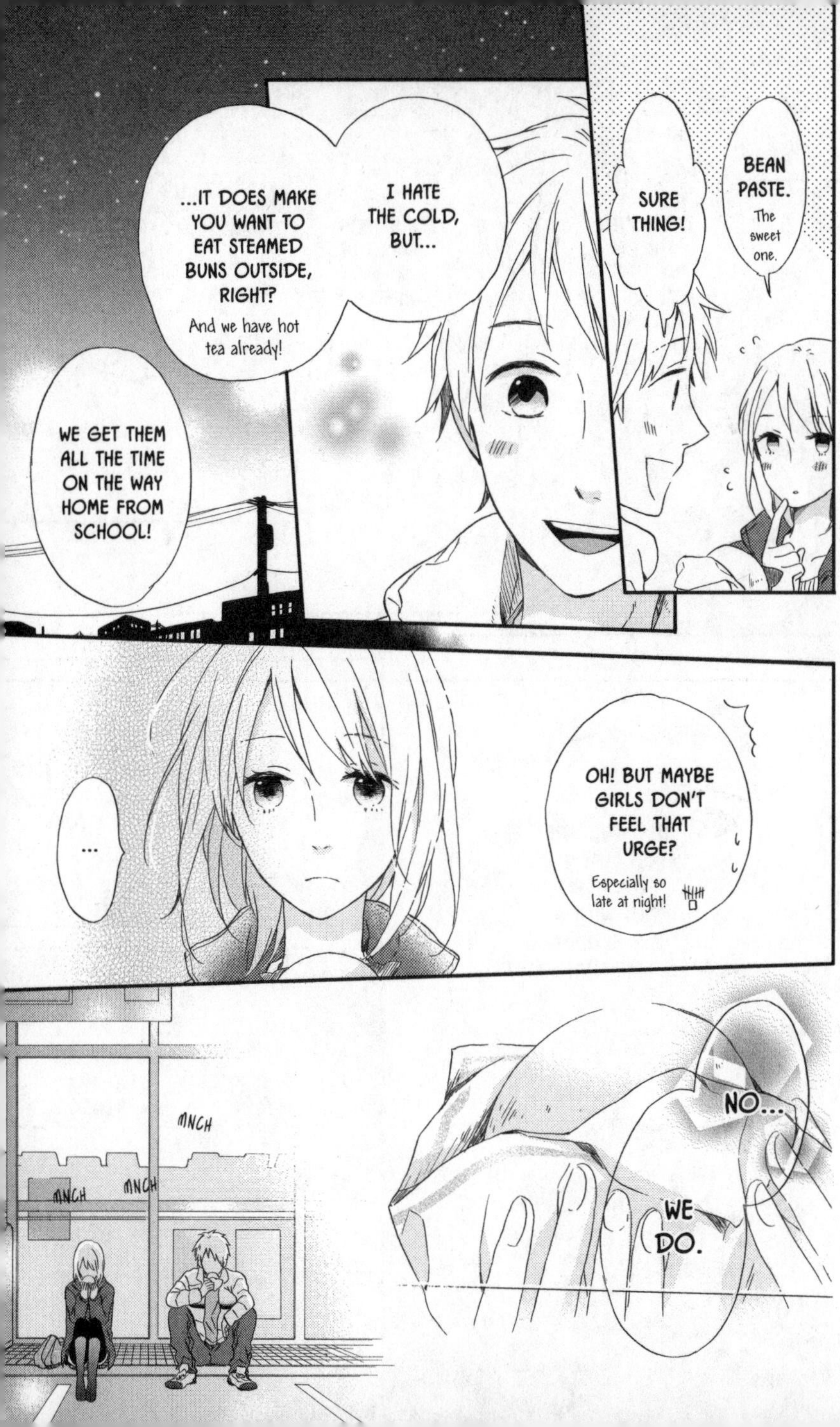
BEAN PASTE.
The sweet one.
SURE THING!
I HATE THE COLD, BUT...
...IT DOES MAKE YOU WANT TO EAT STEAMED BUNS OUTSIDE, RIGHT?
And we have hot tea already!
WE GET THEM ALL THE TIME ON THE WAY HOME FROM SCHOOL!
OH! BUT MAYBE GIRLS DON'T FEEL THAT URGE?
Especially so late at night!
...
NO...
WE DO.
MNCH
MNCH
MNCH

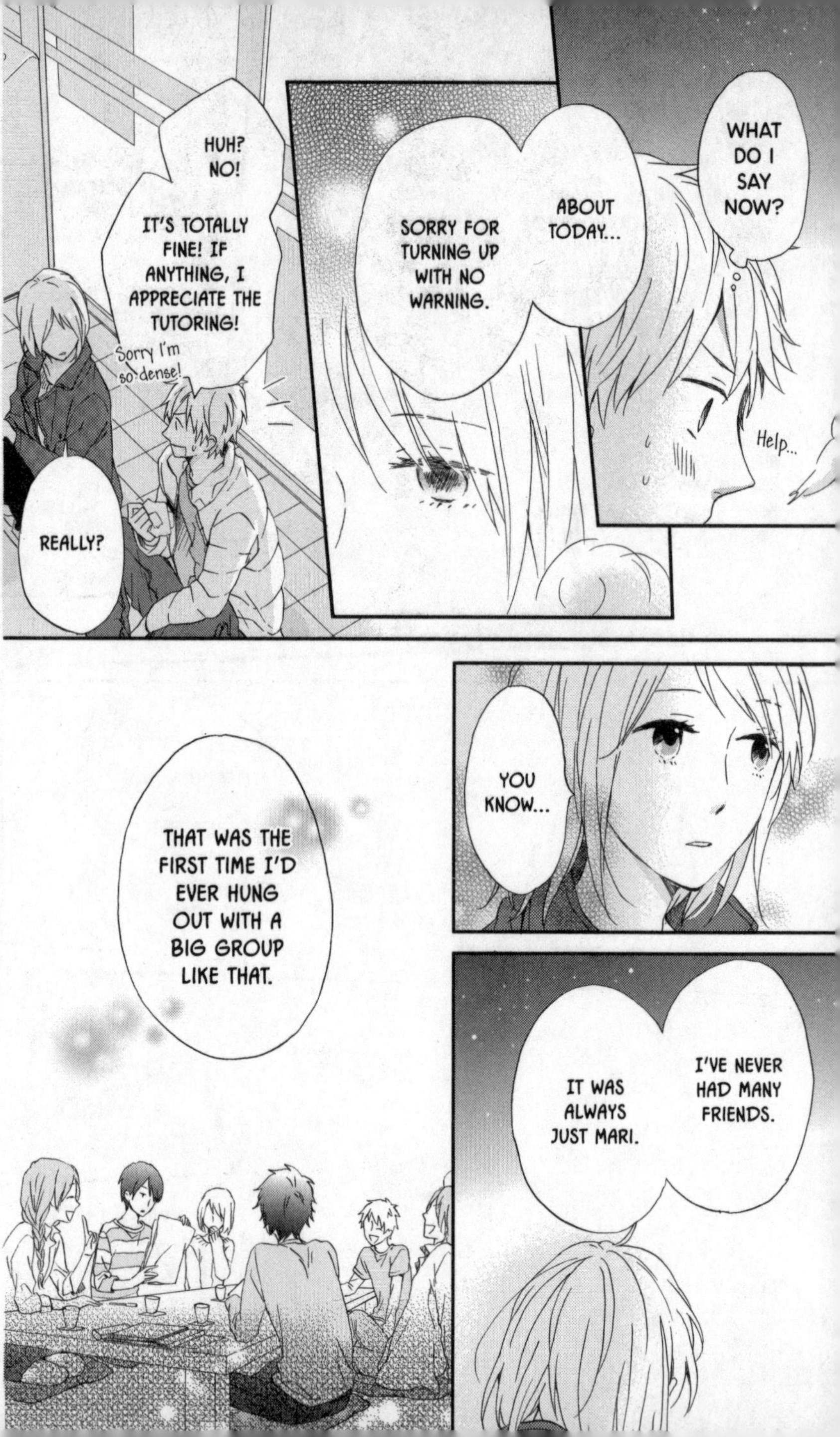
WHAT DO I SAY NOW?
Help...
ABOUT TODAY...
SORRY FOR TURNING UP WITH NO WARNING.
HUH? NO!
IT'S TOTALLY FINE! IF ANYTHING, I APPRECIATE THE TUTORING!
Sorry I'm so dense!
REALLY?
YOU KNOW...
I'VE NEVER HAD MANY FRIENDS.
IT WAS ALWAYS JUST MARI.
THAT WAS THE FIRST TIME I'D EVER HUNG OUT WITH A BIG GROUP LIKE THAT.

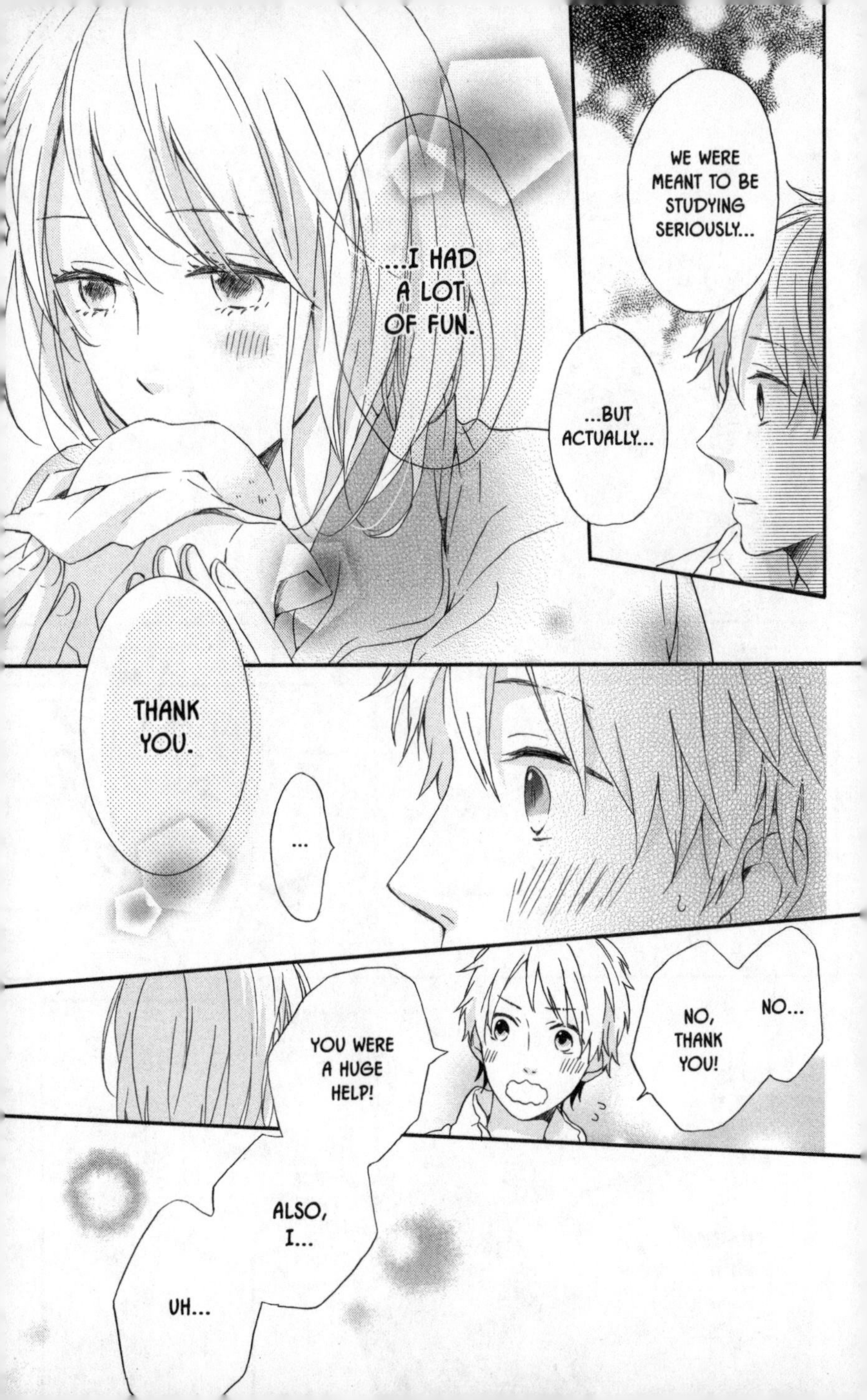
WE WERE MEANT TO BE STUDYING SERIOUSLY...
...BUT ACTUALLY...
...I HAD A LOT OF FUN.
THANK YOU.
...
NO...
NO, THANK YOU!
YOU WERE A HUGE HELP!
ALSO, I...
UH...

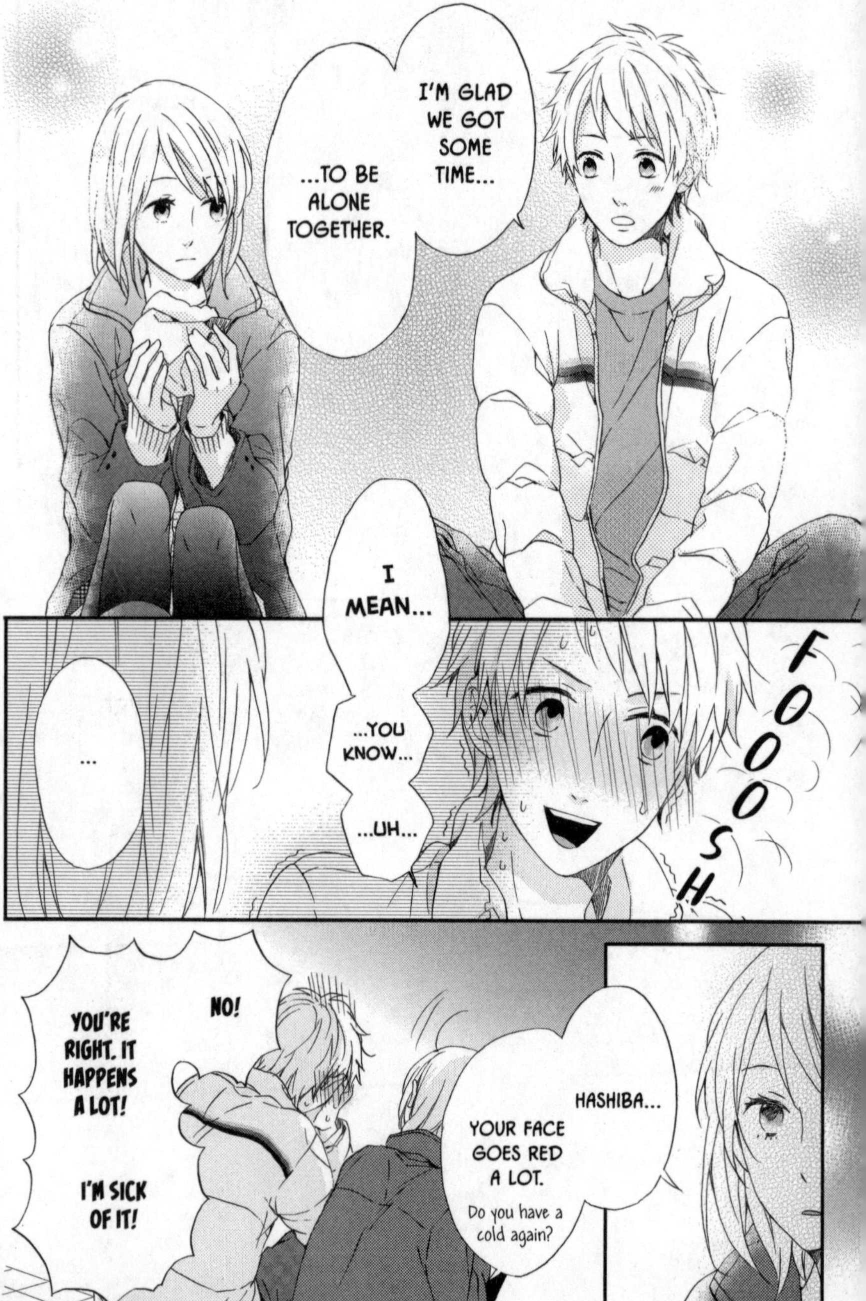
I'M GLAD WE GOT SOME TIME...
...TO BE ALONE TOGETHER.
I MEAN...
FOOOOSH
...YOU KNOW...
...UH...
...
HASHIBA...
YOUR FACE GOES RED A LOT.
Do you have a cold again?
NO!
YOU'RE RIGHT. IT HAPPENS A LOT!
I'M SICK OF IT!

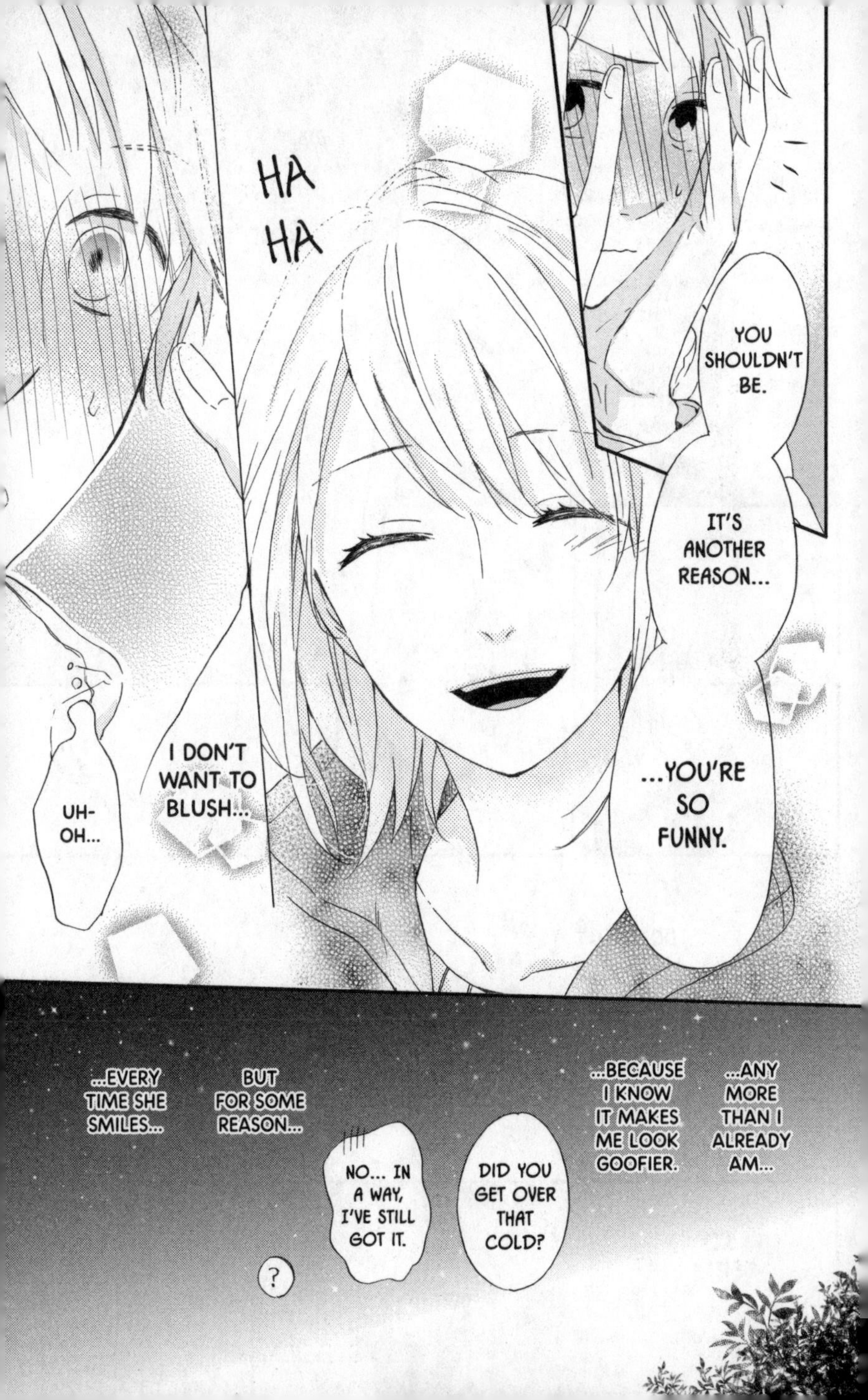
YOU SHOULDN'T BE.
IT'S ANOTHER REASON...
...YOU'RE SO FUNNY.
HA HA
I DON'T WANT TO BLUSH...
UH-OH...
...ANY MORE THAN I ALREADY AM...
...BECAUSE I KNOW IT MAKES ME LOOK GOOFIER.
DID YOU GET OVER THAT COLD?
NO... IN A WAY, I'VE STILL GOT IT.
BUT FOR SOME REASON...
...EVERY TIME SHE SMILES...
?

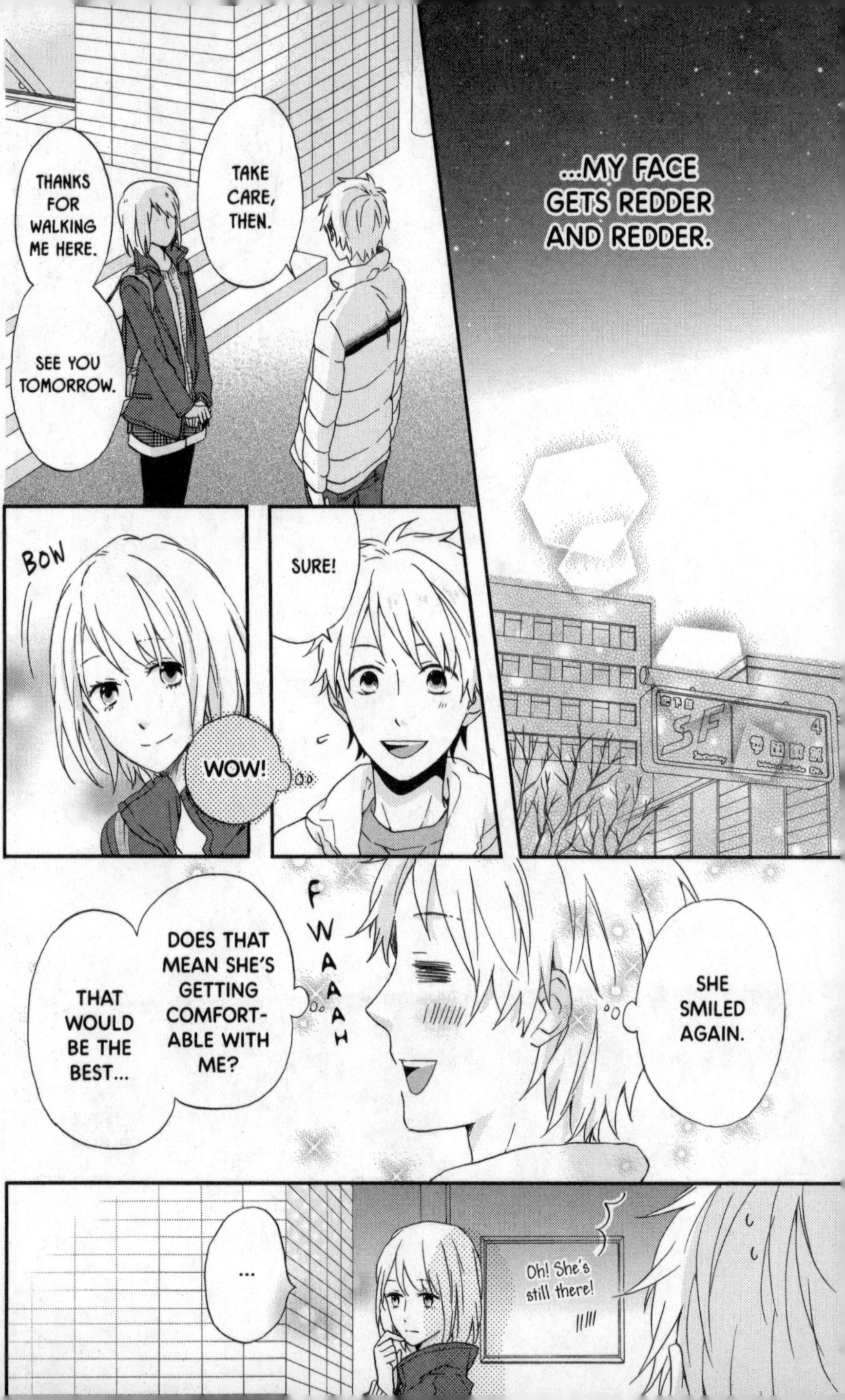
...MY FACE GETS REDDER AND REDDER.
TAKE CARE, THEN.
THANKS FOR WALKING ME HERE.
SEE YOU TOMORROW.
SURE!
BOW
WOW!
SHE SMILED AGAIN.
FWAAAAH
DOES THAT MEAN SHE'S GETTING COMFORT-ABLE WITH ME?
THAT WOULD BE THE BEST...
Oh! She's still there!
...

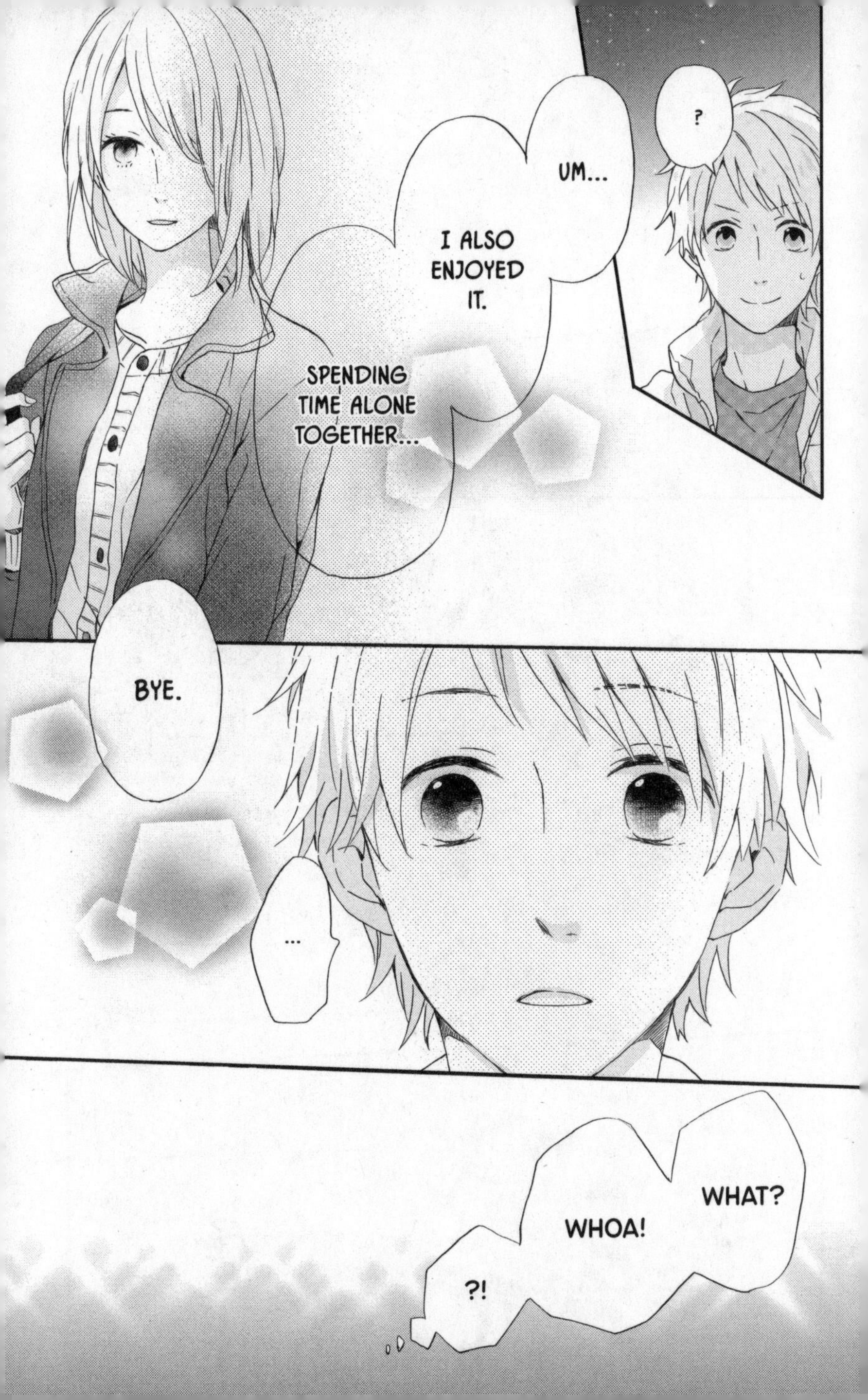

?
UM...
I ALSO ENJOYED IT.
SPENDING TIME ALONE TOGETHER...
BYE.
...
WHAT?
WHOA!
?!

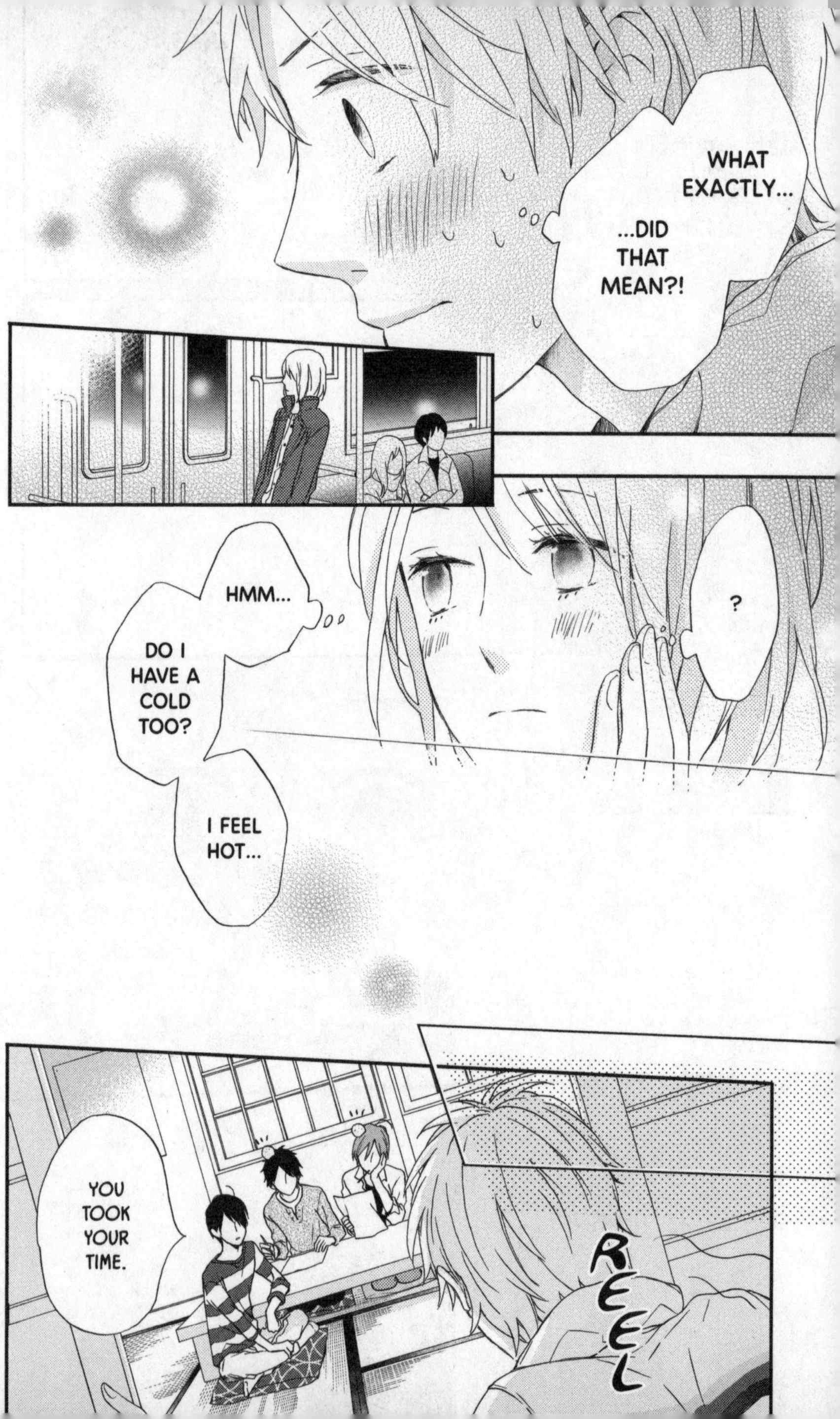
WHAT EXACTLY...
...DID THAT MEAN?!
?
HMM...
DO I HAVE A COLD TOO?
I FEEL HOT...
REEL
YOU TOOK YOUR TIME.

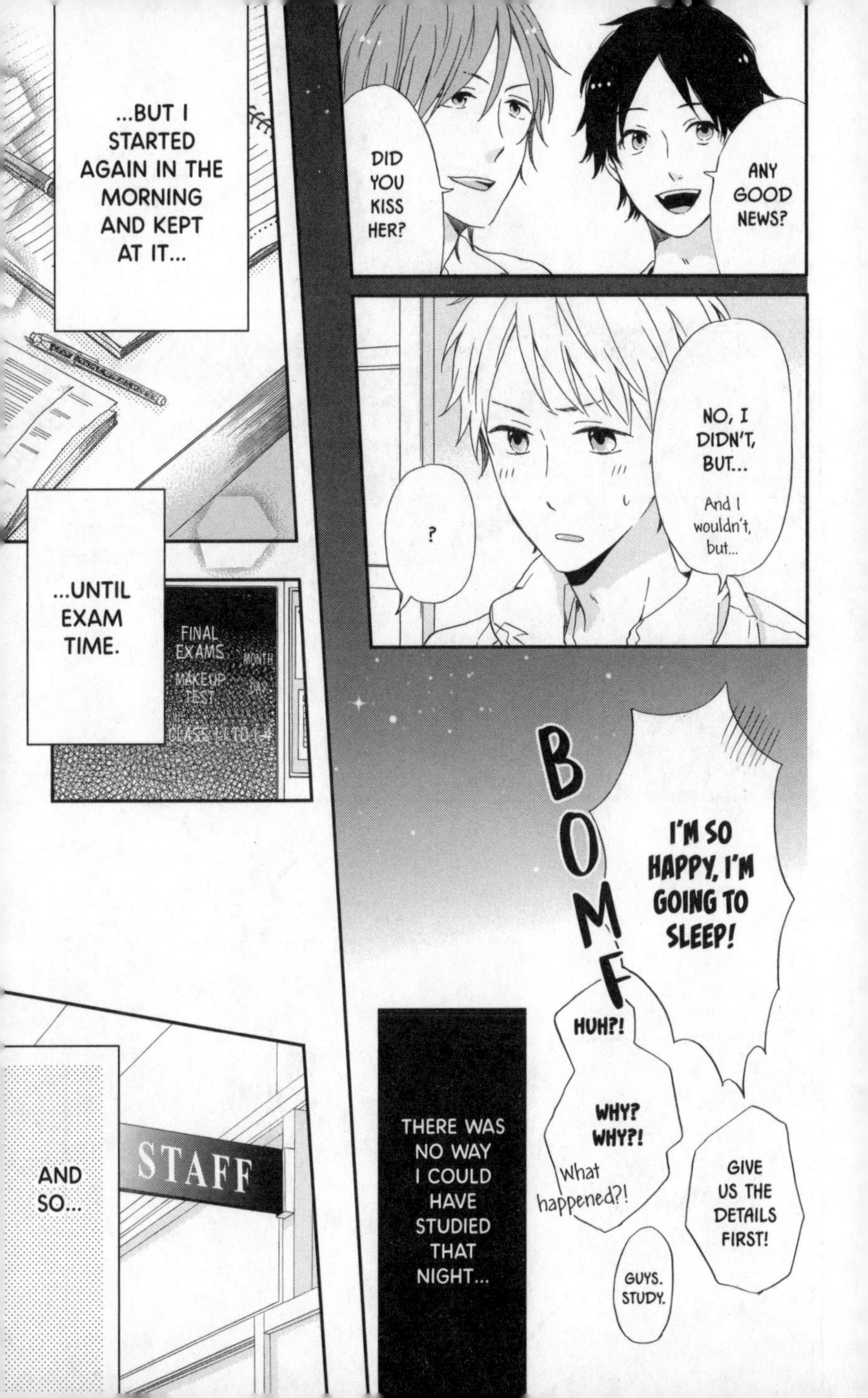
ANY GOOD NEWS?
DID YOU KISS HER?
NO, I DIDN'T, BUT...
And I wouldn't, but...
?
BOMF
I'M SO HAPPY, I'M GOING TO SLEEP!
HUH?!
WHY? WHY?!
What happened?!
GIVE US THE DETAILS FIRST!
GUYS. STUDY.
THERE WAS NO WAY I COULD HAVE STUDIED THAT NIGHT...
...BUT I STARTED AGAIN IN THE MORNING AND KEPT AT IT...
...UNTIL EXAM TIME.
FINAL EXAMS
MONTH
MAKEUP TEST
DAY
CLASS 1-1 TO 1-4
AND SO...
STAFF

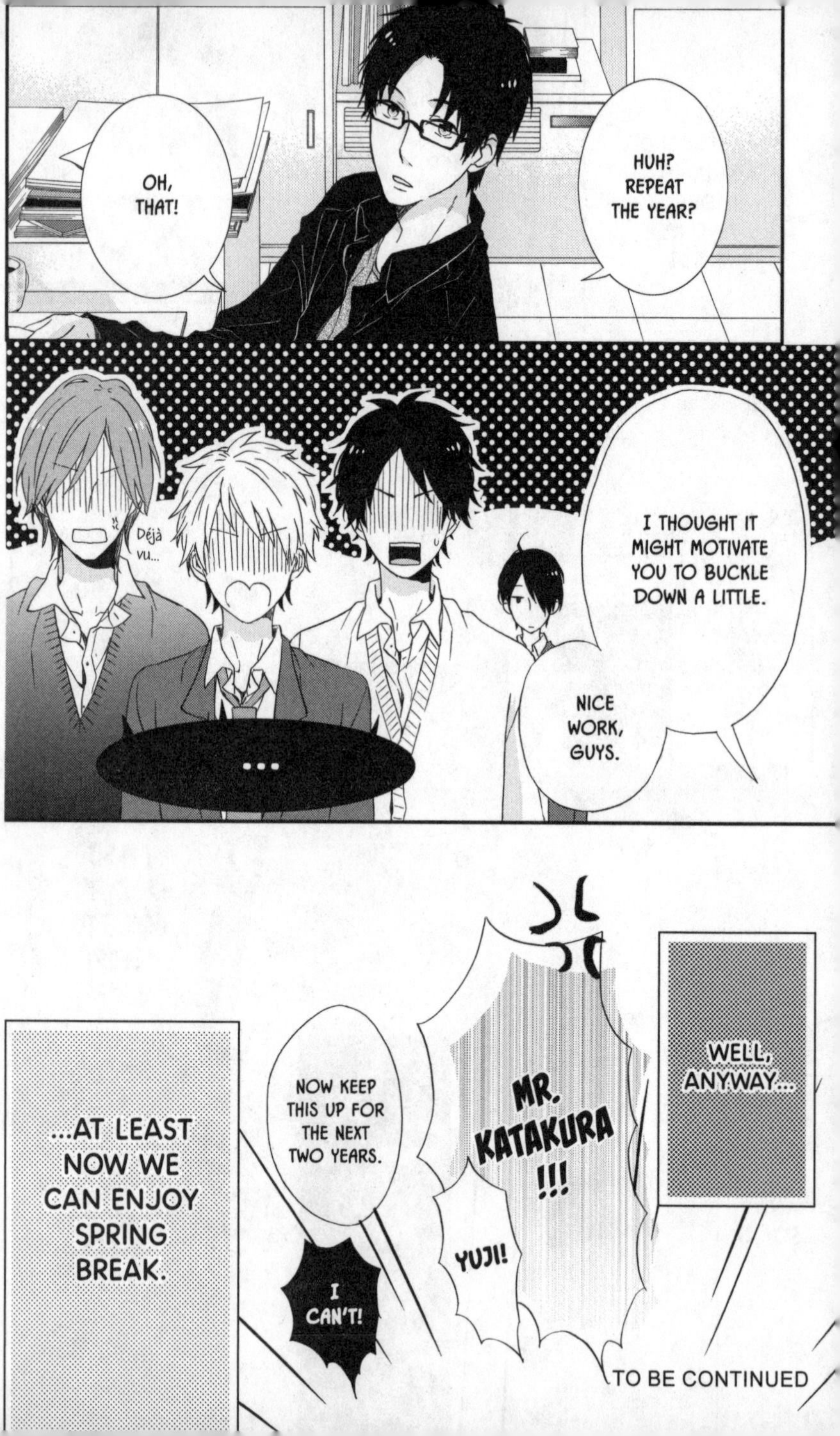
HUH? REPEAT THE YEAR?
OH, THAT!
I THOUGHT IT MIGHT MOTIVATE YOU TO BUCKLE DOWN A LITTLE.
NICE WORK, GUYS.
...
Déjà vu...
WELL, ANYWAY...
NOW KEEP THIS UP FOR THE NEXT TWO YEARS.
MR. KATAKURA!!!
YUJI!
I CAN'T!
...AT LEAST NOW WE CAN ENJOY SPRING BREAK.
TO BE CONTINUED

RAINBOW DAYS

I drew this for a postcard included in *The Margaret*.
It's a flirty Natchan.
My editor liked it, which made me happy.
I actually love using flowers as a background for boys,
so I hope to draw something like this again! 【●´ｴ`●】

RAINBOW DAYS

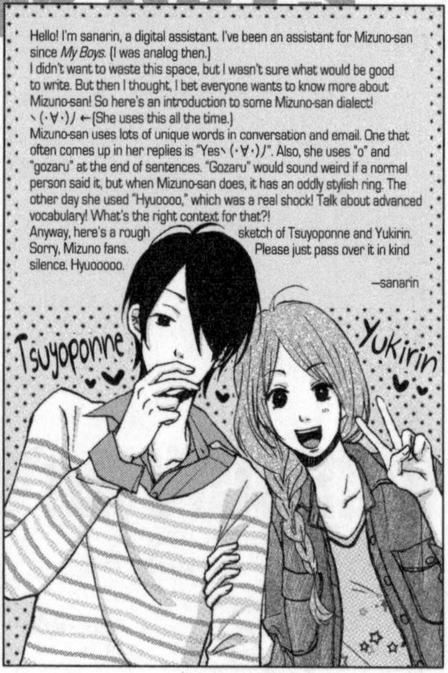
Hello! I'm sanarin, a digital assistant. I've been an assistant for Mizuno-san since *My Boys*. (I was analog then.)
I didn't want to waste this space, but I wasn't sure what would be good to write. But then I thought, I bet everyone wants to know more about Mizuno-san! So here's an introduction to some Mizuno-san dialect!
ヽ(・∀・)ﾉ ←(She uses this all the time.)
Mizuno-san uses lots of unique words in conversation and email. One that often comes up in her replies is "Yesヽ(・∀・)ﾉ". Also, she uses "o" and "gozaru" at the end of sentences. "Gozaru" would sound weird if a normal person said it, but when Mizuno-san does, it has an oddly stylish ring. The other day she used "Hyuoooo," which was a real shock! Talk about advanced vocabulary! What's the right context for that?!
Anyway, here's a rough sketch of Tsuyoponne and Yukirin. Sorry, Mizuno fans. Please just pass over it in kind silence. Hyuooooo.
—sanarin
Tsuyoponne
Yukirin

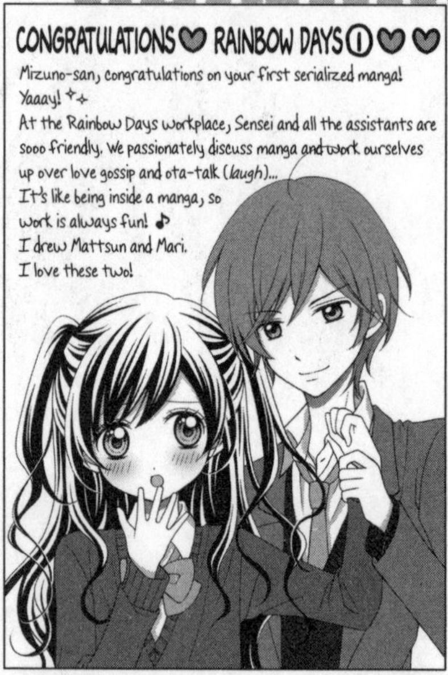
CONGRATULATIONS ♥ RAINBOW DAYS ① ♥ ♥
Mizuno-san, congratulations on your first serialized manga! Yaaay!
At the Rainbow Days workplace, Sensei and all the assistants are sooo friendly. We passionately discuss manga and work ourselves up over love gossip and ota-talk (*laugh*)...
It's like being inside a manga, so work is always fun! ♪
I drew Mattsun and Mari.
I love these two!

MY ASSISTANTS DREW THESE FOR ME PAGE ♥

Top left: Nanami-chan Koyama
Top right: sanarin
Bottom left: nao-san

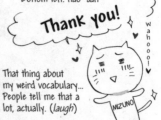

Thank you!

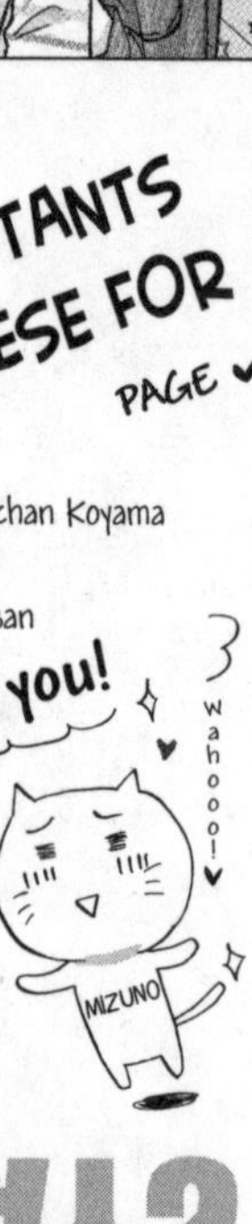
wahoooo!
MIZUNO

That thing about my weird vocabulary... People tell me that a lot, actually. (*laugh*)

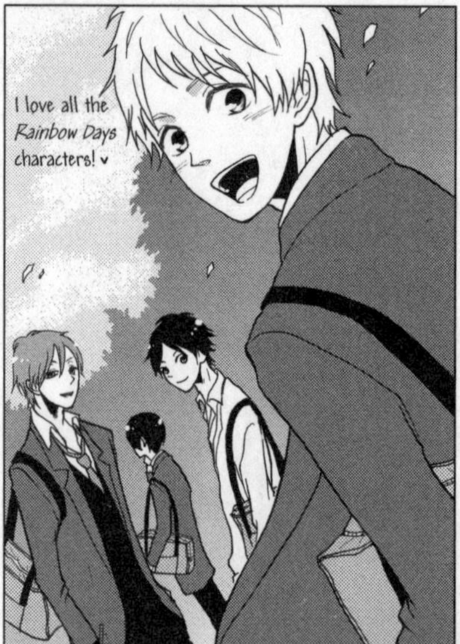
I love all the *Rainbow Days* characters! ♥

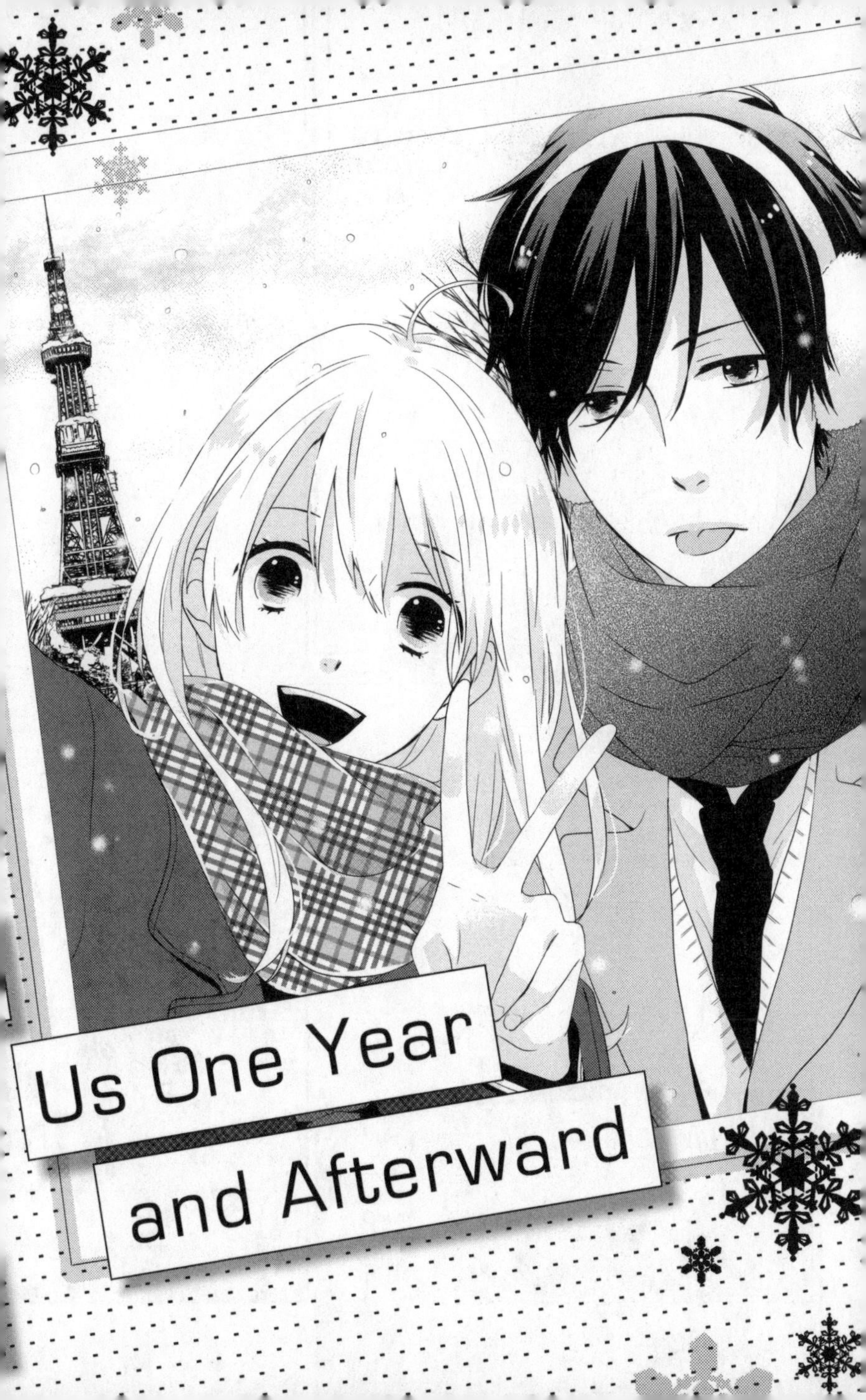
Us One Year
and Afterward

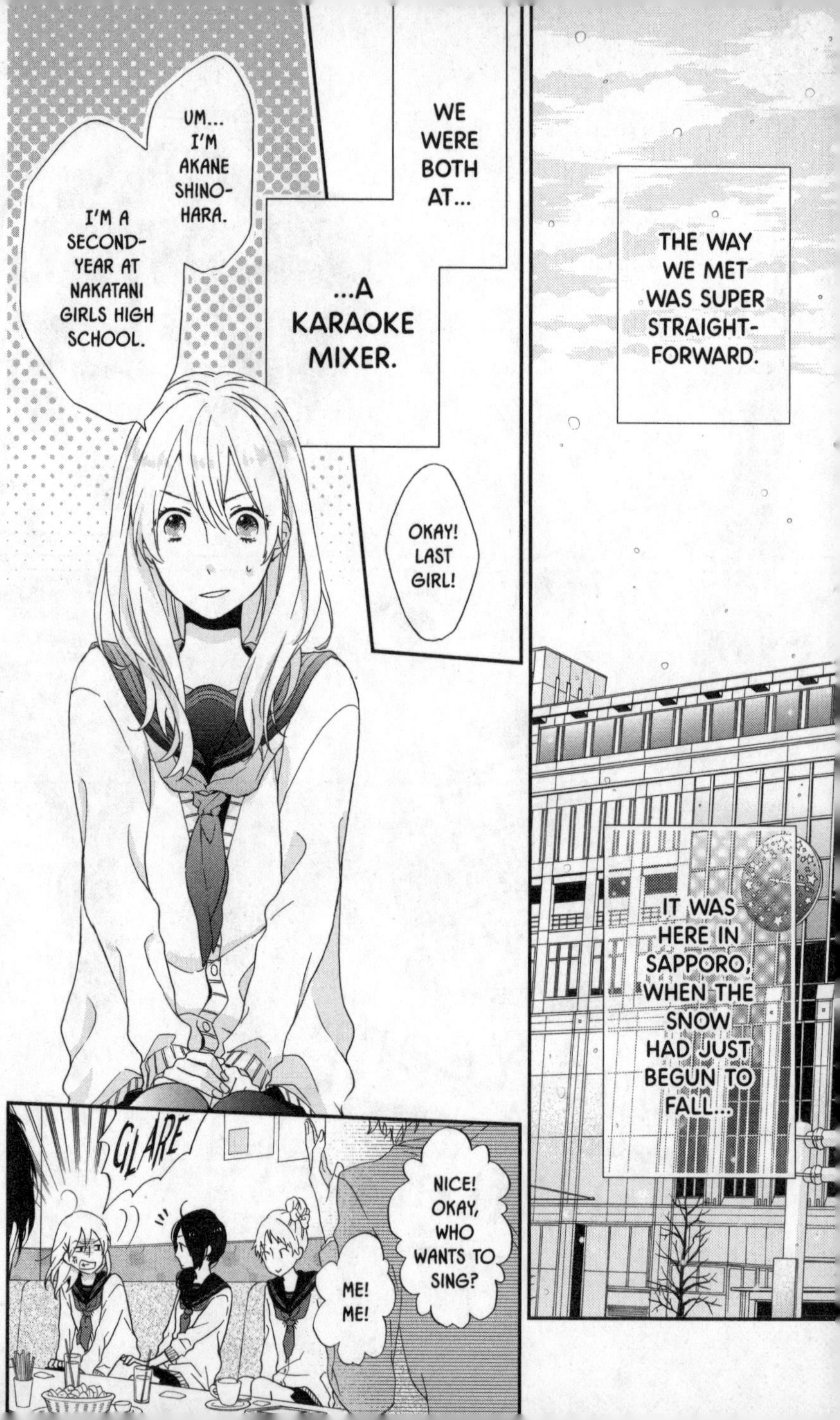
THE WAY WE MET WAS SUPER STRAIGHT-FORWARD.
IT WAS HERE IN SAPPORO, WHEN THE SNOW HAD JUST BEGUN TO FALL...
WE WERE BOTH AT...
...A KARAOKE MIXER.
OKAY! LAST GIRL!
UM... I'M AKANE SHINO-HARA.
I'M A SECOND-YEAR AT NAKATANI GIRLS HIGH SCHOOL.
NICE! OKAY, WHO WANTS TO SING?
ME! ME!
GLARE

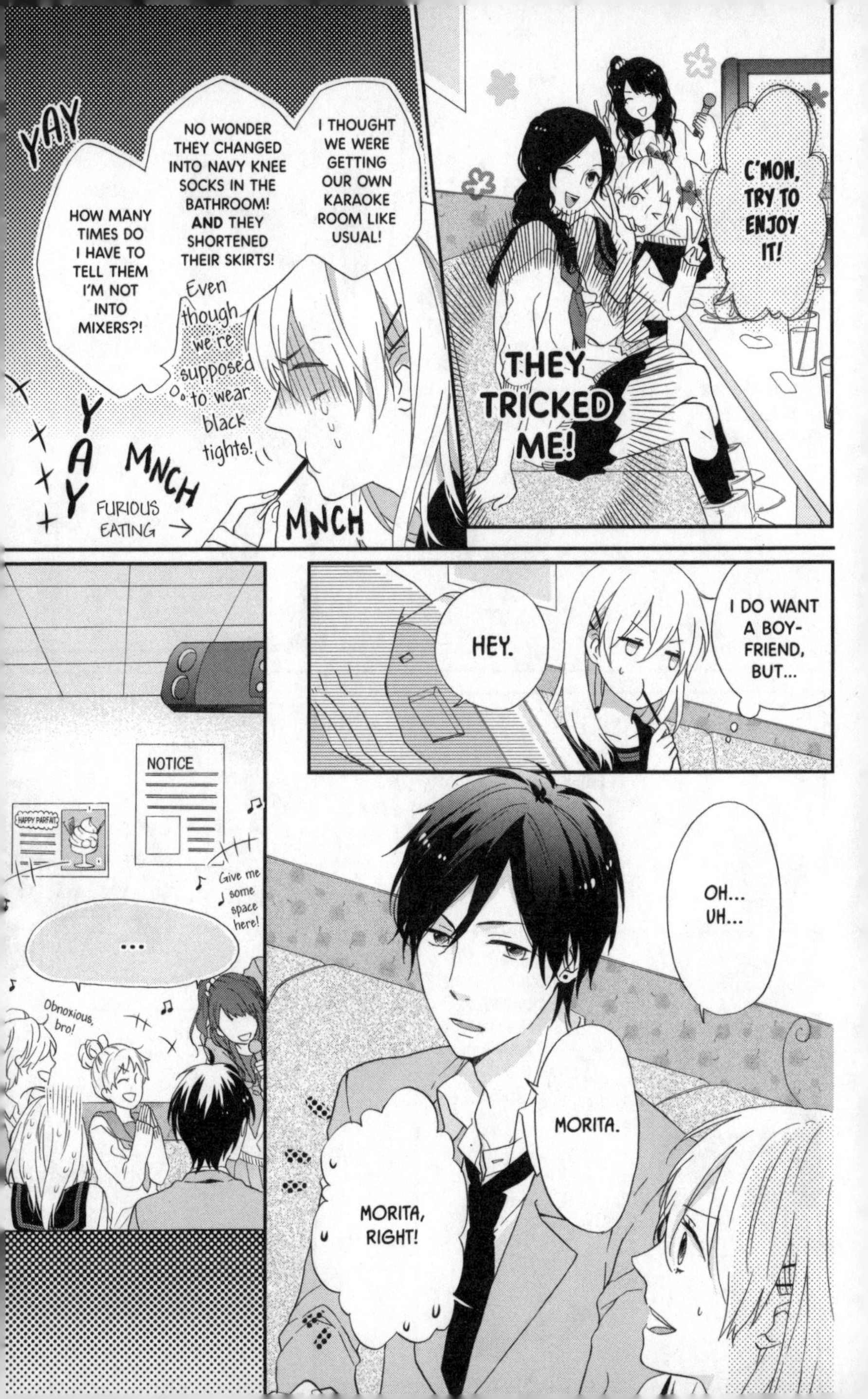
C'MON, TRY TO ENJOY IT!
THEY TRICKED ME!
I THOUGHT WE WERE GETTING OUR OWN KARAOKE ROOM LIKE USUAL!
NO WONDER THEY CHANGED INTO NAVY KNEE SOCKS IN THE BATHROOM! AND THEY SHORTENED THEIR SKIRTS!
HOW MANY TIMES DO I HAVE TO TELL THEM I'M NOT INTO MIXERS?!
Even though we're supposed to wear black tights!
YAY
YAY
MNCH
MNCH
FURIOUS EATING →
I DO WANT A BOY-FRIEND, BUT...
HEY.
OH... UH...
MORITA.
MORITA, RIGHT!
NOTICE
HAPPY PARFAIT
Give me some space here!
...
Obnoxious, bro!

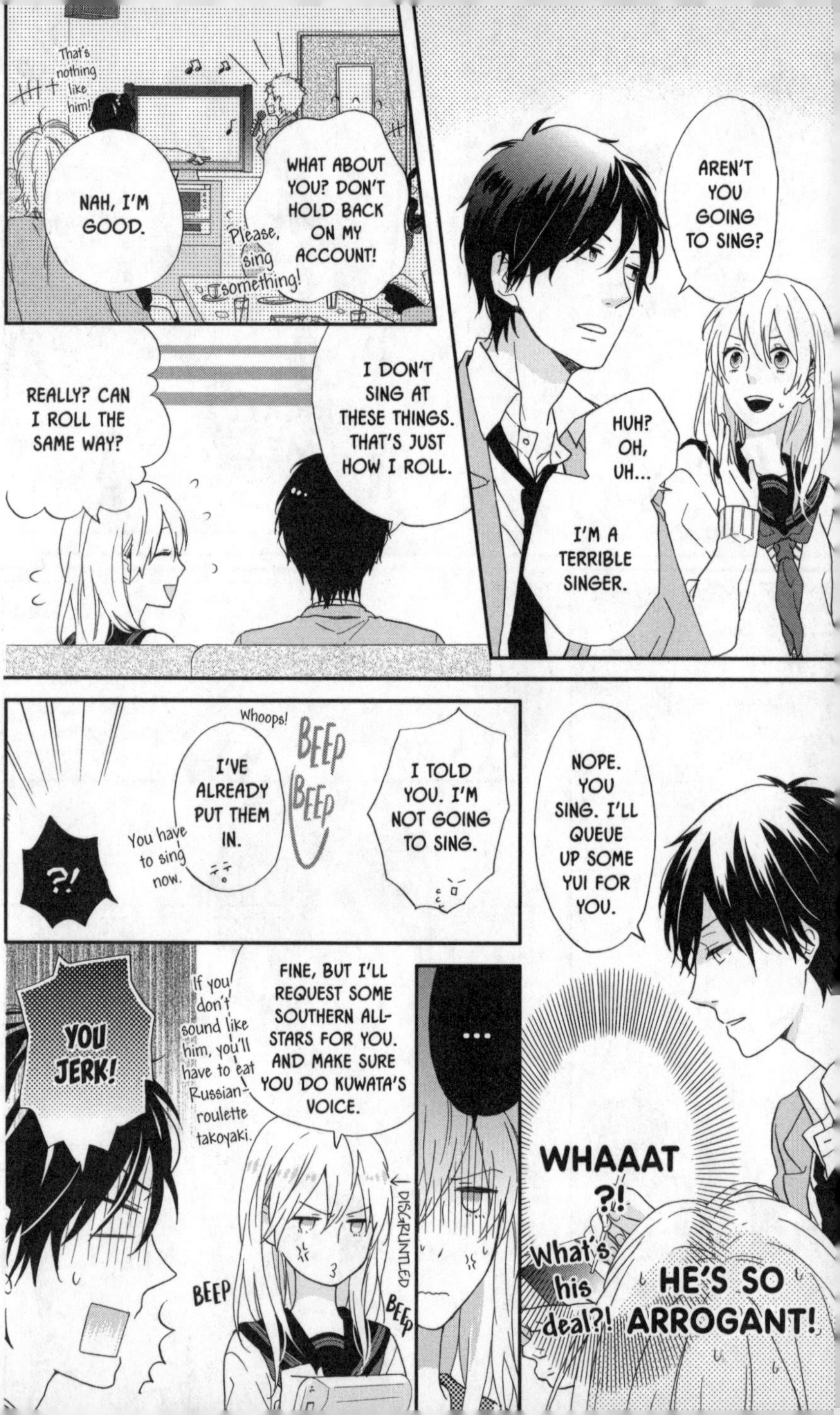
AREN'T YOU GOING TO SING?
HUH? OH, UH...
I'M A TERRIBLE SINGER.
WHAT ABOUT YOU? DON'T HOLD BACK ON MY ACCOUNT!
Please, sing something!
That's nothing like him!
NAH, I'M GOOD.
I DON'T SING AT THESE THINGS. THAT'S JUST HOW I ROLL.
REALLY? CAN I ROLL THE SAME WAY?
NOPE. YOU SING. I'LL QUEUE UP SOME YUI FOR YOU.
WHAAAT?!
HE'S SO ARROGANT!
What's his deal?!
I TOLD YOU. I'M NOT GOING TO SING.
BEEP BEEP
Whoops!
I'VE ALREADY PUT THEM IN.
You have to sing now.
?!
...
FINE, BUT I'LL REQUEST SOME SOUTHERN ALL-STARS FOR YOU. AND MAKE SURE YOU DO KUWATA'S VOICE.
If you don't sound like him, you'll have to eat Russian-roulette takoyaki.
YOU JERK!
DISGRUNTLED
BEEP
BEEP

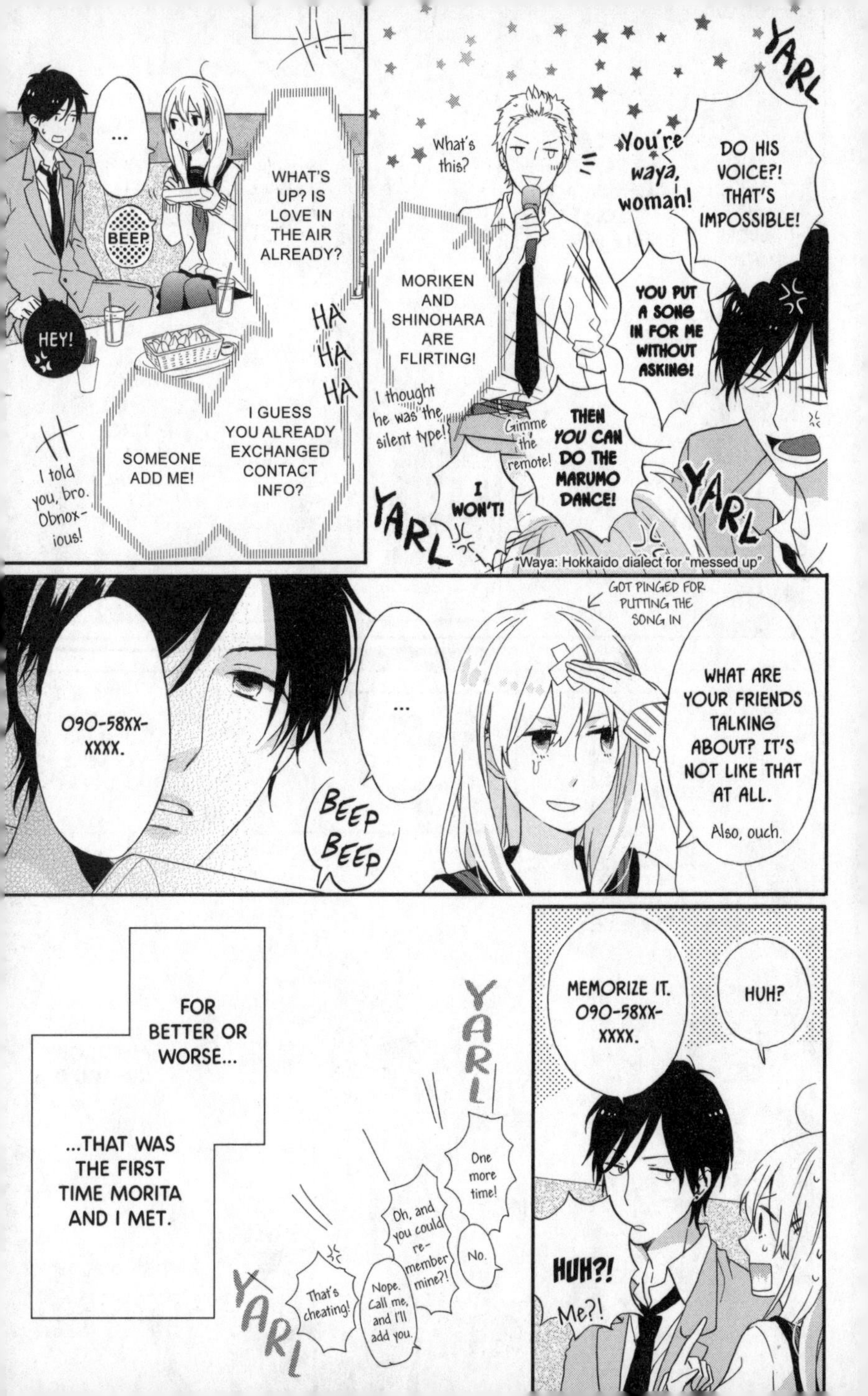
YARL
DO HIS VOICE?! THAT'S IMPOSSIBLE!
You're waya, woman!
What's this?
YOU PUT A SONG IN FOR ME WITHOUT ASKING!
THEN YOU CAN DO THE MARUMO DANCE!
Gimme the remote!
YARL
I WON'T!
YARL
MORIKEN AND SHINOHARA ARE FLIRTING!
I thought he was the silent type!
*Waya: Hokkaido dialect for "messed up"
WHAT'S UP? IS LOVE IN THE AIR ALREADY?
HA HA HA
...
BEEP
I GUESS YOU ALREADY EXCHANGED CONTACT INFO?
SOMEONE ADD ME!
HEY!
I told you, bro. Obnoxious!
GOT PINGED FOR PUTTING THE SONG IN
WHAT ARE YOUR FRIENDS TALKING ABOUT? IT'S NOT LIKE THAT AT ALL.
Also, ouch.
...
BEEP BEEP
090-58XX-XXXX.
HUH?
MEMORIZE IT. 090-58XX-XXXX.
HUH?!
Me?!
YARL
One more time!
No.
Oh, and you could re-member mine?!
Nope. Call me, and I'll add you.
That's cheating!
YARL
FOR BETTER OR WORSE...
...THAT WAS THE FIRST TIME MORITA AND I MET.

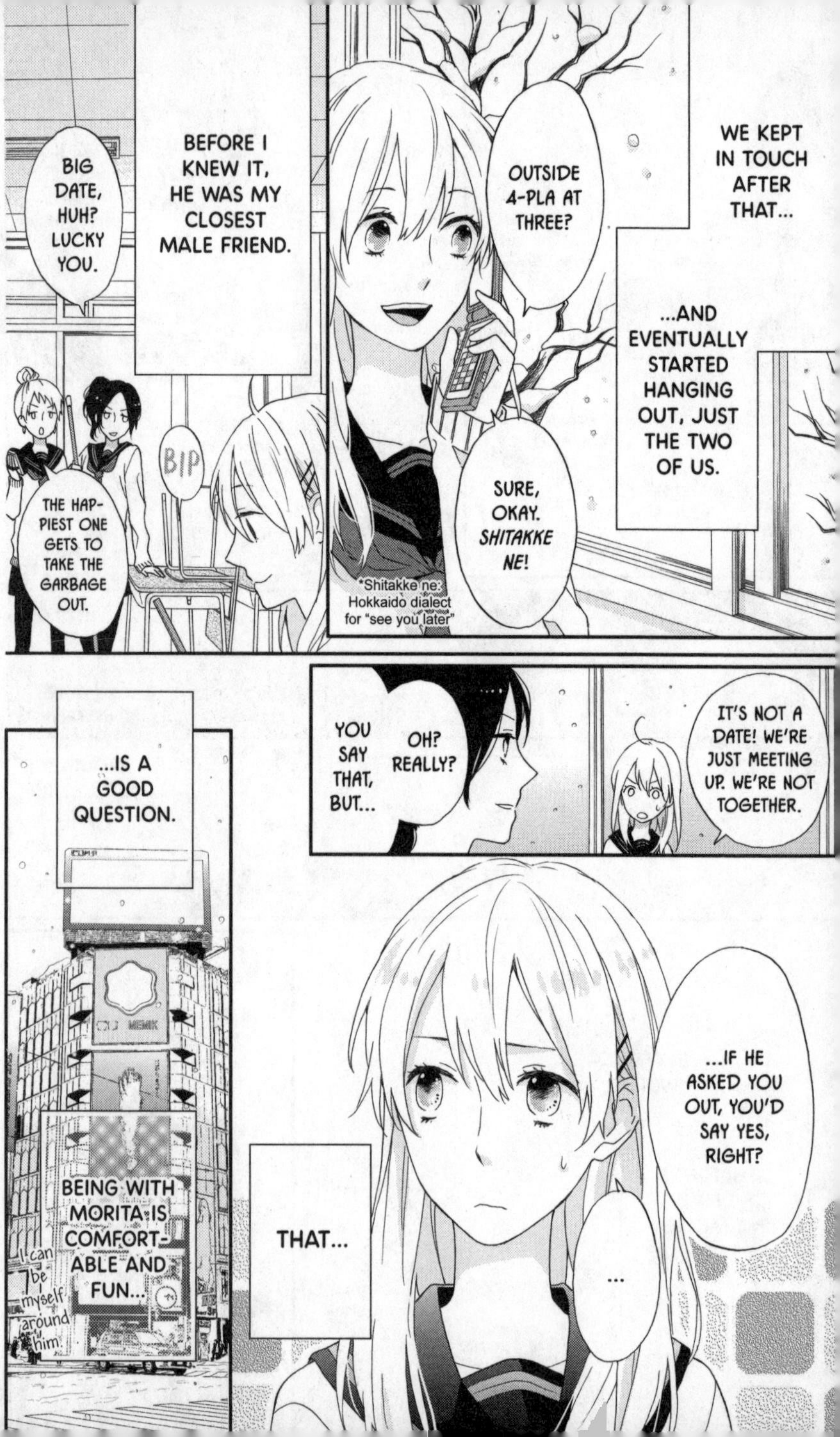
WE KEPT IN TOUCH AFTER THAT...
OUTSIDE 4-PLA AT THREE?
...AND EVENTUALLY STARTED HANGING OUT, JUST THE TWO OF US.
SURE, OKAY. SHITAKKE NE!
*Shitakke ne: Hokkaido dialect for "see you later"
BEFORE I KNEW IT, HE WAS MY CLOSEST MALE FRIEND.
BIG DATE, HUH? LUCKY YOU.
BIP
THE HAP-PIEST ONE GETS TO TAKE THE GARBAGE OUT.
IT'S NOT A DATE! WE'RE JUST MEETING UP. WE'RE NOT TOGETHER.
OH? REALLY?
...
YOU SAY THAT, BUT...
...IF HE ASKED YOU OUT, YOU'D SAY YES, RIGHT?
...
THAT...
...IS A GOOD QUESTION.
BEING WITH MORITA IS COMFORT-ABLE AND FUN...
I can be myself around him.

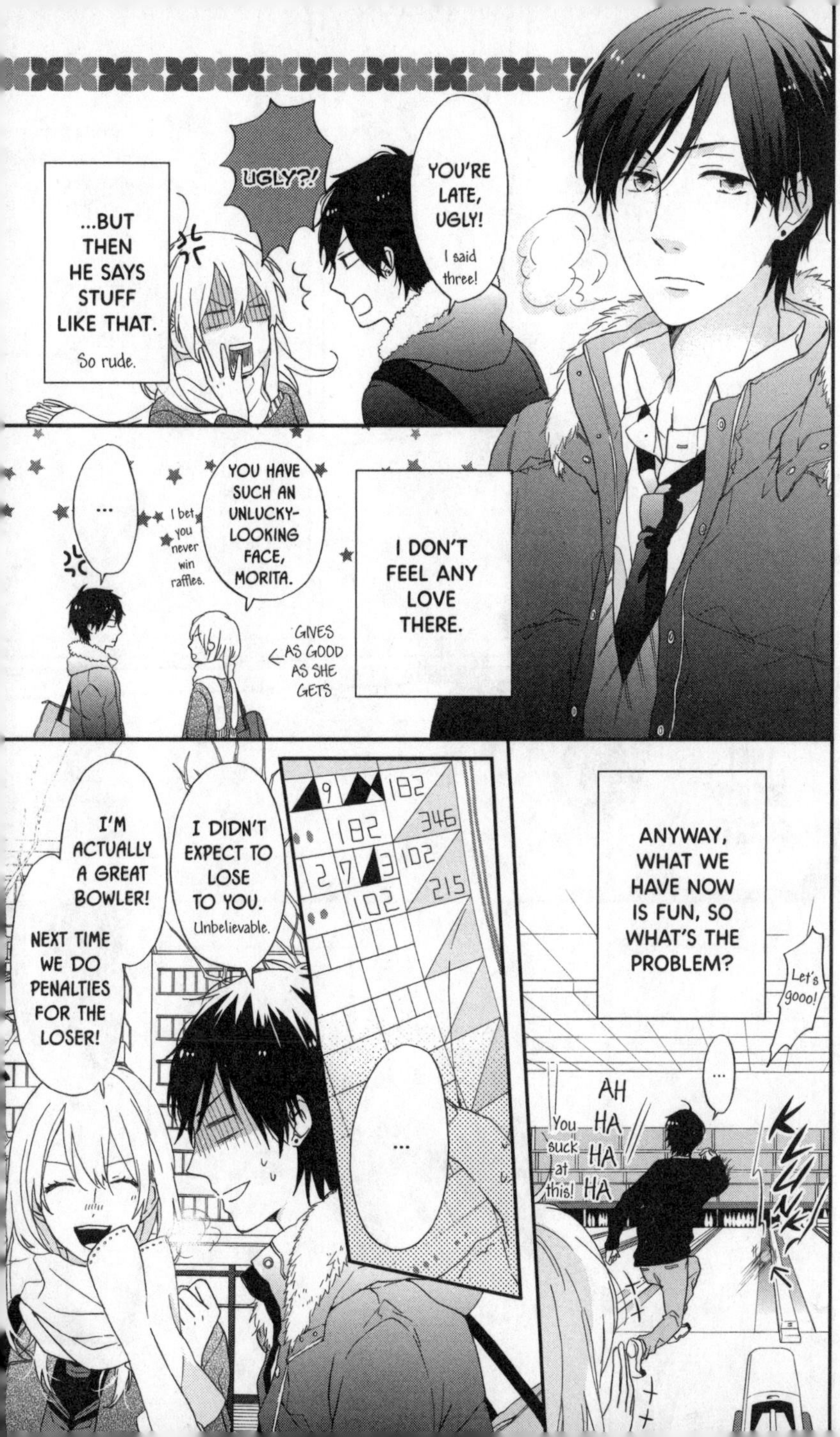
YOU'RE LATE, UGLY!
I said three!
UGLY?!
...BUT THEN HE SAYS STUFF LIKE THAT.
So rude.
YOU HAVE SUCH AN UNLUCKY-LOOKING FACE, MORITA.
I bet you never win raffles.
...
GIVES AS GOOD AS SHE GETS
I DON'T FEEL ANY LOVE THERE.
ANYWAY, WHAT WE HAVE NOW IS FUN, SO WHAT'S THE PROBLEM?
Let's gooo!
...
KLUNK
AH HA HA HA
You suck at this!
...
I DIDN'T EXPECT TO LOSE TO YOU.
Unbelievable.
I'M ACTUALLY A GREAT BOWLER!
NEXT TIME WE DO PENALTIES FOR THE LOSER!

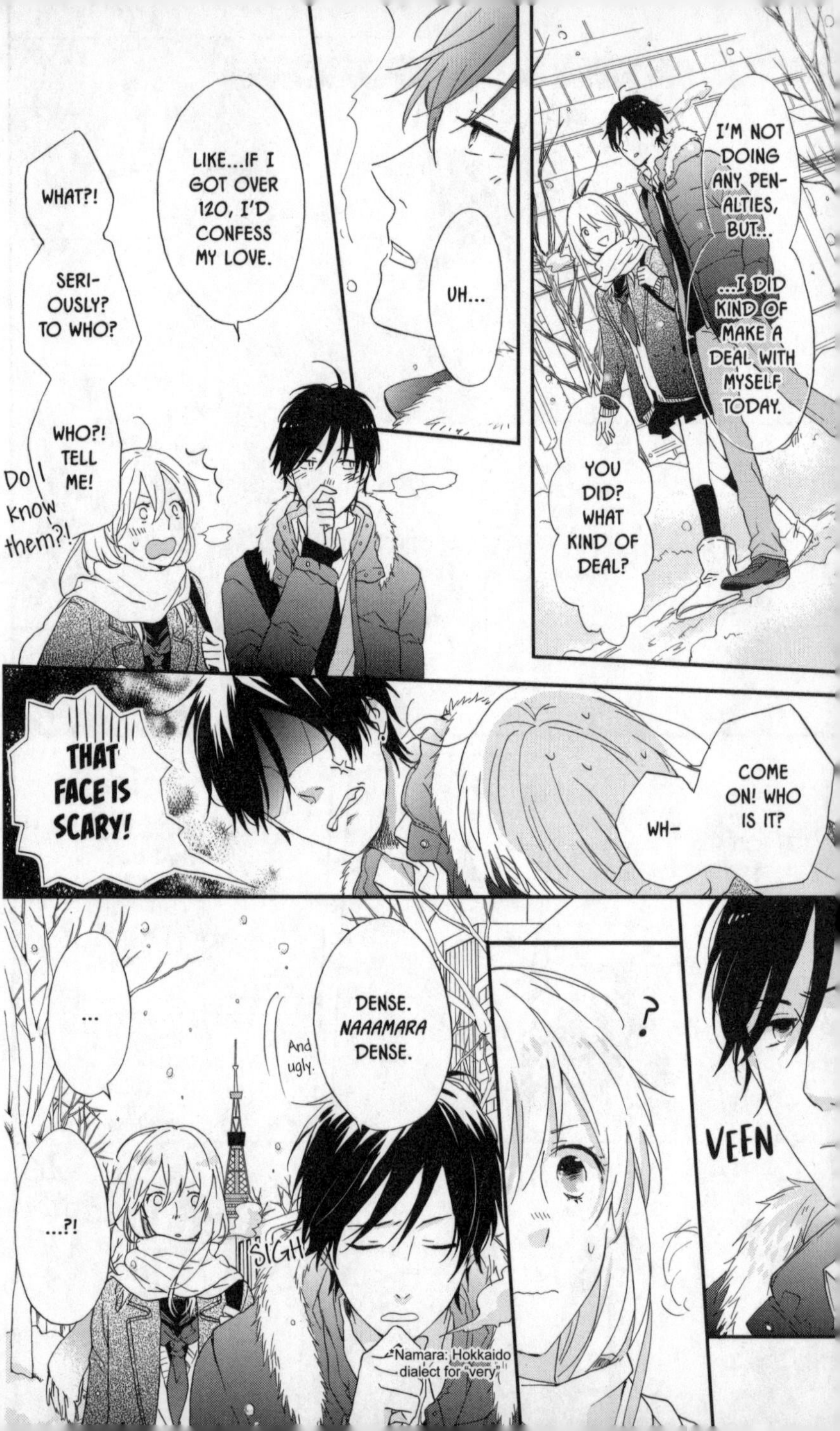
I'M NOT DOING ANY PEN-ALTIES, BUT...
...I DID KIND OF MAKE A DEAL WITH MYSELF TODAY.
YOU DID? WHAT KIND OF DEAL?
UH...
LIKE...IF I GOT OVER 120, I'D CONFESS MY LOVE.
WHAT?!
SERI-OUSLY? TO WHO?
WHO?! TELL ME!
Do I know them?!
COME ON! WHO IS IT?
WH-
THAT FACE IS SCARY!
VEEN
?
DENSE. NAAAMARA DENSE.
And ugly.
...
SIGH
...?!
*Namara: Hokkaido dialect for "very"

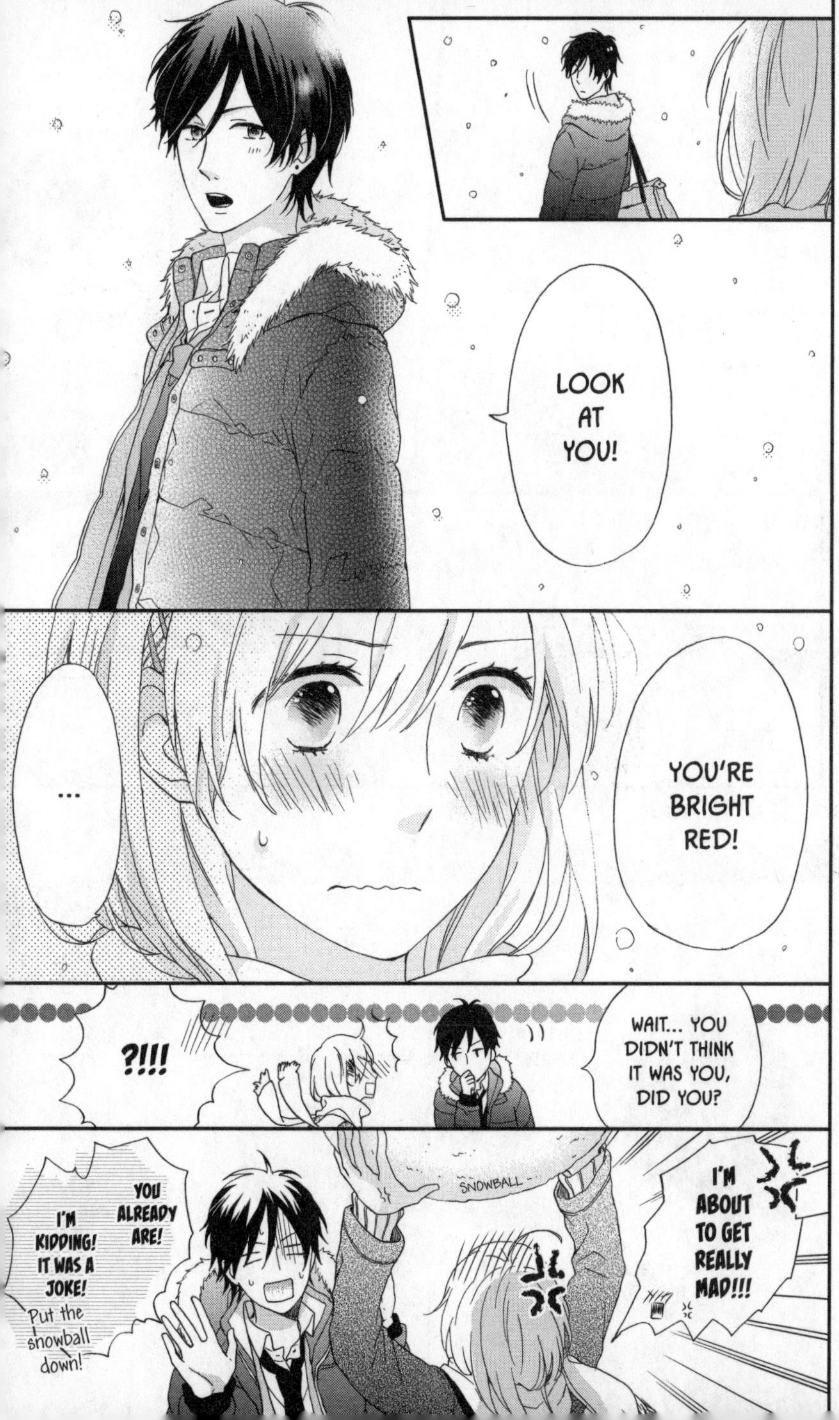
LOOK AT YOU!
YOU'RE BRIGHT RED!
...
WAIT... YOU DIDN'T THINK IT WAS YOU, DID YOU?
?!!!
I'M ABOUT TO GET REALLY MAD!!!
SNOWBALL
YOU ALREADY ARE!
I'M KIDDING! IT WAS A JOKE!
Put the snowball down!

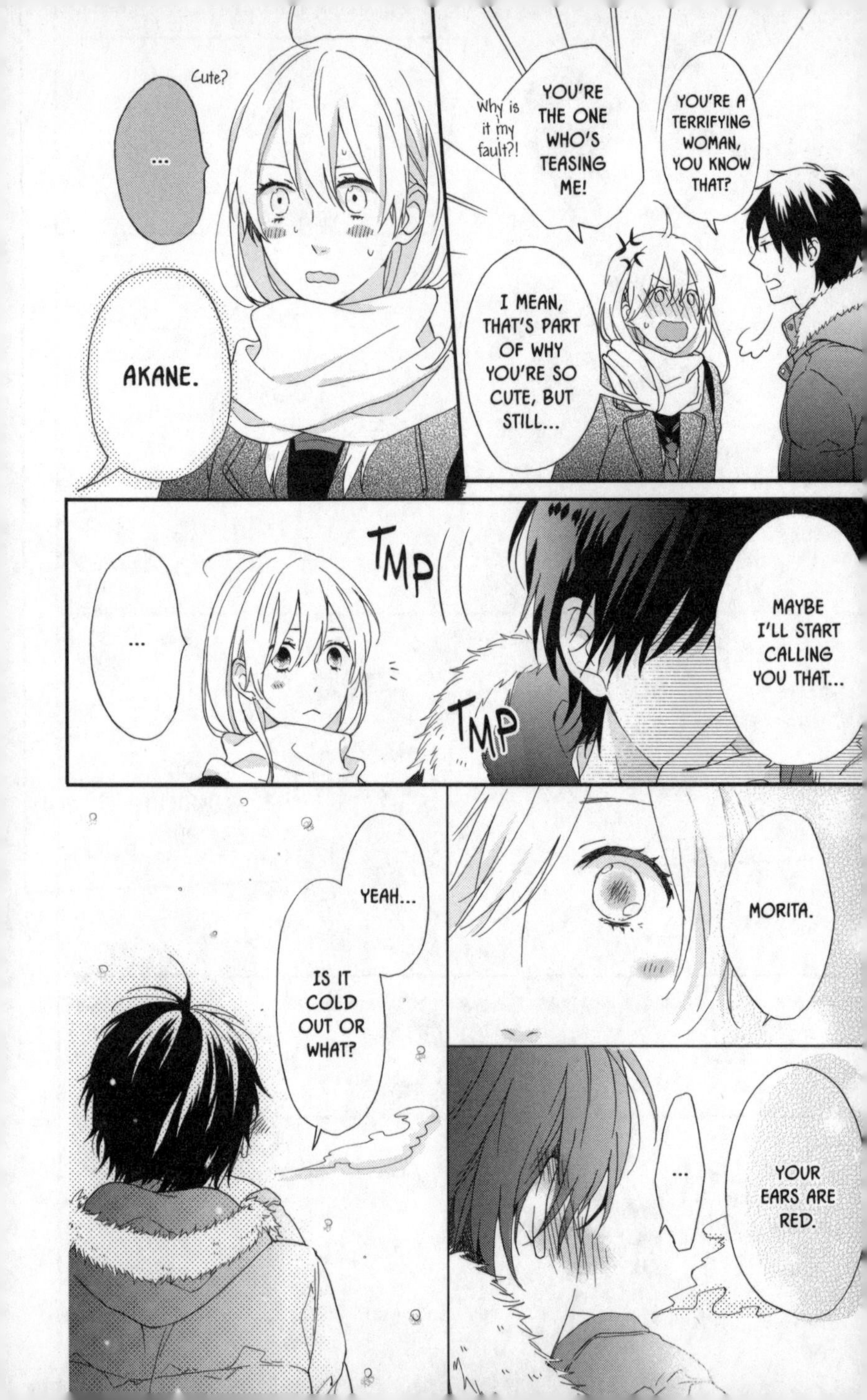
YOU'RE A TERRIFYING WOMAN, YOU KNOW THAT?
YOU'RE THE ONE WHO'S TEASING ME!
Why is it my fault?!
I MEAN, THAT'S PART OF WHY YOU'RE SO CUTE, BUT STILL...
Cute?
...
AKANE.
MAYBE I'LL START CALLING YOU THAT...
TMP
TMP
...
MORITA.
YOUR EARS ARE RED.
...
YEAH...
IS IT COLD OUT OR WHAT?

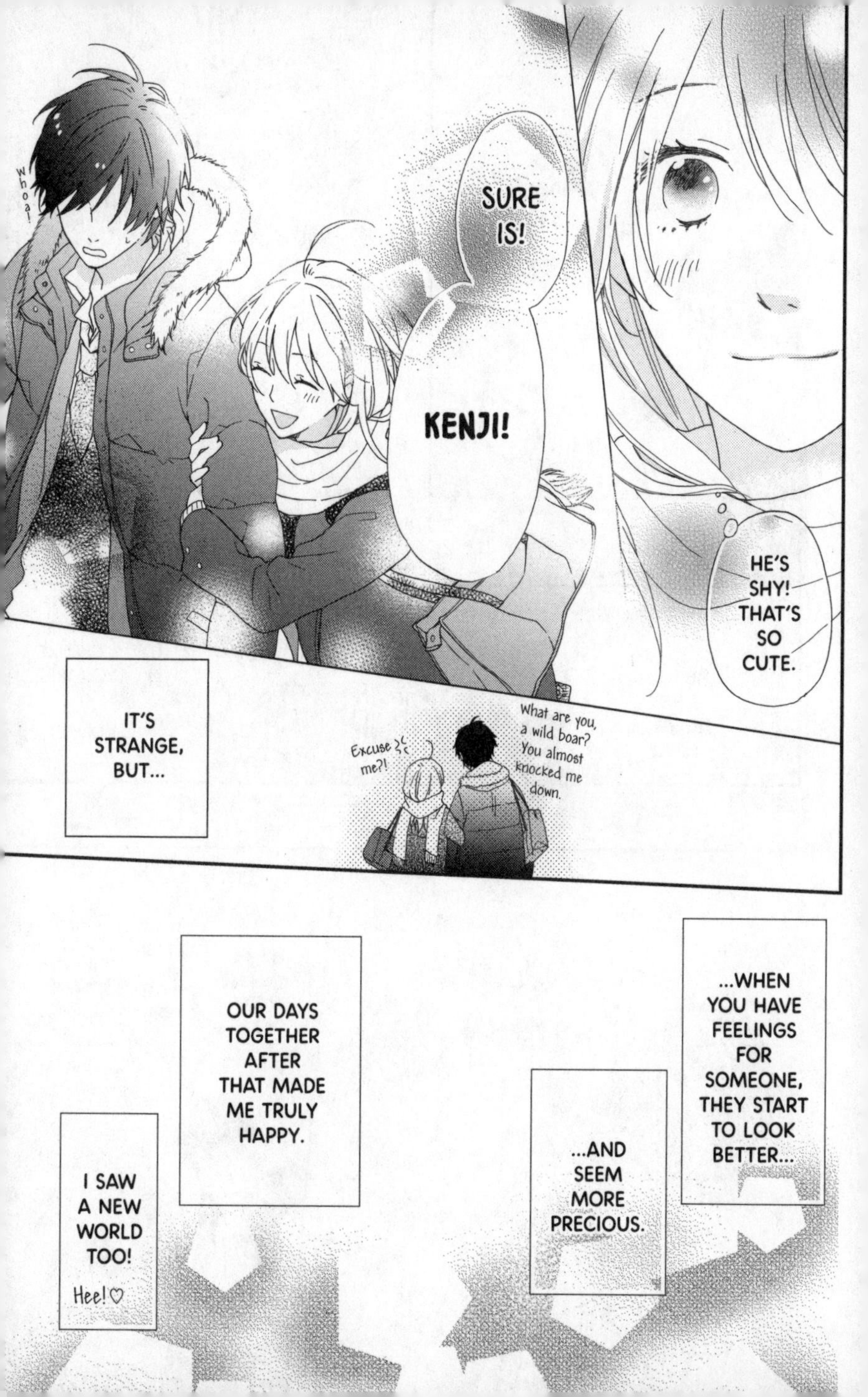
HE'S SHY! THAT'S SO CUTE.
SURE IS!
KENJI!
Whoa!
What are you, a wild boar? You almost knocked me down.
Excuse me?!
IT'S STRANGE, BUT...
...WHEN YOU HAVE FEELINGS FOR SOMEONE, THEY START TO LOOK BETTER...
...AND SEEM MORE PRECIOUS.
OUR DAYS TOGETHER AFTER THAT MADE ME TRULY HAPPY.
I SAW A NEW WORLD TOO!
Hee!♡

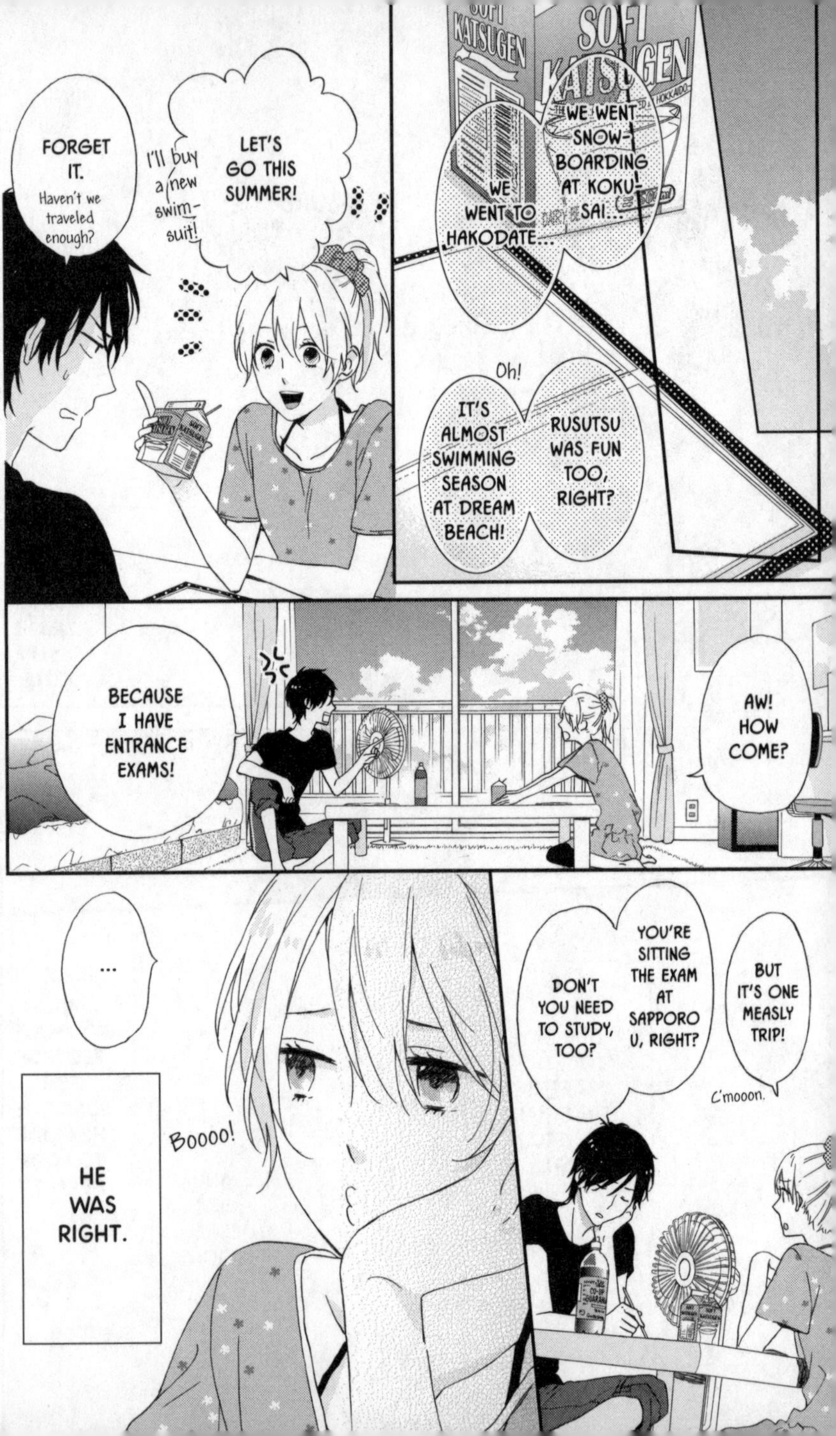
SOFT KATSUGEN
SOFT KATSUGEN
WE WENT SNOW-BOARDING AT KOKU-SAI...
WE WENT TO HAKODATE...
Oh!
RUSUTSU WAS FUN TOO, RIGHT?
IT'S ALMOST SWIMMING SEASON AT DREAM BEACH!
LET'S GO THIS SUMMER!
I'll buy a new swim-suit!
FORGET IT.
Haven't we traveled enough?
AW! HOW COME?
BECAUSE I HAVE ENTRANCE EXAMS!
BUT IT'S ONE MEASLY TRIP!
C'mooon.
YOU'RE SITTING THE EXAM AT SAPPORO U, RIGHT?
DON'T YOU NEED TO STUDY, TOO?
...
Boooo!
HE WAS RIGHT.

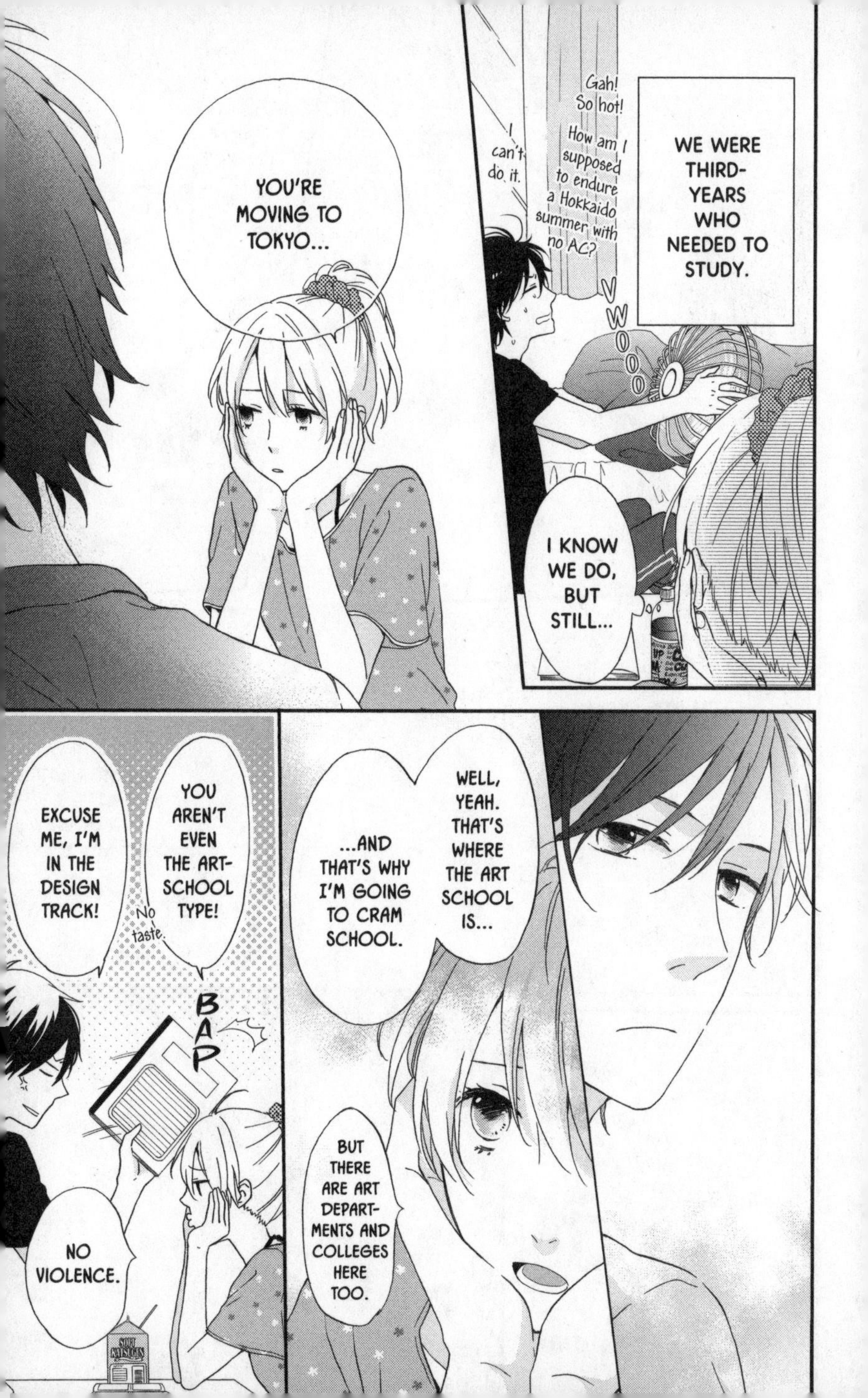
WE WERE THIRD-YEARS WHO NEEDED TO STUDY.
Gah! So hot! How am I supposed to endure a Hokkaido summer with no AC?
I can't do it.
VWOOO
I KNOW WE DO, BUT STILL...
YOU'RE MOVING TO TOKYO...
WELL, YEAH. THAT'S WHERE THE ART SCHOOL IS...
...AND THAT'S WHY I'M GOING TO CRAM SCHOOL.
BUT THERE ARE ART DEPARTMENTS AND COLLEGES HERE TOO.
YOU AREN'T EVEN THE ART-SCHOOL TYPE!
No taste.
EXCUSE ME, I'M IN THE DESIGN TRACK!
BAP
NO VIOLENCE.

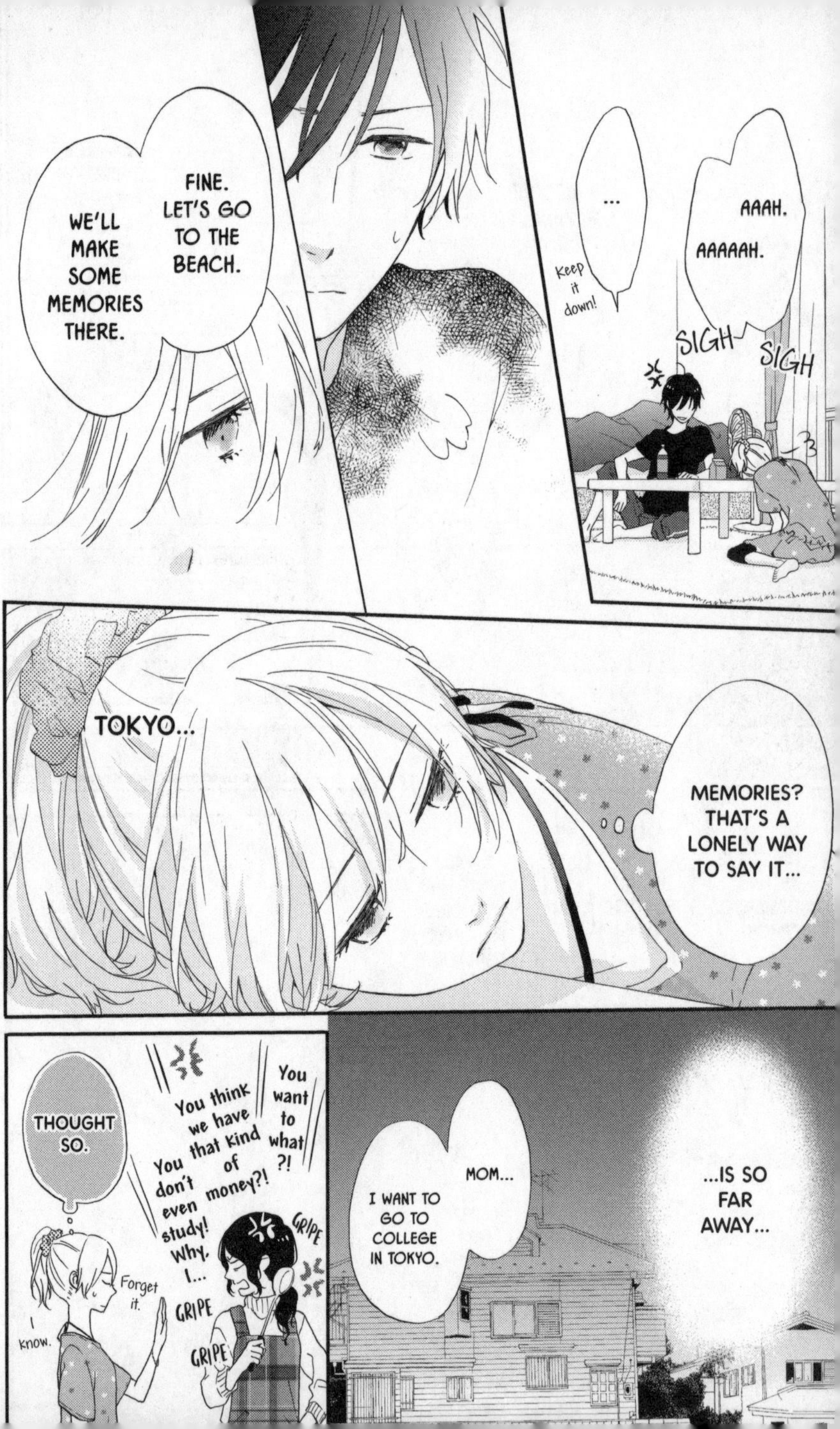
AAAH.
AAAAAH.
...
Keep it down!
SIGH
SIGH
FINE. LET'S GO TO THE BEACH.
WE'LL MAKE SOME MEMORIES THERE.
MEMORIES? THAT'S A LONELY WAY TO SAY IT...
TOKYO...
...IS SO FAR AWAY...
MOM...
I WANT TO GO TO COLLEGE IN TOKYO.
You want to what?!
You think we have that kind of money?!
You don't even study! Why, I...
GRIPE
GRIPE
GRIPE
THOUGHT SO.
Forget it.
I know.

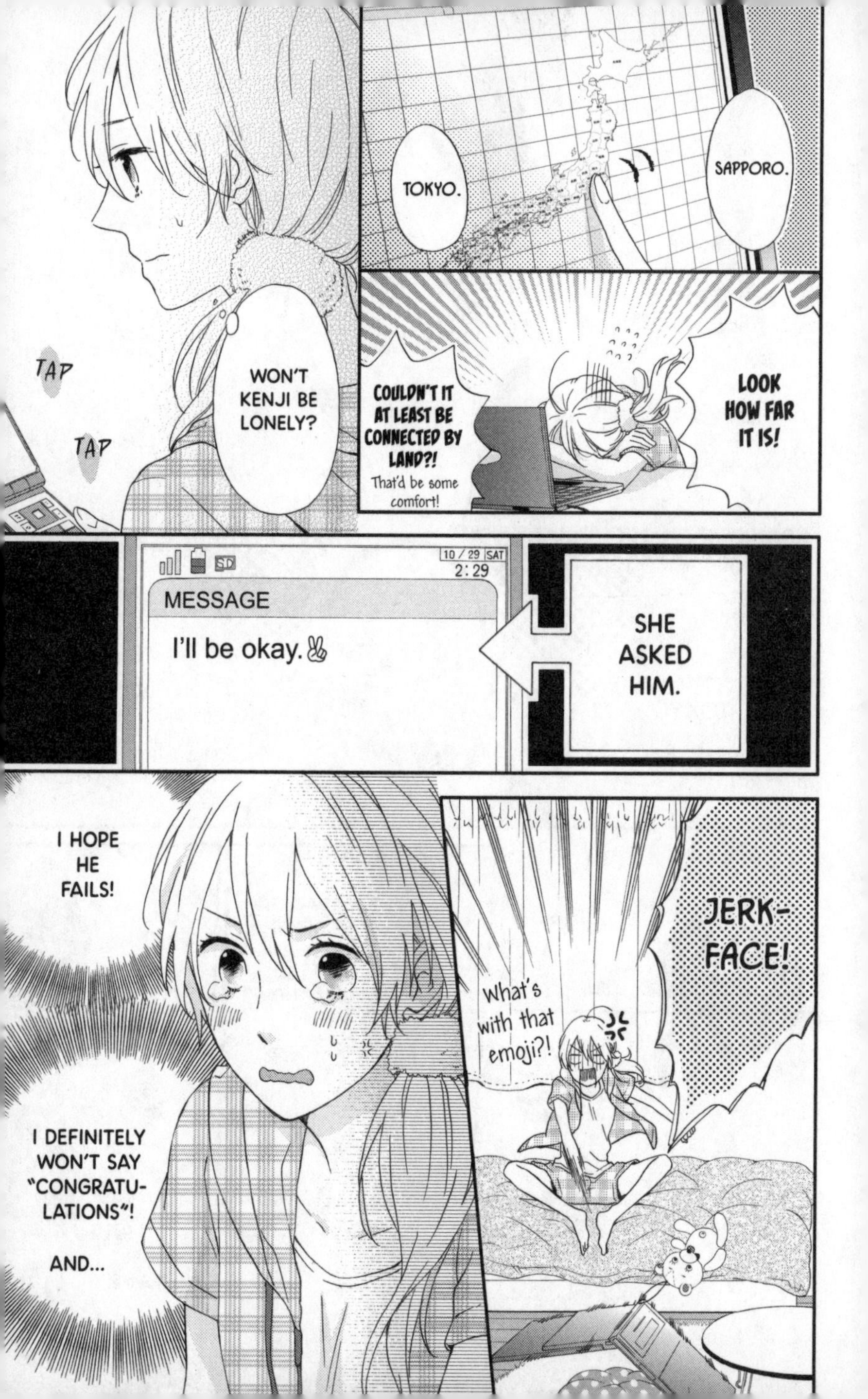
SAPPORO.
TOKYO.
LOOK HOW FAR IT IS!
COULDN'T IT AT LEAST BE CONNECTED BY LAND?!
That'd be some comfort!
WON'T KENJI BE LONELY?
TAP
TAP
SHE ASKED HIM.
10 / 29 SAT
2:29
MESSAGE
I'll be okay. ✌
JERK-FACE!
What's with that emoji?!
I HOPE HE FAILS!
I DEFINITELY WON'T SAY "CONGRATULATIONS"!
AND...

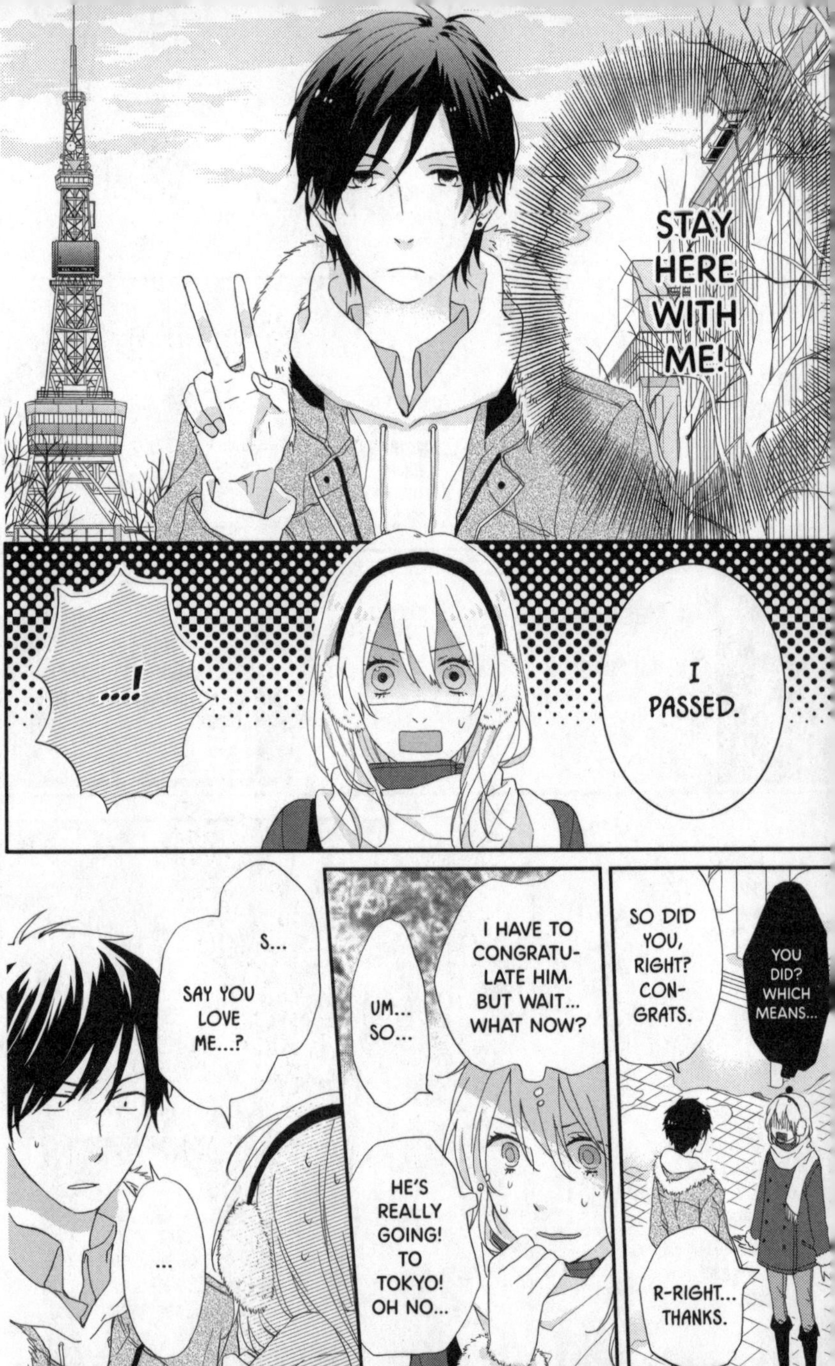
STAY HERE WITH ME!
I PASSED.
...!
YOU DID? WHICH MEANS...
SO DID YOU, RIGHT? CON-GRATS.
R-RIGHT... THANKS.
I HAVE TO CONGRATU-LATE HIM. BUT WAIT... WHAT NOW?
UM... SO...
HE'S REALLY GOING! TO TOKYO! OH NO...
S...
SAY YOU LOVE ME...?
...

OH, AND I'M LEAVING TOMORROW.

C-CONGRA-

SORRY! I DIDN'T MEAN THAT!

UM... LISTEN!

WHAT KIND OF MISTAKE WAS THAT?!

HUH?

YEEK! I MESSED UP!

AKANE?

HIS LAST DAY?

OH NO... I SERIOUSLY HAVE NO IDEA WHAT I'M GOING TO DO.

ARE YOU LISTENING?

THE VERY LAST?

This is going way too fast!

WAIT!!!

YEAH. I'M STAYING IN A DORM, BUT THE MOVERS ONLY HAD TOMORROW OPEN.

Spring is their busy season.

HUH?! TO... TOMOR-ROW?!

SO, YOU KNOW... THIS IS MY LAST DAY HERE.

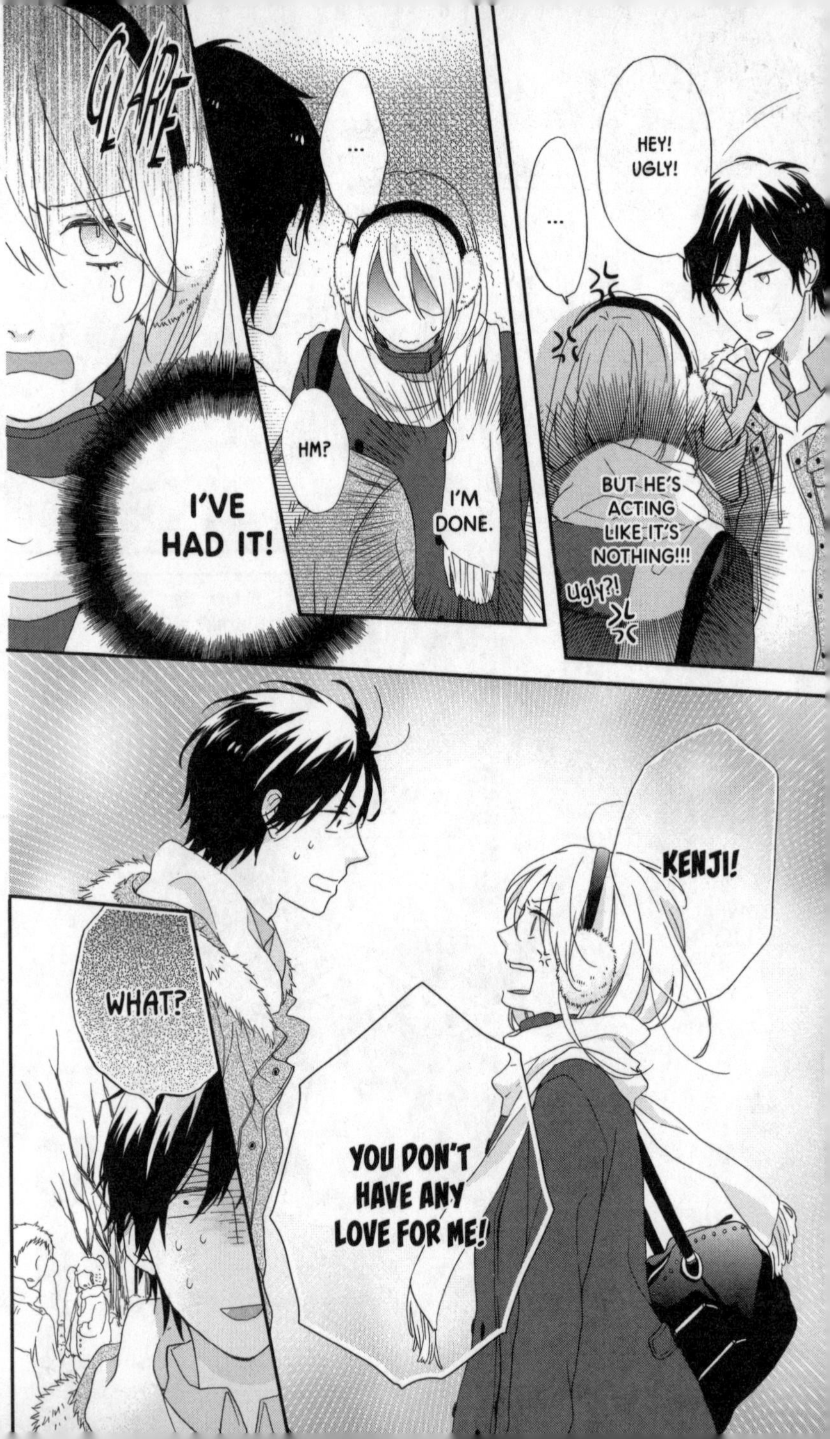
HEY! UGLY!
...
BUT HE'S ACTING LIKE IT'S NOTHING!!!
Ugly?!
...
HM?
I'M DONE.
GLARE
I'VE HAD IT!
KENJI!
YOU DON'T HAVE ANY LOVE FOR ME!
WHAT?

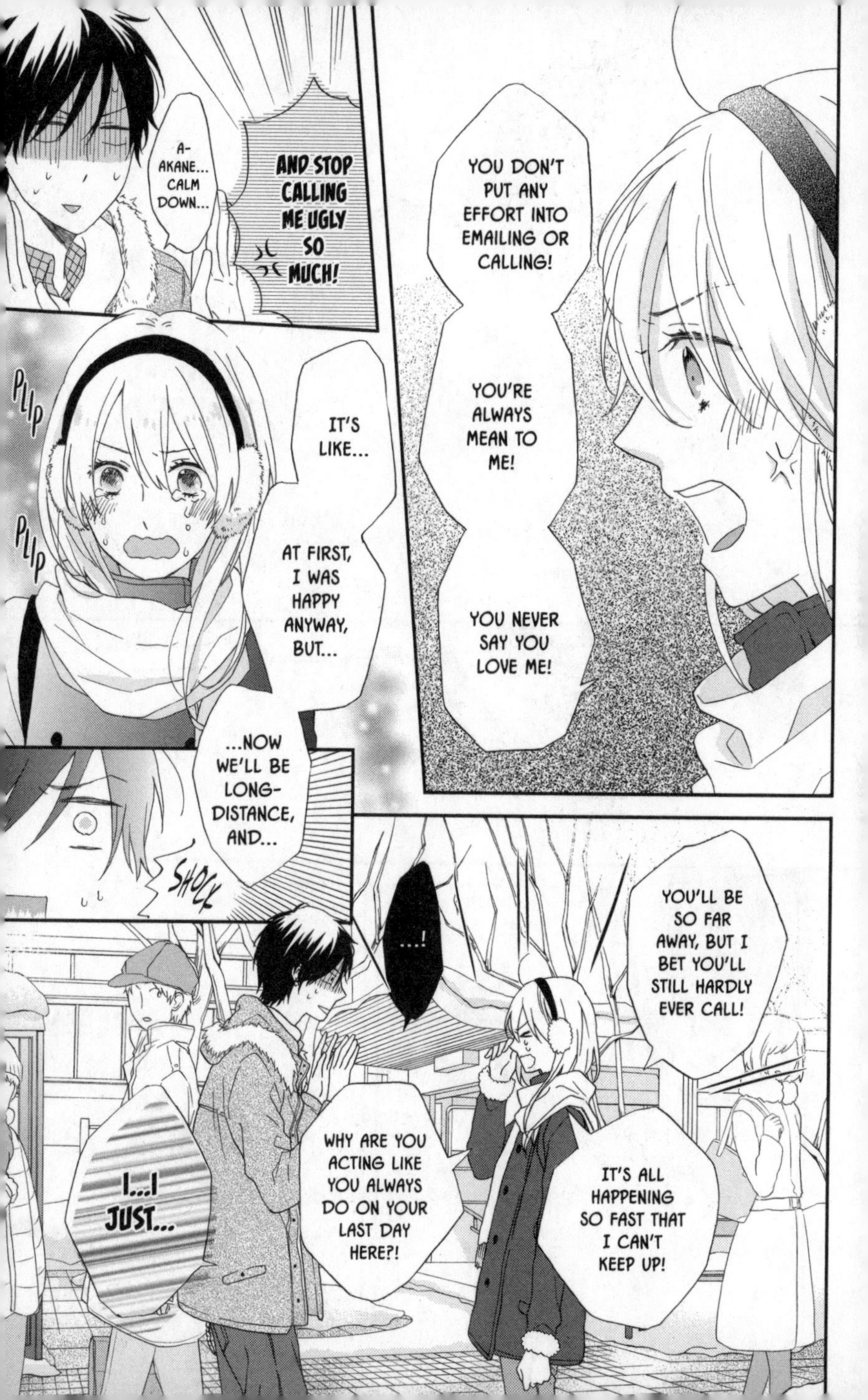
YOU DON'T PUT ANY EFFORT INTO EMAILING OR CALLING!
YOU'RE ALWAYS MEAN TO ME!
YOU NEVER SAY YOU LOVE ME!
AND STOP CALLING ME UGLY SO MUCH!
A-AKANE... CALM DOWN...
IT'S LIKE...
PLIP
PLIP
AT FIRST, I WAS HAPPY ANYWAY, BUT...
...NOW WE'LL BE LONG-DISTANCE, AND...
SHOCK
YOU'LL BE SO FAR AWAY, BUT I BET YOU'LL STILL HARDLY EVER CALL!
IT'S ALL HAPPENING SO FAST THAT I CAN'T KEEP UP!
...!
WHY ARE YOU ACTING LIKE YOU ALWAYS DO ON YOUR LAST DAY HERE?!
I...I JUST...

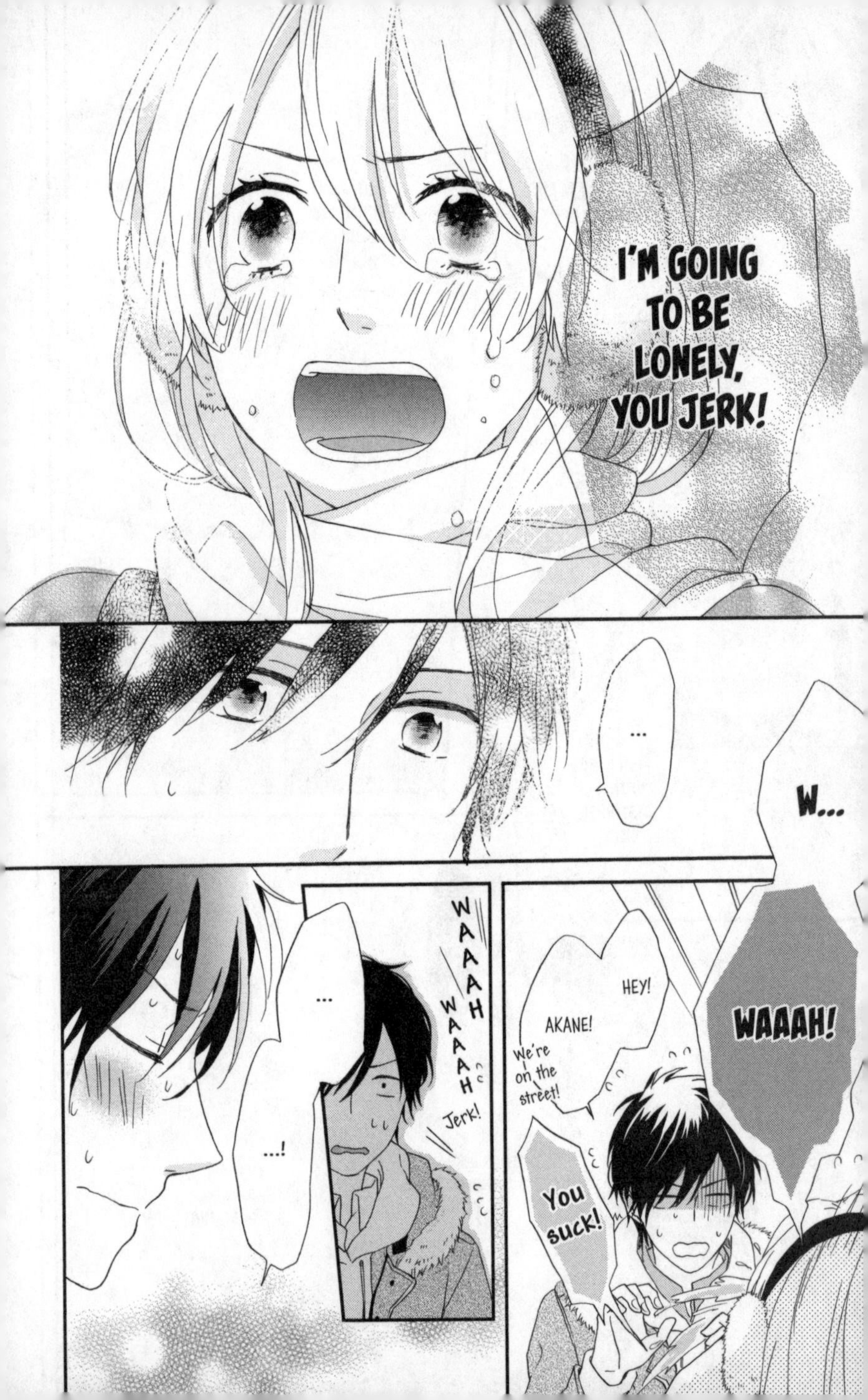
I'M GOING TO BE LONELY, YOU JERK!
W...
...
WAAAH!
HEY!
AKANE!
We're on the street!
You suck!
WAAAAH
WAAAAH
Jerk!
...
...!

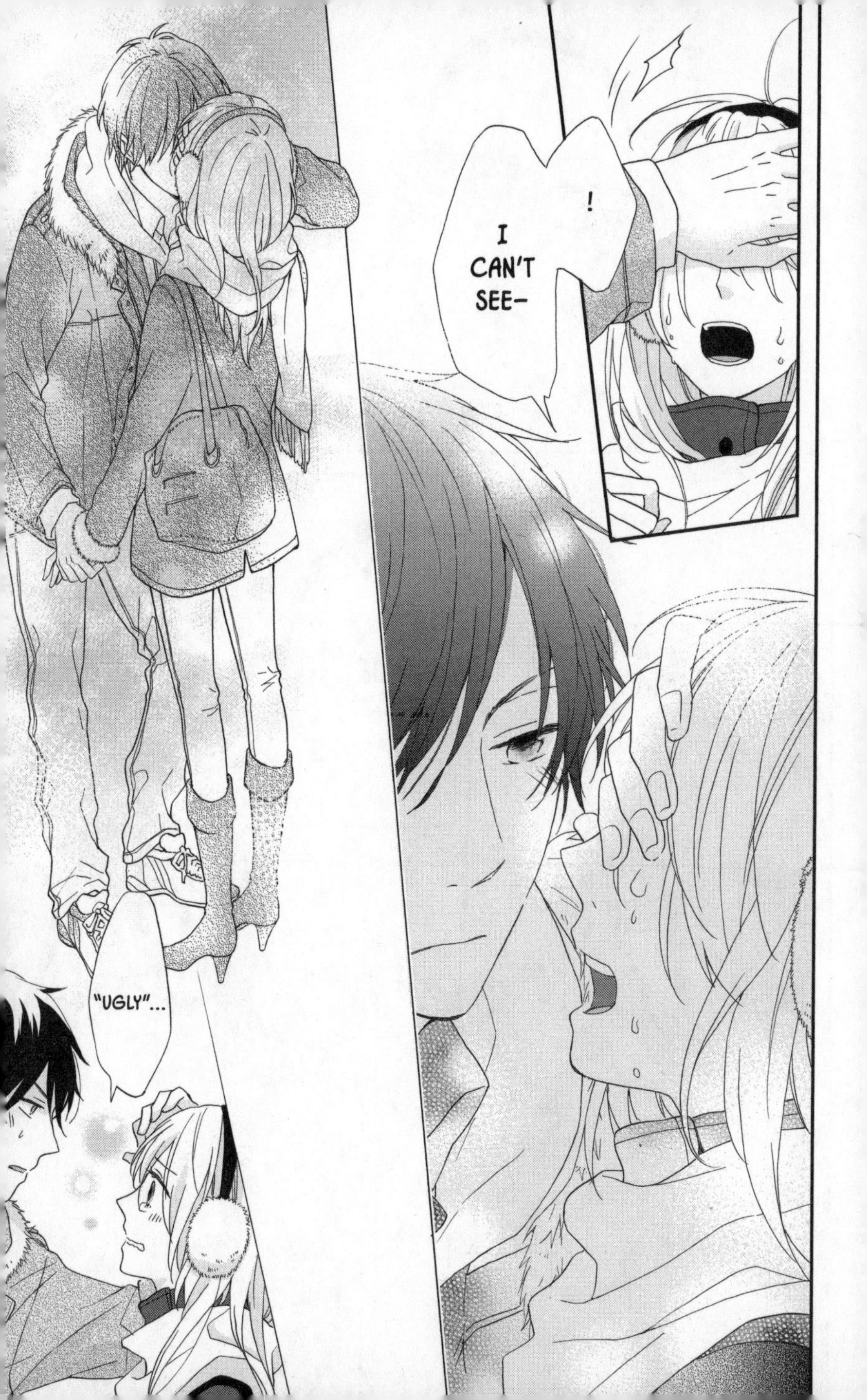
!
I CAN'T SEE–
"UGLY"...

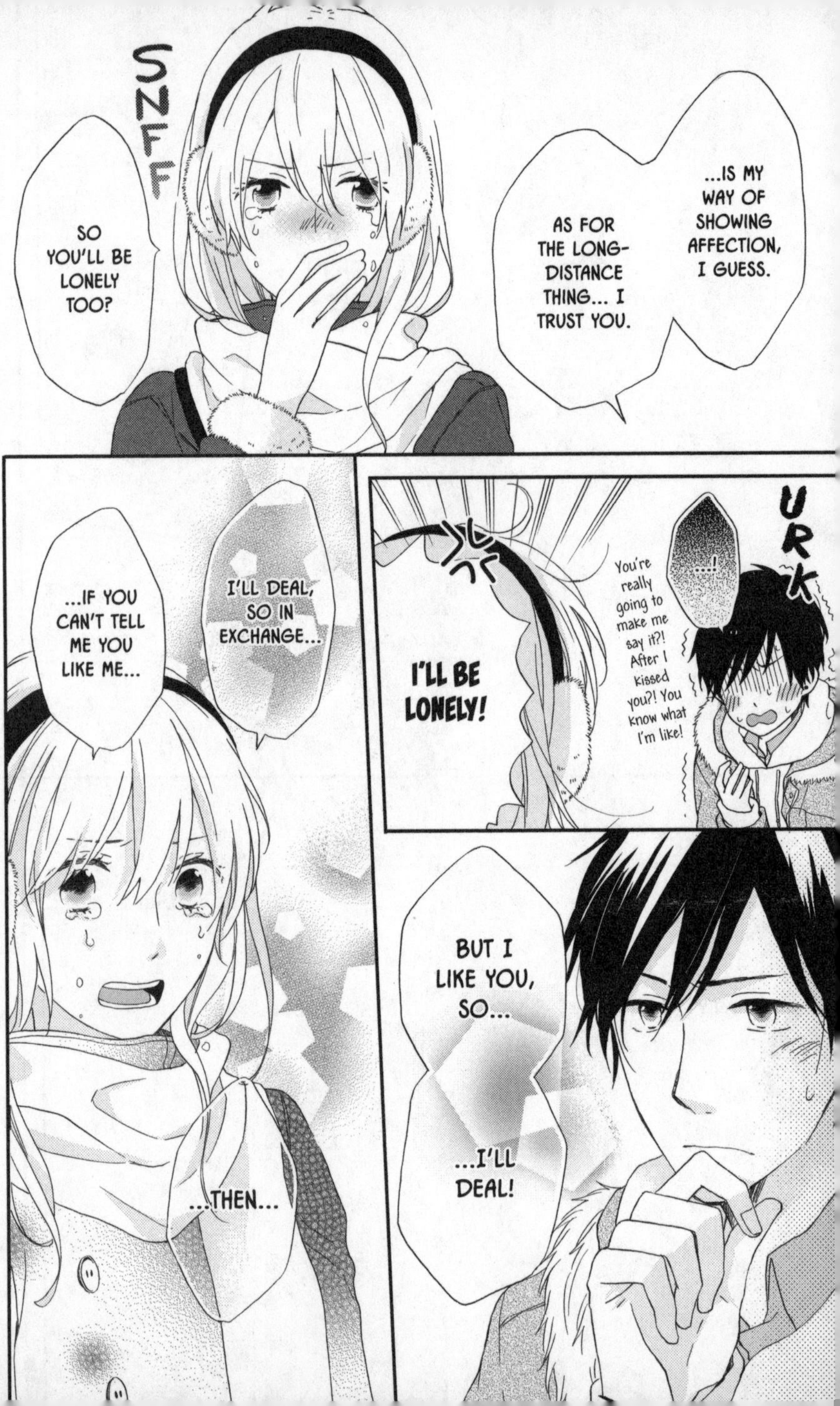
...IS MY WAY OF SHOWING AFFECTION, I GUESS.
AS FOR THE LONG-DISTANCE THING... I TRUST YOU.
SNFF
SO YOU'LL BE LONELY TOO?
URK
...!
You're really going to make me say it?! After I kissed you?! You know what I'm like!
I'LL BE LONELY!
BUT I LIKE YOU, SO...
...I'LL DEAL!
I'LL DEAL, SO IN EXCHANGE...
...IF YOU CAN'T TELL ME YOU LIKE ME...
...THEN...

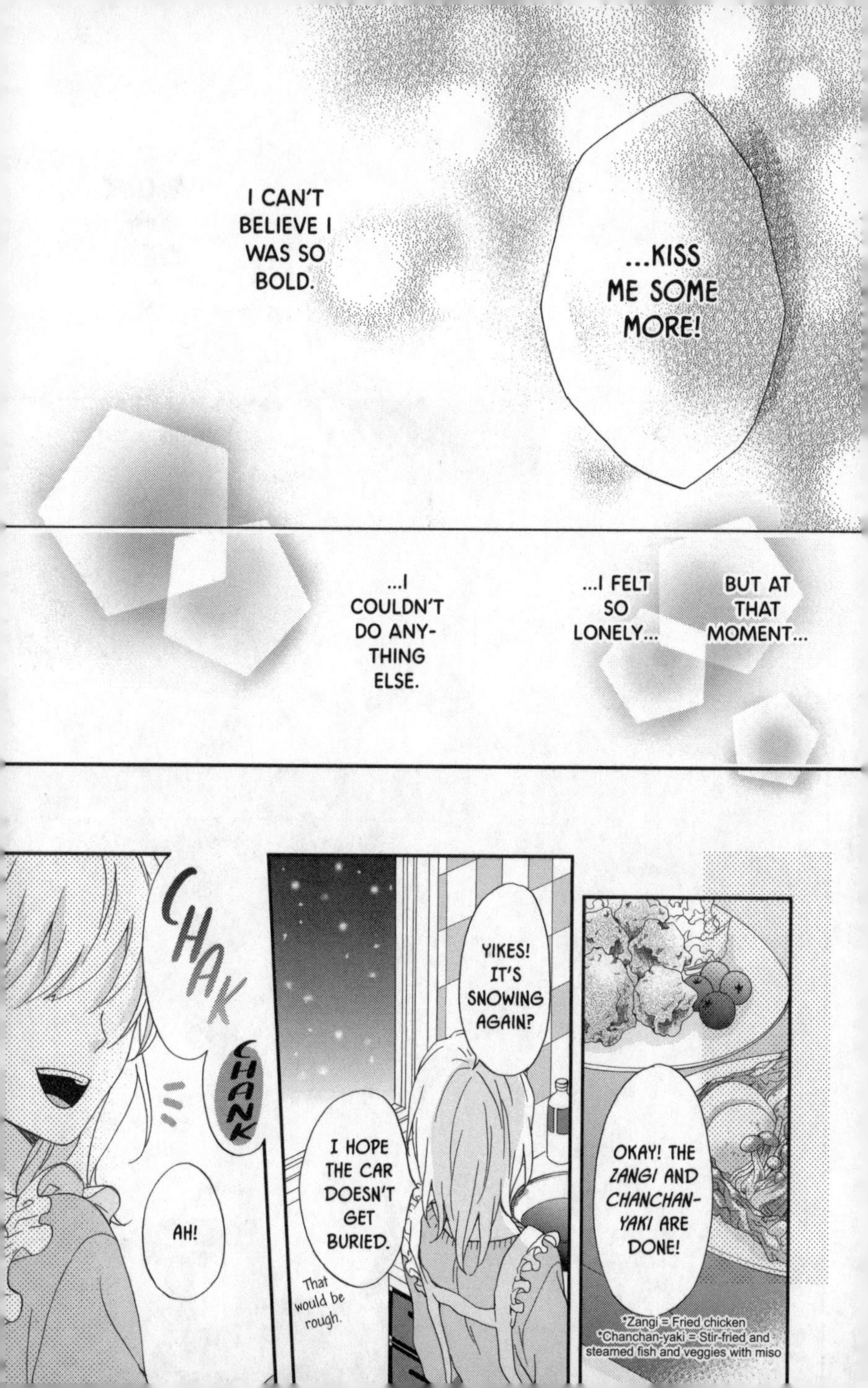
...KISS ME SOME MORE!
I CAN'T BELIEVE I WAS SO BOLD.
BUT AT THAT MOMENT...
...I FELT SO LONELY...
...I COULDN'T DO ANY-THING ELSE.
OKAY! THE ZANGI AND CHANCHAN-YAKI ARE DONE!
*Zangi = Fried chicken
*Chanchan-yaki = Stir-fried and steamed fish and veggies with miso
YIKES! IT'S SNOWING AGAIN?
I HOPE THE CAR DOESN'T GET BURIED.
That would be rough.
CHAK
CHANK
AH!

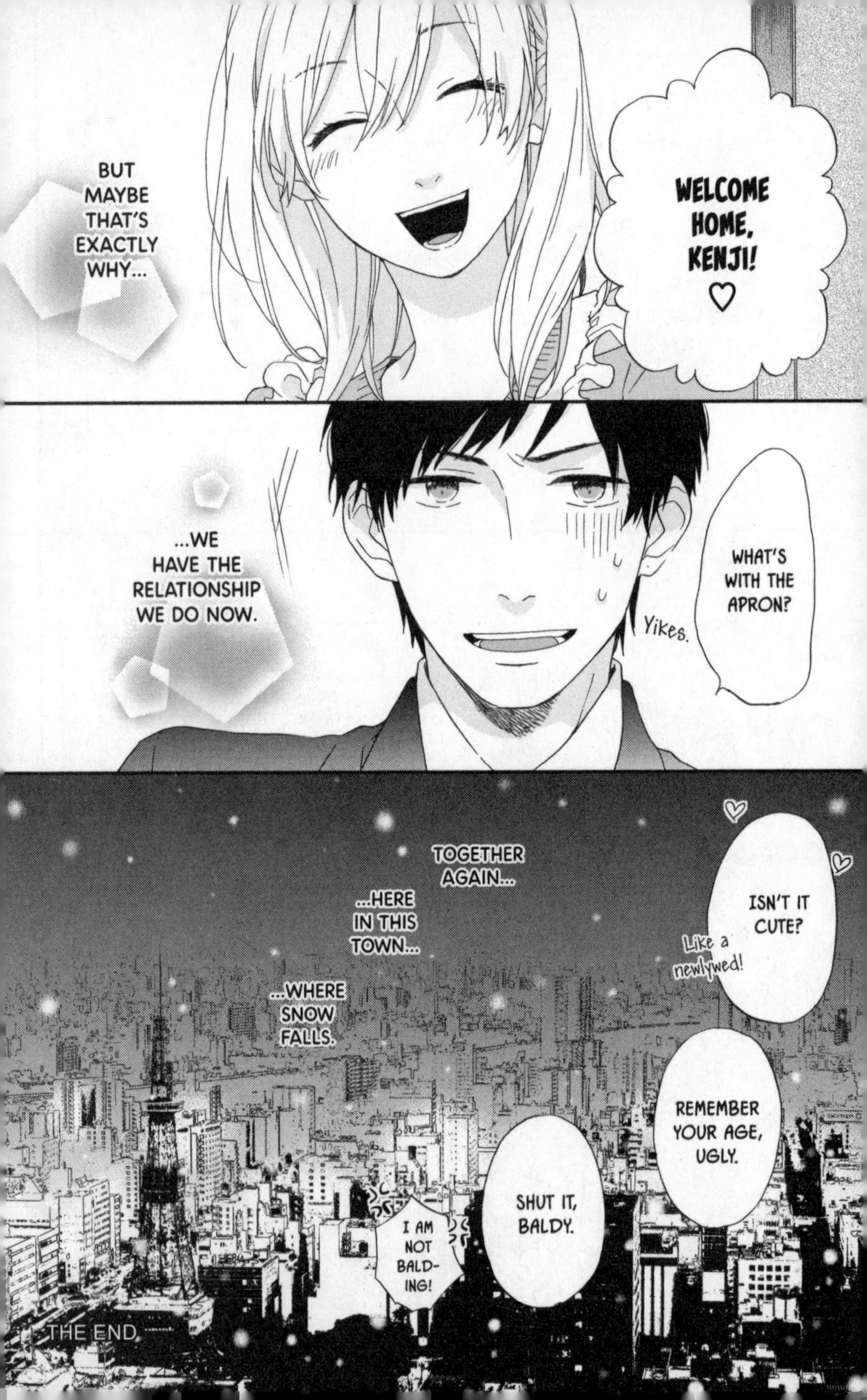
WELCOME HOME, KENJI! ♡
BUT MAYBE THAT'S EXACTLY WHY...
WHAT'S WITH THE APRON?
Yikes.
...WE HAVE THE RELATIONSHIP WE DO NOW.
ISN'T IT CUTE?
Like a newlywed!
TOGETHER AGAIN...
...HERE IN THIS TOWN...
...WHERE SNOW FALLS.
REMEMBER YOUR AGE, UGLY.
SHUT IT, BALDY.
I AM NOT BALDING!
THE END

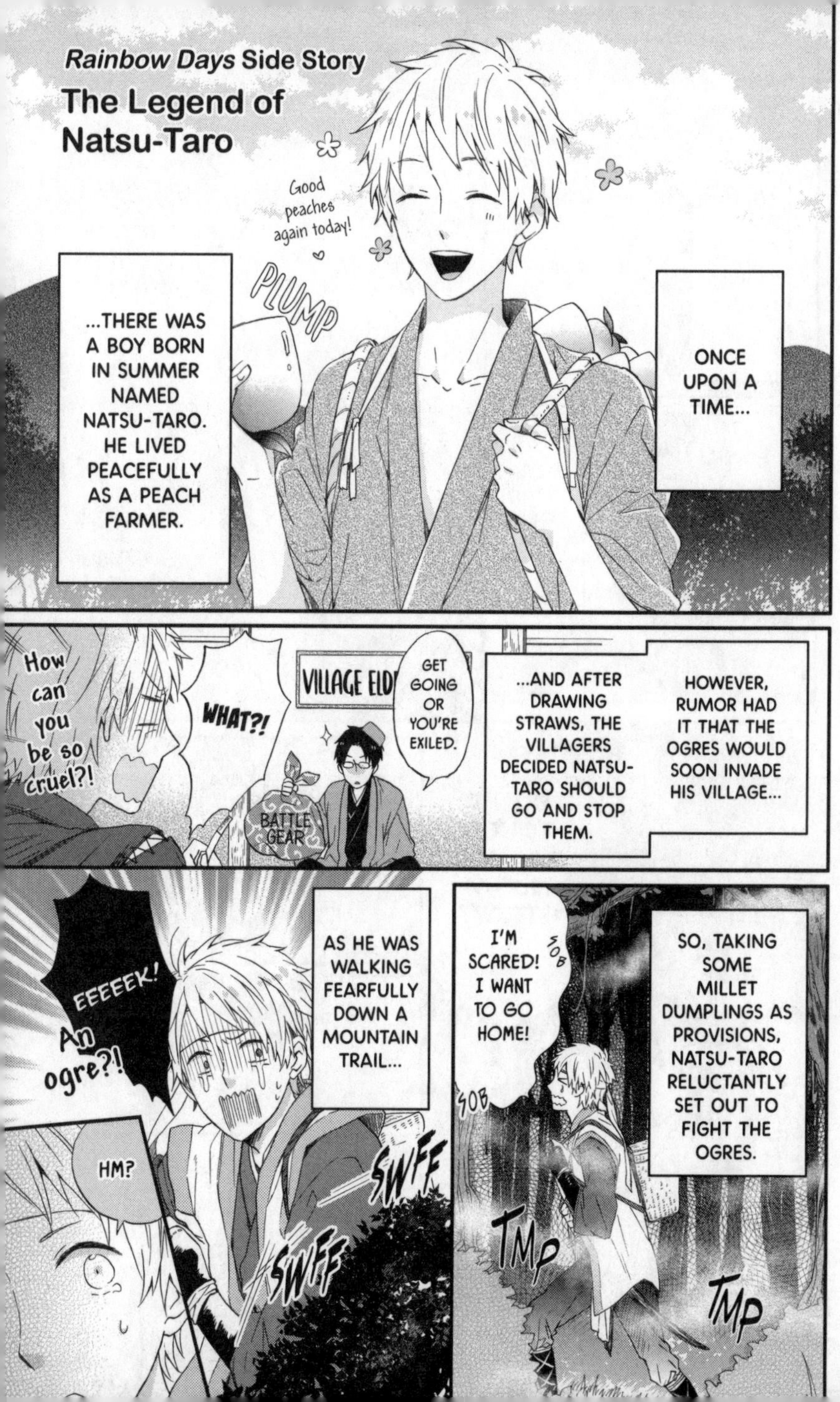
Rainbow Days Side Story
The Legend of Natsu-Taro
ONCE UPON A TIME...
Good peaches again today!
PLUMP
...THERE WAS A BOY BORN IN SUMMER NAMED NATSU-TARO. HE LIVED PEACEFULLY AS A PEACH FARMER.
HOWEVER, RUMOR HAD IT THAT THE OGRES WOULD SOON INVADE HIS VILLAGE...
...AND AFTER DRAWING STRAWS, THE VILLAGERS DECIDED NATSU-TARO SHOULD GO AND STOP THEM.
GET GOING OR YOU'RE EXILED.
VILLAGE ELD
WHAT?!
How can you be so cruel?!
BATTLE GEAR
SO, TAKING SOME MILLET DUMPLINGS AS PROVISIONS, NATSU-TARO RELUCTANTLY SET OUT TO FIGHT THE OGRES.
I'M SCARED! I WANT TO GO HOME!
SOB
SOB
TMP
TMP
AS HE WAS WALKING FEARFULLY DOWN A MOUNTAIN TRAIL...
EEEEEK! An ogre?!
SWFF
SWFF
HM?

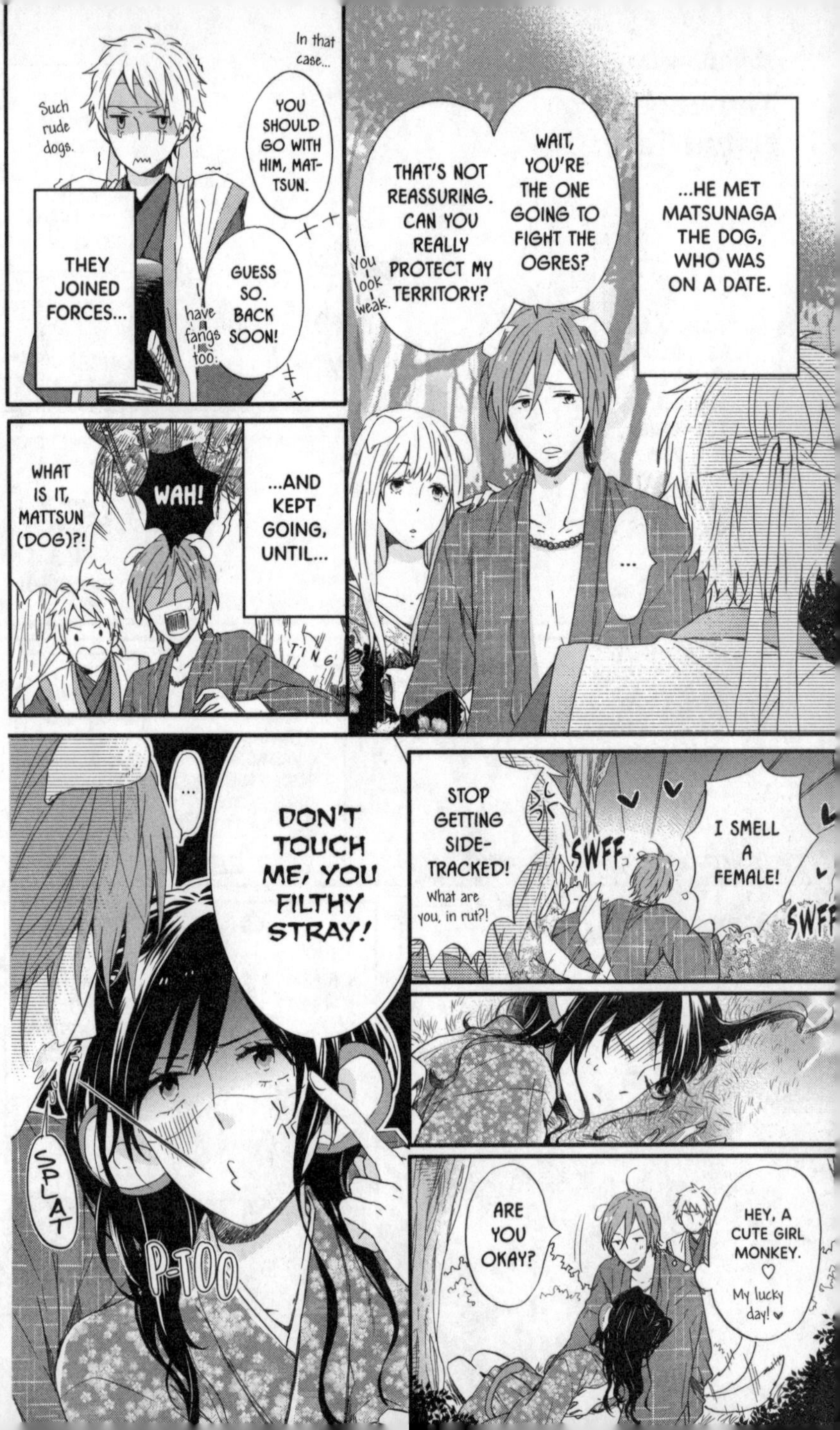
...HE MET MATSUNAGA THE DOG, WHO WAS ON A DATE.
WAIT, YOU'RE THE ONE GOING TO FIGHT THE OGRES?
THAT'S NOT REASSURING. CAN YOU REALLY PROTECT MY TERRITORY?
You look weak.
...
In that case...
YOU SHOULD GO WITH HIM, MAT-TSUN.
Such rude dogs.
THEY JOINED FORCES...
GUESS SO. BACK SOON!
I have fangs too.
...AND KEPT GOING, UNTIL...
WAH!
WHAT IS IT, MATTSUN (DOG)?!
TING
I SMELL A FEMALE!
SWFF
STOP GETTING SIDE-TRACKED!
What are you, in rut?!
SWFF
HEY, A CUTE GIRL MONKEY. ♡
My lucky day! ♥
ARE YOU OKAY?
...
DON'T TOUCH ME, YOU FILTHY STRAY!
SPLAT
P-TOO

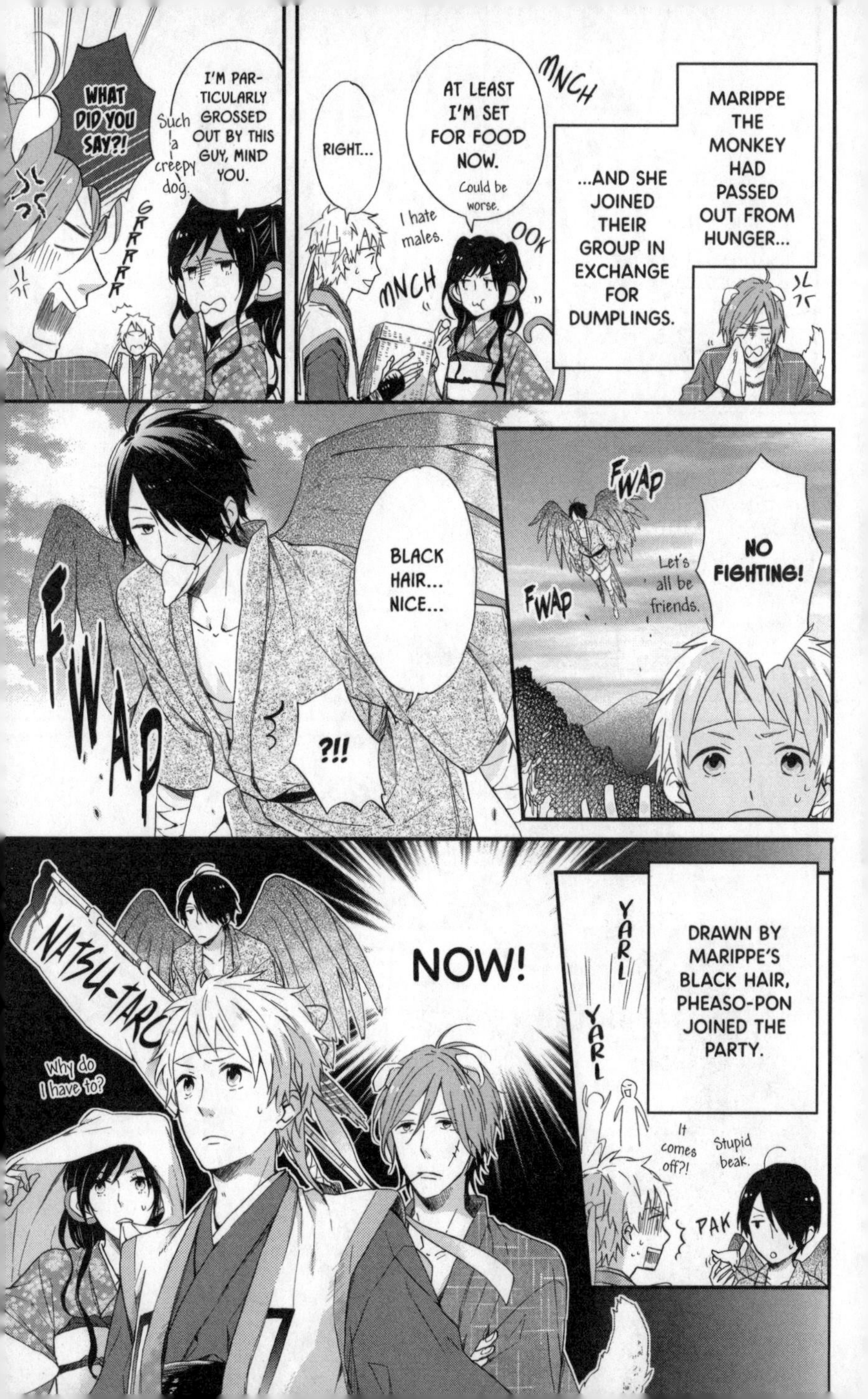
MARIPPE THE MONKEY HAD PASSED OUT FROM HUNGER...
...AND SHE JOINED THEIR GROUP IN EXCHANGE FOR DUMPLINGS.
MNCH
AT LEAST I'M SET FOR FOOD NOW.
Could be worse.
RIGHT...
I hate males.
OOK
MNCH
I'M PARTICULARLY GROSSED OUT BY THIS GUY, MIND YOU.
Such a creepy dog.
WHAT DID YOU SAY?!
GRRRRR
FWAP
FWAP
NO FIGHTING!
Let's all be friends.
BLACK HAIR... NICE...
?!!
FWAP
DRAWN BY MARIPPE'S BLACK HAIR, PHEASO-PON JOINED THE PARTY.
YARL
YARL
It comes off?!
Stupid beak.
PAK
NOW!
NATSU-TARO
Why do I have to?

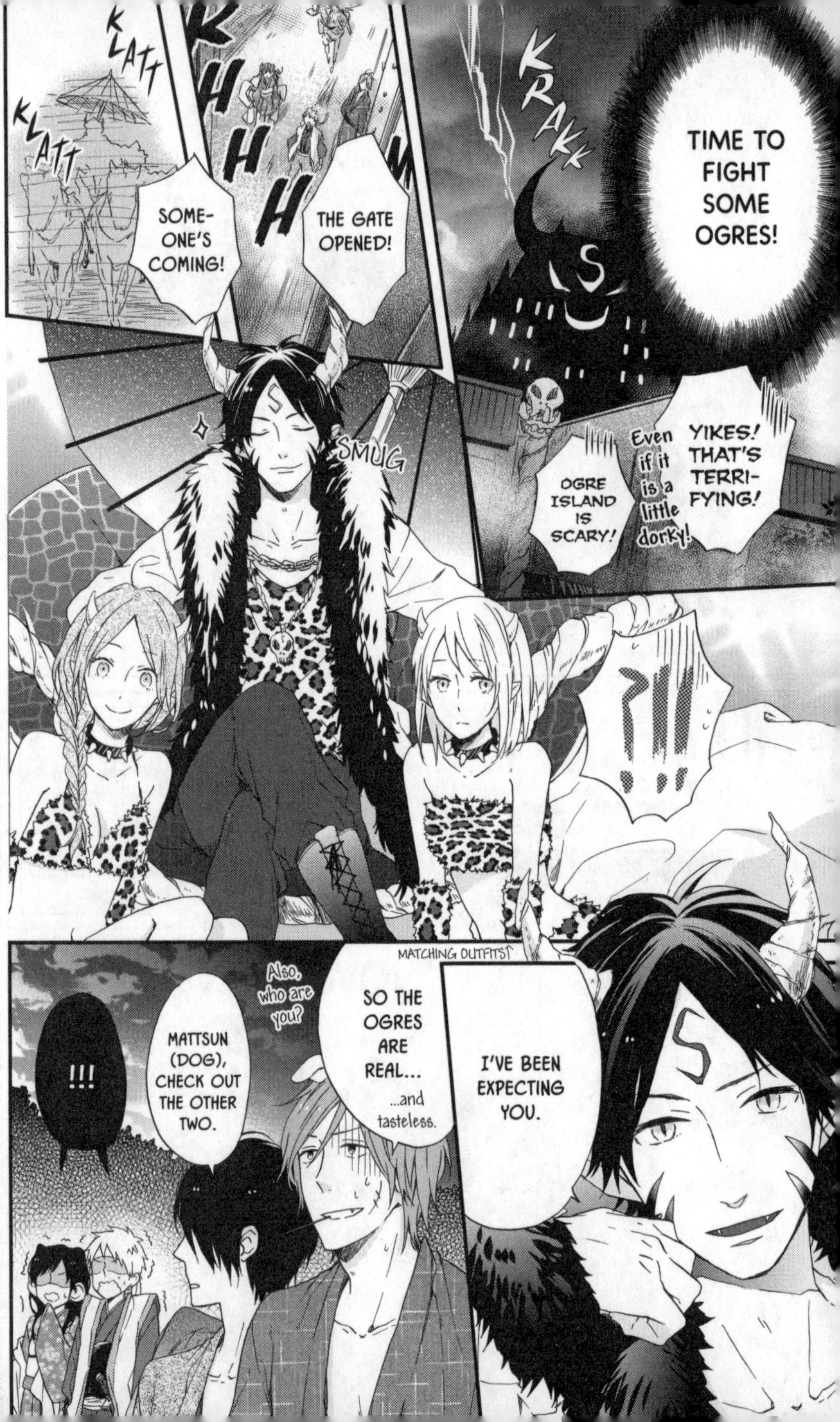
KRAKK
TIME TO FIGHT SOME OGRES!
KHHHH
THE GATE OPENED!
KLATT
KLATT
SOME-ONE'S COMING!
YIKES! THAT'S TERRI-FYING!
Even if it is a little dorky!
OGRE ISLAND IS SCARY!
SMUG
MATCHING OUTFITS!
?!!
I'VE BEEN EXPECTING YOU.
SO THE OGRES ARE REAL...
...and tasteless.
Also, who are you?
MATTSUN (DOG), CHECK OUT THE OTHER TWO.
!!!

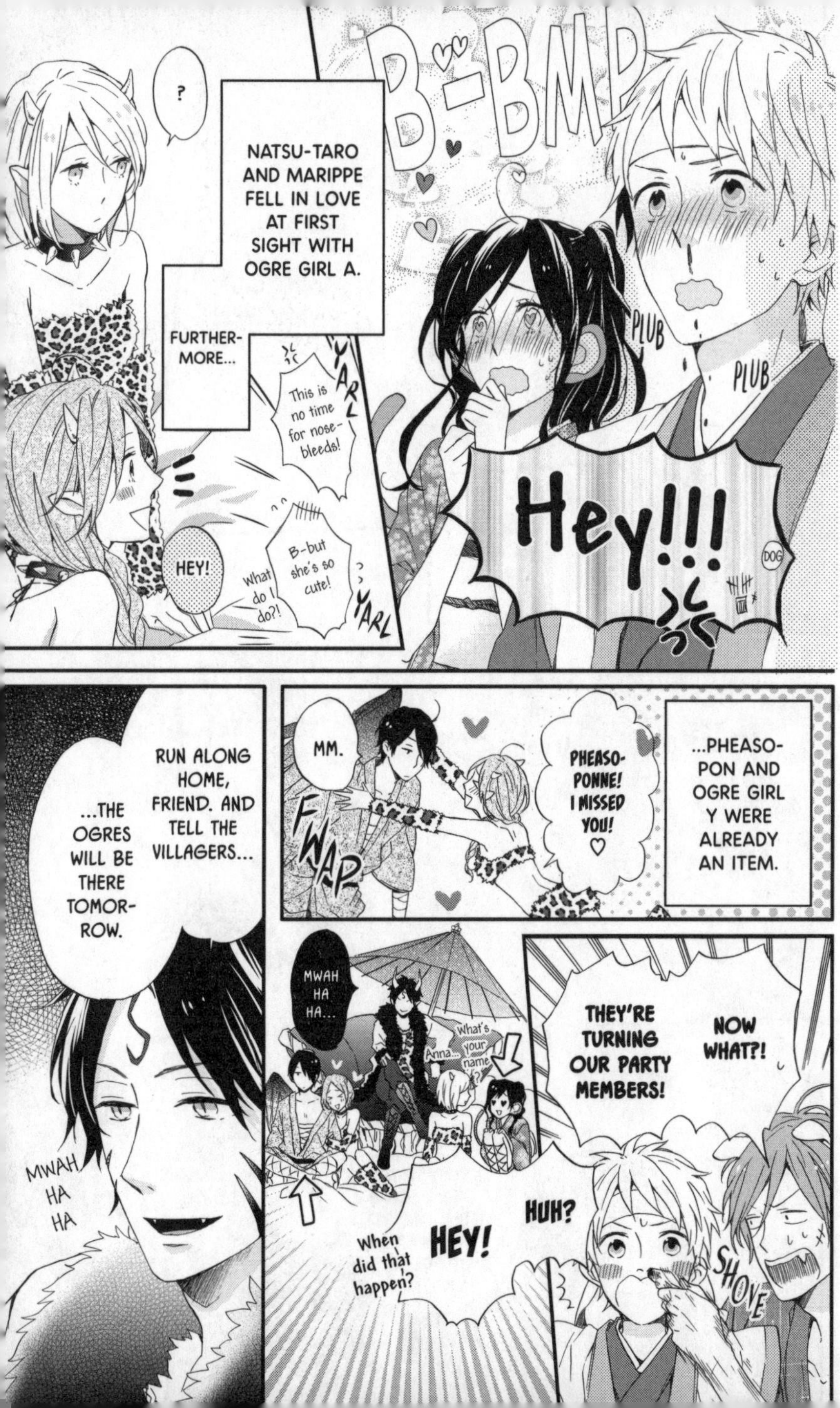
B-BMP
PLUB
PLUB
Hey!!!
DOG
NATSU-TARO AND MARIPPE FELL IN LOVE AT FIRST SIGHT WITH OGRE GIRL A.
?
FURTHER-MORE...
YARL
This is no time for nose-bleeds!
B-but she's so cute!
What do I do?!
YARL
HEY!
...PHEASO-PON AND OGRE GIRL Y WERE ALREADY AN ITEM.
PHEASO-PONNE! I MISSED YOU! ♡
MM.
FWAP
NOW WHAT?!
THEY'RE TURNING OUR PARTY MEMBERS!
SHOVE
HUH?
HEY!
When did that happen?
MWAH HA HA...
What's your name?
Anna...
RUN ALONG HOME, FRIEND. AND TELL THE VILLAGERS...
...THE OGRES WILL BE THERE TOMOR-ROW.
MWAH HA HA

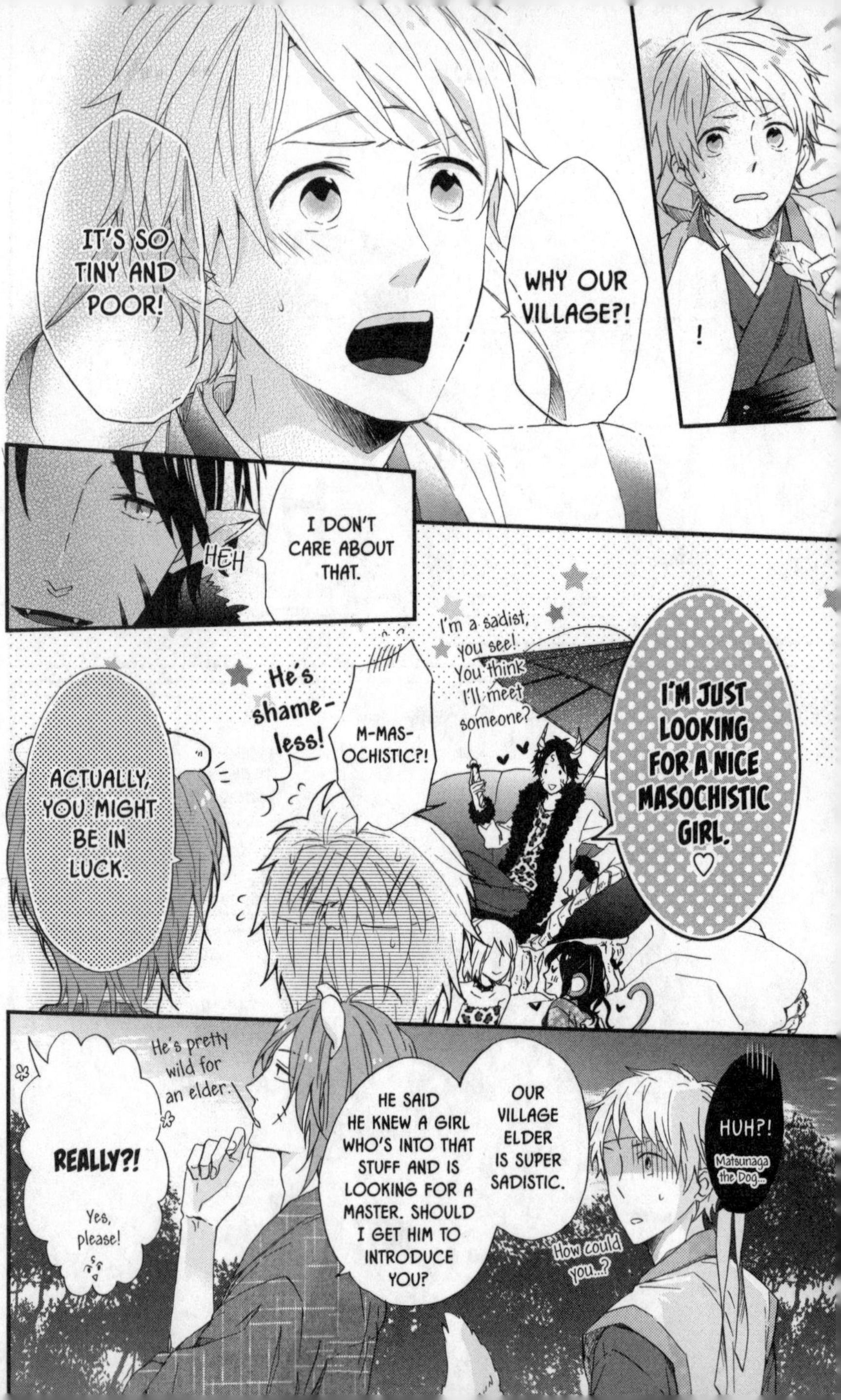
!
WHY OUR VILLAGE?!
IT'S SO TINY AND POOR!
I DON'T CARE ABOUT THAT.
HEH
I'M JUST LOOKING FOR A NICE MASOCHISTIC GIRL. ♡
I'm a sadist, you see! You think I'll meet someone?
M-MAS-OCHISTIC?!
He's shame-less!
ACTUALLY, YOU MIGHT BE IN LUCK.
HUH?!
Matsunaga the Dog...
How could you...?
OUR VILLAGE ELDER IS SUPER SADISTIC.
HE SAID HE KNEW A GIRL WHO'S INTO THAT STUFF AND IS LOOKING FOR A MASTER. SHOULD I GET HIM TO INTRODUCE YOU?
He's pretty wild for an elder.
REALLY?!
Yes, please!

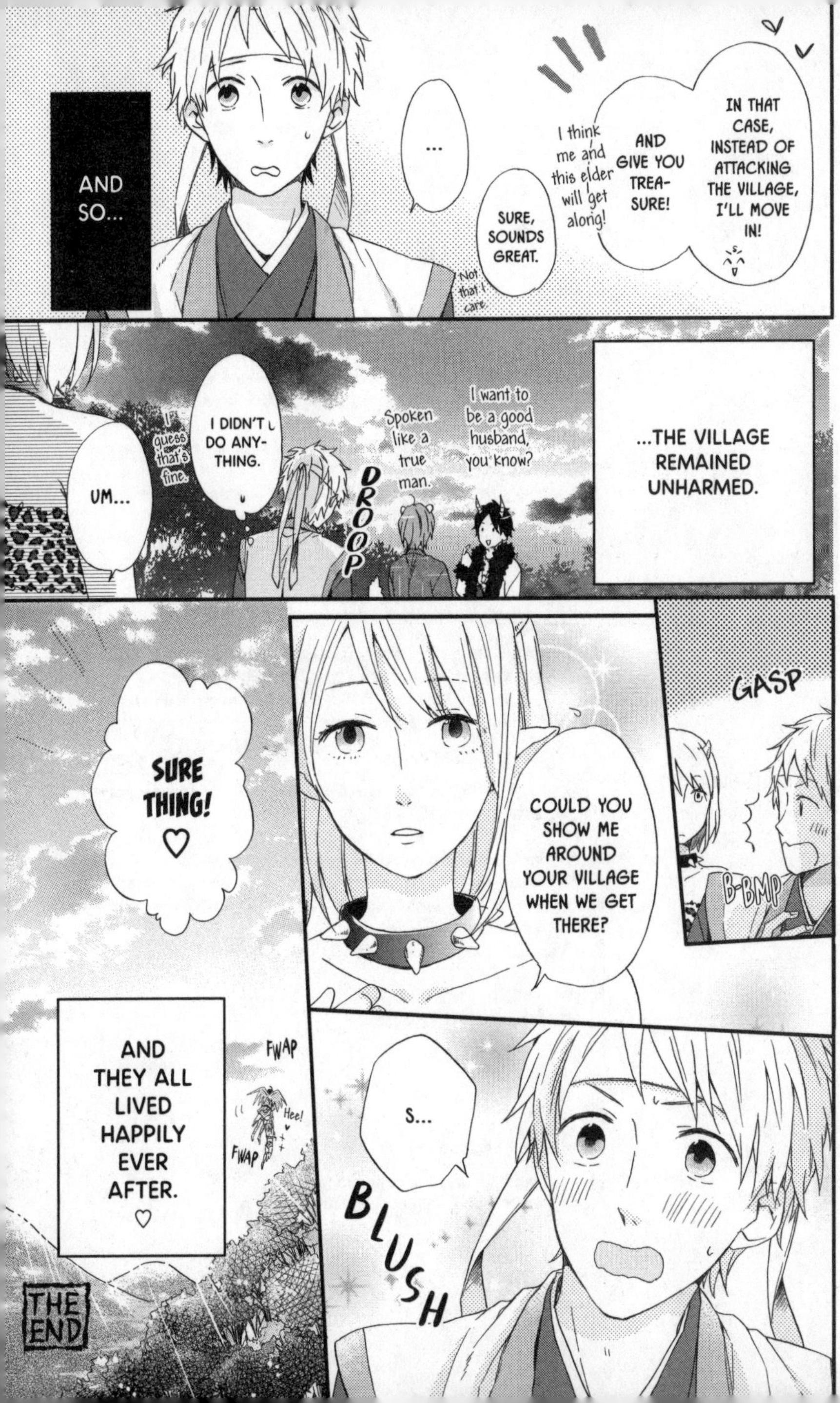
IN THAT CASE, INSTEAD OF ATTACKING THE VILLAGE, I'LL MOVE IN!
AND GIVE YOU TREASURE!
I think me and this elder will get along!
SURE, SOUNDS GREAT.
Not that I care
...
AND SO...
...THE VILLAGE REMAINED UNHARMED.
I want to be a good husband, you know?
Spoken like a true man.
DROOP
I DIDN'T DO ANYTHING.
I guess that's fine.
UM...
GASP
B-BMP
COULD YOU SHOW ME AROUND YOUR VILLAGE WHEN WE GET THERE?
S...
BLUSH
SURE THING! ♡
FWAP
Hee!
FWAP
AND THEY ALL LIVED HAPPILY EVER AFTER. ♡
THE END

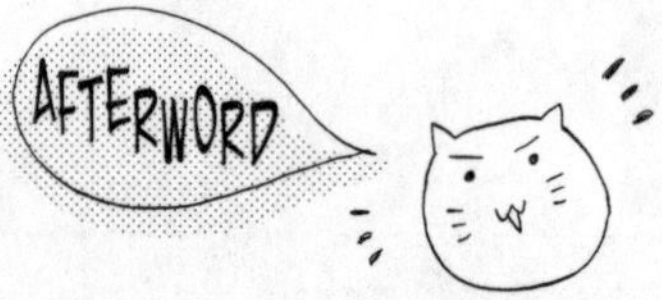
AFTERWORD

Hello to both longtime readers and new readers! Minami Mizuno here.
Thank you for buying my fourth published book of manga!

This one is *Rainbow Days* volume 1—my first book title that includes a volume number! ♡♡
Rainbow Days started as a one-shot, so when I got the okay to make it a series, I was over the moon!
I say this a lot, but...I like drawing guys. ♡
I like girls too, but it frustrates me that I can't draw them the way I imagine them.
Urk... I've got to keep working at it.

I also love getting letters from readers about which character is their favorite. It's fun that everyone has their own reasons for liking who they do. ♥ Incidentally, I still enjoy reading the letters that arrive mentioning character names from *Seishun Trickers*. ♥

Especially this person... →

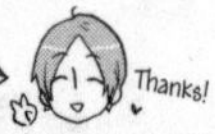
Thanks!

If you like any characters from *Rainbow Days*, please let me know! That'd be wonderful! For me!

For my last one-shot manga, the theme was "place," so I drew a story set in Sapporo, Hokkaido, my hometown. There's a bit of dialect in it too!
Both the main characters are types I like, so it felt like the storyboard was done in no time. (*laugh*)
Actually, it made me think, "If only I could always be this fast..."

So with luck, volume 2 will be out soon!
I hope we can meet again there! ♥

Bye now!
Minami Mizuno

- Blog: http://mizunoiro.jugem.jp
- Twitter: http://twitter.com/mizuno007

When I was working on the original *Rainbow Days*
one-shot, I experienced the kind of fateful encounter
that makes you go, "This is the one!"

I met the pen barrel of my dreams. For G-pen nibs.
Next I'd like to meet the barrel of my dreams
for round pen nibs. And quickly, if possible!

Minami Mizuno

Minami Mizuno was born on July 30 in Sapporo, Japan.
She debuted with *Tama ni wa Konna Watashi to Anata*
(We Get like This Sometimes, You and I) in 2006.
Rainbow Days was nominated for the 40th Kodansha Manga Award
in 2016, and her subsequent work, *We Don't Know Love Yet*,
was nominated for the 66th Shogakukan Manga Award in 2020.

Rainbow Days

Volume 1
Shojo Beat Edition

Story and Art by
Minami Mizuno

TRANSLATION + ADAPTATION **Max Greenway**
TOUCH-UP ART + LETTERING **Inori Fukuda Trant**
DESIGN **Shawn Carrico**
EDITOR **Nancy Thistlethwaite**

NIJIIRO DAYS © 2011 by Minami Mizuno
All rights reserved.
First published in Japan in 2011 by SHUEISHA Inc., Tokyo.
English translation rights arranged by SHUEISHA Inc.

Printed in Canada

Published by VIZ Media, LLC
P.O. Box 77010
San Francisco, CA 94107

10 9 8 7 6 5 4 3 2 1
First printing, December 2022

viz.com   shojobeat.com

Ao Haru Ride

STORY AND ART BY
IO SAKISAKA

Futaba Yoshioka thought all boys were loud and obnoxious until she met Kou Tanaka in junior high. But as soon as she realized she really liked him, he had already moved away because of family issues. Now, in high school, Kou has reappeared, but is he still the same boy she fell in love with?

Sometimes the greatest romantic adventure isn't falling in love— it's what happens after you fall in love!

IMA KOI

Now I'm in Love

STORY & ART BY
Ayuko Hatta

After missing out on love because she was too shy to confess her feelings, high school student Satomi blurts out how she feels the next time she gets a crush—and it's to her impossibly handsome schoolmate Yagyu! To her surprise, he agrees to date her. Now that Satomi's suddenly in a relationship, what next?

A fresh romance from Io Sakisaka,
leading shojo manga creator and author of *Ao Haru Ride*!

Love Me,
Love Me Not

Story and Art by
IO SAKISAKA

Four friends share the springtime of their youth together

Fast friends Yuna and Akari are complete opposites—Yuna is an idealist, while Akari is a realist. When lady-killer Rio and the oblivious Kazuomi join their ranks, love and friendship become quite complicated!

In this warmhearted romantic comedy, mistaken identity leads to a blossoming romance between two boys.

My Love Mix-Up!

Art by **Aruko**
Story by **Wataru Hinekure**

Aoki has a crush on Hashimoto, the girl in the seat next to him in class. But he despairs when he borrows her eraser and sees she's written the name of another boy—Ida—on it. To make matters more confusing, Ida sees him holding that very eraser and thinks Aoki has a crush on him!

SHORTCAKE CAKE

CAKE

STORY AND ART BY
suu Morishita

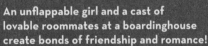

An unflappable girl and a cast of lovable roommates at a boardinghouse create bonds of friendship and romance!

When Ten moves out of her parents' home in the mountains to live in a boardinghouse, she finds herself becoming fast friends with her male roommates. But can love and romance be far behind?

RATED T TEEN

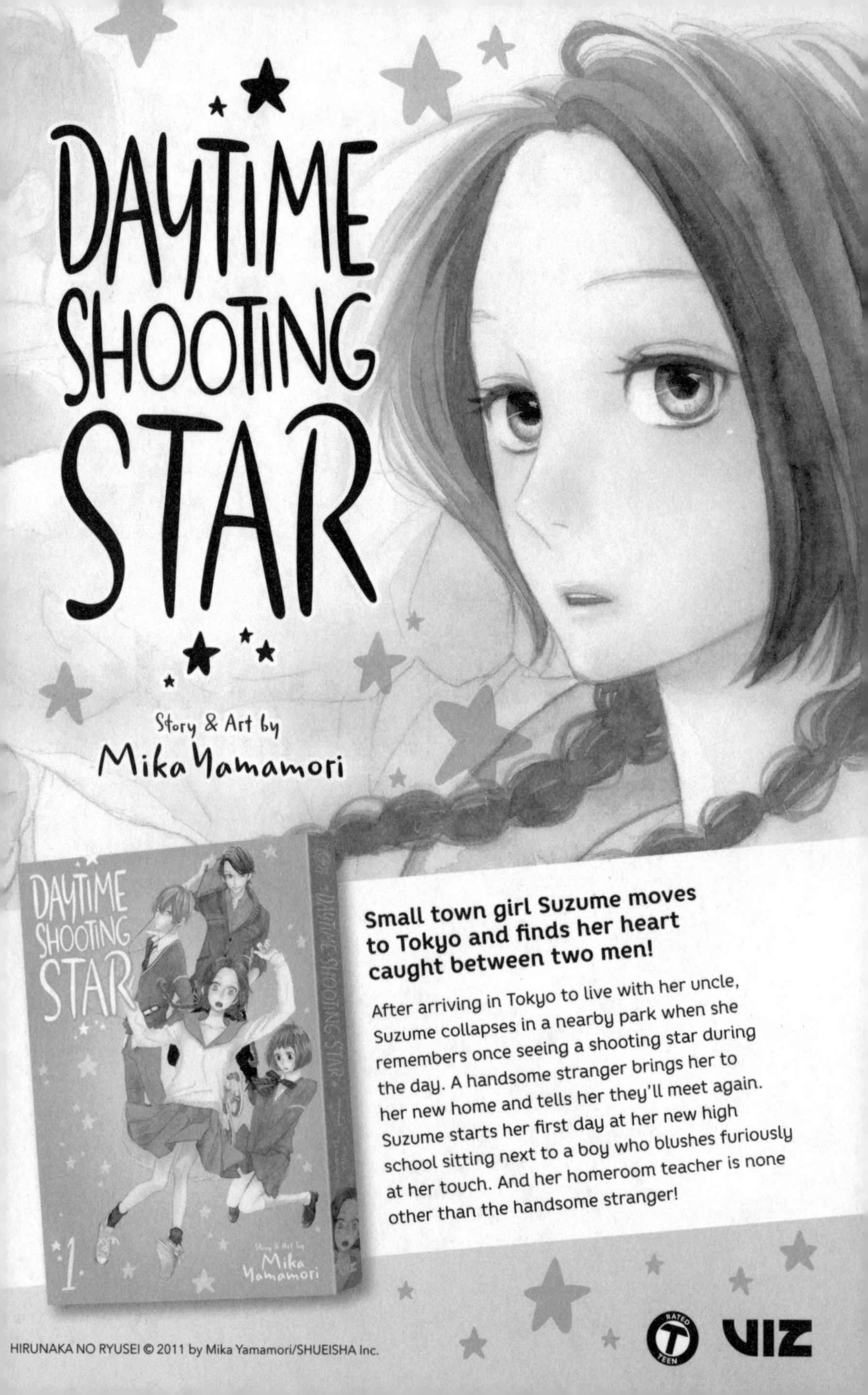
DAYTIME SHOOTING STAR
Story & Art by
Mika Yamamori
DAYTIME SHOOTING STAR
1
Story & Art by Mika Yamamori
Small town girl Suzume moves to Tokyo and finds her heart caught between two men!
After arriving in Tokyo to live with her uncle, Suzume collapses in a nearby park when she remembers once seeing a shooting star during the day. A handsome stranger brings her to her new home and tells her they'll meet again. Suzume starts her first day at her new high school sitting next to a boy who blushes furiously at her touch. And her homeroom teacher is none other than the handsome stranger!
RATED T TEEN
VIZ
HIRUNAKA NO RYUSEI © 2011 by Mika Yamamori/SHUEISHA Inc.

Stop!

You may be reading the wrong way.

In keeping with the original Japanese comic format, this book reads from right to left—so action, sound effects, and word balloons are completely reversed to preserve the orientation of the original artwork. Check out the diagram shown here to get the hang of things, and then turn to the other side of the book to get started!

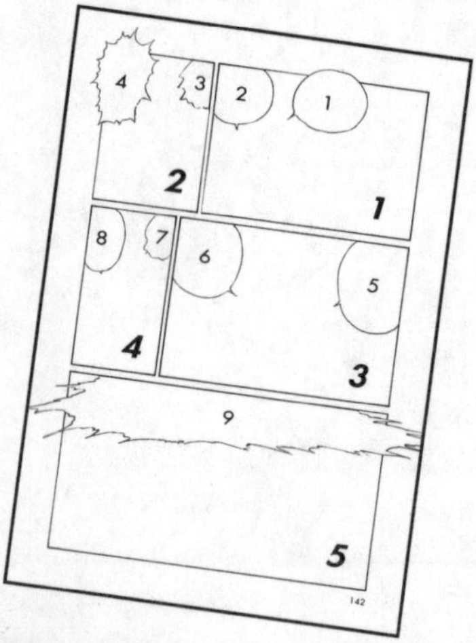

1
2
1
3
4
2
5
6
3
7
8
4
9
5
142

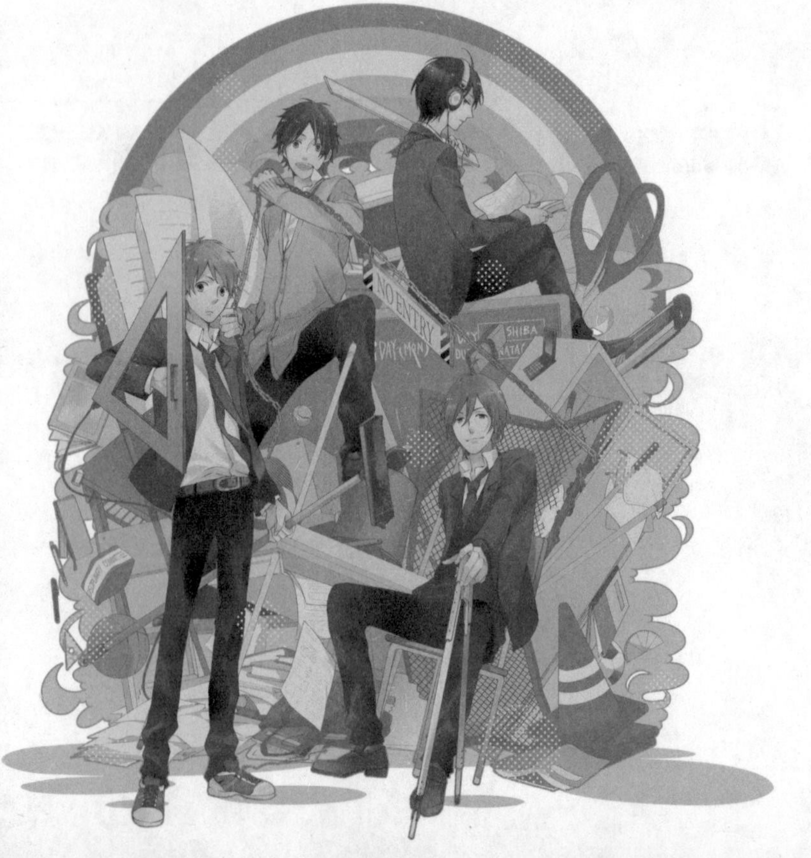

NO ENTRY
SHIBA